Foreign Direct Investment, China and the World Economy

Also by Peter J. Buckley

THE MULTINATIONAL ENTERPRISE REVISITED (*with Mark Casson*)

THE MULTINATIONAL ENTERPRISE AND THE GLOBALIZATION OF KNOWLEDGE

THE CHALLENGE OF INTERNATIONAL BUSINESS

CANADA-UK BILATERAL TRADE AND INVESTMENT RELATIONS (*with Christopher L. Paes and Kate Prescott*)

THE CHANGING GLOBAL CONTEXT OF INTERNATIONAL BUSINESS

FOREIGN DIRECT INVESTMENT AND MULTINATIONAL ENTERPRISES

INTERNATIONAL STRATEGIC MANAGEMENT AND GOVERNMENT POLICY

THE FUTURE OF MULTINATIONAL ENTERPRISE (*with Mark Casson*)

INTERNATIONAL TECHNOLOGY TRANSFER BY SMALL AND MEDIUM-SIZED ENTERPRISES (*co-edited with Jaime Campos and Eduardo White*)

MULTINATIONAL ENTERPRISES IN LESS DEVELOPED COUNTRIES (*co-edited with Jeremy Clegg*)

MULTINATIONAL FIRMS, COOPERATION AND COMPETITION IN THE WORLD ECONOMY

THE STRATEGY AND ORGANIZATION OF INTERNATIONAL BUSINESS (*co-edited with Fred Burton and Hafiz Mirza*)

STUDIES IN INTERNATIONAL BUSINESS

INTERNATIONAL BUSINESS: Economics and Anthropology, Theory and Method

Foreign Direct Investment, China and the World Economy

Peter J. Buckley
Professor of International Business, University of Leeds, UK

palgrave
macmillan

Selection and Editorial Content © Peter J. Buckley 2010
Foreword © Klaus Macharzina 2010
Individual chapters © the contributors 2010

All rights reserved. No reproduction, copy or transmission of this publication may be made without written permission.

No portion of this publication may be reproduced, copied or transmitted save with written permission or in accordance with the provisions of the Copyright, Designs and Patents Act 1988, or under the terms of any licence permitting limited copying issued by the Copyright Licensing Agency, Saffron House, 6-10 Kirby Street, London EC1N 8TS.

Any person who does any unauthorized act in relation to this publication may be liable to criminal prosecution and civil claims for damages.

The authors have asserted their rights to be identified as the authors of this work in accordance with the Copyright, Designs and Patents Act 1988.

First published 2010 by
PALGRAVE MACMILLAN

Palgrave Macmillan in the UK is an imprint of Macmillan Publishers Limited, registered in England, company number 785998, of Houndmills, Basingstoke, Hampshire RG21 6XS.

Palgrave Macmillan in the US is a division of St Martin's Press LLC, 175 Fifth Avenue, New York, NY 10010.

Palgrave Macmillan is the global academic imprint of the above companies and has companies and representatives throughout the world.

Palgrave® and Macmillan® are registered trademarks in the United States, the United Kingdom, Europe and other countries

ISBN-13: 978-0-230-51598-7   hardback

This book is printed on paper suitable for recycling and made from fully managed and sustained forest sources. Logging, pulping and manufacturing processes are expected to conform to the environmental regulations of the country of origin.

A catalogue record for this book is available from the British Library.

A catalogue record for this book is available from the Library of Congress.

10	9	8	7	6	5	4	3	2	1
19	18	17	16	15	14	13	12	11	10

Printed and bound in Great Britain by
CPI Antony Rowe, Chippenham and Eastbourne

Contents

Notes on Contributors	vii
Foreword by Professor Klaus Macharzina	ix
1 Introduction Peter J. Buckley	1

Section I   Theory — 5

2 Regaining the Edge for International Business Research Peter J. Buckley and Donald R. Lessard	7
3 Stephen Hymer: Three Phases, One Approach? Peter J. Buckley	14
4 Firm Configuration and Internationalisation: A Model Peter J. Buckley and Niron Hashai	25
5 Edith Penrose's Theory of the Growth of the Firm and the Strategic Management of Multinational Enterprises Peter J. Buckley and Mark Casson	53

Section II   Chinese Outward Foreign Direct Investment — 79

6 The Determinants of Chinese Outward Foreign Direct Investment Peter J. Buckley, Jeremy Clegg, Adam Cross, Xin Liu, Hinrich Voss and Ping Zheng	81
7 Historic and Emergent Trends in Chinese Outward Direct Investment Peter J. Buckley, Adam Cross, Hui Tan, Xin Liu and Hinrich Voss	119

Section III   Foreign Direct Investment in China — 163

8 Cultural Awareness in Knowledge Transfer to China – The Role of *Guanxi* and *Mianzi* Peter J. Buckley, Jeremy Clegg and Hui Tan	165

9 Is the Relationship between Inward FDI and Spillover Effects Linear? An Empirical Examination of the Case of China 192
   Peter J. Buckley, Jeremy Clegg and Chengqi Wang

10 Inward FDI and Host Country Productivity: Evidence from China's Electronics Industry 216
   Peter J. Buckley, Jeremy Clegg and Chengqi Wang

11 China's Inward Foreign Direct Investment Success: Southeast Asia in the Shadow of the Dragon 239
   Peter J. Buckley, Jeremy Clegg, Adam Cross and Hui Tan

12 The Impact of Inward Foreign Direct Investment on the Nature and Intensity of Chinese Manufacturing Exports 270
   Chengqi Wang, Peter J. Buckley, Jeremy Clegg and Mario Kafouros

13 The Impact of Foreign Direct Investment on the Productivity of China's Automotive Industry 284
   Peter J. Buckley, Jeremy Clegg, Ping Zheng, Pamela A. Siler and Gianluigi Giorgioni

14 The Impact of Foreign Ownership, Local Ownership and Industry Characteristics on Spillover Benefits from Foreign Direct Investment in China 305
   Peter J. Buckley, Chengqi Wang and Jeremy Clegg

15 Organisation and Action in a Chinese State-owned Service Intermediary: The Case of Sinotrans 327
   Peter J. Buckley, Jeremy Clegg and Hui Tan

Section IV   Foreign Direct Investment and Policy   363

16 Foreign Direct Investment in Ireland: Policy Implications for Emerging Economies 365
   Peter J. Buckley and Frances Ruane

17 A Simple and Flexible Dynamic Approach to Foreign Direct Investment Growth: The Canada–United States Relationship in the Context of Free Trade 386
   Peter J. Buckley, Jeremy Clegg, Nicolas Forsans and Kevin T. Reilly

Index   419

Notes on Contributors

Peter J. Buckley is Professor of International Business and Director of the Centre for International Business, University of Leeds (CIBUL) UK.

Mark Casson is Professor of Economics, University of Reading.

Jeremy Clegg is Jean Monnet Professor of European Integration and International Business Management, Leeds University Business School.

Adam Cross is Senior Lecturer in International Business, Leeds University Business School.

Nicolas Forsans is Lecturer in Strategic Management, Leeds University Business School.

Gianluigi Giorgioni is Senior Lecturer at the Liverpool Business School, Liverpool John Moores University, Liverpool.

Niron Hashai is Senior Lecturer in International Business and Strategic Management, Jerusalem School of Business Administration, The Hebrew University.

Mario Kafouros is Lecturer in International Business, Leeds University Business School.

Donald R. Lessard is the Epoch Foundation Professor of International Management and Deputy Dean at the MIT Sloan School of Management.

Xin Liu is Head of Global Risk Solutions, China, BNP Paribus Hong Kong.

Klaus Macharzina is Emeritus Professor at the University of Hohenheim, Stuttgart, Germany where he served as chaired Professor of Business Management from 1976–2005. He is the Founding Director of the Research Centre for Export and Technology Management (EXTEC), and has been the Editor of Management International Review for about 30 years. Previous appointments include academic positions at the

Universities of Munich, Augsburg and Lancaster, UK, where he occupied the Wolfson Chair of International Accounting from 1974–1976. He is Past President of the European International Business Academy (EIBA). He is a Fellow of the Academy of International Business and EIBA, and has served as Dean of the EIBA Fellows.

Kevin T. Reilly is Senior Lecturer in Economics, Leeds University Business School.

Frances Ruane is Director of the Economic and Social Research Institute in Dublin.

Pamela A. Siler is Senior Lecturer, Economics, Dundee Business School, University of Abertay.

Hui Tan is Reader in Strategy, School of Management, Royal Holloway, University of London.

Hinrich Voss, Roberts Academic Research Fellow, Leeds University Business School.

Chengqi Wang is Associate Professor and Reader in International Business Nottingham University Business School.

Ping Zheng is Senior Lecturer in International Business, Harrow Business School, University of Westminster.

Foreword by Professor Klaus Macharzina

One of the most prolific and inspiring writers in International Business has prepared a reader in which he republishes those articles that in one way or the other, can be qualified as *Peter Buckley's* hit list covering the last three years or so. Several of the papers have been co-authored by Jeremy Clegg, some three to four papers by Adam Cross, Chengqi Wang and Hui Tan, and two articles by Ping Zheng, Hinrich Voss and Xin Liu, respectively. Other co-authors include Don Lessard, Niron Hashai, Mark Casson, Mario Kafouros, Pamela Siler, Gianluigi Giorgioni, Frances Ruane, Nicolas Forsans and Kevin Reilly. So the team of authors included in this volume represents an interesting mixture of highly distinguished scholars and young academics from different countries.

The book has the title 'Foreign Direct Investment, China and the World Economy'; it is structured in four sections: theory, Chinese outward foreign direct investment, foreign direct investment in China, and policy. As is documented by ten papers, clearly Peter Buckley's regional emphasis over the last two decades has been on China. Two of those papers deal with determinants and trends of Chinese outward foreign direct investment, two papers look at spillover effects of inward foreign direct investment in China, and two papers discuss special spillover effects on productivity in the electronics and automotive industry, respectively. One paper is on China's inward foreign direct investment success, one on export performance, and another one on cultural awareness; lastly, a case-study of Sinotrans, the Chinese state-owned service intermediary, rounds the picture. The foreign direct investment policy papers have appeared in 'The World Economy' and are related to Ireland and Canada.

As a general pattern the empirical research papers dealing with China start with an analysis of the literature and a focused theoretical discussion from which hypotheses are derived. The empirical test of those hypotheses mainly relies on published official Chinese data, provided e.g. by China's State Administration of Foreign Exchange, the Ministry of Commerce or the State Statistical Bureau of China. Other sources employed include yearbooks of the industries under study. The empirical evidence of the cultural awareness and the Sinotrans is primary data collected by fieldwork using in-depth interviews with multiple interviewees in the selected case companies.

The spillover papers generate interesting results and add to the literature in so far as curvilinear relationships between foreign direct investment from Chinese MNEs and productivity spillovers could be found, especially for low-technology and labour-intensive industries, but not for other (Western) firms. Also there is evidence that foreign direct investment seems to promote exports from China. In the study on Chinese foreign direct outward investment (OFDI) it is shown that the latter seems to be associated with high levels of political risk in, and cultural proximity to, host countries throughout, and with host market size and geographic proximity and host natural resource endowments. Also the authors found that Chinese OFDI is similar to, yet distinct from the standard model of emerging country OFDI. There is of course the general problem that the secondary data used suffer from the drawback of a considerable time-lag between the years of publication of the data and the publication of the actual papers, and eventually their republication in a reader. As a consequence there is almost no empirical evidence included in the book about Chinese investment behaviour and its effects in the post WTO period. So there is room for future research, of course also with a view to India which I suspect Peter and some of the other authors are already studying.

In the theory section the 'historical' papers on Stephen Hymer and Edith Penrose caught my special attention. The former paper distinguishes three phases (PhD, neoclassical, Marxist) in Hymer's work and argues that those phases – although not reconcilable at first glance – can be reconciled around the central core of an economic theory of the multinational corporation that was truly dynamic reflecting the rapid changes in the world economy co-evolving with Hymer's thought. How intriguing it would have been to learn about Hymer's reflection on our present world economic crisis!

To me the Penrosian paper is the strongest among the entire collection of high quality essays. It represents, in my opinion, a successful attempt to merge two distinct theories by way of formalising Penrose's Theory of the Growth of the Firm and combining it with the Buckley and Casson model of the Multinational Enterprise. The resulting model is a two-dimensional generalisation of the one-dimensional Penrose theory. The (Penrosian) entrepreneur or management has identified a technological innovation generated by the (Buckley and Cassonian) R&D team who may generate a series of product innovations (growth 1). Management by way of market entry takes each product to a series of national markets (growth 2). Multinationality arises because each national market is sourced by local production. The limits of growth are related to its costs which increase due to the declining productivity of human resources, the R&D team on the one hand and management team on the other. Would it be an idea to expand the model and take it from multinationality to globalisation because of global markets, global sourcing and regional R&D centres spread over the globe and located in regions with superior talent and competences in certain areas? This, by the way, as a future project could serve as a conceptual platform supporting the third pillar in the book's title, namely the 'World Economy' which seems to be a little under-represented in the present collection.

I hope by highlighting some selected flashes of the all-in-all rich contents I have succeeded in trying to make potential readers curious about, and hungry for this fine book. In my opinion it is of high quality and has value. Even in a world of increasingly electronic publishing where you have almost unlimited access to published articles we still need that kind of focused volumes which integrate the material scattered over many outlets. Moreover, I strongly believe in the superiority of presenting such material in the form of a book (rather than a screen) you can hold in your hands and enjoy reading. Congratulations to the Editor. With this volume he has managed very well to achieve the standard that he set jointly with Don Lessard at the outset when demanding: 'This requires researchers ... to be crystal clear in their theoretical derivations and advances, and to defend rigour at all costs.'

1
Introduction

This volume of my collected papers from 2005–8 continues my interest in the theory of international business (Section I) and policies towards foreign direct investment (FDI) (Section IV) but has a major concentration on China, both as regards outward foreign direct investment (OFDI) from China (Section II) and FDI in China (Section III). My research on China has been facilitated by working with colleagues in the Centre for International Business, University of Leeds (CIBUL) and by CIBUL's participation in the White Rose East Asia Centre (WREAC), a collaboration with the East Asian Studies Department of the University of Leeds and with the University of Sheffield. China has become such an important element of the global economy that its influence cannot be ignored in almost any field of endeavour. The phenomenal impact of FDI in China and its (largely trade-related) consequences has been well documented and now there is a significant literature on the phenomenon of outward investment from China too.

The book is set up by a joint piece with Don Lessard which attempts to pick up from my question as to whether the international business (IB) research agenda is running out of steam (Buckley, 2002). It suggests that IB theorists should aim at mid-range theories that emphasise context and focus on issues as well as disciplines. The second paper in this section focuses on Stephen Hymer's theoretical work. Hymer, a key figure in the development of the theory of the multinational enterprise (MNE) wrote a seminal thesis in 1960 that set the tone for much that followed. This paper suggests that three seemingly separate phases of Hymer's work contain a set of common attributes that unify his lifetime's work. Chapter 4, co-written with Niron Hashai, continues a tradition of modelling the activities of the MNE undertaken by Niron, Mark Casson and myself. This paper represents a discreet choice model that analyses location and control decisions in internationalising firms. This contribution has the goal of examining the dynamics of MNEs in contrast to a 'stages' model of internationalisation. Edith Penrose's (1959) *Theory of the Growth of the Firm* has important implications for the strategy of MNEs but these have not often been integrated with models of the internationalisation of the firm. Chapter 5 (with Mark Casson) attempts such an integration and provides a tractable model that gives an account of the trade off between product diversification and foreign market penetration. This model incorporates the speed of entry into foreign markets, geographical expansion patterns, sequential decision making and learning.

Chapter 6 (written with CIBUL co-authors) examines the determinants of Chinese outward foreign direct investment and uses this example to test theory. The explanation of foreign direct investment (FDI) from an emerging economy, where most investors were State Owned Enterprises and 'naïve', even first-time, foreign investors, represents a stiff test for theories designed to explain mature, Western MNEs. However, the paper shows that the internalisation theory of the MNE (Buckley and Casson, 1976) can withstand such an examination. The explanation relies on a special theory that relates Chinese OFDI to the particular context of its home country where capital market imperfections channelled funds to foreign investors on a favourable basis. This emphasis on the institutional background of Chinese OFDI is developed in Chapter 7 where the policy background is related to Chinese firms' outbound strategy.

Section III is the longest in the book and it examines a truly vital element in globalisation – the vast flows of foreign direct investment into China since liberalisation. Many of the contributions examine the spillover effects of FDI in China on domestic firms. These external effects impact on domestic firms' productivity, technological expertise, competitive and exporting abilities and are not uncontested – results from the many investigations of spillover effects from different contexts find mixed results. The investigations reported in Chapters 9, 10, 12, 13 and 14 represent contributions to the debate across a range of industries and contexts in China. The transfer of technology to China through FDI is a major concern of both the host country (which wishes it to diffuse throughout the economy) and to the MNE doing the transfer (which wishes it to be effective and to improve the performance of the global company). Chapter 8 examines the role of cultural awareness facilitating this transfer and the particular of *guanxi* ('relationships') and *mianzi* ('face'). Chapter 15 examines aspects of the transformation of a state-owned company – Sinotrans – as it moves towards becoming a global competitor. Finally, Chapter 11 is a first attempt to access the impact of China's success in attracting FDI on some of its neighbours and competitors as host countries.

Foreign direct investment and policy is the subject of Section IV. Chapter 16 presents the case of Ireland as an exemplar for emerging countries in attracting FDI. This chapter (with Frances Ruane) shows the benefits of consistency and rationality in long term policy making. The final chapter puts FDI and trade into a model of FDI growth in the context of the Canada-US relationship as economic integration accelerates.

Professor Peter J. Buckley
Leeds University Business School
University of Leeds
May 2009

Section I
Theory

2
Regaining the Edge for International Business Research

Peter J. Buckley and Donald R. Lessard

The domain of international business

The key to international business is that it approaches empirical phenomena at a variety of levels of analysis, using a variety of theoretical frameworks. The most important levels of analysis are the individual manager, the firm, the industry, and the environment. In each category there is vast heterogeneity. Figure 2.1 illustrates this interaction between issues and theories. It has levels of analysis on the vertical axis and the basic social sciences on the horizontal axis as systems of thinking about the phenomena. It would also be possible to replace fundamental disciplines by the primary management disciplines (marketing, finance, strategy, etc.).

Over the history of international business, different phases of research have privileged one level or another in order to give clarity to the analysis. For instance, internalisation theory (Buckley and Casson, 1976) and the product cycle hypothesis (Vernon, 1966) privilege the level of the firm. Analysis of global strategy privileges the industry level, and institutional analysis has the macroenvironment at its core. Almost in parallel with these developments, individual managers have been studied, investigating in particular national differences in management attitudes and decision-making (Hofstede, 1980, 1991), but often out of firm or macro-context.

This poses a number of problems for the international business research community. It is possible to argue that the objective of research should be a multilevel, multidiscipline 'unified' theory. However, this is likely to be so bland that it is unlikely to be dignified with the term 'theory'. Rather better is a community of scholars that cuts across disciplines and levels with a shared core. 'International business is best when it is a collective enterprise' (Buckley, 2002).

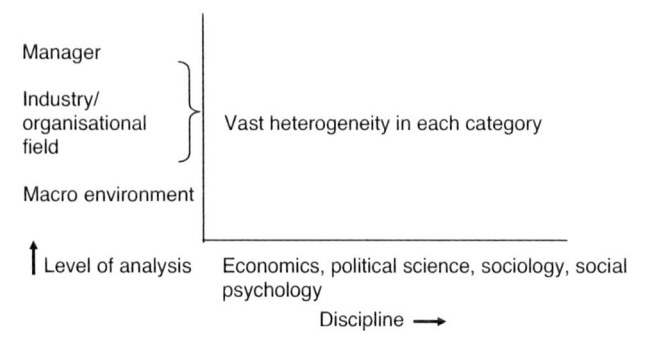

Figure 2.1 The domain of international business.

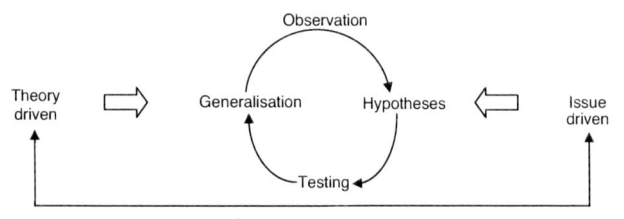

Figure 2.2 A recursive view of research in international business.

Multiple relevant literatures can be focused on a core idea. Figure 2.2 shows such a process involving theory ('theory driven') – the rocks on which researchers stand, constructs and maps of the real empirical phenomena ('issue driven') in an integrated cycle. The schema in Figure 2.2 applies both to the individual researcher and to the research community. Applying this model to the research community in international business allows specialisation in the processes and in the levels of analysis to which the process is applied. The third stage shown in Figure 2.2 can, it is argued, be aided by mapping the phenomena to give a visual approach to outlining the issues (Mitchell, 2004).

The founders of the field of international business were convinced of the need for an open, eclectic approach to theory. Successive 'chapters of dominance' have narrowed their credible frame of reference. In many approaches to 'global strategy', there are no places (countries, institutions, cultures).[1] The global strategy analysis of the 1980s onwards focused on the industry level, leaving the environment as a black box. These approaches also focused almost exclusively on the 'Triad' (North America, Europe and Japan), leaving emerging countries to be latterly discovered with the emergence, particularly, of China and India.

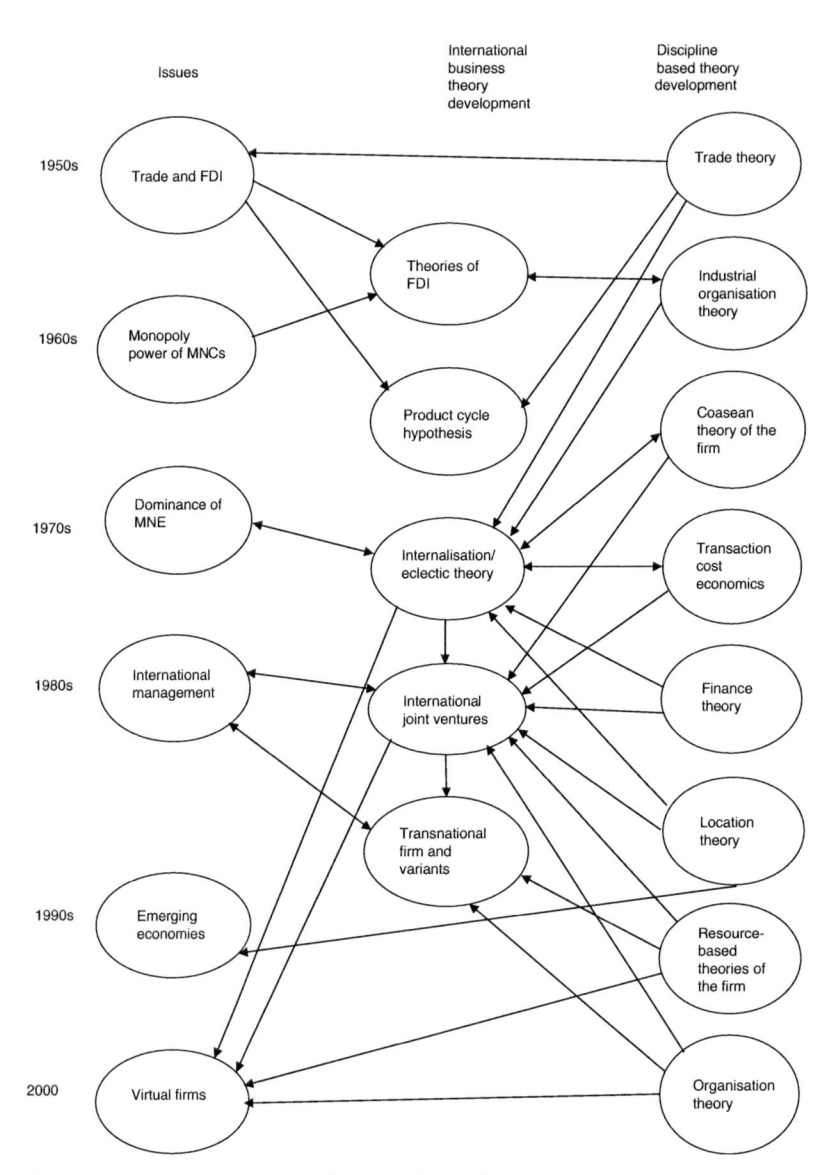

Figure 2.3 Early international business issue–theory interaction.

This recursive process is illustrated in Figure 2.3 for the period spanning the mid-1960s to the mid-1970s. It is a caricature, which does not reflect the complexity and messiness of this interaction, but we hope that those who were active in this period or have had read the early international business literature carefully will recognise the major elements we have traced out.

Initially, issues drove the development of IB as a field. As noted by many pioneers,[2] IB scholarship arose in response to the observation of 'foreign direct investment' as opposed to trade as the leading international economic phenomenon, one that was largely ignored by academia and policy-makers to that point. However, by the mid-1970s IB's reach was increasingly theory driven, even if many of the phenomena that had inspired those theories had already changed markedly.[3] By the early 1980s, internalisation theory had emerged as the dominant positive theory of international business, the antecedents for the normative framing of the balance between localisation and global integration were in place, and the normative 'ideal' of the transnational had emerged (Bartlett and Ghoshal, 1989).

This recursive approach worked quite well in this early period, but there is a danger as the phenomenological and theoretical fields become more complex. That danger is that a 'mix and match' approach to theories from outside the domain of international business will be superficially understood, badly applied, and inappropriately interpreted. Rather than advancing, microvariations in theory and phenomenon tend to cycle. Perhaps, what is needed is a 'refocus' on one or more big questions. There is a binding value in common theory in the sense of a common language to describe commonly accepted results. This is the virtue of the focus on a single 'big question' (Buckley, 2002) or at least a core set of issues.

One way forward is to use the method of distinguishing general from special theories. General theories are attempts at universal laws. Special theories achieve empirical content by placing restrictions on the general. Buckley and Casson (1976) had a general theory of the internalisation of markets. (Markets are internalised by firms until the benefits of further internalisation are outweighed by the costs.) Empirical relevance is then achieved by creating a number of special theories that show, at certain specific times and places, where the benefits (or costs) of internalisation are particularly strong – in vertically integrated process industries or linked, knowledge-intensive industries, for instance.

Issues of the philosophical basis of enquiry also arise. If the world is a 'linear variable space' then time and place do not matter, case studies are invalid, and we can search for universal laws. If, however, context – both spatial and temporal – is important, we need to take care to specify the applicability of 'general' laws.

A complementary way forward, therefore, is to document phenomena that challenge generality. However, mere description is not enough. What is required is to articulate in what ways the observation challenges existing theory (or the attempt to generalise theory), or indicates a theoretical void. This requires a clear reference to a specific theory, not a cataloguing of the various theories that could explain this phenomenon.

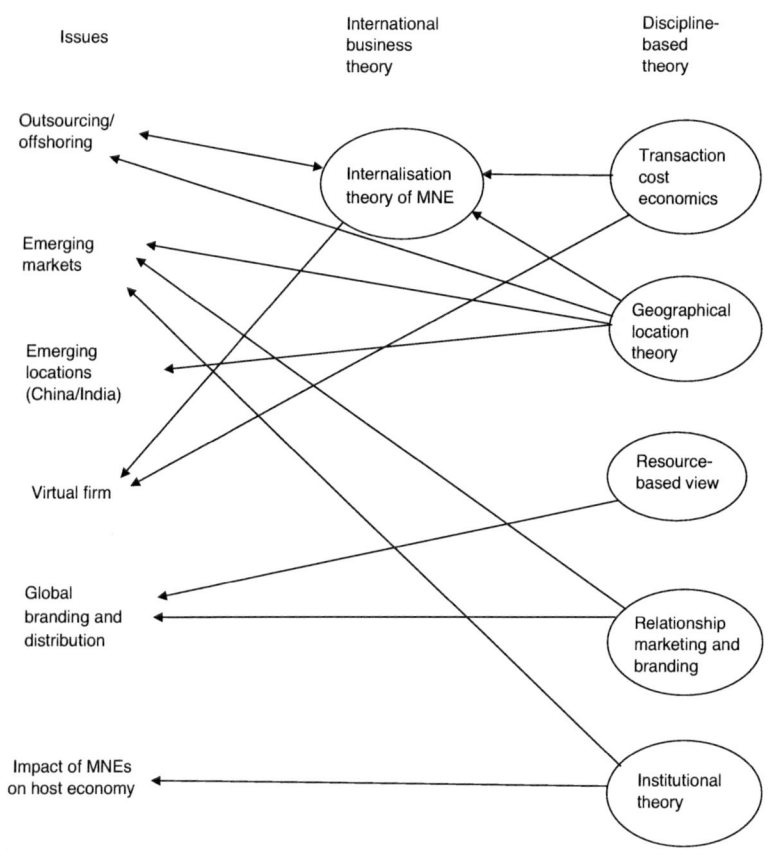

Figure 2.4 The 'missing middle'.

International business has too many kitchen sink papers that show that an eclectic model can explain the observed phenomenon. What it needs is a sharper edge in bringing forward phenomena that challenge and sharpen the 'theoretical rocks' that we stand on.

Figure 2.4 is a (perhaps somewhat exaggerated) illustration of the current problem. It shows that, in explaining current issue-driven phenomena, there is a 'missing middle' of international business theory. Important issue-driven features of the global economy are identified but are explained directly by discipline-based theory with no intermediation by international business theorists. This is in contrast to at least the pre-2000 position as shown in Figure 2.3, and it is to this problem that international business scholars need to direct their attention.

Summary

As a community, international business researchers need to find ways of making their own (discipline-based) approaches accessible to others operating in the community and their phenomenological observations relevant across disciplines. This requires researchers to be open minded, to be crystal clear in their theoretical derivations and advances, and to defend rigour at all costs. Major advances can be made if every 'theory driven' international business article begins with a statement of its derivation from theory and ends with its contribution to theory, however, incremental. Often, theoretical derivations are lost in extensive literature reviews and theoretical contributions are underweighted compared with contributions to practice or methodology. 'Issue driven' contributions should identify how/why the observation challenges/ sharpens theory, making specific reference to the relevant theory rather than just collecting interesting artefacts. By failing to do either, the international business research community often undersells itself.

Acknowledgements

This paper was inspired by the Second Annual Emerging Research Frontiers in International Business Studies Conference at Michigan State University East Lansing, 16th–19th September, 2004, and to papers and comments by participants, especially Lorraine Eden, Bernard Yeung, Will Mitchell, Tamer Cavusgil, Tim Devinney, Peter Murmann, Arvind Parkhe and Michael Gibbert.

Notes

1. See, for example, Prahalad and Doz (1987), Porter (1980).
2. This point was sharply presented by Jack Behrman in the 2004 meetings.
3. The clearest case in point is Vernon (1966) and Vernon (1979).

References

Bartlett, C.A. and Ghoshal, S. (1989) *Managing Across Borders: The Transnational Solution*, Harvard Business School Press: Boston, MA.
Behrman, J. (2004) Comment presented at the AIB conference, Stockholm 2004 (Pioneer's session).
Buckley, P.J. (2002) 'Is the international business research agenda running out of steam?' *Journal of International Business Studies* 33(2): 365–373.
Buckley, P.J. and Casson, M. (1976) *The Future of the Multinational Enterprise*, Macmillan: London.
Hofstede, G. (1980) *Culture's Consequences: International Differences in Work Related Values*, Sage Publications: Beverly Hills, CA.
Hofstede, G. (1991) *Cultures and Organisations*, McGraw-Hill: London.
Mitchell, W. (2004) 'Research methods in international business', Second annual emerging research frontiers in international business studies conference, Michigan State University, 16–19 September 2004.
Porter, M.E. (1980) *Competitive Strategy: Techniques for Analysing Industries and Competitors*, Free Press: New York.
Prahalad, C.K. and Doz, Y. (1987) *The Multinational Mission: Balancing Global Demands and Global Vision*, Free Press: New York.
Vernon, R. (1966) 'International trade and international investment in the product cycle', *Quarterly Journal of Economics* **80**: 190–207.
Vernon, R. (1979) 'The product life cycle hypothesis in a new international environment', *Oxford Journal of Economics and Statistics* **41**: 255–267.

3
Stephen Hymer: Three Phases, One Approach?
Peter J. Buckley

Introduction

Stephen Hymer (1934–1974) is regarded as a seminal figure in the establishment of the theory of the multinational enterprise (MNE) and a founder of the academic subject of international business. This reputation is largely built on Hymer's thesis, written in 1960 (published only as Hymer 1976) but also on his later writings which, after Hymer's conversion to Marxism, took a critical view of the activities of MNEs and their impact on the world economy from the viewpoint of a radical economist.

This paper suggests that there were three phases in Hymer's work. The first phase was the 1960 PhD thesis, the second is a neoclassical phase represented by his strange 1968 paper in French in *Revue Economique*, and the third his 'radical phase'.

The intriguing question, which this paper explores, is whether these three phases are consistent, contradictory or non-overlapping sets.

The three phases of Hymer's work

Phase 1: The thesis: The International Operations of National Firms (1960)

Hymer's thesis deserves the epithet 'seminal'. Its title is significant. Hymer saw firms as primarily national and their international operations were seen as expansions from their home, national, base rather as a firm might diversify from its original industry. This parallel is instructive.

In Hymer's view firms have a nationality in three senses. First, they have a legal nationality which provide legal constraints on the firm's behaviour. Second, most shareholders reside in a certain nation and the firm is obliged to pay dividends in a certain currency. Third, managers have a nationality and this may affect their allegiance and behaviour. Hymer's firms are committed to earning and (their shareholders) to receiving profits in their 'own' currency. Firms have a distinct, definitive nationality. They are in no sense 'global' firms.

Hymer made a profound and enduring distinction between portfolio and direct foreign investment. The distinguishing feature between the two is that direct foreign investment (DFI) implies control of the operation whilst portfolio foreign investment confers a share of ownership, but not control. This is important because the traditional theory of investment based on differential interest rates, after accounting for the risk premium, does not explain DFI. This profound empirical observation prepared the ground for a separate and separable theory of DFI. It was supported by the following stylised facts.

1. There was little, or no, correlation between high interest rates and inflows of DFI.
2. Cross DFI occurred. Firms of country A were investing in country B at the same time (and often in the same industry) as country B's firms were investing in country A.
3. Most DFI (in Hymer's observation period) was undertaken by firms of one nationality – the USA. Thus the motivation must be other than interest rate differentials.
4. There was distinct, definite pattern of industrial composition of DFI. Some industries were characterised by a great deal of DFI, others by little. And, DFI took place in both directions between countries simultaneously.

The motivation for DFI was the desire to control foreign operations. It was often profitable to control enterprises in more than one country in order to remove competition. Some firms have advantages in a particular activity and may find it profitable to exploit these advantages by establishing foreign operations. They need to do this in order to fully appropriate the returns from these advantages. The profits from these operations are related to control. A minor motivation relates to the diversification advantages of international operations. (In fact, DFI is a poor way to diversity. The need to control operations necessitates putting more investment in one location than would be dictated by an optimal portfolio, which would tend to be more widely spread.)

Hymer thus begins where the firm already has an advantage, developed in its home market. There are managerial or organisational advantages which favour centralised or at least unified decision making. The direction of DFI will also be influenced by the ease of entry into particular foreign locations.

Hymer further needed to explain why the firm does not license its advantage to a third party, given that the foreign firm necessarily incurs costs of operating in an alien environment. (The costs of information in operating in a foreign market he may have seen as a fixed cost.) Hymer's answer was made up of two parts. First, there is not necessarily joint maximisation of profits if two firms pursue their own course. Integration increases joint profits. Second, the two firms (licensor and licensee) may have a different valuation of the worth of the 'patent' on the advantage. This arises because of asymmetric information. The owner knows the value better than the buyer. This conflict of evaluations causes uncertainty. There is also the danger of the owner losing the advantage by diffusion (intended or unintended on the part of the licensee).

The external market, and, in particular, market imperfections play a huge role in Hymer's contribution. Imperfections allow exploitation of advantages and these are specifically imperfections in the market for knowledge. The thesis starts 'one stage too far forward' (Buckley and Casson, 1976, p. 69) and pays no attention to the process of generating the advantage. In particular, the innovation process is not linked to its exploitation.

Hymer's thesis must be one of the most photocopied and circulated documents in business academia. It was largely disseminated, however, by the 1969 publication of Kindlberger's *American Business Abroad*. It was through the lens of his supervisor's publication that Hymer's work reached a wider public and the Hymer/Kindleberger theory was named. The thesis finally appeared in book form in 1976.

A major source of controversy has been the issue of whether Hymer took on board the issue of internalisation (Dunning and Rugman, 1985; Horaguchi and Toyne, 1990; Kindleberger, 1969). In the thesis, Hymer generally used the term 'integration' although he once uses the phrase 'the firm internalises or supersedes the market' on page 48 (Pitelis, 2002). He was to take up the Coasean approach (Coase, 1937) in the second phase of his contribution.

Phase 2: Post-thesis, the 1968 neoclassical article

Hymer's (1968) *Revue Economique* paper is an engima. It was written in French and is regarded by its translators to be written in poor French.

It does appear to have been written in 1968 as it contains references to publications of that year. The article contains many mistakes (see, Mark Casson's 1990 introduction) and it misquotes Coase. Perhaps, the 'quotations' from Coase are meant to be Hymer's paraphrasing. The article has no clear conclusion it just ends. Despite this, the piece is wide-ranging and (as usual with Hymer) insightful.

The paper not only includes a discussion of internalisation, it integrates this notion with external market imperfections to give a satisfying explanation of the direction of growth of the international expansion of firms (Buckley, 1990). Hymer's Coasian, neoclassical theory of the international firm embraces both horizontal and vertical integration. Not only does this work show that market power and internalisation are not competing explanations of international expansion, it also demonstrates that both are necessary for a complete explanation. Hymer shows the systemic interaction between them. To paraphrase Casson (1990, pp. 3–4) internalisation in an industry of a given size determines the number of firms, and therefore, also industrial concentration and market structure. Market structure feeds back in two ways. First, it governs the opportunities for further horizontal expansion of the firm within the industry. Thus, high industrial concentration encourages the firm to expand by diversifying. Second, imperfections in competition at one stage of production induce price distortions within a multi-stage production process and so create an incentive for backward or forward integration.

As Casson points out, Hymer has moved on from the preoccupation of his thesis with technological advantages to emphasise the role of large firms in the international division of labour. (Here, is a link to the concerns of Marxist thinkers.) The emphasis is indeed upon backward integration into raw materials rather than on the way that preparatory technology is exploited (taken up by Buckley and Casson, 1976). Again, there is a link to Hymer's later concern with the problems of labour in the primary sectors of less developed countries.

Hymer follows Coase in seeing internalisation as a general theory of the existence of firms. The international firm is a special case where market imperfections and the direction of the internalisation of markets takes the firm's control across national boundaries.

Hymer focuses on imperfections in the capital market in this paper. These imperfections explain why shareholders prefer to diversify themselves rather than hold shares in 'pre-diversified' firms. Again the underlying rationale arises from indivisibilities in information. The multidivisional firm can be explained by the internal allocation of capital mimicking an external bank. Profits are reallocated by retention and reinvestment (this explains the large firm's preference for retaining profits rather than paying out dividends). This anticipates the argument that internal forward markets coordinate vertically linked supply chains (Buckley and Casson, 1976, p. 37). However, the discipline of the market constrains managers of even the largest firms. This is a distinctly neo-classical paper emphasising marginalist principles.

Phase 3: The radical economist and critic of international capitalism

The three phases of Hymer's work are not temporarily distinct. As a Canadian, Hymer was critical of foreign (particularly US) domination of Canadian industry. In 'Direct foreign investment and the national interest' (1966), Hymer took a critical stance, but the early work's purpose is 'to analyse rather than prescribe' (Hymer, 1966, p. 201). It is notable that there is little or no discussion of policy issues in Hymer's dissertation.

Hymer's approach evolved into a 'on the one hand, on the other' type of analysis as exemplified by his 1970 piece 'The efficiency (contradictions) of Multinational Corporations' (Hymer, 1970a) which showed that the dual nature of the multinational corporation arose from its external market dominance combined with its ability to achieve efficiency by successful coordination of internally controlled markets.

Later pieces were hostile to multinational corporations as agents of an international capitalist system which was causing inequality, poverty and distortions in the world economy.

Hymer never changed his view on the welfare impact MNEs from the original duality of welfare gains (from the replacement of an imperfect external market by a more perfect internal one or where a new market is created where none existed before – the internalisation of an externality) and welfare loses (where MNEs maximise profits by restricting the output of goods and services or where vertical integration is used as a barrier to entry) (Buckley, 1990). Further, MNEs may reduce social efficiency because they provide a more suitable mechanism for exploiting a collusive agreement than does a cartel. By internalising a collusive agreement, MNEs make the enforcement of collusion more effective (Casson, 1985).

However, Hymer began to place more emphasis on global macrodynamics (Rowthorne, 1971). In contrast to Buckley and Casson's approach which addresses dynamic benefits from internal markets on the grounds that an internal market allows greater inter-plant integration and cross functional integration between production, marketing and R&D which in the long run, they argue, will stimulate both the undertaking of R&D and its effective implementation in production and marketing. Hymer took a malign view of MNE dynamics.

In 'The efficiency contradictions of multinational corporations' (1970a), Hymer begins with the famous quote from D.H. Robertson that multinational corporations (firms in the original) are 'islands of conscious power in an ocean of unconscious co-operation' (Hymer, 1970a, p. 441). Hymer questions whether such powerful MNEs can be analysed by economics alone, but his argument rests almost solely on economics. Hymer examines and contrasts the division of labour between firms coordinated by markets with the division of labour within firms, he notes scale effects (big firms, small countries) and questions the extent of trickle-down to less developed countries. He further notes the supranational power of MNEs. The conclusion however is a list of advantages and disadvantages of MNEs with the reader left to attach weights to the points and arrive at a view of the balance – duality again.

'The multinational corporation and the law of uneven development' (Hymer, 1972b) is futuristic in outlook. Hymer examines the hierarchical division of labour implanted by firms on states and regions. Hymer contrasts Marshall and Marx. Both, he believes, stress the internal division of labour but Marx stressed the authoritarian and unequal nature of this relationship based on the cohesive power of property. Hymer believed that Marshall's answer, based on cooperation between labour and capital and on the power of the market to reconcile individual freedom and collective production was an inadequate response. Hymer argues that the increasing size and power of firms as MNEs subverted the power of the market and that conscious coordination widened whilst market directed division of labour contracted. This is Coasean dualism at a macro and dynamic level with a strong (unsubstantiated, as Hymer acknowledges) assumption of weakening global market forces.

Hymer goes on to project that increasing specialisation by MNEs will force the global economy to become increasingly locationally or spatially specialised with a hierarchy of specialised locations (and therefore nations) emerging. Hymer's condemnation of the role of MNEs spreading inequality cannot disguise his admiration (like Marx) for its dynamism. Surprisingly, the Epilogue to the paper is anti-pessimistic. Countervailing forces will pressurise the centre – although this is seen to come from 'alternative methods of organising the international economy' such as regional planning, rather than from competitive forces and innovation.

Similarly, in 'The internationalisation of capital' (Hymer, 1972a), although MNEs, through their internal division of labour, are wasteful and corporate structure is seen as 'divide and rule' Hymer again believes that the contradictions within the system will force ultimately beneficial change. This would partly be due to competition from Europe and Japan to the world hegemon – USA – and partly to the fact that capitalism is not satisfying and does not fulfil human needs. Here Hymer anticipates the anti-globalisation movement (Cohen *et al*.s 1979).

Perhaps, one's view of this period of Hymer's writing depends on whether Marx is regarded as providing the correct interpretation of long-run social and economic dynamics or whether he is seen as a minor post-Ricardian economist.

The three phases – discussion

As we move through the three phases Hymer's work evolves from the micro (transactions and the firm) to the macro (the world system) although the emphasis is always on the multinational corporation as the main actor. The combination of the market imperfections or 'firm-specific advantages' of the thesis with Coasean internalisation gives a rounded approach which, nevertheless, lacks a dynamic at the level of the firm in that Hymer's focus on innovation is weak. This basic analytical apparatus feeds through into the radical critique of later work when a macro-dynamic based on Marx is introduced.

The three phases – commonalities

Six common attributes of Hymer's work feed through all the phases of his *oeuvre*.[1]

First, the analysis is always economics based or, at least, economistic. The analytical apparatus does not include cultural elements nor does the explanation rely on 'managerial capitalism'. The discipline of the market ensures that even though large firms may have a distinct 'personality' (Hymer, 1968), deviations in behaviour from a profit-maximising firm can be indulged only within very definite limits (Casson, 1990).

Second, hierarchy is central to the explanation. Initially, this is observed within the firm. In later writings, hierarchy is seen as a key feature of the global economy.

Third, power is crucial. Power is observed in industrial concentration, in spatial concentration, in monopoly and monopsony. Market imperfections, especially those in information and in the capital market are major drivers of the explanation of outcomes in the world economy. Yet, the discipline of the market can constrain power as in the disciplinary threat of takeovers to the policies of multinational corporations.

Fourth, boundaries are critical. The boundaries of the firm in the early writings (Hymer, 1960, 1968) are vital, even as regards the title of the thesis – 'The international operations of national firms'. National boundaries play a major role in determining the world's distribution of income. Nationalism is a driving force and the example of Canada (earlier) and less developed countries (later) exemplify this. The combination of boundaries and neoclassical economics give Hymer a major intellectual engine – the notion of substitution at the margin.

Fifth, the role of communications and the control of information loom large, particularly within the firm. Good examples of this occur in the 1968 paper and in 'Multinational corporations and the division of labour' (Hymer, 1979), where Fig. 1 shows 'degrees of downstream coupling'.

Sixth, disequilibrium is a feature of Hymer's continuing world view.[2] Graham (2002) feels that Hymer was constantly searching for an explanation of long run non-equilibrium dynamics in the world economy – a view very close to classical Marxism. Hymer (1975) saw Marx as trying to uncover the 'economic laws of motion of modern society' and Hymer's later work might be seen as an attempt to introduce a dynamic into the basically static analysis of international firms which he had created. Graham distinguishes a true dynamic (non-equilibrium) analysis from one where a new static equilibrium is obtained when a system is perturbed away from an old such equilibrium. The path that Hymer chose to develop (along Marxist lines) differed from that taken by most international business academics, which is to try to introduce innovation into the system (see for instance, Buckley and Casson, 1976). If this is a correct interpretation, then Hymer's vision can be rescued from the wreck of Marxism and Marxist theory. The search for a dynamic analysis of the world economy on non-comparative static equilibrium lines still has to be completed.

The argument that Hymer's three phase contribution can be seen as evolutionary rather than separate or contradictory has to cope with the discontinuity in Hymer's thought brought about by his conversion to Marxism and his concern with less developed countries such as Ghana. In my view, neither of these perceived discontinuities undermines the six common attributes of Hymer's work. The Marxian framework is best regarded as a macro-dynamic element which is progressively and increasingly emphasised as Hymer observed globalisation advancing. Here, Hymer diverged from conventional international business economics which concentrates on innovation as the driving force in the world economy (Buckley and Casson, 2003).

When Hymer was writing, as now, 'the third world' was at the sharp end of the interface between MNEs and their environment. The 'colonisation' of Canada by foreign capital occurred at high levels of GDP and the question arose whether the effects of FDI were different in less developed countries. To Hymer, the problems of FDI were put into sharper relief by poverty in the host country. Hymer spent time in Trinidad and Chile but his strongest engagement was with Ghana (Hymer, 1970b; Hymer and Green, 1965, 1966; Hymer and Resnick, 1969)[3] immediately following his graduation from M.I.T. Here, MNEs are but one facet of the interaction between a 'modern' and a 'traditional' society, analysed at a time when an independent state (Ghana) was emerging from a colony (the Gold Coast). Even here, the themes of hierarchy, power, boundaries and communication are analysed in Hymer's economics-based analytical system where disequilibrium is all too evident.

Conclusion

Hymer's work on the multinational corporation was fundamental to the development of international business theory. This paper has argued that three separate phases of his career and writing can be reconciled around the central core of an economic theory of the multinational corporation that was truly dynamic and that reflected the rapid changes in the world economy co-evolving with his thought. In Hymer's work it is a necessary condition for the existence of the multinational corporation that it possesses a 'firm specific advantage' and a sufficient condition that the firm can obtain more profit by exploiting the advantage internally than licensing it out to external organisations. The multinational corporation is both efficiency improving in the way that it integrates internal markets in goods, services, capital and information whilst at the same time such firms create distortions by the use of monopoly and monopsony power. Hymer constantly strives to cast his work into a dynamic frame. He chose to do this via Marxian macro dynamics rather than through a microdynamic analysis of innovation at the firm level.

Acknowledgements

This paper was originally presented at the Academy of International Business Annual Meeting in Stockholm, July 2004 and I would like to thank the participants and other panellists for their comments and especially the panel organiser, Christos Pitelis. I would also like to thank Bernard Wolf, Monty Graham, Christos Pitelis and Mark Casson for their insightful comments on the post-conference paper.

Notes

1. It should be re-iterated that Hymer died young and as Monty Graham pointed out, it is possible that 'Hymer as Marxist' may have been a transitional phase giving way to post-Marxism or some other mode. Sadly, we shall never know.
2. I owe this insight to Monty Graham's notes for the Stockholm Conference, from Graham (2002).
3. Hymer prepared the statistical abstract to Kay (1972) in collaboration with the editor. Kay planned the book 'as a joint venture with Stephen Hymer and Reginald Green. The statistical abstract was finally completed in collaboration with Stephen Hymer, but his influence on the whole work goes much further. Without the advantages of long discussions with him, his comments on my numerous drafts and his many brilliant insights this book could hardly have been written' (Kay, Preface, p. xviii).

References

Buckley, P.J. (1990) Problems and developments in the core theory of international business. *Journal of International Business Studies*, 21(4), 657–665.
Buckley, P.J. and Casson, M. (1976) *The Future of the Multinational Enterprise*. London: Macmillan.
Buckley, Peter J. and Casson, M. (2003) The future of the multinational enterprise in retrospect and in prospect. *Journal of International Business Studies*, 34(2), 219–222.
Casson, M. (1985) Multinational monopolies and international cartels. In P.J. Buckley and M. Casson (eds), *The Economic Theory of the Multinational Enterprise*. London: Macmillan.
Casson, M. (1990) The large international 'corporation': An analysis of some motives for the international integration of business by Stephen Hymer. Introduction. In M. Casson (ed.), *Multinational Corporations*. Cheltenham: Edward Elgar.
Coase, R.H. (1937) The nature of the firm. *Economica*, 4, 386–405.
Cohen, R.B., Felton, N., Nkosi, M. and van Liere, J. (1979) *The Multinational Enterprise: A Radical Approach. Papers by Stephen Herbert Hymer*. Cambridge: Cambridge University Press.
Dunning, J.H. and Rugman, A.M. (1985) The influence of Hymer's dissertation on the theory of foreign direct investment. *American Economic Review*, 75(2), 228–232.

Graham, E.M. (2002) The contributions of Stephen Hymer: One view. *Contributions to Political Economy*, 21, 27–41.
Horaguci, H. and Toyne, B. (1990) Setting the record straight, Hymer, internalisation theory and transaction cost economics. *Journal of International Business Studies*, 21(3), 487–494.
Hymer, S.H. (1960) *The International Operation of National Firms: A Study of Direct Foreign Investment*. Doctoral dissertation, Massachusetts Institute of Technology.
Hymer, S.H. (1966) Direct foreign investment and the national interest. In P. Russell (ed.), *Nationalism in Canada*. Toronto: McGraw-Hill.
Hymer, S.H. (1968) The multinational corporation: An analysis of some motives for international business integration. *Revue Economique*, XIX(6), 949–973.
Hymer, S.H. (1970a) The efficiency (contradictions) of multinational corporations. *American Economic Review*, LX(2), 441–448.
Hymer, S.H. (1970b) Economic forms in pre-colonial Ghana. *Journal of Economic History*, XXX(1), 33–50.
Hymer, S.H. (1972a) The internationalization of capital. *Journal of Economic Issues*, 6(1), 91–111.
Hymer, S.H. (1972b) The multinational corporation and the law of uneven development. In J. Bhagurat (ed.), *Economics and World Order from the 1970s to the 1990s*. New York: Collier Macmillan.
Hymer, S.H. (1975) International politics and international economics: A radical approach. In L. Lindberg, R. Alford, C. Crouch, & C. Offe (eds), *Stress and Contradiction in Modern Capitalism*. Lexington, MA: Lexington Books.
Hymer, S.H. (1976) *The International Operations of National Firms: A Study of Direct Foreign Investment*. Cambridge, MA: MIT Press.
Hymer, S.H. (1979) The multinational corporation and the international division of labour. In R.B. Cohen, N. Felton, M. Nkosi and J. Van Liere (eds), *The Multinational Enterprise: A Radical Approach. Papers by Stephen Herbert Hymer*. Cambridge: Cambridge University Press.
Hymer, S.H. and Green, R.H. (1965) Investment in the Ghana cocoa industry: Some problems of structure and policy. *Economic Bulletin*, IX(1), 16–23.
Hymer, S.H. and Green, R.H. (1966) Cocoa in the Gold Coast: A study in the relationship between African farmers and agricultural experts. *Journal of Economic History*, XXVI(3), 299–319.
Hymer, S.H. and Resnick, S. (1969) A model of an agrarian economy with non-agricultural activities. *American Economic Review*, 493–506.
Kay, G.B. (ed.) (1972) *A Political Economy of Colonialism in Ghana: A Collection of Documents and Statistics*. Cambridge: Cambridge University Press (with a statistical abstract prepared in collaboration with Stephen Hymer).
Kindleberger, C.P. (1969) *American business abroad*. New Haven, CT: Yale University Press.
Pitelis, C.N. (2002) Stephen Hymer: Life and the political economy of multinational corporate capital. *Contributions to Political Economy*, 21, 9–26.
Rowthorne, R. (1971) *International Big Business 1957–1967. A study of comparative growth*. Cambridge: Cambridge University Press (in collaboration with Stephen Hymer).

4
Firm Configuration and Internationalisation: A Model

Peter J. Buckley and Niron Hashai

Introduction

The 'economic school' of thought has been tremendously influential in International Business (IB) research. Scholars adhering to this school (e.g., Anderson and Gatignon, 1986; Buckley and Casson, 1976; Dunning, 1977, 1988; Hennart, 1993; Hirsch, 1976; Rugman, 1981, 1986) focus on the advantages gained from internalising the firm's foreign activities during its international expansion. Internalisation enables the firm to minimise the cost of economic transactions by better exploiting underutilised firm-specific capabilities (e.g., managerial skills and technology), which are superior to those of indigenous competitors.

Notwithstanding the central role that the 'economic school' plays in IB research, a few shortcomings characterise this literature. First, it is mostly confined to a 'home country-host country' view, thus neglecting the fact that a firm may often expand *in parallel* to foreign markets and to resource abundant countries. Second, with a few exceptions (e.g., Buckley and Casson, 1976, 1998), the 'economic school' treated the firm as a 'black box' and did not distinguish between the motivations to internationalise different value adding activities of the firm. Third, this school was mainly focused on static analyses of the choice between alternative foreign market servicing modes, thus neglecting the dynamic dimension of firm internationalisation. Finally, in many cases, scholars coming from this school have explicitly or implicitly assumed that the internationalising firm possesses some kind of 'home-based' competitive advantage, hence neglecting the potential impact that 'host country' knowledge resources may have on the competitiveness of internationalising firms (Cantwell, 1995; Dunning and Narula, 1995; Kuemmerle, 1997; Zanfei, 2000).

The current paper offers a method to overcome these shortcomings by using a discrete choice model that follows the reasoning of the 'economic school', analyses the economic cost of different kinds of transactions and identifies those that minimise overall costs. We make a few simplifying assumptions for the sake of clarity, but our model offers a method to simultaneously include a foreign market and a resource abundant country, to open the 'black box' of the firm and to predict the location and control modes of specific value adding activities, to allow a dynamic dimension to firm internationalisation and to reflect the role of host country knowledge resources.

Next, we briefly detail the relevant literature in the context of our proposed model. The features of our model and its underlying assumptions are presented in Section 2. Then we formulate and solve the model and specify the criteria according to which firms are expected to make their location and control decisions. We follow this by extending the static formulation into a dynamic one and finally we conclude and present suggestions for further research.

Literature review

Essentially, the 'economic school' views internationalisation as engagement in cross border activities motivated by rational economic considerations (e.g., Buckley and Casson, 1976, 1998; Dunning, 1977, 1988; Hirsch, 1976; Martin and Salomon, 2003; Rugman, 1981, 1986). Firms choose their foreign market-servicing mode by evaluating the cost of different transactions and selecting the mode that minimises overall costs.

Dunning's Eclectic Paradigm (Dunning, 1977, 1988) probably offers the most holistic description of the conditions of foreign market-servicing strategy of firms using ownership, location and internalisation advantages as explanatory variables. Ownership advantages reflect firm-specific, technological, marketing or managerial knowledge, such as privileged access to resources not available to competitors. Location advantages represent the comparative cost of materials, labour and natural resources accessed by enterprises operating in a particular host country as well as the relative proximity to potential foreign markets and suppliers. Internalisation advantages apply to the case, where a firm prefers to exploit its ownership advantage within its organisational boundaries, rather than by licensing or the use of other modes of externalisation (Buckley and Casson, 1976, 1998; Hennart, 1993; Martin and Salomon, 2003; Rugman, 1981, 1986).

Within the 'economic school' of thought, our model specifically builds on Hirsch's (1976) path breaking paper. This paper has influenced many classic internationalisation models (e.g., Buckley and Casson, 1976; Rugman, 1981) as well as more recent ones (Martin and Salomon, 2003). Hirsch's paper was especially pioneering in its focus on the interaction between supply and demand factors in the explanation of firm's choice between FDI and exports. These factors are: differences in production costs between the home and host countries, the cost of possessing and transferring proprietary know-how, the excess cost of marketing in the host country compared to the domestic market and the additional costs of controlling and coordinating foreign operations compared to domestic ones.

The current paper extends the basic building blocks of Hirsch (1976). First, the paper presents a formal model that explains the configuration of internationalising firms in a world that is made up of the home country, a target country (where the firm's foreign market exists) as well as a resource abundant country. By simultaneously including a foreign market and a foreign resource abundant country, we expand beyond conventional home-host country analyses.

Second, our model refers to the cost of executing various value adding activities in different locations, intra-firm and inter-firm knowledge flow costs and the cost of product flows to customers. Essentially, our model presents internationalisation (i.e. the expansion of a firm's activities beyond its national boundaries) as a consequence of the firm's decisions on its optimal configuration, where the overall costs of operations and flows are minimised.

We define a firm's configuration as the location of, and control over value-adding activities. We follow Buckley and Casson (1976); Casson (2000) and Hirsch (1976) and focus on three major value-adding activities: (1) R&D – creation of knowledge and consumable technology, (2) production – transforming inputs into outputs, (3) marketing – which includes promotion, sales, distribution and after-sales services.

The firm's location and control decisions are both determined by the *interrelation* between the cost of executing these value-adding activities in various locations, knowledge flow costs between these activities (Buckley and Carter, 2004; Kogut and Zander, 1993; Martin and Salomon, 2003) and the cost of product flows to the market. The location decision is *where* to locate each value-adding activity so that the overall costs are minimised. The control decision is *which* value-adding activity to *internalise* (own or control) and which to *externalise* (i.e., perform outside the firm's boundaries through arms-length transactions, licensing or outsourcing) in order to minimise costs.

Third, our model offers a dynamic extension to the firm's decisions on its optimal location and control configuration. This is done by returning to the underlying logic of the product cycle framework (Vernon, 1966). While the framework has been criticised for being too deterministic and being relevant mainly to the technology-based products (Melin, 1992), it has remained central in IB literature. In the framework, products typically pass through the phases of introduction, growth and maturity (and finally decline). The location of new products is influenced by the proximity of innovators to their home country customers. In the introductory phase, when products are not yet standardised, the innovators locate production activities at home in order to facilitate interaction between R&D and production. During the growth phase, the demand for products expands into additional markets and, over time, the innovators locate production activities in proximity to consumers in these countries. As products continue to mature, they become more and more standardised. First mover advantages are dissipating and production cost considerations become critical. During the maturity phase, production will be transferred to countries that enjoy cost advantages. Hence, according to the product cycle framework, over time the relative importance of R&D and knowledge flow costs decline compared to that of production, marketing and product flows.

Finally, our model also refers to host country knowledge resources by considering the question of where R&D activities of the internationalising firm should be located. The internationalisation of knowledge creation (often referred to as R&D) activities is receiving increasing attention in the literature (e.g., Cantwell, 1995; Dunning and Narula, 1995; Kuemmerle, 1997; Patel and Pavitt, 1991; Patel and Vega, 1999; Pearce and Papanastassiou, 1996, 1999; Zanfei, 2000) and hence should be incorporated in the firm's choice of its optimal configuration.

We employ a discrete choice model to analyse the decision-making of an internationalising firm regarding the location and control of its value-adding activities. The main advantage of such a model is the ability to enumerate all the possibilities, evaluate them separately and rank them according to different criteria. Then, alternatives that are dominated by others are eliminated, and at the end of the process the remaining alternatives are evaluated according to inequalities between specific variables. This approach follows the reasoning of 'economic school' (e.g., in Buckley and Casson, 1976; Casson, 2000; Hirsch, 1976;

Martin and Salomon, 2003; Rugman, 1981) by asserting that profit maximisation is achieved through minimising the costs of the firm's value-adding activities, the costs of knowledge flows between value-adding activities and the cost of product flows to customers.

The deficiency of this methodology is that as the number of variables increases, we face a 'combinatorial explosion' since the number of permutations accelerates accordingly (Casson, 2000), chap. 3. In order to overcome this problem, some simplifying assumptions are made. While these assumptions may in some cases change the firm's decision set, our main point is to demonstrate a solvable method that enables a more holistic and rigorous view of the location and control dilemmas of internationalising firms. We return to this point in Section 6.

The model

Structure

Consider a firm that produces a single consumer good in a single plant. As mentioned earlier, three types of activity are involved in the firm's operations: R&D (denoted by R), Production (denoted by P) and Marketing (denoted by M). There are three possible locations: A, the home country, B, a destination country, where the firm's main foreign market exists, and W, a resource-abundant country, where production inputs are expected to be the cheapest. We assume that the market in country B is large enough to justify the operation of dedicated value-adding activities. Thus, the home market does not play a role in the location and control decisions of the firm.

In order to simplify the model, we assume that the location of value-adding activities is mutually exclusive – there is no duplication of identical value-adding activities in different countries. In practice, internationalising firms may locate a specific value-adding activity in multiple locations, so the above assumption implies that for each value-adding activity (R, P or M), a major location is chosen by the firm.

While P can be located at any of three locations, R and M must be located at A – near the firms' headquarters or at B – close to the firm's market. This assumption reflects the view that there is not much sense in locating R&D or marketing at W, away from both the firm's headquarters (which are assumed to be located in A) and its market. This view is consistent with the view of many scholars regarding the location of marketing activities (Dunning, 1988; Hirsch, 1976; Johanson and Vahlne, 1977, 1990) and that the location of R&D in low cost countries is still unusual (Dunning and Narula, 1995; Kumar, 2001; Pearce and Papanastassiou, 1996, 1999; Rao, 2001).

Following these assumptions, a firm operating in the above-mentioned world has a relatively small number of location possibilities to choose from: 2 (for R) ×3 (for P) ×2 (for M) = 12 possibilities. This view is portrayed in Figure 4.1 and formally detailed in the following sections.

An R&D laboratory is denoted by a circle, a production plant by a square and a marketing facility by a diamond. Flows of products are denoted by thick lines while flows of knowledge are denoted by thin lines. An arrow indicates the direction of flow. Three main types of linkage are identified: K_{R-P}, flow of knowledge from R&D to production and vice versa, K_{M-R}, flow of knowledge from marketing to R&D and vice versa, and T_{i-j} (i,j = A, B, W; $i \neq j$), flow of products from the production plant to the market. Product flow is one-way, but knowledge

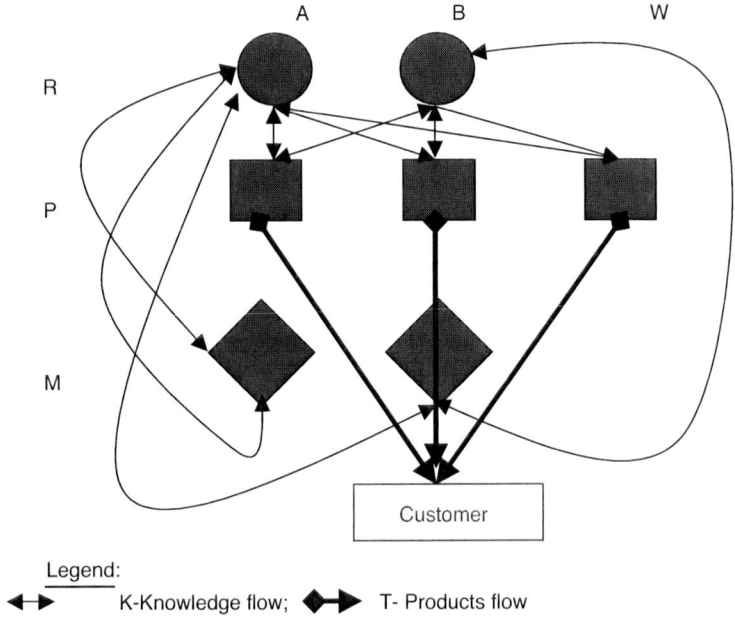

Figure 4.1 Alternative locations of value-adding activities.
K, Knowledge flow; T, products flow; R, R&D; P, production; M, marketing. A, Home country; B, destination country; W, resource-abundant country.

flows are two-way. This is because there is always feedback in knowledge flows between different value-adding activities.

K_{R-P} includes details on the product design and manufacturing instructions. K_{M-R} enables state of the art know-how to be transferred to the marketing personnel, as well as getting market feedback from the market regarding product design and competitors' technology. There is no flow of knowledge between the production and marketing; the transmission of knowledge between these two entities is entirely intermediated by R&D. This simplification implies that the market feedback is processed in the R&D laboratory before it is implemented in production, and that the R&D personnel have to approve product specifications before they are transferred to the marketing people.

Based on the set of location possibilities detailed in Figure 4.1, it is possible to formulate the control decision of the firm over each of its value-adding activities. We include two modes of control:

(a) *Internalisation* – Operating a value-adding activity within the boundaries of the firm.
(b) *Externalisation* – Operating a value-adding activity outside the firms' boundaries through arms length transactions, licensing or outsourcing.

We ignore externalisation of local value-adding activities, as this is not part of this paper's main focus. Hence the firm's decision whether to internalise or externalise a value-adding activity is narrowed down to R&D (in B), production (in B and/or W) and marketing (in B).

Adding the control decision to the location decision, discussed earlier, naturally increases the number of alternatives faced by the internationalising firm. In sum, there are 45 alternative configurations. Table 4.1 details the possible set of configurations. For each of the 12 location alternatives (numbered 1–12), the relevant control alternatives are specified (denoted, for instance, as '12a', '12b', '12c', etc.). The sign 'ex' is used to indicate a value-adding activity that is externalised. We denote the location of a value-adding activity (R, P, M) by its sign and the country symbol (A, B, W). Knowledge flows between two value-adding activities are denoted by 'K' and the symbols of the relevant activities (for instance, $K_{RA-PB-ex}$ indicates knowledge flows from the R&D laboratory in A to the externalised production site in B). Product flows are denoted by 'T' and the symbols of origin and destination countries (for instance, T_{A-B} indicates product flow from country A to country B). Hence, Table 4.1 includes the location of R, P

Table 4.1 Alternative firm configurations.

No.	R&D	Knowledge flow R&D–production	Production	Transportation to customers	Marketing	Knowledge flow marketing – R&D
1	R_A	K_{RA-PA}	P_A	T_{A-B}	M_A	K_{MA-RA}
2	R_A	K_{RA-PB}	P_B	T_{B-B}	M_A	K_{MA-RA}
2a	R_A	$K_{RA-PB-ex}$	P_{B-ex}	T_{B-B}	M_A	K_{MA-RA}
3	R_A	K_{RA-PW}	P_W	T_{W-B}	M_A	K_{MA-RA}
3a	R_A	$K_{RA-PW-ex}$	P_{W-ex}	T_{W-B}	M_A	K_{MA-RA}
4	R_A	K_{RA-PA}	P_A	T_{A-B}	M_B	K_{MB-RA}
4a	R_A	K_{RA-PA}	P_A	T_{A-B}	M_{B-ex}	$K_{MB-ex-RA}$
5	R_A	K_{RA-PB}	P_B	T_{B-B}	M_B	K_{MB-RA}
5a	R_A	$K_{RA-PB-ex}$	P_{B-ex}	T_{B-B}	M_B	K_{MB-RA}
5b	R_A	K_{RA-PB}	P_B	T_{B-B}	M_{B-ex}	$K_{MB-ex-RA}$
5c	R_A	$K_{RA-PB-ex}$	P_{B-ex}	T_{B-B}	M_{B-ex}	$K_{MB-ex-RA}$
6	R_A	K_{RA-PW}	P_W	T_{W-B}	M_B	K_{MB-RA}
6a	R_A	$K_{RA-PW-ex}$	P_{W-ex}	T_{W-B}	M_B	K_{MB-RA}
6b	R_A	$K_{RA-PW-ex}$	P_{W-ex}	T_{W-B}	M_{B-ex}	$K_{MB-ex-RA}$
6c	R_A	K_{RA-PW}	P_W	T_{W-B}	M_{B-ex}	$K_{MB-ex-RA}$
7	R_B	K_{RB-PA}	P_A	T_{A-B}	M_A	K_{MA-RB}
7a	R_{B-ex}	$K_{RB-ex-PA}$	P_A	T_{A-B}	M_A	$K_{MA-RB-ex}$
8	R_B	K_{RB-PB}	P_B	T_{B-B}	M_A	K_{MA-RB}
8a	R_B	$K_{RB-PB-ex}$	P_{B-ex}	T_{B-B}	M_A	K_{MA-RB}
8b	R_{B-ex}	$K_{RB-ex-PB}$	P_B	T_{B-B}	M_A	$K_{MA-RB-ex}$
8c	R_{B-ex}	$K_{RB-ex-PB-ex}$	P_{B-ex}	T_{B-B}	M_A	$K_{MA-RB-ex}$
9	R_B	K_{RB-PW}	P_W	T_{W-B}	M_A	K_{MA-RB}
9a	R_B	$K_{RB-PW-ex}$	P_{W-ex}	T_{W-B}	M_A	K_{MA-RB}
9b	R_{B-ex}	$K_{RB-ex-PW}$	P_W	T_{W-B}	M_A	$K_{MA-RB-ex}$
9c	R_{B-ex}	$K_{RB-ex-PW-ex}$	P_{W-ex}	T_{W-B}	M_A	$K_{MA-RB-ex}$
10	R_B	K_{RB-PA}	P_A	T_{A-B}	M_B	K_{MB-RB}
10a	R_B	K_{RB-PA}	P_A	T_{A-B}	M_{B-ex}	$K_{MB-ex-RB}$
10b	R_{B-ex}	$K_{RB-ex-PA}$	P_A	T_{A-B}	M_B	$K_{MB-RB-ex}$
10c	R_{B-ex}	K_{RB-PA}	P_A	T_{A-B}	M_{B-ex}	$K_{MB-ex-RB-ex}$
11	R_B	$K_{RB-ex-PB}$	P_B	T_{B-B}	M_B	K_{MB-RB}
11a	R_B	$K_{RB-PB-ex}$	P_{B-ex}	T_{B-B}	M_B	K_{MB-RB}
11b	R_B	K_{RB-PB}	P_B	T_{B-B}	M_{B-ex}	$K_{MB-ex-RB}$
11c	R_B	$K_{RB-PB-ex}$	P_{B-ex}	T_{B-B}	M_{B-ex}	$K_{MB-ex-RB}$
11d	R_{B-ex}	$K_{RB-ex-PB}$	P_B	T_{B-B}	M_B	$K_{MB-RB-ex}$
11e	R_{B-ex}	$K_{RB-ex-PB-ex}$	P_{B-ex}	T_{B-B}	M_B	$K_{MB-RB-ex}$
11f	R_{B-ex}	$K_{RB-ex-PB}$	P_B	T_{B-B}	M_{B-ex}	$K_{MB-ex-RB-ex}$
12d	R_{B-ex}	$K_{RB-ex-PW}$	P_W	T_{W-B}	M_B	$K_{MB-RB-ex}$
12e	R_{B-ex}	$K_{RB-ex-PW-ex}$	P_{W-ex}	T_{W-B}	M_B	$K_{MB-RB-ex}$
12f	R_{B-ex}	$K_{RB-ex-PW-ex}$	P_{W-ex}	T_{W-B}	M_{B-ex}	$K_{MB-ex-RB-ex}$
12g	R_{B-ex}	$K_{RB-ex-PW}$	P_W	T_{W-B}	M_{B-ex}	$K_{MB-ex-RB-ex}$

and *M* operations for each alternative, an indication whether these activities are externalised or not and the specification of the relevant knowledge and product flows.

Flow costs

Next, we define the costs of value-adding activities and flows. For convenience, the denotations used in Table 4.1 also represent the cost of the relevant value-adding activities and flows.

Product flows

Product flow costs (*T*) include the cost of transportation, tariffs and non-tariff barriers (Hirsch, 1976). These costs are referred to as 'transportation costs'. We assume that international transportation costs are higher than local ones (Helpman and Krugman, 1985; Hirsch, 1976; Hirsch and Hashai, 2000; Krugman, 1991, 1995). Thus, we determine that:

$$T_{local} < T_{international}. \tag{1a}$$

For the sake of simplicity, we assume that the international product flow costs are identical between A, B and W. Thus, we can define the difference between local and international flows as:

$$\Delta T = T_{local} - T_{international}.$$

We also assume that:

$$T_{external} = T_{internal} \tag{1b}$$

This is because the main cost that is captured by *T* is the products' transportation costs. Additional costs such as the costs of controlling the transportation of products to customers. costs of delays in supply and faults in shipped goods are expected to be negligible in comparison to the transportation cost.

Knowledge flows

Knowledge flows costs (*K*) include formal as well as informal firm-specific knowledge that flows between the firm's value-adding activities (Buckley and Carter, 2004; Casson, 2000; Hirsch, 1976; Kogut and Zander, 1993; Martin and Salomon, 2003).

We assume that:

$$K_{local} < K_{international} \tag{2a}$$

As recently noted by Buckley and Carter (2004), international knowledge flow costs are higher than the local knowledge flow costs, because of the greater complexity of control (Hirsch, 1976), cultural differences (Hofstede, 1980; Kogut and Singh, 1988) and language differences (Rangan and Adner, 2001).

For the sake of simplicity, we assume that the differences in international knowledge flow costs are identical between A, B and W. Thus, the difference between local and international knowledge flows is defined as:

$$\Delta K = K_{local} - K_{international}.$$

Knowledge flow costs are assumed to be more expensive when an external value-adding activity is involved. The reason for this is the need to control external activities, disinformation that might occur in the process, and the costs of dishonesty and opportunism. The flow of knowledge between an internal and external value-adding activity is more exposed to mistakes and disinformation in comparison to an internal knowledge flow, while the knowledge flow between two external value-adding activities is even more costly for the firm (Anderson and Gatignon, 1986; Buckley and Casson, 1976, 1979; Dunning, 1977, 1988, 2000; Hirsch, 1976; Kogut and Zander, 1993; Martin and Salomon, 2003; Rugman, 1981; Williamson, 1975, 1985). We therefore assume that

$$K_{internal-internal} < K_{internal-external} < K_{external-external}, \tag{2b}$$

and that the cost difference between these terms is equal and denoted by:

$$\Delta K' = K_{internal-internal} - K_{internal-external} = K_{internal-external} - K_{external-external}.$$

Operation costs

R&D

The output of an R&D laboratory can be transferred (via K_{R-P}) to production sites at A, B and W. In addition, there is an extensive flow of know-how between the marketing entity and R&D laboratory (via K_{M-R}).

We assume that:

$$R_A < R_B \tag{3a}$$

The fact that a firm's knowledge resources are often based on its home country implies that the operation of R&D will probably be cheaper at the home country. This is consistent with Hirsch's view of the creation of firm-specific proprietary know-how (Hirsch, 1976) and with other studies that identified specific home country advantages in the location of R&D (Dunning, 1988; Patel and Pavitt, 1991; Pearce and Papanastassiou, 1996). These costs advantages are reinforced by the costs stemming from the liability of foreignness (Hymer, 1976) in operating in B as well as the superior information links and knowledge exchange that a firm is expected to have with Universities and government authorities in its home country. We denote: $\Delta R = R_B - R_A$ as the difference between the R&D cost in A and B.

Nevertheless, according to (2a), savings on knowledge flow costs facilitate cost advantages in locating the R&D laboratory abroad in proximity to foreign production or to marketing activities (Patel and Vega, 1999; Pearce and Papanastassiou, 1996). Hence, the final decision concerning location would be the outcome of the comparative costs of operations (R, P and M) and knowledge flow costs.

While the cost of R&D activities in B is expected to exceed that of R&D activities in A, externalisation of R&D activities in B may decrease this cost differential. An externalised R&D laboratory is expected to be cheaper than an internalised one, because of savings on once-and-for-all set up costs and savings on fixed costs. Indigenous partners in B may use their existing R&D laboratories in B and thus enjoy economies of scale and scope in generating knowledge, thus enjoying a cost advantage over a newly established (or acquired) R&D lab (Narula and Dunning, 1998). These costs advantages are even greater if one considers the impact of cultural distance (Hofstede, 1980; Kogut and Singh, 1988) that again give advantages to indigenous partners from B over the A firm in its relations with the local universities and government in B. We therefore assume that

$$R_{B-ex} < R_B \tag{3b}$$

where R_{B-ex} denotes an external R&D laboratory and R_B denotes an internal one. The cost difference between internal and external R&D activities is denoted by $\Delta R' = R_{B-ex} - R_B$.

Production

Production costs are assumed to be cheapest at W. W is assumed to be comparatively endowed with production inputs compared to A and B. For example, W may be a labour-abundant developing country with cheaper labour costs than A or B. It is also assumed that production in the home country is cheaper than production in the destination country. This assumption stems from the liability of foreignness (Hymer, 1976) as well as the superior information links and connections a firm is supposed to have with suppliers, government authorities and other institutions in its home country (Buckley and Casson, 1976; Casson, 1994; Kogut and Singh, 1988; Mariotti and Piscitello, 1995). Thus we assume that:

$$P_W < P_A < P_B \qquad (4a)$$

We denote the differences between these production costs as: $\Delta P = P_i - Pj$, $(i, j = A, B, W, i \neq j)$. For the sake of simplicity, we assume that the production cost differential is equal between each pair of countries: $\Delta P_{B-A} = \Delta P_{A-W}$. Inequality (4a) implies that the cost differential between P_B and P_W is twice as much as the cost differential between P_A and P_W, hence: $\Delta P_{B-W} = 2 \times \Delta P_{A-W}$.

We assume that external execution of international production (in B or W) is cheaper than producing internally. The reason for this is that an external operation usually does not require the large investment necessary to establish a production facility, because the indigenous partner/subcontractor in the destination country may leverage on existing plants and production lines. For the same reason, an indigenous partner may save some of the fixed costs of production, thus enabling manufacture at a lower cost. Moreover, the liability of foreignness and cultural distance (Hofstede, 1980; Hymer, 1976; Kogut and Singh, 1988; Mariotti and Piscitello, 1995) again gives an advantage to indigenous partners/subcontractors (from B or W) over firm A in bargaining power and connections with local suppliers and government. We therefore assume that

$$P_i - \text{ex} < P_i \ (i = B, W) \qquad (4b)$$

where $P_{i-\text{ex}}$ denotes external production and P_i denotes internal production. The cost difference between internal and external production is denoted by $\Delta P' = P_{i-\text{ex}} - P_i \ (i = B, W)$.

Marketing

The costs of marketing are assumed to be lower in the destination country, in comparison with the home country:

$$M_B < M_A \qquad (5a)$$

The fact that maintaining a marketing force (sales and post-sale services personnel) abroad involves additional costs that may be avoided in the home country (e.g., renting of additional offices and expatriate worker costs), proximity of marketing to the firm's customers, is assumed to be of much greater importance if the firm has to serve a large mass of customers (Hirsch, 1989). The savings on promotion costs, on sales persons' and technicians' travelling costs, on distribution control costs and on transportation of spare parts, together with the quick response to customer needs and the ability to collect data on market trends in a much more efficient way, are all part of the explanation why it is cheaper to locate marketing activities in the destination market (Almor and Hirsch, 1995; Hirsch, 1989). We denote $\Delta M = M_A - M_B$ as the difference between marketing activities costs in A and B.

The cost of external operation of marketing in B is assumed to be lower than the internal operation. This assumption stems from the high fixed costs required to establish a marketing infrastructure that is able to market the product and provide after-sale services abroad. Indigenous firms that are well acquainted with the market and have already established their marketing infrastructure may save these costs. Moreover, the liability of foreignness is even more significant in marketing than in production: cultural and economic differences (Contractor, 1990; Hofstede, 1980; Kogut and Singh, 1988; Linder, 1961), accessibility to distribution channels, connection with the media and government authorities – are all crucial factors that give the indigenous marketing entity an advantage over a foreign one. Thus we assume that

$$M_{B-ex} < M_B \qquad (5b)$$

where M_{B-ex} denotes an external marketing operation and M_B denotes the internal one. The cost difference between internal and external marketing operation is denoted by $\Delta M' = M_{B-ex} - M_B$.

Solution of the location and control decisions

We expect the internationalising firm to choose the configuration with the lowest overall cost. The overall cost of each configuration can be calculated by summing the costs of each value-adding activity, together with the relevant product and knowledge flow costs. Which configuration will be chosen depends on the relative magnitude of costs. The easiest way to understand the general properties of the solution is first to eliminate any configuration that is clearly dominated by another. Then we compare the remaining configurations in terms of the major trade-offs involved and their magnitude. This is done by comapring the costs of 12 location alternatives and then evaluating for each location alternative the cost of internal versus external operations.

The location decision

Based on inequalities (1)–(5), configurations 7–10 are dominated by others. Configuration 7, for instance, is dominated by configuration 1. These configurations differ only in the location of R&D laboratory. In configuration 1, R&D is located in A and in configuration 7, it is located in B. The location of R&D in A is cheaper than in B (inequality (3a)) and also implies cheaper knowledge flow costs between R, P and M since only local knowledge flows are involved (inequality (2a)). Likewise, it can be shown that configuration 7a is also dominated by configuration 1, configurations 8, 8a, 8b and 8c are dominated by configurations 11, 11a, 11d and 11e, respectively, configurations 9 and 9b are dominated by configuration 3, configurations 9a and 9c are dominated by configuration 3a, and configuration 10, 10a, 10b and 10c are dominated by configurations 12, 12a, 12d and 12e, respectively. The dominated configurations are denoted with italics in Table 4.1.

Thus, we are left with 31 configurations, representing eight location configurations. Table 4.2 presents a set of necessary and sufficient conditions for the selection of each of the eight location configurations as the preferred one. This set of necessary and sufficient conditions enables us to compare the eight location configurations according to the specific product attributes and to choose the configuration that minimises overall costs.

The interpretation of Table 4.2 is as follows. Configuration 1 is the preferred configuration of an internationalising firm if *all* the inequalities, specified under configuration 1, exist. For example if $\Delta K_{R-P} + \Delta P > \Delta T$, configuration 1 ($R$, P and M located at A) will be preferred over configuration 2 (R and M located at A, P located at B) since the cost of knowledge flows between R and P and the extra cost of producing in B is higher than the savings on transportation (product flow) costs that result from the comparative proximity of the plant in B to the market. Configuration 1 is preferred over configuration 3 if $\Delta K_{R-P} > \Delta P$, and so on. Thus, per each location configuration, Table 4.2 details the set of inequalities that should exist for the specific location configuration to be the least cost one.

Although we cannot present a single term that identifies the superiority of a given configuration, i.e. satisfies the necessary and sufficient conditions to select it, we can introduce a single term that specifies the *necessary* condition to select a configuration, as detailed in the *final row* of the cost comparison of each configuration.

The necessary condition can be calculated as the sum of the inequalities that constitute the set of necessary and sufficient conditions to

Table 4.2 Decision criteria between location configurations.

Configuration No.	Selection Criteria	Notes
1	**Ra, Pa, Ma**	
2	$\Delta K_{R-P}+\Delta P>\Delta T$	
3	$\Delta K_{R-P}>\Delta P$	
4	$\Delta K_{M-R}>\Delta M$	
5	$\Delta K_{R-P}+\Delta P+\Delta K_{M-R}>\Delta T+\Delta M$	result of 2 & 4
6	$\Delta K_{R-P}+\Delta K_{M-R}>\Delta P+\Delta M$	result of 3 & 4
11	$\Delta R+\Delta P>\Delta T+\Delta M$	
12	$2\Delta K_{R-P}+\Delta R>\Delta P+\Delta M$	
	Necessary condition: $3\Delta K_{R-P}+\Delta K_{M-R}+2\Delta R>2\Delta T+3\Delta M$	
2	**Ra, Pb, Ma**	
1	$\Delta T>\Delta K_{R-P}+\Delta P$	
3	$\Delta T>2\Delta P$	
4	$\Delta T+\Delta K_{M-R}>\Delta K_{R-P}+\Delta P+\Delta M$	result of 1 & 5
5	$\Delta K_{M-R}>\Delta M$	
6	$\Delta K_{M-R}+\Delta T>\Delta M+2\Delta P$	result of 3 & 5
11	$\Delta R>\Delta K_{R-P}+\Delta M$	
12	$\Delta R+\Delta T>2\Delta P+\Delta M$	result of 3 & 11
	Necessary condition: $\Delta K_{M-R}+2\Delta T+\Delta R>2\Delta K_{R-P}+3\Delta P+2\Delta M$	
3	**Ra, Pw, Ma**	
1	$\Delta P>\Delta K_{R-P}$	
2	$2\Delta P>\Delta T$	
4	$\Delta P+\Delta K_{M-R}>\Delta K_{R-P}+\Delta M$	result of 1 & 6
5	$2\Delta P+\Delta K_{M-R}>\Delta T+\Delta M$	result of 2 & 6
6	$\Delta K_{M-R}>\Delta M$	
11	$\Delta R+2\Delta P>\Delta K_{R-P}+\Delta T+\Delta M$	
12	$\Delta R>\Delta M$	
	Necessary condition: $2\Delta R+\Delta K_{M-R}+5\Delta P>2\Delta K_{R-P}+2\Delta T+3\Delta M$	
4	**Ra, Pa, Mb**	
1	$\Delta M>\Delta K_{M-R}$	
2	$\Delta K_{R-P}+\Delta P+\Delta M>\Delta T+\Delta K_{M-R}$	result of 1 & 5
3	$\Delta K_{R-P}+\Delta M>\Delta P+\Delta K_{M-R}$	result of 1 & 6
5	$\Delta K_{R-P}+\Delta P>\Delta T$	
6	$\Delta K_{R-P}>\Delta P$	
11	$\Delta R+\Delta P>\Delta K_{M-R}+\Delta T$	
12	$\Delta R+\Delta K_{R-P}>\Delta K_{M-R}+\Delta P$	
	Necessary condition: $\Delta M+3\Delta K_{R-P}+2\Delta R>3\Delta K_{M-R}+2\Delta T$	

Table 4.2 Decision criteria between location configurations – *continued*

Configuration No.	Selection Criteria	Notes
5	**Ra, Pb, Mb**	
1	$\Delta T+\Delta M>\Delta K_{R-P}+\Delta P+\Delta K_{M-R}$	result of 2 & 4
2	$\Delta M>\Delta K_{M-R}$	
3	$\Delta T+\Delta M>2\Delta P+\Delta K_{M-R}$	result of 2 & 6
4	$\Delta T>\Delta K_{R-P}+\Delta P$	
6	$\Delta T>2\Delta P$	
11	$\Delta R>\Delta K_{R-P}+\Delta K_{M-R}$	
12	$\Delta R+\Delta T>\Delta K_{M-R}+2\Delta P$	result of 6 & 11
	Necessary condition: $\Delta M+3\Delta T+2\Delta R>2\Delta K_{R-P}+3\Delta K_{M-R}+5\Delta P$	
6	**Ra, Pw, Mb**	
1	$\Delta P+\Delta M>\Delta K_{R-P}+\Delta K_{M-R}$	result of 3 & 4
2	$\Delta M+2\Delta P>\Delta K_{M-R}+\Delta T$	result of 3 & 5
3	$\Delta M>\Delta K_{M-R}$	
4	$\Delta P>\Delta K_{R-P}$	
5	$2\Delta P>\Delta T$	
11	$\Delta R+2\Delta P>\Delta T+\Delta K_{R-P}+\Delta K_{M-R}$	
12	$\Delta R>\Delta K_{M-R}$	
	Necessary condition: $\Delta M+5\Delta P+2\Delta R>2\Delta K_{R-P}+2\Delta T+3\Delta K_{M-R}$	
11	**Rb, Pb, Mb**	
1	$\Delta T+\Delta M>\Delta R+\Delta P$	
2	$\Delta K_{R-P}+\Delta M>\Delta R$	
3	$\Delta K_{R-P}+\Delta T+\Delta M>\Delta R+2\Delta P$	
4	$\Delta K_{M-R}+\Delta T>\Delta R+\Delta P$	
5	$\Delta K_{R-P}+\Delta K_{M-R}>\Delta R$	
6	$\Delta T+\Delta K_{R-P}+\Delta K_{M-R}>\Delta R+2\Delta P$	
12	$\Delta T+\Delta K_{R-P}>2\Delta P$	
	Necessary condition: $5\Delta K_{R-P}+5\Delta T+3\Delta K_{M-R}+3\Delta M>8\Delta P+6\Delta R$	
12	**Rb, Pw, Mb**	
1	$\Delta P+\Delta M>\Delta K_{R-P}+\Delta R$	
2	$2\Delta P+\Delta M>\Delta R+\Delta T$	result of 3 & 11
3	$\Delta M>\Delta R$	
4	$\Delta K_{M-R}+\Delta P>\Delta R+\Delta K_{R-P}$	result of 6 & 11
5	$\Delta K_{M-R}+2\Delta P>\Delta R+\Delta T$	result of 6 & 11
6	$\Delta K_{M-R}>\Delta R$	
11	$2\Delta P>\Delta T+\Delta K_{R-P}$	
	Necessary condition: $3\Delta P+\Delta K_{M-R}+2\Delta M>3\Delta R+\Delta T+6\Delta K_{R-P}$	

select a given configuration. The mathematical reasoning of this is straightforward. If the terms α, β, γ and δ fulfil the following relations

$$\alpha > \beta \qquad (6a)$$

and

$$\gamma > \delta \qquad (6b)$$

then it implies that

$$\alpha + \gamma > \beta + \delta \qquad (6c)$$

Following inequalities (1)–(5) and as indicated in the 'Notes' column of Table 4.2, some inequalities are implied by others (for example, if configuration 1 is preferred over configurations 2 and 4, it is preferential to configuration 5 as well). Hence, we do not need to sum all the inequalities, but only those that are 'stand-alone' (i.e. are not results of other inequalities).

The necessary condition is a single inequality that assures us that a specific configuration dominates all others. For example if $3\Delta K_{R-P} + \Delta K_{M-R} + 2\Delta R > 2\Delta T + 4\Delta M$, configuration 1 will dominate all other configurations. The savings on knowledge cost flows (both K_{R-P} and K_{M-R}), together with the relatively cheap cost of R_A will be higher than the additional cost that results from transportation to the market in B, and location of M in A rather than in B.

The necessary condition enables us to speculate on the location configurations of firms with different product attributes. The basic logic of these speculations is that if a certain cost variable (R, P, M, K_{R-P}, K_{M-R} or T) has higher values in products with specific attributes, the cost difference of these variables is also expected to be higher. This observation is intuitively reasonable and stems from the following mathematical conventions:

if $\alpha \to \infty$ and $\beta \to \infty$ then $(\alpha - \beta) \to \infty$ (7a)

if $\alpha \to 0$ and $\beta \to 0$ then $(\alpha - \beta) \to 0$ (7b)

For example, as High Technology (HT) products are more knowledge-intensive than Low Technology (LT) products, we expect that R, K_{R-P}, K_{M-R} and M are higher in HT products compared to LT ones (Almor and Hirsch, 1995; Buckley and Casson, 1976; DuBois, Toyne and Oliff, 1993; Hirsch, 1989; Kogut and Zander, 1993; Martin and Salomon, 2003). The fact that R, K_{R-P} and K_{M-R} are relatively higher in

HT products implies that their cost difference is also probably relatively higher. Thus, whenever a high value of these terms is required in order to satisfy the necessary condition of a location configuration (e.g., configurations 1 and 4), they are likely to be chosen by HT firms. One interesting implication of this observation is that the choice of configurations 1 and 4 for producers of HT products does not depend on production costs at all, as opposed to the view of many scholars (e.g., DuBois *et al.*, 1993; Dunning, 1977, 1988, 2000; Hirsch, 1976; Kotabe and Swan, 1994).

Another example applies to producers of intangible products (which have negligible transportation costs) that do not require intensive marketing interactions with their customers, as they are fairly standard (Hirsch, 1989). Such products might be, for instance, standard (ready-made) software packages or computer games. Since M and T are assumed to be low in these products, we expect ΔM and ΔT to be relatively low as well (e.g. *as opposed* to location configuration 5). Producers of standard intangible products are therefore expected to select location configurations that require high values of ΔM and ΔT less frequently than producers of other products.

Finally, Table 4.2 enables us to specify the necessary conditions for the emergence of 'knowledge asset seeking' FDI in the host country (Dunning and Narula, 1995). This is expected to occur when either configuration 11 or configuration 12 are the preferred location configuration (since both configurations imply the location of R&D activities in B). Essentially, in the case where production is located in B (configuration 11), knowledge asset seeking FDI is expected to occur when the savings on knowledge flow between R&D and production and transportation costs exceed the extra costs of production and R&D in B. On the other hand, in the case where production is located in W (configuration 12) knowledge asset seeking FDI is expected to occur when the savings on production costs exceed the extra costs of R&D in B, transportation from W to B and knowledge flow between R&D and production.

The control decision

Having defined the set of necessary and sufficient conditions to select a location configuration, we can now elaborate the decision rules and compare between internal and external modes of control. Inequalities (1b), (2b), (3b), (4b) and (5b) imply that:

Configurations 2a, 3a, 5a, 6a, 11a and 12a are preferential to configurations 2, 3, 5, 6, 11 and 12, respectively, in cases where the savings on external foreign production are higher than the savings on internal knowledge flows between R&D and production, i.e. if:

$$\Delta P' > PR > \Delta K'_{R-P} \tag{8a}$$

Configurations 4a, 5b, 6c, 11b and 12c are preferential to configurations 4, 5, 6, 11 and 12, respectively, in cases where the savings on external foreign marketing operations are higher than the savings on internal knowledge flows between marketing and R&D, i.e. if:

$$\Delta M' > \Delta K'_{M-R} \tag{8b}$$

Configurations 5c, 6b, 11c and 12b are preferential to configurations 5, 6, 11 and 12, respectively, in cases where the cumulative savings on external foreign production and marketing operations are higher than the cumulative savings on internal knowledge flows between R&D and production and between marketing and R&D, i.e., if:

$$\Delta P' + \Delta Ml > \Delta K'_{R-P} + \Delta K'_{M-R} \tag{8c}$$

Configurations 11d and 12d are preferential to configurations 11 and 12, respectively, in cases where the savings on external foreign R&D activities are higher than the cumulative savings on internal knowledge flows between R&D and production and between marketing and R&D, i.e., if:

$$\Delta R' > \Delta K'_{R-P} + \Delta K'_{M-R} \tag{8d}$$

Configurations 11e and 12e are preferential to configurations 11 and 12, respectively, in cases where the cumulative savings on external foreign R&D and production are higher than the cumulative savings on internal knowledge flows between R&D and production and between marketing and R&D, or more specifically if:

$$\Delta R' + \Delta P' > 2\Delta K'_{R-P} + \Delta K'_{M-R} \tag{8e}$$

Configurations 11f and 12f are preferential to configurations 11 and 12, respectively, in cases where the cumulative savings on external foreign R&D and marketing operations are higher than the cumulative savings on internal knowledge flows between R&D and production and between marketing and R&D, or more specifically if:

$$\Delta R' + \Delta M' > \Delta K'_{R-P} + 2\Delta K'_{M-R} \tag{8f}$$

Configurations 11g and 12g are preferential to configurations 11 and 12, respectively, in cases where the cumulative savings on external foreign R&D, production and marketing operations are higher than the cumulative savings on internal knowledge flows between R&D and production and between marketing and R&D, or more specifically if:

$$\Delta R' + \Delta P' + \Delta M' > 2\Delta K'_{R-P} + 2\Delta K'_{M-R} \qquad (8g)$$

Inequalities (8a)–(8f) imply under which conditions externalisation of R&D, production and marketing activities is preferred over internalisation of these value-adding activities. Moreover, following the reasoning presented in inequalities (6a)–(6c) regarding the preference of certain location configurations over others, we can deduce that inequality (8 g) that sums inequalities (8a)–(8f) serves as the *necessary* condition to prefer externalisation to internalisation, since this inequality has to exist for inequalities (8a)–(8f) to exist.[1]

We can now articulate additional expectations regarding the internalisation and externalisation preferences of firms with different product attributes. For instance, as knowledge cost flows are expected to be higher in HT products than in LT products (DuBois *et al.*, 1993; Hirsch, 1976; Kogut and Zander, 1993; Martin and Salomon, 2003), we anticipate their cost differential to be higher as well, and thus producers of HT products are expected to have a greater tendency to internalise value-adding activities than producers of LT products.

For intangible products (e.g. software), per unit production costs are negligible compared to knowledge flow costs, implying that knowledge flow cost differences are probably higher than production costs ones. This implies, for instance, that configurations 2, 3, 5, 6, 11 and 12 are expected to be costlier than configurations 2a, 3a, 5a, 6a, 11a and 12a, respectively, for manufacturers of intangible products. Thus, producers of intangible products are also expected to prefer the configurations that imply internalisation of foreign production activities.

A dynamic perspective

The firm's decision regarding its preferred configuration will clearly change over time. We use insights from the product cycle framework (Vernon, 1966) to provide a dynamic extension to the static model discussed earlier. Strictly speaking, the proposed dynamic extension applies only to an internationalising firm that starts out by selling a HT product, which over time (following the familiar product cycle trajectory) is standardised and becomes a LT product.

The product cycle refers to three major phases in the evolution of firm's sales of specific products: introduction, growth and maturity. During these phases, the volume of sales is expected to increase and may be described as an S-shape curve. In order to simplify our discussion, we refer only to two periods of time in the worldwide cycle of a product: *Period 1* – the period where the volume of sales is low but sales are growing rapidly and *Period 2* – the period where the firm faces a substantial market for its product, but sales are not growing fast. Our dynamic extension applies to the expected change in firm configuration between these two periods.

Essentially we argue that the relative cost of each value-adding activity and flow out of the firm's overall costs (i.e., the percentage that this activity or flow cost constitutes out of overall costs) changes between periods 1 and 2. Following Vernon (1966), we assume that the following relationships exist (the numbers 1 and 2 together with the activity/flow cost symbol denote their cost in periods 1 and 2, respectively).

The relative cost of R&D (compared to other value adding activities) is expected to decline over time, since the product becomes standardised:

$$R_1 > R_2 \tag{9}$$

As the number of changes in product specifications reduces, the relative cost of knowledge flows between R and P is expected to reduce as well:

$$(K_{R-P})_1 > (K_{R-P})_2 \tag{10}$$

As production volume increases, the relative cost of production is expected to increase compared to other costs (e.g., R&D). Although the absolute per unit production cost may decline, production share in overall costs increases as production runs become longer and the units are more standardised, implying that:

$$P_1 < P_2 \tag{11}$$

The relative cost of transportation is expected to increase too in parallel with the increase in production volumes, as relatively more units will be shipped in period 2 than in period 1:

$$T_1 < T_2 \tag{12}$$

The relative cost of marketing is expected to increase as sales volume increases and competition intensifies:

$$M_1 < M_2 \tag{13}$$

As the number of changes in product specifications and customers' feedback regarding the product (e.g., requests for changes in specifications, fixing bugs) declines, the relative cost of knowledge flows between M and R is expected to decrease:

$$(K_{M-R})_1 > (K_{M-R})_2 \tag{14}$$

Inequalities (9)–(14) imply that over time, the relative importance of K_{R-P}, K_{M-R} and R declines, whereas the relative importance of P, T and M rises. In order to understand how these changes affect the firm's choice of its preferred configuration, we assume that in the long run (i.e. period 2): $K_{R-P} \to 0$, $K_{M-R} \to 0$ and $R \to 0$. Following inequality (7b), this means that in the long run: $\Delta K_{R-P} \to 0$, $\Delta K_{M-R} \to 0$ and $\Delta R \to 0$. As the relevant costs become negligible, the cost difference between different locations and control modes of R becomes negligible and the cost difference between knowledge flows becomes negligible as well. On the other hand ΔP, ΔT and ΔM are expected to remain constant or to increase.

Applying the above assumptions to the relationships detailed in Table 4.2 imply that in period 2, configurations that include more value-adding activities that are located outside the home country (A) are expected to dominate others, namely: configurations 6 and 12 dominate configurations 1, 3 and 4 and configurations 5 and 11 dominate configuration 2. This happens because knowledge flow costs become negligible in period 2. We can therefore deduce that the firm's *location* choice, once its product has matured, is limited only to location configurations 5, 6, 11 and 12. While the relationships between these configurations are not clear, it is evident that configurations requiring international knowledge flows become more attractive in period 2, thus firms are expected to increase their international dispersion and locate more value-adding activities outside their home country, over time.

Referring to the necessary conditions that apply to each configuration in Table 4.2, the fact that $\Delta K_{R-P} \to 0$, $\Delta K_{M-R} \to 0$ and $\Delta R \to 0$ implies that the necessary conditions to choose between four remaining configurations, *during period 2*, change as detailed in Table 4.3.

It can be seen from Table 4.3 that the choice between location configurations 5, 6, 11 and 12 depends on the magnitude of product flow costs difference (ΔT), production costs difference (ΔP) and marketing costs difference (ΔM). This implies that the long-term location configuration of firms whose product follows the patterns anticipated by the product cycle framework may be predicted based on the product-specific attributes. For instance, we may anticipate that over time distance-sensitive products, i.e., products for which the ratio of per unit

Table 4.3 Necessary conditions for choosing a location configuration (period 2).

Configuration No.	Necessary condition
5	$\Delta M + 3\Delta T > 5\Delta P$
6	$\Delta M + 5\Delta P > 2\Delta T$
11	$6\Delta T + 3\Delta M > 8\Delta P$
12	$3\Delta P + 2\Delta M > \Delta T$

transportation costs to per unit production cost is relatively high, incur a larger ΔT than products which are not distance-sensitive (DuBois *et al.*, 1993; Helpman and Krugman, 1985; Hirsch and Hashai, 2000). As high values of ΔT are required in order to satisfy the necessary condition of several location configurations (e.g., configurations 5 and 11) in the long run, these configurations are likely to be chosen by firms producing distance-sensitive products.

Incorporating the control *mode* choice into the dynamic extension reveals that during period 2, the factors that favoured internal operation have weakened while the factors favouring external operation have become stronger. The reduction in knowledge flow costs difference compared to production and marketing cost difference indicates that once the firm's product has matured, inequalities (8a)–(8c) as well as (8e)–(8 g) are likely to exist and thus the external operation of M and P will become more economic. This implies that over time, pressures for externalisation increase and internationalising firms are expected to prefer to externalise foreign production and marketing activities. Hence, following our earlier discussion on internal and external operations, during period 2 configurations 5a, 5b and 5c will be preferential to configuration 5; configurations 6a, 6b and 6c will be preferential to configuration 6; configurations 11a, 11b, 11c, 11e, 11f and 11 g will be preferential to configuration 11; and configurations 12a, 12b, 12c, 12e, 12f and 12 g will be preferential to configuration 12.

Conclusion

In this chapter, we followed the reasoning of 'economic school' of thought to offer a method for the analysis of location and control decisions of internationalising firms. The choice between alternative configurations is captured as a systematic comparison between the costs of value-adding activities and the cost of product and knowledge flows, where the configurations that exhibit the lowest cost are the preferred ones. We have demonstrated the applicability of our approach in a world consisting of three countries and have shown how superior location and control configurations can be identified. Moreover, we were able to considerably shorten the criteria of choice among various location and control configurations by introducing the appropriate sufficient and necessary conditions.

Our proposed model goes beyond classic models adhering to the 'economic school' in several directions. First, the model relates *simultaneously* to a destination country (i.e., the country where the firm's foreign market exists) and a resource-abundant country (i.e., where production is assumed to be the cheapest). This approach enables us to capture a more realistic view of the dilemmas facing internationalising firms than most models of internationalisation that usually relate only to one of the above-mentioned countries or, at best, treat them separately.

Second, we distinguish between the costs of performing specific value-adding activities and the costs of flows. This enables us to get a clearer view of the location and control dilemmas of internationalising firms. In our view, location and control decisions are the outcome of the comparative costs of operations and (mainly knowledge) flows. Operation and flow costs often counteract each other (e.g., when production is cheaper in a specific foreign country, but knowledge flow costs favour proximity of production to R&D, or when externalisation is cheaper but knowledge flows to externalised activities are more expensive). This counter-balancing impact should be considered more specifically as is done in this paper.

Third, we offer a dynamic extension to the firm's internationalisation process based on the economic, rather than the familiar behavioural arguments of the so called stages model of internationalisation (e.g., Calof and Beamish, 1995; Johanson and Vahlne, 1977, 1990; Johanson and Wiedersheim-Paul, 1975). In that respect, our model implies that over time value-adding activities are expected to be not only more internationally dispersed but also more externalised. While this view is consistent with the view of stages model regarding the gradual internationalisation of firms' value-adding activities, it contrasts the stages model which argues that firms internalise their foreign value-adding activities over time.

Fourth, our model places 'knowledge assets seeking' (Dunning and Narula, 1995) within the firm's overall location and control dilemmas and specifies the conditions to internationalise and internalise R&D. By doing this, we integrate the accumulating literature on the internationalisation of R&D (e.g., Cantwell, 1995; Kuemmerle, 1997; Patel and Vega, 1999; Pearce and Papanastassiou, 1996, 1999; Zanfei, 2000) with the basic reasoning of 'economic school' of thought.

Finally, while our model is based on several simplifying assumptions, the model's strength actually lies in the ability to change these assumptions, offer alternative ones and analyse the impact of changing specific assumptions on the model's results. In fact, our model can be modified in many different ways. One modification is to allow duplication of identical value-adding activities across borders. This, of course, complicates the decision making of the firm, as there are then $3 \times 7 \times 3 = 63$ possible location configurations to choose from. Allowing duplication of value-adding activities across borders requires incorporating the impact of returns to scale into the model, which stems from concentration and dispersion of value-adding activities. Additionally, it is possible to modify the model; it also applies to the home market of the internationalising firm, to allow reverse production cost ratios between country A and B (e.g., analyse what happens when production in A is costlier than production in B), to allow the location of R&D and marketing activities in the resource-abundant country (e.g., the location of R&D facilities or Customer Relations Management centres in India or China) or to allow multiple stages of production and thus include the international division of labour in the model. These modifications nat-urally complicate the model but by using linear programming analysis tools, it should be possible to offer criteria for the solution of these problems as well. Hence, the proposed model may be only the foundation of a new research avenue that may shed light on the interrelations between firms' configurations and internationalisation.

Acknowledgements

Niron Hashai wishes to thank the Recanati Fund at the Hebrew University for its financial support.

Note

1 Still inequality (8g) does not guarantee the existence of all other inequalities and this is why it cannot serve as the necessary and sufficient condition for the control decision.

References

Almor, T. and Hirsch, S. (1995) Outsiders' response to Europe 1992: Theoretical considerations and empirical evidence. *Journal of International Business Studies*, 26(2), 223–238.

Anderson, E. and Gatignon, H. (1986) Modes of entry: A transactions cost analysis and propositions. *Journal of International Business Studies*, 17(3), 1–26.

Buckley, P.J. and Carter, M.J. (2004) A formal analysis of knowledge combination in multinational enterprises. *Journal of International Business Studies*, 35(5), 371–384.

Buckley, P.J. and Casson, M. (1976) *The Future of the Multinational Enterprise*. London: Macmillan.

Buckley, P.J. and Casson, M. (1979) A theory of international operations. In J. Ghertman and J. Leontiades (eds), *European research in International Business*. Amsterdam: North Holland.

Buckley, P.J. and Casson, M. (1998) Analysing foreign market entry strategies: Extending the internalisation approach. *Journal of International Business Studies*, 29(3), 539–561.

Calof, J.L. and Beamish, P.W. (1995) Adapting to foreign markets: Explaining internationalization. *International Business Review*, 4(2), 115–131.

Cantwell, J. (1995) The globalisation of technology: What remains of the product cycle model? *Cambridge Journal of Economics*, 19(1), 155–174.

Casson, M. (1994) Why are firms hierarchical. *International Journal of the Economics of Business*, 1(1), 47–76.

Casson, M. (2000) *The Economics of International Business – A New Research Agenda*. Cheltenham: Edward Elgar.

Contractor, F.J. (1990) Ownership patterns of US joint ventures abroad and the liberalization of foreign government regulation in the 1980's: Evidence from the benchmark surveys. *Journal of International Business Studies*, 21(1), 55–73.

DuBois, F.L., Toyne, B. and Oliff, M.D. (1993) International manufacturing strategies of US multinationals: A conceptual framework based on four-industry study. *Journal of International Business Studies*, 22(2), 307–333.

Dunning, J.H. (1977) Trade, location of economic activity and the MNE: A search for an eclectic paradigm. In B. Ohlin, P.O. Hesselborn and P.M. Wijkman (eds), *The International Allocation of Economic Activities. Proceedings of a Nobel Symposium in Stockholm*. London: Macmillan.

Dunning, J.H. (1988) The eclectic paradigm of international production: A restatement and some possible extensions. *Journal of International Business Studies*, 19(1), 1–31.

Dunning, J.H. (2000) The eclectic paradigm as an envelope for economic and business theories of MNE activity. *International Business Review*, 9(2), 163–190.

Dunning, J.H. and Narula, R. (1995) The R&D activities of foreign firms in the United States. *International Studies of Management and Organization*, 25(1 and 2), 39–73.

Helpman, E. and Krugman, P.R. (1985) *Market Structure and Foreign Trade – Increasing Returns, Imperfect Competition and the International Economy*. Cambridge, MA: MIT Press.

Hennart, J.F. (1993) Explaining the swollen middle: Why most transactions are a mix of 'market' and 'hierarchy'. *Organization Science*, 4(4), 529–547.

Hirsch, S. (1976) An international trade and investment theory of the firm. *Oxford Economic Papers, 28*, 258–270.

Hirsch, S. (1989) Services and service intensity in international trade. *Weltwirtschaffliches Archiv – Review of World Economics, 125*(1), 45–60.

Hirsch, S. and Hashai, N. (2000) Arab Israeli potential trade: The role of distance sensitive products. *The International Trade Journal, 14*(1), 1–35.

Hofstede, G. (1980) *Culture's Consequences: International Differences in Work-related Values.* Beverley Hills, CA: Sage.

Hymer, S.H. (1976) *The International Operations of National Firms: A Study of Direct Foreign Investment.* 1960 PhD thesis. Cambridge, MA: MIT Press.

Johanson, J. and Vahlne, J.-E. (1977) The internationalization process of the firm – A model of knowledge development and increasing foreign market commitment. *Journal of International Business Studies, 8*(1), 23–32.

Johanson, J. and Vahlne, J.-E. (1990) The mechanism of internationalisation. *International Marketing Review, 7*(4), 11–24.

Johanson, J. and Wiedersheim-Paul, F. (1975) The internationalisation of the firm – Four Swedish cases. *Journal of Management Studies, 12*, 305–322.

Kogut, B. and Singh, H. (1988) The effect of country culture on the choice of entry mode. *Journal of International Business Studies, 19*(3), 411–423.

Kogut, B. and Zander, U. (1993) Knowledge of the firm and the evolutionary theory of the Multinational Corporation. *Journal of International Business Studies, 24*(4), 625–645.

Kotabe, M. and Swan, S. (1994) Offshore sourcing: Reaction, maturation and consolidation of US multinationals. *Journal of International Business Studies, 25*(1), 115–140.

Krugman, P. (1991) Increasing returns and economic geography. *Journal of Political Economy, 99*, 483–499.

Krugman, P. (1995) *Development, Geography and Economic Theory.* MIT Press: Cambridge, MA.

Kuemmerle, W. (1997) Building effective R&D capabilities abroad. *Harvard Business REview, March–April*, 61–70.

Kumar, N. (2001) Determinants of location of overseas R&D activities of multinational enterprises: The case of US and Japanese Corporations. *Research Policy, 30*(1), 159–174.

Linder, S.B. (1961) *An Essay on Trade and Transformation.* New York: Wiley.

Mariotti, S. and Piscitello, L. (1995) Knowledge costs and location of FDI's within the host country: Empirical evidence from Italy. *Journal of International Business Studies, 26*(4), 815–841.

Martin, X. and Salomon, R. (2003) Knowledge transfer capacity and its implications for the theory of the multinational corporation. *Journal of International Business Studies, 34*(4), 356–373.

Melin, L. (1992) Internationalization as a strategy process. *Strategic Management Journal, 13*, 99–118.

Narula, R. and Dunning, J.H. (1998) Explaining international R&D alliances and the role of governments. *International Business Review, 7*(4), 377–397.

Patel, P. and Pavitt, K. (1991) Large firms in the production of the world's technology: An important case of non-globalisation. *Journal of International Business Studies, 22*(1), 1–22.

Patel, P. and Vega, M. (1999) Patterns of internationalisation of corporate technology: Location vs. home country advantages. *Research Policy, 28*(2 and 3), 145–155.

Pearce, R. and Papanastassiou, M. (1996) R&D networks and innovation: Decentralised product development in multinational enterprises. *R&D Management, 26*(4), 315–333.

Pearce, R. and Papanastassiou, M. (1999) Overseas R&D and the strategic evolution of MNEs: Evidence from laboratories in the UK. *Research Policy, 28*(1), 23–41.

Rangan, S. and Adner, R. (2001) Profits and the internet: Seven misconceptions. *MIT Sloan Management Review, Summer*, 44–53.

Rao, P.M. (2001) The ICT revolution, internationalization of technological activity, and the emerging economies: Implications for global marketing. *International Business Review, 10*(5), 571–596.

Rugman, A.M. (1981) *Inside the Multinationals: The Economics of Internal Markets*. New York: Columbia University Press.

Rugman, A.M. (1986) New theories of the multinational enterprise: An assessment of internalization theory. *Bulletin of Economic Research, 38*(2), 101–119.

Vernon, R. (1966) International investment and international trade in the product cycle. *Quarterly Journal of Economics, 80*, 190–207.

Williamson, O.E. (1975) *Markets and hierarchies: Analysis and anti-trust applications*. New York: Free Press.

Williamson, O.E. (1985) *The economic institutions of capitalism*. New York: Free Press.

Zanfei, A. (2000) Transnational firms and changing organization of innovative activities. *Cambridge Journal of Economics, 24*(5), 515–554.

5
Edith Penrose's Theory of the Growth of the Firm and the Strategic Management of Multinational Enterprises

Peter J. Buckley and Mark Casson

Introduction

Foss (2002, p. 148) says 'Penrose's work is, in the crucial dimensions, at variance with economic orthodoxy ... It should be thought of as a contribution to economic heterodoxy' Penrose and Pitelis (2002, pp. 19 *et seq.*), in describing Fritz Machlup as 'Edith's supervisor' at Johns Hopkins says 'A fascinating paradox is how Machlup, a doyen of neo-classical economics, should have been partially responsible for a work so far removed from the mainstream'. Penrose has also been claimed as a feminist economist (Best and Humphries, 2003). Our argument is that Penrose sought to create a theory of the growth of the firm which was logically consistent and empirically tractable. Her subsequent adoption as grandmother of the resource based view has only limited validity, based on a selective reading of her work and in defiance of its holistic qualities. See the debate between Rugman and Verbeke (2002, 2004) and Kor and Mahoney (2004) and Lockett and Thompson (2004), the latter based on Penrose's (1960) analysis of the Hercules Powder Company.

This paper presents a formalisation of Penrose's model contained in the *Theory of the Growth of the Firm* (1959) and applies it to the strategic decisions of multinational enterprises (MNEs). Previous research on Penrose and the multinational firm (e.g., Dunning, 2003; Pitelis, 2002, 2004) has focused on Penrose's overall contributions to strategic decisions in MNEs. This paper focuses solely on her 1959 model and compares it to the model of Buckley and Casson (1976). Interesting contrasts are found and a synthetic approach suggests that this combination is a useful basis for further theorising about the MNE and its strategic decisions.

In contrasting Penrose's theory with that of Buckley and Casson (1976), we shall see that the former's concentration on product diversification can be considered complementary to the latter's emphasis on innovation. Combining the two gives a satisfying model of the strategic management decisions within an MNE and opens up a new research agenda.

A simple formal model of Penrose's theory of the growth of the firm

The key to formalising Penrose's ideas is the recognition that she reformulated the familiar cost functions used in the theory of the firm. She argued that the average cost of output is independent of the scale of production, but increases with respect to the rate of growth. Thus in so far as the average cost curve is U-shaped, it is U-shaped with respect, not to the scale of production, as commonly assumed, but to the rate of growth.

The simplest way to understand this postulate is to recognise that average costs are increased by *adjustments* in the rate of output. Changing the rate of output has a bigger impact on average cost than setting *steady state* output at a higher or lower level. Changes in the rate of output dislocate the allocation of resources. This is particularly true for human resources. Employees are usually most productive when they repeat the same routines; furthermore, when their work is repetitive, productivity may improve as a result of learning on the job. As a firm grows, the internal division of labour has to change, and this forces people to change their roles. Their previous learning of job-specific skills becomes obsolete, as they return to the start of the 'learning curve' in their new job.

Change is expensive in other ways too. Plant and machinery have to reallocated to different uses, and this process needs to be managed, creating additional demands on the management team. As the management team grows, new recruits need to be trained. Through leaving their previous employment with another firm, and joining the expanding firm, these recruits incur the same costs of retraining as those who have changed their jobs within the firm. Indeed, their training costs are greater because they know little about the institutional context of their job. To train recruits, experienced managers have to be diverted from their usual work, adding to the dislocation described above.

Costs of change may be related either to the absolute amount of change or the proportional amount of change. A case can be made for both, but in the Penrose model it is the proportional and not the absolute amount of change that matters. In alternative models of growth, however, the absolute amount of change is key.

The formalisation of Penrose's theory is based on Buckley and Casson's (2004) recent interpretation of her major work (Penrose, 1959). The model analyses a firm that grows through diversification at a steady rate. The central point of the model is that the firm faces 'costs of growth' which increase, not with the size of the firm, but with its rate of growth. The key to the model is the specification of these costs of growth.

Penrose viewed the firm as a 'bundle of resources' because she saw resources – in particular human resources – as both the key to the firm's success and the principal constraint on its growth. According to her theory, the tacitness of information – on which modern resource-based theory places so much emphasis – not only protects the secrets of the firm's entrepreneurial success, but also inhibits the assimilation of the additional human resources required to sustain its growth. The growth rate of the firm reflects a balance between the entrepreneurial dynamism which drives its diversification, and the difficulty of enlarging the firm's management team to exploit the resultant opportunities.

In the basic model, the profitability of the firm is independent of its size and depends only on its rate of growth. This leads to a simple formula for the value of a growing firm, as determined by the present value of its future profit stream. Managers serving shareholder interests will maximise this value, whilst managers pursuing their own objectives – such as status – may maximise growth instead. Penrose considered both objectives; the differences are small, however, because maximising profits not only maximises shareholder value but also facilitates the internal financing of growth (see also Baumol, 1967; Marris, 1964).

Penrose's central point is that there is, in principle, no limit to the size to which a firm can grow.

- There are limits to the extent to which a firm can grow within a single market, which are set by the overall size of the market and the existence of competitors within it. But a firm can evade any such market size constraint by diversifying into other markets.
- It is often said that because of U-shaped average cost curves, there is a unique optimal size of firm at which average cost is a minimum.

However, the logic of the U-shaped average cost curve applies to physical plant and equipment rather than to a managerial unit such as a firm. A firm that cannot expand beyond optimum plant size can expand by increasing the number of plants it operates, either through replicating plants in the same market (horizontal integration), moving into other stages of production in the same market (vertical integration) or diversifying into different markets.
- Misleading analogies have been employed to suggest that there is a limit to the size of firm. Marshall's metaphor of the firms in an industry resembling the 'trees in a forest' is misleading because it ignores the fact that firms can regenerate themselves through managerial succession. More significant still, firms can merge with each other to sustain their growth, and metamorphose into new forms, as when a small firm with highly-centralised autocratic management merges with other small firms and turns into a large highly-decentralised multi-divisional firm. As a legal and contractual entity, a firm can in principle endure for ever.
- Managerial diseconomies of scale are often said to limit the size of firms, but such limiting factors are more properly regarded as diseconomies of growth. In other words, the costs that limit the size of a firm at any time are costs that limit its continued growth, rather than costs associated with the size to which it has already grown. It is therefore more appropriate to use the concept of an optimum rate of growth of a firm than an optimum size of firm.
- In terms of international expansion, Penrose can be interpreted as considering foreign subsidiaries as autonomous companies. As such, they are beyond the reach of the firm's administrative coordination. The absence of authoritative communication would thus put them beyond the boundary of the firm. There is a potential modification of our formalisation in which the rate of growth of firms of different sizes is the same up to the extent of the reach of coordination and then zero beyond it. This is not a realistic interpretation of modern multinational firms, especially given managerial learning and technological breakthroughs in communication and control of international expansion.

When analysing growth, the natural analogue of a theory of the optimal size of firm is a theory of the optimal growth rate of the firm, and this is essentially what Penrose provides. Because size of firm does not matter, there is no reason to believe that the firm's growth rate will vary systematically over its lifetime, and so it is reasonable to postulate the existence of a steady state rate of growth. The existence of such a steady state implies that, in the limit, firms can last forever and so, with a constant rate of growth, they can eventually approach infinite size. To many observers of the corporate scene in the 1950s, it seemed as if large firms like General Motors would, indeed, con0tinue to grow forever. Although this may now appear an extreme possibility, it was considered quite plausible at the time that Penrose was writing.

Let the size of the firm be measured by x. If growth proceeds continuously at a constant proportional rate g then the size of the firm will increase exponentially:

$x = X \exp(gt)$

To simplify the subsequent discussion it is useful to normalise the size of the firm on its foundation to unity, $X = 1$. In terms of Penrose's theory, size is most naturally measured by the number of markets served by the firm; the normalisation therefore means that when the firm is newly established it operates in a single market.

All variables are non-negative unless otherwise stated. Discrete variables, such as the number of markets, are treated as though they were continuous.

For expository purposes it is useful to set out the model in three stages, with the final stage representing the model actually used in this paper.

Stage 1

Suppose that the profit generated by a representative market is A, where A is a constant independent of the size of the firm. As the number of markets grows at the rate g, total profit grows at the same rate:

Profit at time $t = Ax = A \exp(gt)$.

If future profits are discounted at the rate r, and $r > g$, then the value of the firm at the time it is founded ($t = 0$) is

$v = \int_0^\infty \exp(-rt) \, Ax \, dt = A / (r - g)$

The factor $1 / (r - g)$, which multiplies into the profit per market, A, indicates the net rate at which profit is capitalised.

The first of the firm's objectives mentioned above corresponds to the maximisation of v. The second objective corresponds to the maximisation of g, subject to a constraint that the value of the firm is sufficient to support a dividend stream of acceptable size. If the dividend stream $d(t)$ grows at the same rate as the firm then

$$d(t) = D \exp(gt)$$

where D is the initial level of dividend payments. To be feasible, initial dividend payments must be less than initial profit, $D \leq A$. Shareholder pressure fixes the minimum acceptable level, D, and managers then set dividends exactly equal to this level as part of their growth-maximising strategy. The value of the dividend stream is

$$v^d = D / (r - g)$$

and the managers maximise g subject to the constraint that

$$v \geq v^d$$

If there are no costs of growth then, since A is a constant, value is maximised by setting growth as high as possible. Since g is constrained to be slightly less than r, this becomes the value-maximising rate of growth. Provided that $A \geq D$ there is no difference between growth-maximisation and value-maximisation: both objectives imply the largest possible rate of growth.

Stage 2

To avoid this trivial result, it is necessary to introduce costs of growth. Let B be a parameter measuring costs that are directly proportional to growth. It is necessary to choose the dimension of B with care: it is the average cost per unit size generated per unit rate of growth. After deducting the cost of growth, net profit at time t becomes $(A - Bg)x$, and the value of the firm at the outset becomes

$$v = (A - Bg)/(r - g)$$

It turns out, however, that costs which are directly proportional to growth do not fundamentally modify the trivial result above. If net profit is positive, $A > Br$, then value-maximising growth is just less than r, exactly as before, whereas if net profit is negative, $A < Br$, then value-maximising growth is zero. But in the latter case the firm has negative value, and so it will not be established in the first place. In the special case where profit is zero, $A = Br$, the firm is just viable and the value-maximising growth rate is indeterminate within the permitted range, $0 \leq g < r$. Thus the growth rate is either just less than r, indeterminate, or the firm is not established, depending upon whether profit is positive, negative, or zero.

Stage 3

To achieve a determinate value-maximising growth inside the permitted range it is necessary to introduce decreasing returns to the rate of growth through a quadratic cost term which reflects the decline of productivity as the rate of growth increases. This quadratic term, Cg^2x, represents the effects of dislocation, as described above. It is quadratic in g, the proportional rate of growth, rather than in gx, which is the absolute rate of growth, because it is the proportional rather than the absolute amount of dislocation which affects average cost.

Net profit at time t becomes $(A - Bg - Cg^2)x$, and the value of the firm becomes

$$v = (A - Bg - Cg^2)/(r - g)$$

This is the fundamental formula for the value of the firm in a theory of the growth of the firm. The formula is implicit throughout Penrose's analysis.

The first order condition for value-maximisation is

$$v_g = ((A - Bg - Cg^2) / (r - g)^2) - ((B + 2Cg) / ((r - g)) = 0$$

where the subscript g denotes the derivative with respect to g. The derivative v_g measures the sensitivity of the firm's value to changes in its rate of growth, and comprises two terms. The first measures the impact of a change in growth on the capitalised value of initial profits, assuming that the profit stream remains unchanged, whilst the second term measures the cost of growth, which is equal to the value of the marginal reduction in the profit stream induced by growth, assuming that the capitalisation rate remains unchanged.

Placing both terms over a common denominator, $(r - g)^2$, and noting that the denominator is always positive over the permitted range $0 \leq g < r$, indicates that the first order condition is satisfied only when the numerator is zero. The numerator is quadratic:

$$(A - Br) - 2Crg + Cg^2 = 0$$

and its solution has two roots. These roots are real if

$A - Br > 0;$ $\qquad A - Br - Cr^2 < 0$

i.e. if growth is profitable at the margin when growth is zero, and profit is negative when growth is equal to the discount rate, $g = r$. Only the smaller of the two roots lies in the permitted range; this root determines the optimal growth rate

$$g^* = r - (r^2 - ((A - Br)/C))^{1/2}$$

Under the assumed conditions, the numerator of the derivative always declines with respect to g, and since the denominator is always positive within the permitted range, v_g switches from positive to negative as g increases in the region of g^*, which guarantees that g^* supports a maximum.

Differentiation of the growth equation shows that under the assumed conditions the partial derivates can be signed as follows:

$$g^*_A > 0; \qquad g^*_B < 0; \qquad g^*_C < 0; \qquad g^*_r < 0$$

Growth is higher, the higher is the profitability of the representative market, A, and the lower are the cost parameters, B, C. B is less important than either A or C because its impact is mediated by the rate of cost of capital, r, which is normally substantially less than unity. The key insight of the growth formula, therefore, is that growth is governed by a fundamental trade-off between the profitability of the representative market, A, and the strength of decreasing returns to growth, as measured by C. Growth is also higher, the lower the cost of capital: an increase in the rate at which future profits are discounted discourages the firm from sacrificing current profit to promote future growth.

When growth is maximised subject to a dividend constraint, growth will expand up to the point where profit is zero, which implies that

$$(A - D) - Bg - Cg^2 = 0$$

This quadratic equation has two roots, and assuming that the dividend constraint is feasible, both are real. The smaller root is negative, and so the larger root must be taken, which is the root that corresponds to a maximum of growth:

$$g^{**} = ((B^2 + 4(A - D)C)^{1/2} - B) / 2C$$

Given the other assumptions, this root lies within the permitted range. Partial differentiation of the growth equation shows that:

$$g^{**}_A > 0; \qquad g^{**}_B < 0; \qquad g^{**}_C < 0; \qquad g^{**}_D < 0$$

Like the value-maximising growth rate g^*, the growth-maximising growth rate g^{**} is heavily dependent on A and C, but only marginally dependent on B, confirming that the optimal growth rate is basically determined by a trade-off between the profitability of individual markets, as measured by A, and decreasing returns to growth, as measured by C. Unlike the value-maximising growth rate, however, the growth-maximising growth rate is independent of the cost of capital r. The capital constraint operates through dividend commitments, D, instead. The higher is D, the less profit the firm can retain to finance set-up costs and entrepreneurial management, and hence the lower is the growth of the firm.

In view of the similarity in the results for value-maximisation and growth-maximisation, the rest of the paper considers just the value-maximising case.

A simple multinational analogue of the Penrose model

In considering not simply the growth of the firm but also its internationalisation, it is important to note that Penrose discusses three main dimensions along which a firm can expand. While the main focus of her discussion is on product diversification, she also considers vertical integration along the supply chain, and geographical diversification which can turn the firm into an MNE. Geographical diversification can be either horizontal – the typical case where technology transfer is involved – or vertical, as exemplified by 'resource seeking' investments. In our model, as in Buckley and Casson (1976), the uni-national firm is simply a special case of a multinational firm.

Each of these three main dimensions has further sub-dimensions. Diversification can involve either different varieties of the same product, or wholly distinct products, or some combination of the two. New product varieties may substitute obsolete varieties, or complement existing varieties, or be independent of each other. Vertical integration can be either forwards – into wholesaling or retailing, for example – or backwards – into component manufacture or raw material supply. Vertical integration can also be applied to the product development process, in which the firm not only undertakes product development but integrates backwards into basic research, or forwards into quality control and warranty repairs. Finally, geographical diversification can be either local, inter-regional, international or global, depending on whether it spans regional boundaries or national boundaries, or covers the entire world.

With so many different dimensions, it is useful to focus the discussion on a single representative case. Vertical integration is therefore ignored; it is assumed that the firm concentrates on just a single stage of production. It innovates an expanding range of products which are then introduced to different national markets.

Suppose to begin with that each new product is launched simultaneously in every national market. Thus the 'markets' into which the growing firm diversifies are, in effect, global markets. Whilst the introduction of products is sequential, their introduction to individual local markets is not.

The fact that the firm serves global markets does not necessarily make it a multinational, however. The firm only becomes a multinational if its location strategy involves production in more than one country. The firm could be simply a specialised exporter which serves all its markets from the same host-country location.

In the Penrose model, an exporter can become a multinational in two possible ways. It can serve some markets through local production, and therefore become multinational as a result of its geographical expansion; alternatively, it can serve each global market from a single plant, but locate different plants in different countries, in which case multinationality is driven by product expansion instead. Multinationality driven by geographical expansion is a response to obstacles to transport and trade – connected, for example, with the perishability of the product, or the need for face-to-face delivery – whilst multinationality driven by product expansion exploits comparative advantage by specialising the production of each product on the location best endowed with the relevant non-tradable inputs.

When geography is the driver, the firm becomes a multinational whilst still a single-product firm, but when the product is the driver it becomes a multinational only when it becomes a multi-product firm. These two effects are combined in globally rationalised production, in which plants in different countries serve not only local markets but act as export platforms for particular products in the range. Case study evidence suggests that single-product firms can be multinational, which suggests that geography is a more important driver than the product. However, the interaction of the geographical dimension and the product dimension is relevant to the analysis of the globally rationalised firm.

A more refined approach to geographical expansion interprets market entry as a sequential process. Instead of entering all national markets simultaneously, the firm enters them one at a time. The basic unit of analysis is no longer an integrated global market for a product, but a particular national market for a particular product. The firm expands sequentially by first introducing one product into one market, and then introducing another product into another market, and so on.

Sequential entry into national markets for individual products can be effected in several ways. Firstly, the firm can expand initially in the product dimension, selling entirely in the home market, and then, once a critical number of products have been introduced, expand the product range into foreign markets. A second method is the converse of this: the firm expands first in the product dimension and then in the geographical dimension. The firm launches its first product into a set of key markets and only introduces its second product once this process is complete; the second product is introduced into the same set of markets, and then the third product; and so on.

A more plausible process is one in which products are innovated into the home market whilst they are in the process of diffusing through international markets. To begin with, the firm introduces its first product into the home market. If this product is successful, it introduces the product to a foreign market in the second period and, shortly afterwards, introduces a second product to its home market to capitalise on its initial success. Next, the first product is introduced to a third country, then the second product is introduced to the second country, and then a new product is introduced to the home market; and so on. The process may be termed a 'innovation-diffusion' process, since products are innovated at the same time that established products are diffusing into national markets.

The innovation-diffusion model also predicts that the rate of introduction of new products into any given market will decline over time, even though the firm is growing at a constant proportional rate. This is because the firm is extending the geographical scope of its markets as it grows. Each stage of growth is marked by the entry of a product into another national market, rather than the innovation of another new product *per se*. Thus the rate of product innovation slows as the number of national markets served increases; more effort goes into diffusion, and less into innovation.

The results generated by the innovation-diffusion model seem to be broadly consistent with evidence about the growth of MNEs in the second half of the twentieth century. Furthermore, the general approach is consistent with both Vernon's product cycle theory of foreign direct investment (Vernon, 1966), and with the Uppsala theory of sequential internationalisation (Johanson and Vahlne, 1977).

Although it goes beyond both. A further development of this approach is presented below.

Table 5.1a Sequential entry into national markets with a fixed product range.

	Location 1	Location 2	Location 3	Location 4
Product 1	1	5	9	13
Product 2	2	6	10	14
Product 3	3	7	11	15
Product 4	4	8	12	16

Table 5.1b The innovation-diffusion model: sequential product innovation with overlapping sequential local entry.

	Location 1	Location 2	Location 3	Location 4
Product 1	1	2	4	7
Product 2	3	5	8	11
Product 3	6	9	12	14
Product 4	10	13	15	16

A contrast between the Penrose model and that of Buckley and Casson

A potential weakness of the Penrose approach to multinationals is that the growth of the firm is driven by product diversification rather than by technological innovation. Empirical evidence points to the crucial role of technology in stimulating the growth of multinational firms. Early post-war US foreign direct investment, for example, was heavily concentrated in technology-intensive industries.

Although Penrose recognised that large firms invested significantly in R&D, she regarded their entrepreneurial capabilities as the main driver of their growth. She believed that there were abundant opportunities for discovering new markets, irrespective of whether R&D was undertaken or not. The main constraint on the growth of the firm was not the need to finance expensive R&D, but the difficulty of expanding the firm at a sufficient rate to exploit all of the opportunities available.

In fact, decreasing returns to R&D provides a simple explanation of how the growth of a technology-intensive firm is constrained. When market opportunities drive firm growth, as in Penrose, then decreasing returns to entrepreneurship and management will constrain growth, while if technological opportunities drive the firm's growth then decreasing returns to R&D will constrain growth instead. There is, therefore, a logical parallel between the limits to growth identified by Penrose, and the limits to growth associated with R&D.

An emphasis on R&D also helps to explain why related diversifications are generally more successful than unrelated diversifications in sustaining the growth of the multinational firm. If new products are generated sequentially from a single integrated programme of research, then the cost of generating any one product can be reduced by using knowledge spill-overs from other products. Furthermore, products generated in this way may also be related in terms of the materials or components from which they are produced, thereby generating supply chain economies once they are in production. Although relatedness can also be achieved through 'bundling' products for sale, or marketing different products to the same group of customers, there is little doubt that the technological relatedness of different products has been a significant factor in boosting the profits and growth of modern multinational firms.

As it happens, the link between R&D and the growth of the firm was an important part of the model of the multinational enterprise developed by Buckley and Casson (1976). This was no accident; they introduced internalisation theory in order to explain the 'pattern of growth' of the MNE in terms of 'a long-run theory' (p. 59), and they concluded their exposition with 'a mathematical model of the growth of the research-intensive firm' (p. 62). Unlike the later work of Dunning (1977), their model did not assume that the firm possessed a given ownership advantage. Instead, it considered the generation of a stream of ownership advantages from a continuous process of R&D. The internalisation of the intangible knowledge flows generated by R&D established a link between the steady state *level* of R&D and the steady state *rate of growth* of production and sales. Just as in Penrose's model, decreasing returns to the growth of the management team restrict the rate of product diversification by an entrepreneurial firm, and hence limit its rate of growth, so in the Buckley and Casson model decreasing returns to the scale of R&D restrict the rate of product innovation by a technology-intensive firm, and hence limit its rate of growth. The similarity between the two theories is not surprising, since Buckley and Casson traced back their ideas, not only on Coase (1937), but also to Penrose (1959) (p. 36, fn 2).

According to Buckley and Casson, R&D activity has a U-shaped average cost curve. This results from the interplay of fixed costs and increasing variable costs. R&D incurs fixed costs due to the indivisible nature of laboratory facilities, and the need for a critical mass of different specialists to be combined within a research team. Beyond a certain scale, however, decreasing returns set in because the advantages of further specialisation diminish, and the team becomes increasingly difficult to manage, as individual researchers start to pursue independent lines of research unrelated to the rest of the team. By contrast, production and marketing operate with constant average costs.

Although Buckley and Casson relate decreasing returns in R&D to the *level* of R&D activity, the output of R&D activity determines the *rate of growth* of the final output of the firm. Thus an analysis of levels in R&D translates naturally into an analysis of growth in terms of output.

In the Buckley and Casson model, R&D generates a continuous stream of new products, each of higher quality than the previous one. Once introduced, each product is sold immediately in a global market; the pattern of internationalisation is summarised in Table 5.2. National markets are highly segmented, on account of transport costs and tariffs, and so each national market is serviced by wholly-owned production and distribution subsidiaries. In each market the firm enjoys market power, derived from the novelty of its product line, and so faces a downward-sloping demand curve. Both the scale of demand, and its price-elasticity, vary between markets, as do average costs.

The firm maximises shareholder value, which is equal to the value of the aggregate profit generated by the local markets, net of the costs of R&D. Sustained R&D leads to continuous improvement in quality, and this in turn maintains steady growth of demand in each market. The higher the level of R&D, the faster is the rate of quality improvement, the faster the growth of demand and aggregate profit, and the higher the cost of R&D. The optimal growth of the firm is determined by a trade-off between growing revenues on the one hand, and the higher costs of R&D on the other. This trade-off determines the rate of

Table 5.2 The Buckley and Casson model: sequential product innovation with simultaneous local entry.

	Location 1	Location 2	Location 3	Location 4
Product 1	1=	1=	1=	1=
Product 2	2=	2=	2=	2=
Product 3	3=	3=	3=	3=
Product 4	4=	4=	4=	4=

optimal level of R&D activity. This in turn determines the rate of quality improvement, and hence the rate of growth of output.

Each incremental improvement in quality yields the same incremental increase in profits. The discounted value of this additional profit is traded off against the marginal cost of generating the improvement in quality. The value-maximising strategy equates the marginal value of an increase in quality to its marginal cost, and determines a rate of quality improvement which is constant over time, and corresponds to a steady state level of expenditure on R&D. The optimal growth rate is an absolute rather than proportional rate, so that the growth of sales is linear in time. The optimal rate of growth is greater, the lower are marginal costs – *i.e.* the lower the salary costs of researchers, and the more slowly decreasing to returns to the scale of research set in. Growth is also greater the higher the marginal value of quality improvement – *i.e.* the more intensive the demand for the product, the lower its price-elasticity, and the lower the cost of capital.

In both the Buckley and Casson and Penrose models, the firm faces a trade-off between faster exploitation of market opportunities on the one hand, and 'costs of growth' on the other. In both cases, costs of growth increase because the productivity of human resources declines as the rate of growth they are required to sustain increases. But there are key differences too.

- In Penrose's model it is the declining productivity of the management team that limits growth, whereas in the Buckley and Casson model it is the declining productivity of scientific researchers instead.
- In Penrose's model declining productivity results from the continuous expansion of the size of the management team whereas in the Buckley and Casson model declining productivity arises from sustaining a constant rate of R&D above the scale which minimises average cost.
- The innovations made by the firm are different too. In the Penrose model, the firm diversifies into new markets, whilst in the Buckley and Casson model it upgrades the quality of a given product.
- Although the firm introduces new products in both cases, in the first case the new products are independent of existing products, whereas in the second case each new product replaces the previous version of the same product.

A weakness of the Buckley and Casson model is that it cannot be used to analyse the sequential nature of international expansion. Sequential entry is predicted only when new markets emerge as a result of the liberalisation of access, or a 'take-off' in local demand stimulated by economic growth. Thus while the Buckley and Casson model can be applied to the entry into 'emerging markets' in 'transition economies', it cannot be applied to sequential entry into mature and accessible markets. It is shown below that this weakness of the Buckley and Casson model is easily overcome.

A reconciliation between the two models

The question arises as to how far it is possible to integrate the Buckley and Casson approach with the basic Penrose model. This section presents a model which attempts to do just this. It is a two-dimensional generalisation of the one-dimensional Penrose model presented in section 2.

The model focuses on a distinctive type of firm, founded by a Schumpeterian entrepreneur (Schumpeter, 1934). The entrepreneur has identified a technological opportunity to generate a range of new products. The entrepreneur is not an inventor, but an innovator; he recognises not merely a technological possibility, but also a latent demand for products that embody the new technology that he plans to exploit. Although product demand is global, national markets are spatially self-contained, and so each needs to be entered separately.

Having identified an opportunity for technological innovation, two further stages are involved in bringing a product to market. The first stage is R&D and the second is market entry – first into the home market and then into foreign markets. Multinationality arises because each national market is sourced by local production.

Each stage involves its own distinctive form of sequential diversification. The firm can only develop one product at a time, and each product can only be introduced into a new market by entering one country at a time. The two stages proceed in parallel. While R&D generates a sequence of product innovations, market entry takes each product and introduces it to a sequence of national markets. Unlike the growth-diffusion model presented above, two separate sets of resources are involved – a team of researchers responsible for product innovation, and a team of managers responsible for market entry. Each process is sequential because this arrangement makes the best use of the human resources involved.

Because of the two dimensions, there are two different growth rates: one associated with a growth in the number of products, g_1, and the other associated with the growth in the number of national markets served, g_2. The two growth rates are distinct, but related: the growth of the product range can be chosen independently of the speed of internationalisation, and *vice versa*; however, conditions which favour faster growth in the product range normally favour faster internationalisation too.

Following the general principles of the Penrose model, it is assumed that the stock of products, x, introduced by the firm grows at a constant proportional rate, g, which is chosen by the firm These products are generated exclusively by the firm's R&D; no technology is licensed in or out to other firms. It is assumed that the firm has already developed a prototype product by the time that it is founded, so that $x = 1$ and time $t = 0$. Thus

$$x = \exp(g_1 t)$$

as in the one-dimensional model. To further simplify the model, it is assumed that the prototype is not sold, so that all the firm's revenue and profit is attributable to its R&D.

The rate of product innovation depends upon the number of scientists employed in R&D. Employment in R&D is n_0. Each scientist receives a fixed salary s_0. There are constant returns to the scale of R&D; other thing being equal, doubling the employment of scientists doubles the rate of new product generation. Due to the real costs of growth, however, the average productivity of scientists declines with the rate of growth of R&D activity; as a result, the real cost of scientific output is $a_0 g$. The parameter a_0 measures the labour-intensity of research; it reflects the interaction between the skills of the scientists and the technological opportunities available. Thus average research productivity is independent of scale, but inversely related to growth.

When growing at rate g_1 with a cumulative stock of products x, the firm must introduce new products at a rate $g_1 x$. With real labour cost $a_0 g_1$, the firm requires $a_0 g^2_1 x$ scientists. When scientific labour is the sole input to R&D, the cost of R&D is therefore $C g^2_1 x$, where $C = a_0 s_0$.

It is assumed that each product, once produced, has the property of a public good within the firm. This has a very specific meaning in the present context; namely that, once developed, product technology can be transferred to any country in the world. Technology is not an absolutely pure public good, because there is a positive cost of transfer to each national market. But it is a public good in the sense that a product does not need to be reinvented for every national market. In other words, R&D generates global products rather than products that can be sold only in a single national market.

National markets vary in size. A large market has a large demand for all products. The operating profit generated by each product in each national market is directly proportional to the size of the market. Each product in each market earns a uniform rate of profit per unit size, z.

Entry into each market requires an input of managerial labour which is directly proportional to market size, y. No learning takes place in the 'roll out' of the product from one market to the next, and so the cost of entry is independent of the number of markets already entered.

All markets are entered at the same speed, independent of their size. The speed of entry is chosen by the firm. Fast entry is effected by employing a large number of managers for a short period of time, and slow entry by employing a smaller number of managers for a longer period of time. No learning takes place with regard to product innovation in a given market, so that the same entry same cost is incurred irrespective of how many previous products have been introduced to the market.

Speeding up entry expedites internationalisation, by bringing forward the time of entry into subsequent markets. It also reduces the productivity of managerial labour, however. With a speed of entry h, total managerial input is $a_1 yh$, where a_1 is a productivity parameter. When managers receive a salary s_1, the cost of entering a market at speed h incurs a management resource cost $a_1 s_1 yh$.

The optimal strategy for the firm, given a positive uniform rate of profit and a commitment to sequential entry, is to enter the largest market first, and then to enter subsequent markets in descending order of size. It is assumed, therefore, that entry is sequenced in descending order of market size.

The precise speed of market entry chosen depends upon the firm's cost of capital, r. Once the optimal speed of market entry has been determined, using the method described below, the value, B, of a new innovated product can be calculated. This value is equal to the discounted value of the operating profits generated by the growing global market for the product, less the discounted value of the costs of product launch in each of the national markets. Since new products are introduced at a rate gx, the value of the output from R&D is $B\, g_1 x$.

The overall value of the firm is therefore

$$v = \int_0^\infty \exp(-rt)\ (B\, g_1 x - C\, g_1^2 x)\, dt = (B\, g_1 - C\, g_1^2) / (r - g_1)$$

The value v is finite if and only if $g_1 < r$. The first order condition for a maximum of v is a quadratic equation, which has real roots if and only if $B < Cr$. The condition for positive profit is $B > C g_1$, and both are satisfied simultaneously only when $g_1 < r$, i.e. when the firm has finite value.

Only the smaller root satisfies this latter condition; this is also the root that fulfils the second order condition for a maximum. Optimal growth is therefore

$$g_1 = r(1 - (1 - (B/Cr))^{1/2})$$

It can be seen that the optimal rate of growth increases with the value of new products, B and decreases with the costs of R&D, C. For a given B, g_1 is a decreasing function of r; a high cost of capital reduces the optimal rate of growth. To complete the solution of the model, it is necessary to determine B.

The optimal speed of internationalisation

Consider the marketing of a representative new product which has just been developed through R&D. A sequential process of internationalisation process can be modelled in the following way.

It is assumed that there is infinite number of national markets, the largest of which has size y^+, and the smallest size zero. They are ranked in descending order of size by a continuous index m. It is assumed for simplicity that market size decreases exponentially with rank, such that the size of the mth market is

$$y(m) = y^+ \exp(-bm)$$

where y^+ is the size of the largest market, and b is a parameter that measures the rate at which size decreases with respect to rank. The parameter b indicates the inequality of market sizes, with a value close to zero indicating relative equality and a high value indicating extreme inequality.

Because there is an infinity of national markets, the internationalisation process continues indefinitely, thereby allowing the firm to expand continuously in the geographical dimension. At the same time, the decreasing size of successive markets means that the total size of the global market remains finite.

By the time the mth market has been reached, sales of the product have cumulated to

$$Y(m) = (y^+/b)(1 - \exp(-bm))$$

and so, as globalisation proceeds, total market size converges exponentially on the 'saturation level' of the global market, y/b. The size of the global market is greater, the greater the size of the largest market, y^+, and the lower the inequality in market size, b.

The speed of market entry is measured by the rate at which the rank of the newest market advances over time. Since the speed of entry, h, is the same for every market,

$$m = ht$$

Cumulative market size converges on the saturation level at a rate bh:

$$Y(t) = (y^+/b)(1 - \exp(-bht))$$

Because markets are entered in order of decreasing size, the proportional rate of growth of the market, g_2, diminishes over time, as a higher proportion of the global market is served:

$$g_2 = bh((y/bY) - 1)$$

As noted earlier, the cost of entry into each market is proportional to its size. If the cost of entry were independent of size, it would soon become uneconomic to enter the smallest markets, and so a rational firm would terminate internationalisation at some point before the global market was saturated. If the firm persisted beyond this point, it would incur significant costs for little benefit, and the consequent drive to minimise these costs would distort the globalisation strategy.

Given earlier assumptions, the number of markets expands at a rate h, and so expenditure on market entry at any time t is

$$c_1 = a_1 s_1 y h^2 = a_1 s_1 h^2 y^+ \exp(-bht)$$

Net cash flow is $zY - c_1$, and so the present value of the product at the time of its launch, u, is

$$u = \int_0^\infty (zY - c_1)\, dt = (y^+/b)[(z/r) - [(z + a_1 b s_1 h^2)/(r + bh)]]$$

The first term, y^+/b, measures the size of the global market, and scales the rest of the expression. The next term, z/r, is the capitalised value of the profit stream from a market of unit size. The remaining two terms – z and $a_1 b r s_1 h^2$ – are deductions from profit, and both are capitalised using a rate of discount $r + bh$. This rate of discount reflects the gradual nature of the build up to the saturation of the global market, which is governed by the product of the inequality parameter, b, and the speed of market entry, h. The first term reflects the deferral of profit, and the second reflects the cost of market entry.

The first order condition for a maximum of u generates a quadratic equation for the optimal speed of market entry, h. One of the roots of the quadratic is positive and the other negative. The second order conditions show that the positive root corresponds to a maximum, h^*:

$$h^* = (r/b)\,((1 + (b/a_1 s_1\, r^2))^{1/2} - 1)$$

It can be seen that speed, h^*, increases with profit, z, and decreases with inequality of market size, b, the real cost of management time, a_1, and the salary level, s_1. It also increases with respect to the cost of capital, r: the higher the rate of discount, the more important it is to generate profits from the smaller markets as early as possible. A faster speed translates into a higher rate of geographical growth, g_2^*.

Substituting the optimal value of h into the valuation of the product gives the optimal value of the product at the time of its development as

$$B = (y^+ z/br)\,(1 - 2(a_1 s_1\, r^2/bz)^{1/2})$$

whence the optimal rate of growth g_1^* becomes

$$g_1^* = r(1 - (1 - (y^+ z/a_0 s_0\, br^2)(1 - 2(a_1 s_1 r^2/bz))^{1/2})$$

It follows that growth is an increasing function of maximum market size, y^+, and profitability, z, and a decreasing function of the inequality of market size, b, the real cost of researchers, a_0, the real cost of management, a_1, and the respective salary levels, s_0, s_1.

A high cost of capital, r, reduces the optimal rate of growth, g_1^*. The present value of the prospective revenues is reduced – especially the revenues generated by the smaller markets which are the last to be entered. Although a higher cost of capital encourages internationalisation to be speeded up, this speed-up is at the expense of higher entry costs, which further reduce the net value of the net profit stream. Thus a higher r reduces the value of B, and thereby reduces the incentive for growth, g_1^*.

It should be noted that the overall growth of the firm's sales depends on the interplay between the two growth rates g_1^*, g_2^*. In its early phase of expansion the firm expands quickly in both the product and geographical dimensions, but gradually converges to an overall growth rate g_1 as the internationalisation process matures.

Synthesis

While Penrose's dismissal of scale effects is plausible in the context of many production processes, it is not particularly plausible where R&D is concerned. Researchers are often motivated by personal curiosity which leads them away from their intended line of research, while the introspective nature of research activity makes it difficult to monitor. Control loss is therefore a genuine concern in large teams. Furthermore, the notion that all research facilities have to start small and then grow as fast as possible is difficult to reconcile with the way that many research establishments are founded on a substantial scale. Many successful firms are able to grow large without continually expanding the sizes of their research facilities.

But while the notion of incremental expansion does not fit well with research, it fits much better with the internationalisation process, although even here the speed with which some firms internationalise has been quite high. Nevertheless, the notion that the speed of internationalisation is constrained by the difficulty of enlarging the management team sufficiently fast is more plausible than an assumption that internationalisation is instantaneous.

It appears, therefore, that while the Penrose model offers a superior account of internationalisation, the Buckley and Casson model offers a superior account of innovation and R&D. This suggests that the two models should be combined by taking the analysis of internationalisation in section 6 and combining it with the approach to innovation summarised in section 4.

Following the Buckley and Casson model, let the costs of R&D be

$$C = C_0 + C_2 q^2$$

where C_0 is the fixed cost of the R&D facility, $C_2 = a_0 s_0$ is a parameter governing variable costs, and q is the output of R&D. Output is measured by the rate of product innovation that it sustains. The cost function corresponds to a U-shaped average cost curve with a minimum at $q = (C_0/C_2)^{1/2}$.

The value of an innovation exploited through an optimal internationalisation strategy is B, as derived above. The value of the firm is

$$v = \int_0^\infty \exp(-rt)(Bq - C_0 - C_2 q^2)\, dt = (Bq - C_0 - C_2 q^2)/r$$

The first order condition for a maximum of value determines the optimal rate of research output, q^*

$$q^* = B/2C_2$$

The second order conditions for a maximum are always satisfied. Substituting for B expresses q^* as an increasing function of market size, y^+, the profitability of sales, z, and a decreasing function of the inequality of market size, b, the real costs of R&D and market entry, a_0,

a_1, the salaries of scientists and managers, s_0, s_1, and the cost of capital, r:

$$q^* = (y^+z/2a_0s_0br)(1 - 2(a_1s_1r^2/bz)^{1/2})$$

In contrast to the exponential growth of the Penrosian model, the firm now grows in the long run at a constant absolute rate q^*. Sales grow faster in the early stages of internationalisation, but converge on this level as the internationalisation process matures. Since the rate of growth is constant in absolute terms, it declines in relative terms, which is consistent with the lifetime growth pattern of a typical firm.

This model is simpler than the pure Penrosian model, and offers a more realistic account of the R&D process. Because it is simpler, if offers greater scope for further development, and can therefore be recommended as a starting point for further research on this subject.

Conclusion

This paper has shown that Penrose's *Theory of the Growth of the Firm* provides a tractable formal model which has important implications for the strategy of MNEs. Its analysis of the appropriate modes of internationalisation can be integrated with a satisfying account of the trade off between (product) diversification and foreign market penetration. The account of speed of entry is an advance on current theories of internationalisation including 'stages' and product cycle based models. There is much profitable work to be done in extending Penrose's implicit model of multi-national enterprise. For now, we can recognise the contribution of Penrose's book to the analysis of geographical expansion patterns, sequential decision making and learning in the MNE as key factors in international strategic management.

Acknowledgements

The authors would like to thank Christos Pitelis for his comments on earlier versions of this article.

References

Barney, J.B., Strategic Factor Markets, *Management Science*, 32, 10, 1985, pp. 1231–1241.

Baumol, W.J., *Business Behavior, Value and Growth*, New York: Harcourt, Brace, Jovanovich 1967.

Best, M.H. and Humphries, J., Edith Penrose: A Feminist Economist?, *Feminist Economics*, 9, 1, 2003, pp. 47–73.

Buckley, P.J. and Casson, M., *The Future of the Multinational Enterprise*, London: Macmillan 1976.

Buckley, P.J. and Casson, M., The Theory of the Growth of the Firm: Extending the Penrose Model, *mimeo* 2004.

Caves, R.E. and Porter, M.E., From Entry Barriers to Mobility Barriers: Conjectural Variations and Contrived Deterrence to New Competition, *Quarterly Journal of Economics*, 91, 3, 1977, pp. 241–262.

Coase, R.H., The Nature of the Firm, *Economica*, 4, 4, 1937, pp. 387–405.

Demsetz, H., Industrial Structure, Market Rivalry, and Public Policy, *Journal of Law and Economics*, 16, 1, 1973, pp. 1–10.

Demsetz, H., *Efficiency, Competition and Policy*, Oxford: Basil Blackwell 1982.

Dunning, J.H., Trade, Location of Economic Activity and the Multinational Enterprise: The Search for an Eclectic Approach, in Ohlin, B. *et al*. (eds), *The International Allocation of Economic Activity*, London: Macmillan 1977.

Dunning, J.H., The Contribution of Edith Penrose to International Business Scholarship, *Management International Review*, 43, 1, 2003, pp. 3–19.

Foss, N.J., *Resources, Firms and Strategies*, Oxford: Oxford University Press 1997.

Foss, N.J., Edith Penrose, Economics and Strategic Management, in Pitelis, C.N. (ed.), *The Growth of the Firm: The Legacy of Edith Penrose*, Oxford: Oxford University Press 2002.

Johanson, J. and Vahlne, J.E., The Internationalisation Process of the Firm: A Model of Knowledge Development and Increasing Market Commitments, *Journal of International Business Studies*, 8, 1, 1977, pp. 23–32.

Kor, Y.Y. and Mahoney, J.T., Edith Penrose's (1959) Contributions to the Resource-based View of Strategic Management, *Journal of Management Studies*, 41, 1, 2004, pp. 183–191.

Lippman, S.A. and Rumelt, R.P., Uncertain Immutability: An Analysis of Interfirm Differences in Efficiency under Competition, *Bell Journal of Economics*, 13, 3, 1982, pp. 418–438.

Lockett, A. and Thompson, S., Edith Penrose's Contributions to the Resource-based View: An Alternative Perspective, *Journal of Management Studies*, 41, 1, 2004, pp. 193–203.

Marris, R.L., *Economic Theory of Managerial Capitalism*, London: Macmillan 1964.

Penrose, E.T., *The Theory of the Growth of the Firm*, Oxford: Blackwell 1959.

Penrose, E.T., The Growth of the Firm: A Case Study: The Hercules Powder Company, *The Business History Review*, 34, 1, 1960, pp. 1–20.

Penrose, P. and Pitelis, C.N., Edith Elura Tilton Penrose: Life Contribution and Influence, in Pitelis, C.N. (ed.), *The Growth of the Firm: The Legacy of Edith Penrose*, Oxford: Oxford University Press 2002.

Peteraf, M.A., The Cornerstones of Competitive Advantage: A Resource-based View, *Strategic Management Journal*, 14, 3, 1993, pp. 179–91.

Pitelis, C.N. (ed.), *The Growth of the Firm: The Legacy of Edith Penrose*, Oxford: Oxford University Press 2002.

Pitelis, C.N., Edith Penrose and the Resource-based View of (International) Business Strategy, *International Business Review*, 13, 4, 2002, pp. 523–532.

Rugman, A.M. and Verbeke, A., Edith Penrose's Contribution to the Resource-based View of Strategic Management, *Strategic Management Journal*, 23, 7, 2002, pp. 769–80.

Rugman, A.M. and Verbeke, A., A Final Word on Edith Penrose, *Journal of Management Studies*, 41, 1, 2004, pp. 205–217.

Schumpeter, J.A., *The Theory of Economic Development*, Cambridge, MA: Harvard University Press 1934.

Teece, D.J., Economics of Scope and the Scope of the Enterprise, *Journal of Economic Behavior and Organization*, 1, 3, 1980, pp. 223–233.

Vernon, R., International Investment and International Trade in the Product Cycle, *Quarterly Journal of Economics*, 80, 2, 1966, pp. 190–207.

Section II

Chinese Outward Foreign Direct Investment

6
The Determinants of Chinese Outward Foreign Direct Investment

Peter J. Buckley, L. Jeremy Clegg, Adam Cross, Xin Liu, Hinrich Voss and Ping Zheng

Introduction

This paper investigates the determinants of foreign direct investment (FDI) by Chinese multinational enterprises (MNEs) over the period 1984 to 2001.[1] The process of China's deepening re-integration with the global economy began, in the modern era, with the 'Open Door' policies of the late 1970s, and accelerated with accession to the World Trade Organisation (WTO) in 2001. Studies of this process generally examine China in terms of its position in global trade flows (e.g., Lall and Albaladejo, 2004); its comparative advantage as a manufacturing location (e.g., Chen *et al.*, 2002; Rowen, 2003); and in the volume, distribution and impacts of *inbound* FDI (e.g., Buckley *et al.*, 2002; Buckley, 2004b).[2] In contrast, understanding of a further dimension to this process – namely, the rise in Chinese outward direct investment (ODI) – remains very incomplete. One reason is the paucity of sufficiently disaggregated data to permit formal analysis of the forces shaping Chinese ODI. The result has been a preponderance of descriptive research on FDI trends (e.g., Taylor, 2002; Deng, 2003, 2004; Wong and Chan, 2003; Buckley *et al.*, 2006) coupled with in-depth case studies on a small number of high-profile Chinese MNEs (e.g., Liu and Li, 2002; Warner *et al.*, 2004).

Using official data from one of the key agencies concerned with China's investment approval process, the State Administration for Foreign Exchange (SAFE), this exploratory study is, to our knowledge, one of the first to model formally the forces driving Chinese ODI. Our focus is on FDI determinants and the extent to which established theoretical explanations of the MNE (much of which concentrates on industrialised country, and especially US, investors) can explain FDI from an emerging economy like China. China is a particularly good test case for the general theory of FDI as it presents many special conditions that are rarely encountered in a single country.

Several indicators point to a strengthening of China's role as an investor country in recent years. By 2004, China was the eighth most important FDI source among developing countries, behind economically more advanced economies such as Hong Kong SAR (Special Administrative Region), South Korea, Republic of China (Taiwan) and Singapore (UNCTAD, 2005a). A recent survey of national investment promotion agencies predicts that China will become a top four source country of FDI over the period 2005–2008 (UNCTAD, 2005b), with African and Asia-Pacific country agencies in particular highlighting the dominant role expected of China, placing it second only to South Africa and the USA in each region, respectively. There is every indication that China will contribute increasingly to global FDI flows over the coming years. These indicators highlight the timeliness of this study.

Chinese outward investors can be regarded as being state-owned in the period under study, since private firms were legally prohibited from investing abroad prior to 2003. Since 1979, when ODI was formally permitted under the 'Open Door' policies, the internationalisation of Chinese firms has been tightly controlled by national and provincial government, either directly, by administrative fiat, or indirectly, via economic policy and other measures designed to advance the economic development agenda (Buckley *et al.*, 2006). Initially, ODI was permitted on a very selective basis. However, in recent years administrative controls have been relaxed, approval processes and procedures streamlined, and the ceiling raised on the amount of foreign exchange that can be committed to individual investment projects (Sauvant, 2005). The process of accelerated outward investment liberalisation and growth can be traced from Deng Xiaoping's tour of South China in 1992 through to the government-led 'go global' (*zou chu qu*) initiative, which was instigated in 1999. This initiative aims to promote the international competitiveness of Chinese firms by further reducing or eliminating foreign-exchange-related, fiscal and administrative obstacles to international investment (Sauvant, 2005). In order to properly understand Chinese ODI, it is therefore important that formal empirical analysis takes full account of this changing institutional context and the idiosyncratic response by Chinese firms that it might engender. In other words, it is necessary to understand the extent to which the investment location decisions of Chinese MNEs, when considered in aggregate, are explicable by received theory, or whether the context and institutional environment of the home country exerts a distinctive effect. Such distinctiveness might be a consequence of the continued pursuit of national economic imperatives, for instance, with state-owned enterprises (SOEs) employed as an instrument of policy.

The paper is organised as follows. First, we review the general theory of FDI and discuss the extent to which it holds for an emerging economy like China, where central planning has greatly influenced the development of the external sector. We do this by considering three potential arguments (namely capital market imperfections, special ownership advantages and institutional factors) for a special theory to be nested within the general theory. We then describe a number of economic and policy variables proposed in the literature to have a significant influence on (industrialised country) FDI flows, and hypothesise on their ability to explain Chinese ODI patterns. We go on to test the special theory in a model of Chinese ODI using official data on individual approved Chinese FDI projects. We find that Chinese ODI is indeed distinctive in certain respects that have implications for theory, particularly the finding for political risk, but that familiar explanations of FDI are relevant, too. We conclude by recommending and commenting on future research directions.

The general theory of FDI

The general principles of the theory of FDI are twofold (Buckley and Casson, 1976). They are that: (1) firms internalise missing or imperfect external markets until the costs of further internalisation outweigh the benefits; and (2) firms choose locations for their constituent activities that minimise the overall costs of their operations. Expansion by the internalisation of markets means that firms use FDI to replace imperfect external markets in intermediate products and knowledge (as exemplified by exporting and licensing) and appropriate the profits from so doing. In the case of emerging economy MNEs, there are likely to be particular imperfections in home country capital markets that may require special applications of the theory, and this, as we shall see, is true of China.

The location aspect of the mainstream or general theory, as encapsulated in Dunning's eclectic paradigm, suggests three primary motivations (Dunning, 1977, 1993):

- foreign-market-seeking FDI;
- efficiency (cost reduction)-seeking FDI;

- resource-seeking FDI (including a subset that is known as strategic-asset-seeking FDI).

The general theory of FDI has been built largely on the experience of industrialised country investors. While in certain respects this can be readily applied to emerging economy investors, there are inevitably gaps. Here, we look critically at the applicability of the general theory. Market-seeking FDI will be undertaken by emerging economy firms for traditional trade supporting reasons – to access distribution networks, to facilitate the exports of domestic producers, and to enhance exports from the host country to other large and rapidly growing markets. Efficiency-seeking FDI will occur when outward investors seek lower-cost locations for operations, in particular in the search for lower-cost labour. Given China's comparatively low labour cost levels this motivation is unlikely, and is not explicitly considered here. Resource-seeking FDI from emerging economies occurs to acquire or secure the supply of raw materials and energy sources in short supply at home. This may well involve Chinese ODI in relatively high-income countries that have significant energy reserves and raw material deposits (e.g., Australia and Canada). It may also involve the search for specific assets such as R&D capacity and output, design facilities and brand names that are embedded in advanced country firms and which can usually be accessed only by takeover of these firms or subdivisions of them (Dunning, 2001).

Various studies also identify an incremental or stages process to firm internationalisation that is linked to geographic and psychic distance (e.g., Johanson and Vahlne, 1977), with firms beginning their international operations in locations geographically close to the home market and in (psychically close) countries where knowledge, relationships and experience have already been established through prior trade business and other interactions. Examples of such behaviour are to be found in work on MNEs from Hong Kong (Lau, 1992, 2003), South Korea (Erramilli *et al.*, 1999), India and Argentina in the 1980s (Ferrantino, 1992; Pradhan, 2003), Brazil (Villela, 1983) and Malaysia (Zin, 1999).

A special theory for Chinese ODI?

The question then arises as to whether FDI from emerging economies and, specifically, from China requires a special theory nested within the general theory above. There are three potential arguments: capital market imperfections, the special ownership advantages of Chinese MNEs and institutional factors.

Capital market imperfections

Capital market imperfections in emerging economies such as China may require a special application of the general theory. Such imperfections may mean that capital is available at below-market rates for a considerable period of time, creating a semipermanent disequilibrium in the capital market that (potential) outward investors can exploit. In this sense, market imperfections may be transformed into ownership advantages by emerging economy firms (Buckley, 2004a). This ability may arise from a number of particular and interrelated imperfections:

(1) state-owned (and state-associated) firms may have capital made available to them at below-market rates (e.g., in the form of soft budget constraints) (e.g., Lardy, 1998; Scott, 2002; Warner *et al.*, 2004);
(2) inefficient banking systems may make soft loans to potential outward investors, either as policy or through inefficiency (e.g., Warner *et al.*, 2004; Child and Rodrigues, 2005; Antkiewicz and Whalley, 2006);
(3) conglomerate firms may operate an inefficient internal capital market that effectively subsidises FDI (e.g., Liu, 2005 on the diversified Chinese conglomerate Haier); and
(4) family owned firms may have access to cheap capital from family members (e.g., Tsai, 2002; Child and Pleister, 2003; Erdener and Shapiro, 2005).

There are good grounds for believing that all four of these imperfections exist in China. State-sponsored soft budget constraints make acquisition by Chinese enterprises a 'normal' mode of entering and penetrating a host economy (Warner *et al.*, 2004). Over-bidding by Chinese MNEs is attributed to the absence of private shareholders and sanguine views of the associated technical, commercial and political risks, to limited fear of failure, close government support and low cost of capital (Ma and Andrews-Speed, 2006).[3] Indeed, the survival of inefficient Chinese firms in general is attributed to the pervasive nature of soft budget constraints promoted by local government and party officials, resulting in the inability of banks and other financial institutions to impose either restructuring or exit on firms (Lardy, 1998). The 'sizeable venture capital' afforded to SOE is exemplified by the State

Council's provision to the China International Trust and Investment Corporation (CITIC) when it was instructed to explore overseas investment opportunities in priority resource sectors (Zhang, 2003). The State Council also directed the transfer of the China Investment and Trust Corporation for Foreign Economic Cooperation and Trade (FOTIC, previously the financial arm of MOFTEC) to the Sinochem Group, effectively giving it an 'internal bank' (Zhang, 2003), while the Beijing steel producer, Shougang Group, was granted the right to start and own a bank, virtually guaranteeing the lifting of a hard budget constraint (Steinfeld, 1998). The acquisition of IBM's personal computer business by Lenovo (concluded in 2005) was generally regarded to have been underwritten by the Chinese government, who at the time held a stake of 57% in the company (*Business Week*, 2004). From this discussion, it appears possible that capital market imperfections may account for the ease with which both natural-resource-seeking FDI (typically in energy and raw materials sectors) and strategic-asset-seeking FDI might be undertaken by Chinese MNEs.

Imperfections in the capital market would become evident if Chinese MNEs had a distinctive foreign investment strategy in terms of location, as exemplified by a perverse reaction to risk and return not predicted by studies on the FDI motivations of industrialised country firms. In the current study, we test for this by including political risk in our determinants of Chinese ODI after controlling for the risk premium, which is proxied by market size and market growth.

Ownership advantages of Chinese MNEs

There is an argument that emerging economy MNEs have developed ownership advantages that allow them to operate certain types of activity in foreign countries more effectively than local firms and industrialised country MNEs. These advantages may include flexibility (Wells, 1983), economising on the use of capital (or resources), benefits accruing from home country embeddedness (i.e., prior familiarity of operating within an emerging market context), and the ability to engage in beneficial relations with firms and other actors in order to provide access to resources controlled by others. The latter advantage, which some term a relational asset (Dunning, 2002; Erdener and Shapiro, 2005), may be revealed as networking skills and may be linked to the Chinese diaspora in the case of Chinese firms.[4] Where these conditions are relatively long-lasting then they provide the case for semi-permanent 'ownership advantages' of emerging economy MNEs – the third element of Dunning's eclectic theory after internalisation and location factors (Dunning, 1993). This argument is less easy to test using aggregate FDI data, however.

Extant theory asserts that the early investments of firms frequently occur in countries with similar cultural background to the home country (Johanson and Vahlne, 1977) or where relational assets in the form of ethnic or familial ties with a specific minority population in the host country can be exploited (Lecraw, 1977; Wells, 1983; Lau, 2003). Within such a network, market information about the most suitable and profitable investment opportunities can circulate with ease, and fruitful commercial relationships can be established that facilitate market entry and development. Investment and commercial risk can be reduced as a consequence (Lecraw, 1977; Zhan, 1995). The importance of networking skills as a special ownership advantage of Chinese firms would be evident if Chinese ODI was associated positively with host countries that are endowed with relevant location-specific relational advantages, such as the presence of an appreciable ethnic Chinese population.

Institutional factors influencing Chinese ODI

The institutional fabric of an emerging economy can determine the ability and will of domestic firms to invest abroad. A straightforward, consistent and liberal policy towards outward FDI will encourage it, while a discretionary and frequently adjusted policy may do the opposite. There is an emerging body of theoretical work that concerns the institution-based view of strategy, or institutional theory for short (North, 1990; Peng, 2002; Meyer and Nguyen, 2005; Wright et al., 2005). This has the potential to help explain distinctiveness in the behaviour of outward-investing Chinese firms. The basic thrust of this contribution is that firms' strategy is shaped by the home institutional environment (more colloquially 'the rules of the game'), which is formally and informally enforced by government and its agents (Scott, 2002) and which bears upon the norms and cognitions that influence investment, including foreign investment, behaviour. High levels of government support, typically in the form of privileged access to raw materials and other inputs, low-cost capital (discussed above), subsidies and other benefits help emerging country firms to offset ownership and location disadvantages abroad (Aggarwal and Agmon, 1990). On the other hand, such investors also often encounter highly bureaucratic and burdensome administrative FDI approval procedures as government, at various levels, seeks to influence the amount, direction and scope of outward capital flows. If this is combined with discriminatory policy tools against certain industries and ownership forms, flows of ODI can be distorted. In such instances, FDI via informal or illegal routes may occur (or indeed be tacitly encouraged).

Given the extent of state control of the Chinese economy (Scott, 2002), the institutional environment is likely to have had far-reaching and profound effects on the internationalisation decision of Chinese firms. Key periods in the evolution of China's FDI approval process are presented in Table 6.1. Because various agencies within the state administration have been required to approve each and every outward FDI project from China (predominantly through the control of foreign exchange), this evolution is likely to have influenced strongly the development, strength and orientation of Chinese MNEs. To illustrate, extant research portrays Chinese ODI of the 1980s and early 1990s as having been directed by government towards supporting the export function of state-owned manufacturers; towards providing stability to the supply of domestically scarce natural resources; and towards the acquisition of information and learning on how to operate at an international level (Ye, 1992; Zhan, 1995; Liu and Li, 2002). In particular, FDI in the energy and minerals sectors was encouraged to meet growing needs at home (Lawrence, 2002). In this sense, China has 'built' some of its MNEs, as did Singapore, South Korea and Malaysia (Heenan and Keegan, 1979; Yeung, 1998; Wang, 2002; Dicken, 2003). FDI, and especially natural resources-oriented FDI, was concentrated by value in the developed countries (Buckley *et al.*, 2006) (see Table 6.2). There is some evidence that latterly Chinese MNEs have internationalised to gain better access to foreign proprietary technology, strategic assets and capabilities (brands, distribution channels, foreign capital markets and so forth), often by acquisition; to exploit new markets; and to diversify business activities in a manner that seeks to improve their international competitiveness (Taylor, 2002; Deng, 2003; Zhang, 2003, Buckley *et al.*, 2006). This development, which has occurred in conjunction with increasing policy openness and liberalisation over the period under study (Sauvant, 2005), has seen Chinese ODI dispersed more widely, especially among the developing countries (see Table 6.2), with both defensive (import-substituting and quota-hopping) and offensive (developing new markets) market-seeking FDI increasingly undertaken (Buckley *et al.*, 2006). This is in addition to the continuance of natural resources-oriented FDI, which now increasingly encompasses developing countries. The promotion of exports and export-oriented FDI also continues. For example, direct government support in the form of export tax rebates, foreign exchange

Table 6.1 Key stages in Chinese ODI policy development.

1979–1985	*Stage 1: Cautious internationalisation* With the 'open-door' policy, Chinese ODI is identified by government as one means of opening and integrating China into the world economy. Chinese state-owned firms start to set up their first international operations. Only state-owned trading corporations under MOFERT (later MOFCOM or the Ministry of Commerce) and provincial and municipal 'economic and technological cooperation enterprises' under the State Economic and Trade Commission (now part of the National Development and Reform Commission [NDRC]) are allowed to invest abroad. Some 189 projects are approved, amounting to around US$197m in value.
1986–1991	*Stage 2: Government encouragement* The government liberalises restrictive policies and allows more enterprises to establish foreign affiliates, provided they have sufficient capital, technical and operational know-how and a suitable joint venture partner. Approval is granted to 891 projects, totalling some US$1.2bn.
1992–1998	*Stage 3: Expansion and regulation* Encouraged by domestic liberalisation, initiated by Deng Xiaoping's journey to the South and the incorporation of enterprise internationalisation into the national economic development policy, subnational-level authorities actively promote the international business activities of enterprises under their supervision, especially in Hong Kong to engage in real estate and stock market speculation. The Asian crisis in 1997 and the subsequent collapse of some enterprises slow down this development. Latterly, concerns about loss of control over state assets, capital flight and 'leakage' of foreign exchange lead to a tightening of approval procedures, notably for projects of US$1m or more. Individual ODI project activity declines, despite an increase of total ODI of US$1.2bn in value terms.
1999–2001	*Stage 4: Implementation of the 'go global' policy* Contradictory policies characterise this period. Further measures to control illicit capital transfers and to regularise ODI towards genuinely productive purposes are introduced. By contrast, ODI in specific industries is actively encouraged with export tax rebates, foreign exchange assistance and direct financial support, notably in trade-related activities that promoted Chinese exports of raw materials, parts and machinery and in light industry sectors like textiles, machinery and electrical equipment. In 2001 this encouragement is formalised in the 10th five-year plan which outlines the 'going global' or *zou chu qu* directive. Total approved ODI rises by US$1.8bn, with an average project value of US$2.6m.

Table 6.1   Key stages in Chinese ODI policy development – *continued*

Since 2001	*Stage 5: Post-WTO period (included here for completeness)* Heightened domestic competitive pressures, owing to the opening of once protected industries and markets to foreign and domestic competitors, forces some Chinese firms to seek new markets abroad. In the 11th five-year plan the Chinese government stresses again the importance of zou chu qu for Chinese firms and the Chinese economy. Although the approval system is decentralised and streamlined to become less burdensome, contradictory regulations still prevail. Direct, proactive support of ODI continues to be limited, aimed mainly at preventing illegal capital outflows and loss of control of state assets.

Source: Yu *et al.* (2005), Zhang (2003), Wong and Chan (2003), Wu and Chen (2001), Guo (1984), Ye (1992), Ding (2000).

assistance and financial support was introduced in 1999 to foster FDI in trade-related activities and to promote Chinese exports, especially in the textiles, machinery and electrical equipment sectors (Wong and Chan, 2003). The effect of home country institutions on the investment behaviour of Chinese MNEs would be evidenced by a correlation between a key policy change and a change in the amount or distribution of Chinese ODI, or both.

The determinants of Chinese ODI: hypotheses

We now review the determinants of FDI derived from theory and hypothesise on their ability to influence the distribution of Chinese ODI.

Market-seeking FDI

Host market characteristics, such as market size, are generally recognised as a significant determinant of FDI flows: as markets increase in size, so do opportunities for the efficient utilisation of resources and the exploitation of economies of scale and scope via FDI (UNCTAD, 1998). Numerous studies (surveyed by Chakrabarti, 2001) show that FDI flow and market size are associated positively. Recent work points to the rise of offensive market-seeking motives driving Chinese MNEs (Taylor, 2002; Zhang, 2003; Deng, 2004; Buckley *et al.*, 2006) and posits that this activity may increasingly be directed towards large markets. Theory suggests that market-oriented, horizontal FDI will be

Table 6.2 Approved Chinese FDI outflows, by host region and economy, 1990–2003 (US$10,000 and %).

	Annual average of ODI stock (%)				
	1990–1992	1993–1995	1996–1998	1999–2001	2002–2003
Total Chinese ODI (US$ 10,000)	133,847.53	176,010.77	235,466.77	377,761.70	1,038,208.76
Percentage distribution by region:					
Developed countries	69.44	64.12	49.95	36.11	22.60
Western Europe	2.62	2.63	2.21	1.72	4.15
European Union (15 countries)	2.29	2.38	2.01	1.58	4.08
Other Western Europe (3 countries)	0.33	0.25	0.20	0.14	0.07
North America	41.59	39.86	31.25	23.67	12.82
Other developed countries	25.22	21.63	16.49	10.71	5.62
Developing countries	30.56	35.88	50.05	63.89	77.40
Africa	4.03	5.18	11.02	16.07	8.40
North Africa (6 countries)	0.20	0.19	0.76	1.13	0.85
Other Africa (46 countries)	3.83	4.99	10.27	14.93	7.55
Latin America and the Caribbean	4.87	4.96	10.04	13.83	7.13
South America (12 countries)	3.64	3.19	8.40	8.89	4.18
Other Latin America and Caribbean (18 countries)	1.23	1.78	1.64	4.94	2.95
Central and Eastern Europe (18 countries)	4.17	5.76	4.85	4.44	4.62
Asia	16.61	18.71	22.22	27.87	56.60
West Asia (Middle East) (12 countries)	1.09	1.17	0.98	1.61	1.46
Central Asia (8 countries)	0.09	0.26	0.49	1.50	0.91
South, East and SE Asia (20 countries)	15.42	17.28	20.74	24.75	54.22
The Pacific (9 countries)	0.88	1.27	1.92	1.69	0.67

Source: Calculated from MOFCOM Almanac of China's Foreign Relations and Trade (various years) and China Commerce Yearbook 2004 (2004).
Note: The total number of recipient countries per region is shown in the region heading. Regions are as per UNCTAD (2003).

associated positively with growth in demand. The market growth hypothesis holds that rapidly growing economies present more opportunities for generating profits than those that are growing more slowly or not at all (Lim, 1983). We therefore derive the following three hypotheses:

Hypothesis 1a: Chinese ODI is associated positively with absolute host market size.
Hypothesis 1b: Chinese ODI is associated positively with host market size per capita.
Hypothesis 1c: Chinese ODI is associated positively with host market growth.

Natural resource endowment

The Chinese government has used ODI to ensure the supply of domestically scarce factor inputs as the Chinese economy has grown (Ye, 1992; Zhan, 1995). Key sectors include minerals, petroleum, timber, fishery and agricultural products (Cai, 1999; Wu and Sia, 2002). Purchases of stakes in Australian mineral and food companies by CITIC and the acquisition of Canada-based PetroKaz by China National Petroleum Corporation (CNPC) are examples (Wu and Sia, 2002). Internalisation theory asserts the importance of equity-based control in the exploitation of scarce natural resources, and so a positive association between the natural resources endowment of countries and Chinese ODI is expected (Buckley and Casson, 1976). Thus:

Hypothesis 2: Chinese ODI is associated positively with host country endowments of natural resources.

Asset-seeking FDI

Chinese ODI has been directed to the acquisition of information and knowledge on how to operate internationally, especially in the 1980s (Ye, 1992; Zhan, 1995; Buckley *et al.*, 2006). In recent years, an expressed goal of state-directed Chinese ODI has been to access advanced proprietary technology, immobile strategic assets (e.g., brands, local distribution networks) and other capabilities abroad (Taylor, 2002; Deng, 2003; Zhang, 2003; Warner *et al.*, 2004), through both greenfield entry and acquisition. It is expected that Chinese MNEs would direct such asset-seeking ODI towards economies with significant levels of human and intellectual capital, and in particular the industrialised countries, to help them to strengthen their competitiveness elsewhere (Dunning *et al.*, 1998; Dunning, 2006). It is worth noting that many acquisitions by Chinese firms, especially in Europe and the USA, have involved a target company that was ailing or insolvent. Proprietary ownership advantage endowments can be proxied by the rate of patenting in the host country. Thus:

> **Hypothesis 3:** Chinese ODI is associated positively with host country endowments of ownership advantages.

Political risk

Internalisation theory predicts that in countries experiencing high political risk, market-oriented firms will tend to substitute arm's length servicing modes (exporting or licensing) for directly owned local production, and that resource-oriented firms are discouraged from committing substantial sunk costs in the form of FDI projects (Buckley and Casson, 1981, 1999). Thus high political risk is generally associated with low values of FDI inflow, *ceteris paribus* (Chakrabarti, 2001). The use of a risk index on its own would beg the question of the return on investment. If higher risk host countries also offer higher returns, then FDI will still flow to them, and an increasing relationship between risk and FDI will be observed. In this study, the role of returns is approximated (as it is in many studies on country risk) by market-related variables, so we can argue that returns of a market-related nature have been controlled for. Similarly, the scope for returns on Chinese investment in natural resources (the most likely motive for investment in risky countries of Central Asia and Africa) is controlled for by the natural resources variable. Because the measure of political risk we use assigns higher values to greater political stability, the general theory of FDI would predict a positive relationship between the dependent and independent variables. Thus:

> **Hypothesis 4:** Chinese ODI is associated negatively with rising levels of host country political risk.

Cultural proximity

The Chinese diaspora is acknowledged to have contributed to the integration of China into the world economy since 1979, especially in positively influencing inbound FDI from Singapore, the Republic of China (Taiwan) and Hong Kong (Henley *et al.*, 1999; Yeung, 1999; Sikorski and Menkhoff, 2000; Ng and Tuan, 2002).[5] Strong economic connections among overseas Chinese and the importance of *guanxi* (the ancient system of personal relationships and social connections based on mutual interest and benefit) in Chinese business dealings may also influence patterns of Chinese ODI (Luo, 1997; Standifird and Marshall, 2000;

Tong, 2003). A number of scholars argue that ethnic and family *guanxi* networks constitute a firm-specific advantage for Chinese MNEs because these help to reduce the business risk and transaction costs (Sung, 1996; Braeutigam, 2003; Erdener and Shapiro, 2005) associated with the identification of business opportunities in certain foreign markets (Zhan, 1995). These networks may also compensate Chinese MNEs for their relatively late entry into international markets (Li, 2003).

This argument suggests that Chinese firms will invest in countries with a large resident population of ethnic Chinese. Such countries are mostly to be found in Asia, which accounts for some 88% of all ethnic Chinese living outside China. In 1990 there were about 37 million overseas Chinese, with the majority (66%) distributed more or less evenly among Indonesia, Thailand, Hong Kong SAR and Malaysia. A further 8% lived in North and South American countries, 2% in European countries and 1% each in Oceania and on the African continent (Poston *et al.*, 1994). Thus:

Hypothesis 5: Chinese ODI is associated positively with the proportion of ethnic Chinese in the host population.

Policy liberalisation

From the discussion above, it is clear that policies on international capital transfers are likely to have greatly influenced patterns and trends in Chinese ODI. Although it is important for completeness that any formal model of Chinese ODI incorporates a policy dimension, lack of transparency in the application of regulations and incentive policies experienced by investors (Wong and Chan, 2003) makes this a difficult aspect to capture. Deng Xiaoping's South China Tour in 1992 was associated with significant domestic market liberalisation. In response to this, numerous subnational-level authorities allowed enterprises under their supervision to internationalise, especially towards Hong Kong SAR, in order to engage in real estate and stock market speculation (Wong and Chan, 2003). Therefore, to investigate the role of institutional liberalisation towards ODI, we introduce a time dummy for 1992. Thus:

Hypothesis 6: Liberalisation of Chinese FDI policy in 1992 increased Chinese ODI.

We control for a number of conventional variables from standard theory to specify correctly the estimated equation, and so to reveal the effects of the main variables, including those to test the special theory applied to Chinese ODI.

Exchange rate

A low or undervalued exchange rate encourages exports but discourages outward FDI (Kohlhagen, 1977; Logue and Willet, 1977; Stevens, 1993). As the home country exchange rate appreciates, more profitable opportunities for outward FDI will occur as foreign currency denominated assets become cheaper. It is possible that a rapid appreciation of the exchange rate, from a low or undervalued position, will more than proportionately increase outward FDI. For this reason, the exchange rate is included as a control variable. An appreciation of the home country's currency *vis-à-vis* other countries should increase ODI into these countries as it is effectively a depreciation in the host country's currency (Scott-Green and Clegg, 1999). In the case of China, the yuan Renminbi (RMB) was *de facto* pegged to the US dollar at a constant nominal level over the period under study (Roberts and Tyers, 2003; Hall, 2004). However, the RMB peg against the US dollar allowed for revaluation of the yuan RMB against other currencies so that the real effective exchange rate of the yuan RMB appreciated by more than 20% between 1995 and 2002 (Hall, 2004). Thus:

> **Hypothesis 7**: A relative depreciation of the host country's currency leads to an increase in Chinese ODI.

Host inflation rate

Volatile and unpredictable inflation rates in a host country discourage market-seeking FDI by creating uncertainty and by making long-term corporate planning problematic, especially in respect of price-setting and profit expectations. High rates of inflation may also lead to domestic currency devaluation, which in turn reduces the real value of earnings in local currency for market-seeking inward-investing firms. High inflation rates tend to check the export performance of domestic and foreign investors and thereby discourage export-oriented FDI by increasing the prices of locally sourced inputs, making it harder to maintain a cost advantage in third markets. We therefore expect a negative relationship between Chinese ODI and host country inflation. Thus:

> **Hypothesis 8**: Chinese ODI is associated negatively with host country inflation rates.

Exports and imports

Exports from China proxy the intensity of trade relations between home and host country by capturing the market-seeking motive of

Chinese firms. During the 1980s and early 1990s, much Chinese ODI took place to provide a local support function for domestic Chinese exporters and to help them increase their hard currency earnings (Wu and Sia, 2002). Typically, such investments were small scale, with local subsidiaries providing information, international trade, transportation and financial services to their Chinese principals and other Chinese firms (Ye, 1992; Zhan, 1995). In some cases, these were vanguard operations for later and more substantial investment. Thus:

> **Hypothesis 9**: Chinese ODI is associated positively with Chinese exports to the host country.

Imports to a home country from a host country also capture the intensity of trade relations. Since they are an indication of the importance of the resources transferred we would expect home country firms to internalise these strategic flows using outward FDI as the key mechanism (Buckley and Casson, 1976). Thus:

> **Hypothesis 10**: Chinese ODI is associated positively with Chinese imports from the host country.

Geographic distance from China

Internalisation theory predicts that market-seeking firms are more likely to serve geographically proximate countries through exports and more distant markets via FDI (Buckley and Casson, 1981). This suggests a substitution of FDI for other modes as distance increases. However, our dependent variable is in the form of the annual flow of Chinese FDI alone (i.e., not in the form of a ratio with exports). As we predict the flow of FDI to be greatest to nearby countries, so we would expect to capture a negative effect of distance on the flow of FDI (Loungani et al., 2002). A physical distance variable is therefore needed to complement our cultural proximity variable, to isolate its effect. We incorporate distance as a control. Thus:

> **Hypothesis 11**: Chinese ODI is associated negatively with geographic distance from China.

Openness to FDI

The more open a country is to international investment, the more attractive it is likely to be as a destination for FDI (Chakrabarti, 2001). We include openness to FDI in our investigation, as a control:

> **Hypothesis 12**: Chinese ODI is associated positively with the degree of openness of the host economy to international investment.

Our hypotheses, their theoretical justification, the proxies we use and the expected signs are detailed in Table 6.3, together with our data sources. We expect the distinctive nature of the factors influencing Chinese ODI to be captured by the collective significance in the main variables that we identify in the table.

The model

Our discussion suggests the following log-linear model:

$$LFDI = \alpha + \beta_1 LGDP + \beta_2 LGDPP + \beta_3 LGGDP + \beta_4 LORE + \beta_5 LPATENT + \beta_6 LPOLI + \beta_7 CP + \beta_8 TD92 + \beta_9 LERATE + \beta_{10} LINF + \beta_{11} LEXP + \beta_{12} LIMP \ \beta_{13} LDIS + \beta_{14} LINFDI + \varepsilon_{it} \quad (1)$$

The data are transformed into natural logarithms as we expect non-linearities in the relationships on the basis of theory and previous empirical work.

Data and method

Our dependent variable is the total amount of foreign exchange approved by SAFE during the project investment process. This includes pre-approved re-invested earnings and intra-company loans, plus in-kind investment up to the total authorised value of a given project, in addition to equity capital.[6] Forty-nine countries are host to Chinese ODI in our data set, of which 22 are members of the Organisation for Economic Cooperation and Development (OECD) and 27 are not (see Appendix).

Two statistical models were used to estimate Eq. (1): pooled ordinary least squares (POLS) and the random effects (RE) generalised least squares method. A fixed effects (FE) model cannot be used since Eq. (1) includes a time dummy variable. A Lagrangian multiplier (LM) test was conducted to identify whether POLS or RE furnished the better model. A value for the LM test that is significantly different from zero means that RE estimation is preferable to that of POLS.

Table 6.3 The determinants of Chinese ODI.

Hypotheses and number	Proxy	Expected sign	Theoretical justification	Main or control variable	Data source
FDI (dependent variable)	Annual outflow of Chinese FDI (see text)				State Administration for Foreign Exchange
Host market characteristics (I): absolute market size (H1a)	*LGDP*: Host country GDP	+	Market seeking	Main	World Bank Development Indicator (2005)
Host market characteristics (II): relative market size (H1b)	*LGDPP*: Host country GDP per capita	+	Market seeking	Alternative main (I)	World Bank Development Indicator (2005)
Host market characteristics (III): market growth (H1c)	*LGGDP*: Annual percentage increase in GDP	+	Market seeking	Alternative main (II)	World Bank Development Indicator (2005)
Natural resource endowment (H2)	*LORE*: the ratio of ore and metal exports to merchandise exports of host country	+	Resource seeking	Main	World Bank Development Indicator (2005)
Asset-seeking FDI (H3)	*LPATENT*: Total (resident plus non-resident) annual patent registrations in host country	+	Strategic asset seeking	Main	World Intellectual Property Organisation (2006)
Political risk (H4)	*LPOLI*: Host country's political risk rating (higher values indicate greater stability	+	Transaction costs	Main	International Country Risk Guide (2005)

Table 6.3 The determinants of Chinese ODI – continued

Hypotheses and number	Proxy	Expected sign	Theoretical justification	Main or control variable	Data source
Cultural proximity to China (H5)	CP: = 1 when percentage of ethnic Chinese in total population is > 1%	+	Region-specific transaction costs	Main	Ohio University (2006); Ma (2003); Kent (2003);
Policy liberalisation (H6)	TD92: Influence of Deng's South China tour (1992)	+	Institutional factors	Main	United Nations Statistics Division (2006)
Exchange rate (H7)	LERATE: Host country official annual average exchange rate against RMB (fixed to dollar)	+	Domestic currency price of foreign assets	Control	World Bank Development Indicator (2005)
Host country inflation rate (H8)	LINF: Host country annual inflation rate	−	Macroeconomic conditions	Control	IMF: World Economic Outlook Database (2005)
Exports (H9)	LEXP: China's exports to the host country	+	Market seeking	Control	China Statistical Yearbook (2005)
Imports (H10)	LIMP: China's imports from the host country	+	Trade intensity	Control	China Statistical Yearbook (2005)
Geographic distance from China (H11)	LDIS: Geographic distance between host and home country (capital)	−	Spatial costs	Control	Calculated using www.geobytes.com
Openness to FDI (H12) FDI stock to host GDP	LINFDI: Ratio of inward	+	Investment policy	Control	UNCTAD FDI database (2006)

Note: all monetary values are in constant (2000) US$ prices.

To investigate heterogeneity within the data we employ a structural break framework. First, we investigate the impact of significant changes in the policy regime dating from 1992. These changes might influence the decision-making of investors across all the variables. Therefore we divide the period into two phases: 1984–1991 and 1992–2001. Second, and as our discussion above has indicated, China's preference to invest in developing countries may indicate a different model of investment behaviour arising from state policy. To investigate this possibility we draw a distinction between developed and developing hosts using their OECD membership status.

Results and discussion

In preliminary regressions, two of the three alternative measures of host market size (growth in GDP and GDP per capita) never attained significance and were therefore not included in the final specification, which is reported in Table 6.6. The absolute host market size variable is retained to capture the market-seeking motive (Hypothesis 1a) and to act as a control (for market returns) in the estimation of the relationship between Chinese ODI and host country risk. The empirical results obtained from the POLS and the RE equations are similar. However, the large and significant LM value indicates in favour of the RE and therefore only the results from RE are discussed. Tables 6.4 and 6.5 present the correlation matrix and variance inflation factor (VIF) test results, which indicate that there are no general problems with the data.

We first discuss the results of the RE model for the main variables (column 2, Table 6.6). We find that host market characteristics (measured by absolute size of economy, *LGDP*), cultural proximity (*CP*) and policy liberalisation (*TD92*) are all significant and correctly signed. These findings support Hypotheses 1a, 5 and 6. By contrast, political risk (*LPOLI*) is found to be significant but with a sign contrary to expectation as predicted in Hypothesis 4. We find that natural resource endowments (*LORE*) and asset-seeking FDI (*LPATENT*) are both insignificant. Therefore Hypotheses 2 and 3 are not supported. We now discuss each of these main findings in more detail.

Absolute host market size (*LGDP*) has a positive influence on Chinese FDI outflows, with a 1% rise in the variable increasing Chinese ODI by 0.35%. This indicates that market seeking was a key motive for Chinese ODI in the period under study (Hypothesis 1a). Cultural proximity (*CP*) is found to have a highly significant and positive effect on

Table 6.4 Correlation matrix.

	LFDI	LGDP	LORE	LPATENT	LPOLI	LERATE	LINF	LEXP	LIMP	LDIS	LINFDI
LFDI	1.0000										
LGDP	0.2188	1.0000									
LORE	0.0044	0.0274	1.0000								
LPATENT	0.0691	0.6684	0.1918	1.0000							
LPOLI	-0.0432	0.4851	0.1789	0.4618	1.0000						
LERATE	0.0745	-0.2606	-0.1282	-0.2237	-0.2760	1.0000					
LINF	-0.0019	-0.2879	0.1739	-0.1421	-0.4528	-0.0978	1.0000				
LEXP	0.4428	0.6565	-0.1286	0.3747	0.3516	0.0414	-0.3952	1.0000			
LIMP	0.3580	0.7282	0.0881	0.4587	0.4022	-0.1296	-0.3211	0.8545	1.0000		
LDIS	-0.1767	-0.0368	0.2335	-0.0844	-0.0098	-0.3316	0.1982	-0.4947	-0.4217	1.0000	
LINFDI	0.1826	-0.2559	-0.1238	-0.2632	0.1313	-0.0067	-0.1856	0.1248	-0.0073	0.0868	1.0000

Table 6.5 Variance inflation factor test.

Variable	VIF	1/VIF
LGDP	7.12	0.140471
LORE	1.58	0.632445
LPATENT	2.18	0.458703
LPOLI	2.02	0.494854
CP	2.17	0.459989
TD92	1.05	0.948919
LERATE	1.47	0.682196
LINF	1.64	0.611576
LEXP	6.61	0.151327
LIMP	7.59	0.131727
LDIS	2.89	0.345584
LINFDI	2.43	0.410728

Chinese ODI (Hypothesis 5). This result suggests that the presence of ethnic Chinese people in the host country has promoted inward investment by Chinese firms. The policy liberalisation variable (TD92) is also positive and significant. This supports the argument that the qualitative changes in Chinese policy that took place in 1992, the year of Deng Xiaoping's visit to the southern provinces, did mark a significant step towards liberalisation in a number of ODI-related areas, and positively influenced the value of approved Chinese ODI for that year (Hypothesis 6). Our interpretation is that policy changes freed SOEs to invest abroad for reasons other than the promotion of exports, that is, they were able to service foreign markets directly.

A major finding is that the coefficient on the index of political risk (LPOLI) indicates an increasing relationship between host country political risk levels and Chinese ODI. We find that a 1% increase in the host country risk index (i.e., a decrease in risk) is associated with a decrease in Chinese ODI of 1.8%. Thus we find no evidence to support Hypothesis 4. This runs counter to the normal findings for this variable, and requires discussion. In line with theory advanced in this paper, capital market imperfections and institutional factors in China may have induced a perverse attitude to risk, which contrasts with that found among industrialised country firms. In other words, Chinese foreign investors seem not to perceive risk in the same way as industrialised country firms. There are a number of reasons why Chinese firms may not behave in the conventional manner. First, Chinese state-owned firms may not be profit-maximisers, or may be maximising subject to government-led institutional influences. Second, the bulk of

Chinese FDI is in developing countries (see Table 6.2), and these are precisely the countries that, as a group, record higher levels of political risk. Much of this investment may have been promoted by political affiliations and connections between China and the developing host country government concerned. The bargaining position of the Chinese government and Chinese firms may have been further strengthened *vis-à-vis* governments in those host countries that attract only modest amounts of investment from the industrialised nations. Third, China's political and ideological heritage in the modern era may have led to Chinese ODI being preferentially directed to fellow communist or ideologically similar countries, many of which also record higher levels of political risk. Fourth, home country embeddedness (i.e., in the current context, the knowledge of operating in an emerging country environment characterised by tight, centralised economic planning) may have provided Chinese firms with ownership advantages that enable them to mitigate the risk associated with operating in equivalent environments abroad. Fifth, Chinese firms may also be prepared to invest in countries generally avoided by industrialised country firms for ethical (e.g., human rights) reasons, with Sudan being an example. Sixth, we should finally note that the relative inexperience of some Chinese firms concerning the establishment and management of large-scale operations abroad may have led to FDI projects being undertaken with insufficient due diligence and attention to associated risks (Wong and Chan, 2003; Ma and Andrews-Speed, 2006). Our finding for risk also highlights potential shortcomings in familiar measures of political risk, which are typically calculated from the point of view of industrialised country firms (World Bank, 2006). Such indices may need to be recalculated to better capture the perceptions of firms from emerging economies like China. Given that our regression specification controls for market returns, it does appear that Chinese behaviour towards conventionally measured host political risk differs from that of developed country investors. In line with the theory put forward earlier, the evidence suggests that capital market imperfections play a role.

Of the main variables we examine, we find no support for Hypothesis 3. The asset-seeking variable (*LPATENT*) in the RE model is insignificant, which suggests that Chinese firms have not been motivated to acquire strategic intellectual capital assets over the period under study.

We now discuss the results for our six control variables. The finding for exports (*LEXP*) is significant and correctly signed, supporting

Hypothesis 9. By contrast, we find that inflation (*LINF*) and imports (*LIMP*) are significant but with signs contrary to expectation as predicted in Hypotheses 8 and 10. Our findings for the exchange rate (*LERATE*), geographic distance (*LDIS*) and market openness (*LINFDI*) are all insignificant. In short, we find no support for Hypotheses 7, 11 or 12.

The two trade-related variables, *LEXP* and *LIMP*, when viewed together, indicate that Chinese ODI has both a conventional and an idiosyncratic nature. As expected, *LEXP* positively affects FDI, which is the conventional finding that FDI follows exports. It also supports the market-seeking motive (Hypothesis 9). This finding concurs with the view that one of the key motivations of Chinese investment has been to promote domestic exports. We find that *LIMP* is also a significant determinant of Chinese ODI but, against expectations (Hypothesis 10), has a negative effect. A 1% increase in China's imports from a host country is associated with a 0.25% reduction in Chinese ODI. This result could be generated by the practice of Chinese investors relocating production from China to other developing countries. In this account, imports of intermediate products to China for processing and re-export are reduced when Chinese firms relocate processing abroad via FDI. By value, most Chinese ODI is in the developing countries (see Table 6.2), and outward investment to these countries to circumvent trade barriers in third markets may have been a motive. In essence, it is possible that some Chinese ODI substitutes for intermediate imports to China.

The coefficient on inflation (*LINF*) is significant and positive, indicating that a 1% increase in the variable is associated with an increase in Chinese ODI of 0.19%. This is contrary to expectation (Hypothesis 8). Such an association might suggest that countries with moderate demand inflation are more attractive to Chinese investors. This link between the variables would be reasonable on the assumption that moderate demand inflation accompanies economic growth. It may also support the view that the investment decisions of Chinese firms are unusually tolerant of less stable countries with respect to local economic conditions. This contrasts with the normal behaviour of profitmaximising industrialised country firms, and again suggests that Chinese firms may be influenced strongly by home country capital market failure and institutional factors.

Changes over time

In order to investigate whether or not Chinese FDI has changed in character over the period in question, we divide our data into two time periods around 1992. This procedure is borne out by the results in columns 3 and 4 of Table 6.6, which contrast sharply. These indicate that different locational determinants and motivations apply over time. Of our main variables, we find that market size (*LGDP*) and cultural proximity (*CP*) were important determinants of Chinese ODI for the period prior to 1991; in the later time period (post-1992), natural resource endowment (*LORE*), political risk (*LPOLI*), cultural proximity (*CP*) and policy liberalisation (*TD92*) are instead significant determinants. We also detect differences across time among the control variables. Before 1991, inflation (*LINF*), geographic distance (*LDIS*) and market openness (*LINFDI*) were important determinants of Chinese ODI, but post-1992 only the two trade-related variables, exports (*LEXP*) and imports (*LIMP*), are significant. These findings are in agreement with the earlier discussion that there has been a significant change in the foreign investment behaviour of Chinese enterprises over time, and that this is at least partly due to the variable policy regime, as suggested by our finding for the policy liberalisation variable (*TD92*), which indicates a surge in ODI for the year 1992. Arguably, this provides further substantiation for the notion that institutional factors have influenced patterns of Chinese ODI. We find that, over the period under study, Chinese firms have moved away from undertaking mainly market-seeking strategies in nearby foreign markets towards the securing of raw materials in riskier markets. These findings reinforce the view that the securement of natural resources has become an imperative in more recent years, in line with Chinese domestic growth, and that this investment has been directed to countries with higher levels of political risk (by Western standards). The fact that *LDIS* is significant and negative for the earlier period but not for the later one shows that geographic proximity of host countries to China was a positive influence only on early Chinese ODI. This development may be an outcome of the growing maturity of Chinese market-seeking investors and the increasing propensity for Chinese firms to engage in natural resources in more spatially distant markets.

The highly significant and positive coefficient for cultural proximity (*CP*) in both time periods (columns 3 and 4) supports our hypothesis that familiarity between populations is important in the flow of Chinese FDI. The facilitating role of the Chinese diaspora persists throughout the period under study, as expected, and suggests that relational assets indeed constitute an ownership advantage for Chinese firms when they invest in countries with a significant Chinese population. In the later period only, ODI is positively associated with

Chinese exports, indicating that a significant part of FDI has followed export trade. These results are consistent with a 'stages approach' to inter-nationalisation being applicable to Chinese ODI, and further research is required.

Host country level of development

Theory suggests that home country market imperfections can exert a significant impact on the decisions of foreign investors. It follows that Chinese government policy may have led to a distinctive pattern of outward FDI by host country. Here, we test this for developed and developing countries by comparing results for the subsamples of OECD and non-OECD countries in columns 5 and 6 of Table 6.6, respectively. Looking at the main variables, we see that market size ($LGDP$) is a significant determinant of Chinese ODI within the OECD group: that is, Chinese investors preferentially seek out larger markets within the OECD countries. This is a conventional result, and captures that part of Chinese FDI that is market seeking. Also significant is the cultural proximity variable (CP). This variable appears to be capturing the tendency for Chinese firms to invest in OECD countries where a sizeable population of ethnic Chinese can be found. The highly significant and positive policy liberalisation variable for OECD countries alone ($TD92$ in column 5 of Table 6.6) again yields insight into the relatively undeveloped state of the FDI decision process by Chinese investors. The policy change in 1992 is associated with a large increase in FDI to the developed world. This implies that the decision to invest was previously tightly circumscribed by government, and this may be the reason why a full and conventional pattern of significance is not observed. However, the pattern of investment flows to the developed economies fits with Chinese government priorities during liberalisation.

It is clear that Chinese ODI in non-OECD countries is not motivated by host market size, and that other motives must therefore be at play. Looking at the control variables, the positive significance of the $LEXP$ variable applies to both OECD and non-OECD countries. This suggests that Chinese ODI follows trade for both categories of country. The strong result for $LEXP$ captures FDI that follows Chinese exports, and is an indicator of the role of host market demand. As we would expect from the argument above concerning the mechanism through which the Chinese import variable ($LIMP$) associates with Chinese ODI, it is the non-OECD group of hosts that records a negative effect. These results indicate that it is specifically those developing countries from which China imports least to which Chinese investors have been

Table 6.6 Results for the determinants of Chinese ODI.

	POLS (1)	REs (2)	REs 1984-91 (3)	REs 1992-01 (4)	REs OECD (5)	REs Non-OECD (6)
LGDP (H1a)	0.3463 (0.1249)***	0.3448 (0.1640)**	0.5085 (0.2787)*	0.2448 (0.2009)	0.6674 (0.3650)*	0.3472 (0.2238)
LORE (H2)	0.1713 (0.0742)**	0.1447 (0.1057)	0.1039 (0.1654)	0.2253 (0.1206)*	-0.0138 (0.3906)	0.1820 (0.1144)
LPATENT (H3)	-0.0223 (0.0309)	-0.0363 (0.0359)	0.0794 (0.0605)	-0.0516 (0.0439)	-0.0752 (0.0773)	-0.0262 (0.0447)
LPOLI (H4)	-2.4762 (0.5822)***	-1.7997 (0.6974)**	-0.7347 (1.0846)	-2.6308 (0.9750)***	-1.8973 (1.8807)	-1.4560 (0.8903)
CP (H5)	1.4779 (0.2588)***	1.4929 (0.4276)***	1.4520 (0.6059)**	1.5338 (0.4634)***	2.0464 (0.8415)**	0.8414 (0.6563)
TD92 (H6)	0.6595 (0.2698)**	0.6961 (0.2534)***		0.8033 (0.3002)***	0.9489 (0.3178)***	0.4104 (0.4021)
LERATE (H7)	0.0471 (0.0337)	0.0688 (0.0463)	0.1032 (0.0638)	0.0246 (0.0618)	0.2319 (0.1866)	0.0142 (0.0540)
LINF (H8)	0.2406 (0.0628)***	0.1891 (0.0734)**	0.4664 (0.1167)***	0.1323 (0.0896)	0.3487 (0.1579)**	0.1320 (0.0914)
LEXP (H9)	0.6934 (0.1084)***	0.6153 (0.1291)***	0.2731 (0.2094)	0.8275 (0.1803)***	0.4062 (0.2053)**	0.8375 (0.1964)***

Table 6.6 Results for the determinants of Chinese ODI – continued

	POLS (1)	REs (2)	REs 1984–91 (3)	REs 1992–01 (4)	REs OECD (5)	REs Non-OECD (6)
LIMP (H10)	−0.2601 (0.0931)***	−0.2544 (0.1027)**	−0.3087 (0.2061)	−0.3098 (0.1204)**	−0.1914 (0.1898)	−0.3677 (0.1374)***
LDIS (H11)	0.1905 (0.2035)	0.1554 (0.2972)	−0.9266 (0.4794)*	0.2885 (0.3400)	0.7452 (0.7360)	0.0171 (0.4259)
LINFDI (H12)	0.0927 (0.0886)	0.0510 (0.1244)	0.3294 (0.1562)**	−0.0589 (0.0439)	−0.1181 (0.2480)	0.1218 (0.1546)
N	402	402	116	286	198	204
LM test	$X^2(1)=15.43$***					
Adj. R^2	0.3642	0.6019	0.6142	0.6024	0.5763	0.6737

Notes: Standard errors are in parentheses.
***, ** and * indicate that the coefficient is significant at the 1, 5 and 10% levels, respectively.

attracted. Inflation (*LINF*) is significant for OECD countries only. This suggests that moderate inflation is a characteristic of those buoyant markets that attracted Chinese firms.

One of the most compelling earlier findings – that our main variable political risk (*LPOLI*) is significant – is lost in both estimations (5) and (6). From this, we infer that, while Chinese ODI is associated with higher levels of host country political risk, the difference in risk in the data is primarily that between developed and developing countries, rather than within these two country groupings. The apparent preference for less developed and risky host countries as against developed hosts is consistent with our argument on the lower cost of capital enjoyed by SOEs, as well as with the relatively unsophisticated country risk evaluation processes of Chinese investors. This result supports our theoretical contention that capital market imperfections in China have been crucial to outward FDI over the period in question.

Conclusions

This paper is one of the first attempts to formally model Chinese ODI. Our motivation is to test the extent to which the mainstream theory that explains industrialised country FDI is applicable to emerging country contexts, and whether special explanations nested within the general theory are needed. We develop a theoretical framework that draws on this body of theory but which allows for both conventional and novel hypotheses to be tested. This is done within a well-specified model using previously unexamined official data on Chinese ODI and by employing a wide range of main and control variables. We find that Chinese ODI has both a conventional and an idiosyncratic dimension.

In terms of our main variables, we find a conventional result for market size. We infer from the significant role played by host country natural resource endowments that the institutional environment has strongly shaped Chinese ODI, leading to significant natural resources-seeking FDI. We also find that policy liberalisation has had a positive influence in stimulating Chinese ODI. This is further evidence of a distinctive explanation, to the effect that home country institutions have played a significant role in determining the flow and direction (OECD compared with non-OECD) of Chinese ODI. Viewed together, these findings are in agreement with the well-publicised expansion of natural resources-seeking activities of Chinese MNEs in recent years, especially to the industrialised countries, in response primarily to domestic economic imperatives (Taylor, 2002; Deng, 2003, 2004).

Although there are indications that Chinese firms have become increasingly acquisitive in recent years, we find that, prior to 2001 (when our data end), ODI was not driven by the motive to acquire strategic assets. Arguably, the asset-seeking hypothesis is more likely to be supported on data for more recent years: for example, as China's 'go global' policy becomes fully implemented and acted upon by firms.

Cultural proximity is found to be a significant factor, indicating that reduced transaction costs and network effects are important in attracting Chinese investors, and that relational assets constitute a special ownership advantage, even for state-owned firms. This supports a role for reduced psychic distance in explaining Chinese ODI. When we examine differences over time, we find that market size, geographic proximity, inflation and market openness are important locational determinants for the period 1984 to 1991, with the distance variable suggesting that the Chinese diaspora and market familiarity have positively influenced the destination of earlier Chinese investment outflows. However, the finding that the cultural proximity variable does not change over time suggests that Chinese ODI is still in an early stage of development, and that more familiar cultures in host countries continue to help promote Chinese inward investment. These findings warrant further investigation on a longer time series of data.

More challenging is the unprecedented finding that Chinese ODI is attracted, rather than deterred, by political risk (as measured conventionally and with market returns controlled for by market size). This suggests that Chinese firms do not perceive or behave towards risk in the same way as do industrialised country firms. In accordance with our theory, we attribute this to the low cost of capital that Chinese firms (for the most part SOEs) enjoy as a consequence of home country capital market imperfections. Indeed, state ownership can be considered as a firm-specific advantage for many Chinese MNEs in this context (Ding, 2000). However, the experience of operating in a highly regulated and controlled domestic environment (i.e., home-country embeddedness) may also be relevant. This experience may have equipped Chinese MNEs with the special ownership advantages needed to be competitive in other emerging economies. Moreover, further augmentation of the ownership advantages of Chinese firms is likely to occur as Chinese MNEs become more experienced internationally (Deng, 2004) and as the Chinese government and its agencies continue to provide political, financial and other support, as implied by our discussion of institution-based theory.

Our study of Chinese outward FDI offers the opportunity to examine how a country with distinctive home country institutions fits with the emerging body of theoretical work on the 'institution-based view of strategy'. Chinese firms that invest abroad have to straddle environments, institutions and rules that differ probably more than for any other outward-investing country in the world. In this paper we have expected contrasts with the conventional model, and we have found evidence for these. Theorising on the strategy of firms, especially those from emerging countries, needs to pay greater attention to the influence of home country institutions. It is arguable that Chinese firms seek foreign investment opportunities in environments that resemble their home environment. Further, it is tenable that Chinese investors are unconstrained by the ethical and governance obligations that are normally expected of Western MNEs today. If so, they may resemble outward investors from the West in an earlier period, and future changes in Chinese firms' behaviour and location decisions can be envisaged, contingent upon the evolution of institutions and rules of the game at home. For the present, Chinese outward investors clearly present marked contrasts from the conventional model in key respects.

There are implications of this research for our understanding of the outward FDI strategies of firms from other emerging markets, such as the other 'BRICs' (Brazil, Russia and India). First, state direction over firms (whether formal or informal) is likely to generate a signature in the locational pattern of outward investment that would not be predicted by the general theory of FDI, which assumes that firms are profit maximisers. The second implication is that liberalisation is a very powerful instrument for emerging economies. This does not simply mean trade liberalisation, but includes the whole range of internal liberalisations possible for countries with a significant state sector or dominant (private or public) firms, or both. The behaviour of domestic firms changes dramatically once competition, or its prospect, is introduced. Firms that performed a social role, such as the SOEs, once divested of this, are able to seek growth. However, China remains distinctive from other emerging economies in that many of its MNEs remain in state hands, even though corporatised in order to focus on commercial objectives. State direction means that these firms still align their operations, whether at home or abroad, with the five-year plans and national imperatives. This is a model that is not replicated, in any general way, in any of the other leading emerging economies.

With respect to further work, an issue requiring investigation, possibly of a qualitative nature, is whether or not and how Chinese investors are influenced (as are industrialised country firms) by concerns of due diligence, risk evaluation and ethical considerations in host countries. Similarly, how patterns of FDI are affected by formal and informal political links between China and other countries (i.e., the supranational institutional framework) also merits further examination.

Acknowledgements

We thank Mark Casson for important comments, Tim Rose for his supportive work, and the referees and Focused Issue editors for their insightful and helpful comments.

Notes

1. In this paper, we take the standard UNCTAD definition of FDI as being an investment involving a long-term relationship and reflecting a lasting interest and control by a firm in an enterprise resident in a foreign country (UNCTAD, 2005a). FDI normally has three components: (1) equity capital (the purchase of shares in the foreign enterprise); (2) reinvested earnings (those earnings not distributed as dividends by foreign affiliates or remitted to the investor enterprise); and (3) intra-company loans or debt transactions (borrowing and lending between parent and foreign affiliate enterprises) (UNCTAD, 2005a).
2. In this study, the terms 'China' and 'Mainland China' are used interchangeably to refer to the People's Republic of China (PRC). For our purposes, the PRC excludes the special autonomous regions of Hong Kong and Macau, unless specifically stated. The Republic of China (Taiwan) is treated as a separate economy. Regions with disputed borders (e.g., the Spratly Islands) are excluded from our definition of the PRC.
3. Although it post-dates the time frame of the current study, the establishment of a special state fund (valued by some at around US$15bn) available to qualifying Chinese firms for the acquisition of foreign brands and companies underscores these points (Swystun et al., 2005).
4. We are grateful to one of the reviewers for this point.
5. Overseas Chinese are defined by Poston et al. (1994: 633) as 'all Chinese living outside mainland China and Taiwan, including *Huaqiao* (Chinese citizens residing abroad), *Huaren* (naturalised citizens of Chinese descent) and *Huayi* (descendants of Chinese parents)'.
6. This also reflects the regulatory framework of Chinese ODI over the majority of the period under study. Until quite recently, Chinese firms were obliged to repatriate overseas earnings to financial authorities at home, while the ability to make inter-company loans was highly restricted under China's foreign exchange controls.

References

Aggarwal, R. and Agmon, T. (1990) 'The international success of developing country firms: role of government-directed comparative advantage', *Management International Review* 30(2): 163–180.

Antkiewicz, A. and Whalley, J. (2006) 'Recent Chinese buyout activities and the implications for global architecture', National Bureau of Economic Research (NBER) Working Paper 12072, NBER, Cambridge, MA.

Braeutigam, D. (2003) 'Close encounters: Chinese business networks as industrial catalysts in Sub-Saharan Africa', *African Affairs* 102(408): 447–467.

Buckley, P.J. (2004a) 'Asian network firms: an analytical framework', *Asia Pacific Business Review* 10(3/4): 254–271.

Buckley, P.J. (2004b) 'The role of China in the global strategy of multinational enterprises', *Journal of Chinese Economic and Business Studies* 2(1): 1–25.

Buckley, P.J. and Casson, M. (1976) *The Future of the Multinational Enterprise*, Macmillan: London.

Buckley, P.J. and Casson, M. (1981) 'The optimal timing of a foreign direct investment', *Economic Journal* 91(361): 75–87.

Buckley, P.J. and Casson, M. (1999) 'A Theory of International Operations', in P.J. Buckley and P.N. Ghauri (eds.) *The Internationalization Process of the Firm: a Reader*, 2nd edn, International Business Thomson: London, pp. 55–60.

Buckley, P.J., Clegg, L.J. and Wang, C. (2002) 'The impact of inward FDI on the performance of Chinese manufacturing firms', *Journal of International Business Studies* 33(4): 637–655.

Buckley, P.J., Cross, A.R., Tan, H., Voss, H. and Liu, X. (2006) 'An investigation of recent trends in Chinese outward direct investment and some implications for theory', Centre for International Business University of Leeds Working Paper.

Business Week (2004) 'Big Blue's Bold Step into China', 20 December: 33–34.

Cai, K.G. (1999) 'Outward foreign direct investment: a novel dimension of China's integration into the regional and global economy', *China Quarterly* 160 (December): 856–880.

Chakrabarti, A. (2001) 'The determinants of foreign direct investments: sensitivity analyses of cross-country regressions', *Kyklos* 54(1): 89–114.

Chen, X., Yung, R.L. and Zhang, B. (2002) *China Manufacturing*, BNP Paribas Peregrine Economics/Sector Update April 2002.

Child, J. and Pleister, H. (2003) 'Governance and management in China's private sector', *Management International* 7(3): 13–24.

Child, J. and Rodrigues, S.B. (2005) 'The internationalization of Chinese firms: a case for theoretical extension?' *Management and Organization Review* 1(3): 381–410.

Deng, P. (2003) 'Foreign direct investment by transnationals from emerging countries: the case of China', *Journal of Leadership and Organizational Studies* 10(2): 113–124.

Deng, P. (2004) 'Outward investment by Chinese MNCs: motivations and implications', *Business Horizons* 47(3): 8–16.

Dicken, P. (2003) *Global Shift: Reshaping the Global Economic Map in the 21st Century*, 4th edn, Sage: London.

Ding, X.L. (2000) 'Informal privatization through internationalization: the rise of *nomenklatura* capitalism in China's offshore business', *British Journal of Political Science* **30**(1): 121–146.

Dunning, J.H. (1977) 'Trade, Location of Economic Activity and the MNE: A Search for an Eclectic Approach', in B. Ohlin, P.O. Hesselborn and P.M. Wijkmon (eds.) *The International Location of Economic Activity*, Macmillan: London, pp. 395–418.

Dunning, J.H. (1993) *Multinational Enterprises and the Global Economy*, Addison-Wesley: Wokingham.

Dunning, J.H. (2001) 'The eclectic (OLI) paradigm of international production: past, present and future', *International Journal of the Economics of Business* **8**(2): 173–190.

Dunning, J.H. (2002) 'Relational Assets, Networks, and International Business Activities', in F.J. Contractor and P. Lorange (eds.) *Cooperative Strategies and Alliances*, Pergamon: Amsterdam, pp. 569–593.

Dunning, J.H. (2006) 'Comment on dragon multinationals: new players in 21st century globalization', *Asia Pacific Journal of Management* **23**(2): 139–141.

Dunning, J.H., van Hoesel, R. and Narula, R. (1998) 'Third World Multinationals Revisited: New Developments and Theoretical Implications', in J.H. Dunning (ed.) *Globalization, Trade and Foreign Direct Investment*, Elsevier: Amsterdam and Oxford, pp. 255–285.

Erdener, C. and Shapiro, D.M. (2005) 'The internationalization of Chinese family enterprises and Dunning's eclectic MNE paradigm', *Management and Organization Review* **1**(3): 411–436.

Erramilli, M.K., Srivastava, R. and Kim, S.-S. (1999) 'Internationalization theory and Korean multinationals', *Asia Pacific Journal of Management* **16**(1): 29–45.

Ferrantino, M.J. (1992) 'Transaction costs and the expansion of third-world multinationals', *Economic Letters* **38**(4): 451–456.

Guo, H. (1984) 'On Establishment of Joint Ventures Abroad', *Almanac of China's Foreign Economic Relations and Trade*, Ministry of Commerce: Beijing, pp. 652–654.

Hall, T. (2004) 'Controlling for risk: an analysis of China's system of foreign exchange and exchange rate management', *Columbia Journal of Asian Law* **17**(2): 433–481.

Heenan, D.A. and Keegan, W.J. (1979) 'The rise of third world multinationals', *Harvard Business Review* **57**(1): 101–109.

Henley, J., Kirkpatrick, C. and Wilde, G. (1999) 'Foreign direct investment in China: recent trends and current policy issues', *The World Economy* **22**(2): 223–243.

International Monetary Fund (IMF) (2005) *World Economic Outlook Database*, [www document] http://www.imf.org/external/pubs/ft/weo/2005/01/data/dbcsubm.cfm. (accessed 26 September 2006).

Johanson, J. and Vahlne, J.-E. (1977) 'The internationalization process of the firm: a model of knowledge development and increasing foreign market commitments', *Journal of International Business Studies* **8**(1): 23–32.

Kent, R.B. (2003) 'A Diaspora of Chinese Settlement in Latin America and the Caribbean', in L.J.C. Ma and C. Cartier (eds.) *The Chinese Diaspora: Space, Place, Mobility, and Identity*, Rowman & Littlefield: Lanham, pp. 117–138.

Kohlhagen, S.W. (1977) 'The Effects of Exchange-Rate Adjustments on International Investment: Comment', in P.B. Clark, D.E. Logue and R. Sweeney (eds.) *The Effects of Exchange Rate Adjustments*, US Government Printing Office: Washington, DC, pp. 194–197.

Lall, S. and Albaladejo, M. (2004) 'China's competitive performance: a threat to East Asian manufactured exports?' *World Development* 32(9): 1441–1466.

Lardy, N.R. (1998) *China's Unfinished Economic Revolution*, Brookings Institution: Washington, DC.

Lau, H.-F. (1992) 'Internationalization, internalization, or a new theory for small, low-technology multinational enterprise?' *European Journal of Marketing* 26(10): 17–31.

Lau, H.-F. (2003) 'Industry evolution and internationalization processes of firms from a newly industrialized economy', *Journal of Business Research* 56(10): 847–852.

Lawrence, S.V. (2002) 'Going global', *Far Eastern Economic Review* 165(12): 32.

Lecraw, D.J. (1977) 'Direct investment by firms from less developed countries', *Oxford Economic Papers* 29(3): 442–457.

Li, P.P. (2003) 'Toward a geocentric theory of multinational evolution: the implications from the Asian MNEs as late-comers', *Asia Pacific Journal of Management* 20(2): 217–242.

Lim, D. (1983) 'Fiscal incentives and direct investment in less developed countries', *Journal of Development Studies* 19(2): 207–212.

Liu, H. and Li, K. (2002) 'Strategic implications of emerging Chinese multinationals: the Haier case study', *European Management Journal* 20(6): 699–706.

Liu, L. (2005) *China's Industrial Policies and the Global Business Revolution: The Case of the Domestic Appliance Industry*, RoutledgeCurzon: London.

Logue, D.E. and Willet, T.D. (1977) 'The Effects of Exchange-Rate Adjustments on International Investment', in P.B. Clark, D.E. Logue and R. Sweeney (eds.) *The Effects of Exchange Rate Adjustments*, US Government Printing Office: Washington, DC, pp. 137–150.

Loungani, P., Mody, A. and Razin, A. (2002) 'The global disconnect: the role of transactional distance and scale economies in gravity equations', *Scottish Journal of Political Economy* 49(5): 526–543.

Luo, Y. (1997) 'Guanxi: principles, philosophies, and implications', *Human Systems Management* 16(1): 43–51.

Ma, L.J.C. (2003) 'Space, Place, and Transnationalism in the Chinese Diaspora', in L.J.C. Ma and C. Cartier (eds.) *The Chinese Diaspora: Space, Place, Mobility, and Identity*, Rowman & Littlefield: Lanham, pp. 1–4.

Ma, X. and Andrews-Speed, P. (2006) 'The overseas activities of China's national oil companies: rationale and outlook', *Minerals and Energy* 21(1): 17–30.

Meyer, K.E. and Nguyen, H.V. (2005) 'Foreign investment strategies and subnational institutions in emerging markets: evidence from Vietnam', *Journal of Management Studies* 42(1): 63–93.

MOFCOM (various years) *Almanac of China's Foreign Relations and Trade*, Ministry of Commerce (MOFCOM): Beijing.

MOFCOM (2004) *China Commerce Yearbook* [Zhongguo shang-wu nianjian] Ministry of Commerce (MOFCOM): Beijing.

National Bureau of Statistics (2005) *China Statistical Yearbook 2005*, China Statistics Press: Beijing.

Ng, L.F.Y. and Tuan, C. (2002) 'Building a favourable investment environment: evidence for the facilitation of FDI in China', *The World Economy* 25(8): 1095–1114.

North, D.C. (1990) *Institutions, Institutional Change and Economic Performance*, Cambridge University Press: Cambridge.

Ohio University (2006) *Distribution of the Ethnic Chinese Population Around the World*, University Libraries, Ohio University [www document] http://cicdatabank.library.ohiou.edu/opac/population.php. (accessed 17 May 2006).

Peng, M.W. (2002) 'Towards an institution-based view of business strategy', *Asia Pacific Journal of Management* 19(2/3): 251–267.

Political Risk Services (PRS) (2005) *International Country Risk Guide* (ICRG), [www document] www.prsgroup.com/ICRG.aspx. (accessed April 2005).

Poston Jr, D.L., Mao, M.X. and Yi, M.-Y. (1994) 'The global distribution of overseas Chinese around 1990', *Population and Development Review* 20(3): 631–645.

Pradhan, J.P. (2003) 'Outward foreign direct investment from India: recent trends and patterns', Jawaharlal Nehru University Working Paper Series, Jawaharlal Nehru University, New Delhi.

Roberts, I. and Tyers, R. (2003) 'China's exchange rate policy: the case for greater flexibility', *Asian Economic Journal* 17(2): 155–184.

Rowen, H.S. (2003) 'Will China take over world manufacturing?' *The International Economy* 17(1): 72.

Sauvant, K. (2005) 'New sources of FDI: The BRICs. Outward FDI from Brazil, Russia, India and China', *Journal of World Investment and Trade* 6(October): 639–709.

Scott, W.R. (2002) 'The Changing World of Chinese Enterprises: An Institutional Perspective', in A.S. Tsui and C.-M. Lau (eds.) *Management of Enterprises in the People's Republic of China*, Kluwer Academic Press: Boston, pp. 59–78.

Scott-Green, S. and Clegg, L.J. (1999) 'The determinants of new FDI capital flows into the EC: a statistical comparison of the USA and Japan', *Journal of Common Market Studies* 37(4): 597–616.

Sikorski, D. and Menkhoff, T. (2000) 'Internationalisation of Asian business', *Singapore Management Review* 22(1): 1–17.

Standifird, S.S. and Marshall, R.S. (2000) 'The transaction cost advantage of *guanxi*-based business practices', *Journal of World Business* 35(1): 21–42.

Stevens, G.V.G. (1993) 'Exchange rates and foreign direct investment: a note', International Finance Discussion Papers, April, No. 444, Board of Governors of the Federal Reserve System, Washington, DC.

Steinfeld, E.S. (1998) *Forging Reform in China: The Fate of State-Owned Industry*, Cambridge University Press: Cambridge.

Sung, Y.-W. (1996) 'Chinese outward investment in Hong Kong: trends, prospects and policy implications', OECD Development Centre Technical Papers, No. 113, Organisation for Economic Cooperation and Development, Paris.

Swystun, J., Burt, F. and Ly, A. (2005) *The Strategy for Chinese Brands: Part 1 – The Perception Challenge*, [www document] http://www.interbrand.com. (accessed 11 January 2006), Interbrand White Paper, Interbrand, New York.

Taylor, R. (2002) 'Globalization strategies of Chinese companies: current developments and future prospects', *Asian Business and Management* 1(2): 209–225.

Tong, S.Y. (2003) 'Ethnic Chinese networking in cross-border investment: the impact of economic and institutional development', Hong Kong Institute of Economics and Business Strategy (HIEBS) Working Paper, University of Hong Kong, Hong Kong.

Tsai, K.S. (2002) *Back-Alley Banking: Private Entrepreneurs in China*, Cornell University Press: Ithaca.

UNCTAD (1998) *World Investment Report 1998: Trends and Determinants*, United Nations: New York and Geneva.

UNCTAD (2003) *World Investment Report 2003: FDI Policies for Development: National and International Perspectives*, United Nations: New York and Geneva.

UNCTAD (2005a) *World Investment Report 2005: Transnational Corporations and the Internationalization of R&D*, United Nations: New York and Geneva.

UNCTAD (2005b) *Prospects for Foreign Direct Investment and the Strategies of Transnational Corporations, 2005–2008*, United Nations: New York and Geneva.

UNCTAD (2006) 'FDI/TNC database', [www document] http:// stats.unctad.org/fdi. (accessed 09 May 2006).

UN Statistics Division (2006) *UN Demographic Yearbook Special Census Topics*, [preliminary release 27 March 2006] [www document] http://unstats.un.org/unsd/demographic/products/ dyb/dybcens.htm. (accessed 17 May 2006).

Villela, A.V. (1983) 'Transnationals from Brazil', in S. Lall (ed.) *The New Transnationals: The Spread of Third World Transnationals*, John Wiley: Chichester, pp. 220–249.

Wang, M.Y. (2002) 'The motivations behind Chinese government-initiated industrial investments overseas', *Pacific Affairs* 75(2): 187–206.

Warner, M., Hong, N.S. and Xu, X. (2004) 'Late development experience and the evolution of transnational firms in the People's Republic of China', *Asia Pacific Business Review* 10(3/4): 324–345.

Wells, L.T. (1983) *Third World Multinationals: The Rise of Foreign Investments from Developing Countries*, MIT Press: Cambridge, MA.

WIPO (World Intellectual Property Organisation) (2006) *Patents and PCT statistics*, [www document] http://www.wipo.int/ ipstats/en/statistics/patents/. (accessed 26 September 2006).

Wong, J. and Chan, S. (2003) 'China's outward direct investment: expanding worldwide', *China: An International Journal* 1(2): 273–301.

World Bank (2005) *World Development Indicators* (WDI) April 2005, ESDS International, (MIMAS) University of Manchester.

World Bank (2006) *Indicators of Governance and Institutional Quality*, [www document] http://siteresources. worldbank. org/INTLAWJUSTINST/Resources/IndicatorsGovernanceand InstitutionalQuality.pdf. (accessed 16 January 2006).

Wu, F. and Sia, Y.H. (2002) 'China's rising investment in Southeast Asia: trends and outlook', *Journal of Asian Business* 18(2): 41–61.

Wu, H.-L. and Chen, C.-H. (2001) 'An assessment of outward foreign direct investment from China's transitional economy', *Europe-Asia Studies* 53(8): 1235–1254.

Wright, M., Filatotchev, I., Hoskisson, R.E. and Peng, M.W. (2005) 'Strategy research in emerging economies: challenging the conventional wisdom', *Journal of Management Studies* 42(1): 1–33.

Ye, G. (1992) 'Chinese transnational corporations', *Transnational Corporations* 1(2): 125–133.

Yeung, H.W.-C. (1998) 'The political economy of transnational corporations: a study of the regionalization of Singaporean firms', *Political Geography* **17**(4): 389–416.

Yeung, H.W.-C. (1999) 'The internationalisation of ethnics Chinese business firms from southeast asia: strategies, processes and competitive advantages', *International Journal of Urban and Regional Research* **23**(1): 88–102.

Yu, A., Chao, H. and Dorf, M. (2005) 'Outbound investments by Chinese companies: the Chinese government approval regime', Topics in Chinese Law, O'Melveny&Myers Research Report, November 2005.

Zhan, J.X. (1995) 'Transnationalization and outward investment: the case of Chinese firms', *Transnational Corporations* **4**(3): 67–100.

Zhang, Y. (2003) *China's Emerging Global Businesses: Political Economy and Institutional Investigations*, Palgrave Macmillan: Basingstoke.

Zin, R.H.M. (1999) 'Malaysian reverse investments: trends and strategies', *Asia Pacific Journal of Management* **16**(3): 469–496.

Appendix

Countries host to Chinese ODI in the data set

OECD countries

Australia, Austria, Canada, Czech Republic, Denmark, Finland, France, Germany, Greece, Hungary, Italy, Japan, Mexico, Netherlands, New Zealand, Poland, Portugal, South Korea, Spain, Sweden, United Kingdom, United States

Non-OECD countries

Algeria, Argentina, Armenia, Brazil, Bulgaria, Chile, Colombia, Croatia, Cyprus, Ecuador, Egypt, Ghana, Hong Kong SAR, India, Indonesia, Israel, Malaysia, Morocco, Nigeria, Philippines, Russia, Singapore, South Africa, Sudan, Thailand, Ukraine, Venezuela

7
Historic and Emergent Trends in Chinese Outward Direct Investment

Peter J. Buckley, Adam Cross, Hui Tan, Xin Liu and Hinrich Voss

Introduction

A substantial body of literature has grown on the prominence of China as a recipient of foreign direct investment (FDI) and its consequences for national economic development and management practice (Branstetter and Lardy, 2006). By contrast, much less attention has been paid to China's position as an FDI source. Given that China attracted an annual average FDI inflow of around US$29bn (or more than 7% of the world's total) in the 1990s, but contributed less than US$2.5bn (around 0.6%) to global outflows, this is perhaps not surprising (UNCTAD, 2006). However, the sharp growth in Chinese outward direct investment (ODI) evident since 2002 (illustrated in Figure 7.1) combined with a number of recent high profile attempts by Chinese enterprises to acquire North American and European firms have brought into relief China's rising status and potential as an *investor* nation. This potential is recognised in a recent UNCTAD survey of investment promotion agencies which predicts that China will become a 'top three' source country for FDI before the end of 2008 (UNCTAD, 2005). It is also highlighted by the Director-General of UNIDO, Kandeh Yumkella, who suggests that annual flows of Chinese outbound investment are likely to reach US$60bn by 2010 (MOFCOM, 2006). If growth rates in Chinese ODI continue and these predictions are realised, China's contribution to global FDI flows is likely to approximate current outflows of the leading industrialised countries.

In this exploratory study, we identify historic and emergent trends detectable in official aggregate data and individual FDI project level data on Chinese ODI for the period 1991 to 2005 with regard to investment destination, activity type, entry mode choice and investment motivation. Our aim is to assess whether or not Chinese ODI conforms to the general model of ODI and to the special case model of emerging country ODI in general, and Asian countries in particular, with respect to the character and evolution of its recent ODI. To do this, we review in the next section selected contributions to the literature on developing country ODI in order to establish a 'received wisdom' or base model against which we can contrast our empirical data from China. We also include some evidence from other Asian countries to control for cultural and regional interactions.[1] We go on to consider how the evolving institutional framework within which Chinese ODI is conducted and, especially, how adjustments to the administrative system and the engagement and disengagement of government at various times, notably following the launch of China's *zou chu qu* or 'go global' policy in 1999, have influenced the internationalisation decisions and motivations of Chinese firms. After providing further evidence for rise of China as an FDI source country, we examine trends in respect of (i) aggregate Chinese ODI stocks and flows; (ii) the spatial distribution of Chinese ODI; (iii) the sectoral distribution, and (iv) the dominant entry mode employed. This is done by reviewing data on accumulated Chinese ODI by host economy as published by the Chinese Ministry of Commerce (MOFCOM) and by analysing previously unpublished data from China's State Administration of Foreign Exchange (SAFE), a government agency that administers, via the banking system, foreign exchange-related matters.[2] In the second part of the paper, we relate detected trends to emergent motivations advanced in the literature as driving the outward FDI activities of Chinese firms. We propose that Chinese ODI is indeed distinctive with respect to a standard model of developing country ODI, which itself is distinctive with respect to industrialised country ODI.

Statistics on outward direct investment (ODI) are compiled by MOFCOM based on a summation of individual firm's direct investment amounts.[3] This aggregation masks the motives of the firms and reflects their choices of entry mode to foreign countries – direct investment is included, while licensing, technology transfer deals and other non-equity modes are excluded by definition. In this paper, we supplement these statistics with unique project level data from SAFE. Official statistics usually disaggregate the total by industry/sector and by destination country, but disaggregation by type of motive usually has to be conducted by analytical techniques such as regression analysis, which is an imperfect method working by inference. In addition, the time factor complicates the analysis. Firms often proceed by gradualism in foreign market entry, following a sequence of exporting, then non-equity modes such as licensing, then direct investment. A second type of sequential entry is from culturally and physically close countries to progressively more remote ones. These time series effects are only partially visible in cross section data. These limitations need to be borne in mind in our analysis.

Theoretical explanations of developing country FDI

Firm and industry level theory

Mainstream international business literature generally explains the strategy of the multinational enterprise (MNE) using the concepts of internalisation (Buckley and Casson, 1976), transaction costs (Hennart, 1988) and monopoly advantage (Hymer, 1960). Together with location advantages, these concepts are synthesised by Dunning (2001) in his eclectic or OLI paradigm. This posits that the decision to internationalise production is predicated upon the interaction of ownership (O) advantages, location (L) advantages and the gains associated with hierarchical (I) over arm's length transacting. Since this theory was developed to explain MNEs from the industrialised countries, its ability to account for developing country FDI has been debated. One view is that an alternative framework to explain late-comer MNEs is needed (e.g., Mathews, 2002; Moon and Roehl, 2001). However, the majority view is that mainstream theory does work, but that special theories nested within the general theory are needed as well (Buckley, Clegg, Cross, Voss, Liu and Zheng, 2007; Lall, 1983; Wells, 1983; Khan, 1986; Lecraw, 1993; Zin, 1999; UNCTAD, 2006).

Special explanations for Asian developing country firms

Lecraw (1993) identifies two key issues that could contribute to a special theory on the internationalisation of developing country firms; namely, *how* do they compete internationally (that is, what is their source of competitive advantage) and *where* do they invest (that is, what drives their location decisions)? In this paper, we also recognise as pertinent issues concerning entry mode choice, the role of home country government and cultural distance between home and host countries.

First, developing country MNEs are said to hold particular ownership advantages over established MNEs, in addition to competitively priced labour (an advantage which normally diminishes as the home economy develops) and that these derive from their experiences and knowledge of operating at home. In other words, the capabilities that firms gain to cope with home country conditions (i.e. 'home country embeddedness') can be leveraged as competitive advantage in similar markets abroad. Erdener and Shapiro (2005), for example, assert that overseas Chinese firms are able to penetrate Asian markets unattractive to industrialised country firms because they are adept at operating successfully in environments characterised by uncertain economic development, opaque regulatory conditions and weak market-enhancing institutions. Similarly, Scott (2002) observes that the ability to exploit culturally-dependent relational assets in Asian countries through personal relationships is a significant source of competitive advantage for overseas Chinese firms. Wells (1977) and Kumar and Kim (1984) demonstrate that developing country firms in general possess older technology which is best exploited in less developed country markets. Developing country firms may also be better able than industrialised country firms at customising particular technologies, products and processes appropriately for other developing country markets. This may be accomplished by downscaling production, by simplifying or substituting local inputs or by increasing the labour intensity of production (Shenkar and Luo, 2004). Developing country firms may also be more flexible and adaptable than industrialised country firms because scale economies are forsaken (Wells, 1983; Erdener and Shapiro, 2005). Lau (2003) argues that this is evidenced by the investments of Hong Kong-based textiles firms in other developing countries. It follows that developing country firms are often found to be involved in manufacturing activity abroad, beginning with labour-intensive production and then graduating over time into more technology and marketing-intensive production, often based on imported technology (Lall, 1983; Wells, 1983; Lecraw, 1993; Zin, 1999).[4] In short, home country embeddedness may enable developing country firms to compete successfully with established MNEs in third markets, as well as with local firms, especially in other developing countries (Aggarwal and Agmon, 1990).

Second, it follows from this discussion that developing country MNEs generally concentrate their investment strategy on other developing countries. In the case of Asian firms this is often in markets geographically close to home (Lau, 2003). In a study of small internationally active South Korean firms, Tallman and Shenkar (1994) found that investments were preferentially sought in Asian countries less economically advanced than Korea, where investing firms often acted as intermediaries in technology flows from developed to less developed host countries. Pang and Komaran (1985) report that Singaporean firms in the 1970s were slow to venture further abroad than Southeast Asia and when they did it was mainly to other, more distant, developing countries such as India. Chen (2003) reports that Taiwanese electronics firms preferentially invested first in Malaysia and Thailand because this enabled them to maintain important links with business networks in Taiwan. Only latterly did they relocate production to mainland China, once requisite industrial networks of buyers and suppliers were in place, to benefit from agglomeration effects and psychic and geographical proximity to home. The trend for Asian firms to preferentially invest in Asia is also evident in aggregate FDI data. For example, UNCTAD (2006), in an analysis of intra- and inter-regional FDI flows between developing countries for the period 2002 to 2004, reports that as much as 96% of Asian FDI (with an annual average value of US$49.8bn) was directed to other Asian developing economies.

Third, the 'stages' (or Uppsala) theory of incremental internationalisation may help to understand the distribution of developing country ODI over time. It proposes a gradual deepening in the engagement of the firm with individual host countries and a gradual widening of the host countries entered on a 'closest first' basis (Johanson and Vahlne, 1977). Thus psychic distance between home and host markets bears upon managerial decision-making. Firms generally invest first in countries that are psychically proximate (that is, culturally similar) to their own because local market knowledge is more readily obtainable. As the firm's international experience, knowledge and opportunities for learning grow, so too does its commitment to more culturally distant countries, since better local market knowledge raises the value of resources to be committed to the market (Brewer, 2007; Dow and Karunaratua, 2006). At the same time, FDI increasingly substitutes for 'arm's length' agency and license contracts. A number of studies provide partial support for this proposition in relation to developing country firms in Asia by showing that they often invest preferentially in countries with strong historical ties or cultural similarity to the home region. For example, Pang and Komaran (1985) found that a large number of Singaporean firms initiated overseas investment activities in Southeast Asia, and later extended this to China, India and other developing countries before making debut entries in Australia and North America. Yang (1997) and Chen (2003) report that one of the main reasons why Taiwanese firms have invested heavily in mainland China is because of the short psychic distance between home and host country. Similarly, Erdener and Shapiro (2005) find that overseas Chinese owners and managers are preferentially attracted to investment opportunities in their ancestral home towns on mainland China because personal connections (that is, relational capital) can be exploited for competitive advantage. To test this theory fully, however, time series data at firm level are required.

Fourth, entry mode choice is an important aspect of the internationalisation of developing country firms. Though little researched, it is generally considered that a large proportion of MNEs from developing countries have preferred the international joint venture (IJV) entry mode (often with minority equity share) because this helps to reduce entry costs and increases the opportunities for learning from the foreign partner (Wells, 1977, 1983; Kumar and Kim, 1984). By contrast, more recent evidence suggests that, when possible, developing country MNEs in Asia (in particular, those from Taiwan and Singapore) choose wholly-owned subsidiaries and majority IJVs over minority ones (e.g., Yeung, 1994). The use of higher equity modes appears positively correlated with later stages in the economic development of the home country, as a consequence of, for example, accumulated experience, greater managerial capacity and improved competitiveness of national firms. It may also reflect improvements in the ability to protect and enforce intellectual property and other proprietary assets abroad. However, industry effects may also be at work. For example, Tallman and Shenkar (1994) report that small Korean companies operating in technology intensive industries generally favour non-equity modes of cooperation to sell explicit technology, while equity IJVs are used in low technology-intensive fields. Perceptions of risk may also impact on the choice of entry mode by Asian firms. For example, a study of Malaysian multinational firms found that 'low risk perceptions were associated with high control modes of entry and high risk perceptions were associated with low control modes of entry' (Ahmed, Mohamad, Tan and Johnson, 2002).

Fifth, at a more aggregate level, research indicates that national governments in developing countries often play a critical role in determining the level and direction of ODI (Aggarwal and Agmon, 1990). On the one hand, control and, effectively, the restriction of ODI has been a major strand of economic policy for many developing countries (UNCTAD, 1996, 2006). Key objectives include prioritising domestic investment levels, preventing capital flight, strengthening foreign exchange reserves and maintaining control of state-owned assets abroad (Sauvant, 2005).

Such controls are generally relaxed over time once an adequate current account surplus has been achieved (UNCTAD, 2006). On the other, developing country MNEs also commonly enjoy high levels of home government support, which may help them to ameliorate certain ownership and location disadvantages (Buckley, Clegg, Cross, Liu, Voss and Zheng, 2007; Aggarwal and Agmon, 1990; Lecraw, 1993). Typically, this takes the form of privileged access to raw materials, cheap capital, government subsidies and other benefits. It has been argued that one of the main reasons why South Korean *chaebols* have been able to invest abroad across a diversified range of industries is the soft budget constraint they enjoy from their close relationship with government and domestic financial institutions (Chow, Holbert, Kelley and Yu, 2004). Similarly, Lau (2003) asserts that strong government support has enabled Korean firms to invest heavily abroad at an early stage in the internationalisation process in a manner not predicted by the 'stages' model. The instrumental role played by developing country governments in setting the institutional framework for ODI activity is confirmed by a number of other studies, notably on Taiwan, Singapore and India (e.g., Pang and Lomaran, 1985; Yeung, 1994).

Aggregation and explanation

This review enables us to establish a standard theoretical explanation of ODI from developing countries, in particular that from Asian economies, against which we can compare trends observed in Chinese ODI (see Table 7.1). This theoretical characterisation suggests six main dimensions. First, developing country firms have special ownership advantages that derive from their home country-embeddedness; second, developing country ODI is generally directed towards other developing countries; third, developing country firms invest preferentially in psychically and geographically close locations where relational assets can be exploited most effectively; fourth, developing country firms over time increasingly target investment opportunities in more advanced economies; fifth, international joint ventures are the preferred entry mode, especially early in the internationalisation process; and sixth, home country government has a strong influence on the level and direction of ODI.

The institutional setting for Chinese ODI

Institutional factors are likely to be an important influence on any country's aggregate ODI flow as at least part of the direction and

Table 7.1 Chinese ODI compared to a standard model of developing country ODI.

Standard model of developing country ODI	Chinese ODI	Our evidence
1. Special ownership advantages of firms ('home country embeddedness')	Yes: Chinese firms enjoy financial advantages especially	SAFE data
2. Early FDI occurs in other developing countries	No: early Chinese ODI was directed mostly to developed countries	SAFE and MOFCOM data
3. FDI occurs in culturally and geographically close countries	No: early Chinese ODI was directed to psychically and geographically distant countries	SAFE and MOFCOM data
4. Later FDI occurs in more advanced economies (cf the 'stages' theory)	No: both early and continued Chinese FDI occurs in more advanced economies	SAFE and MOFCOM data
5. IJVs are the main entry mode (especially in early FDI)	No: both IJVs and wholly-owned affiliates are used	SAFE
6. Home government importance	Yes: but nuanced	SAFE and MOFCOM data

nature of that ODI will be determined by source nation factors (Buckley and Casson, 1976). However, institutional factors are dynamic and government policy changes over time. This section shows the influence of the Chinese institutional framework on Chinese ODI.

Since the late 1970s the Chinese government has determined to a considerable degree the legal, regulatory and financial framework of ODI, either directly, by administrative fiat (via the approval process and foreign exchange controls), or indirectly, using economic policy implementation and other measures (Buckley, Clegg, Cross, Voss, Rhodes and Zheng, 2008). Moreover, as the ultimate owner of state-owned enterprises (SOEs) (which dominated Chinese ODI prior to 2003), the government (at various levels) has effectively been the key operational decision-taker in the majority of formally approved investment projects. However, policy has often been ambivalent and inconsistent, with national and sub-national government at various times supporting, pushing and constraining Chinese ODI (Buckley, Clegg, Cross, Voss, Rhodes and Zheng, 2008). Key stages in the evolution of

Table 7.2 Key stages in the development of Chinese ODI policy.

1979–1985	**Stage One: Cautious internationalisation** With the 'open-door' policy, Chinese state-owned firms start to set up their first international operations. Only state-owned trading corporations under MOFCOM and provincial and municipal 'economic and technological cooperation enterprises' under the State Economic and Trade Commission (SETC) are allowed to invest abroad. The State Council was the only authority to examine and approve overseas investments, irrespective of investment size. The government adopted a cautious approach, favouring investment in kind (know-how and physical assets) to avoid excessive capital outflows. Prior to 1984, there were no regulations regarding ODI. Between 1984 and 1985 MOFTEC enacted two directives on the examination and approval of proposals to establish non-trading companies abroad. Only 189 projects were approved, amounting to about US$197mn.
1986–1991	**Stage Two: Government encouragement** The government liberalised restrictive policies and allowed more enterprises apply to establish foreign affiliates, provided they had sufficient capital, technical and operational know-how and a suitable joint venture partner. Standardised regulations were drafted to cover the approval process. Approval was granted to 891 projects, totalling some US$1.2bn.
1992–1998	**Stage Three: Expansion and regulation** Encouraged by domestic liberalisation, initiated by "Paramount Leader" Deng Xiaoping's journey to the South, sub-national level authorities rushed into international business activities with companies under their supervision, especially in Hong Kong to engage in real estate and stock market speculation. The Asian crisis in 1997 and the subsequent collapse of companies such as GITIC slowed down this development. Latterly, concerns about loss of control over state assets, capital flight and 'leakage' of foreign exchange saw a tightening of approval procedures and in particular a stricter and more rigorous screening and monitoring process. These measures sought to ensure that Chinese capital was invested abroad for genuinely productive purposes. The State Planning Commission and SAFE were required to examine projects valued at US$1mn or more, prior to referral to MOFTEC for final approval. Individual ODI project activity declines, despite an increase of total ODI of US$1.2bn.

Table 7.2 Key stages in the development of Chinese ODI policy – *continued*

1999–2001	**Stage Four: The 'go global' policy period** Contradictory policies characterised this period. Further measures to control illicit capital transfers and to regularise ODI towards genuinely productive purposes are introduced. In parallel, ODI in specific industries is actively encouraged with export tax rebates, foreign exchange assistance and direct financial support, notably in trade-related activities that promoted Chinese exports of raw materials, parts and machinery and in light industry sectors like textiles, machinery and electrical equipment. In 2001 this encouragement is formalised within the 10th five year plan which outlined the *'going global'* or *'zou chu qu'* directive. Total approved ODI rises by US$1.8bn, with an average project value of US$2.6mn.
Since 2001	**Stage Five: Post WTO period** In the outline of the latest five year plan, the 11th, the Chinese government stressed again the importance of *'zou chu qu'* for Chinese firms and the Chinese economy. Nevertheless, direct and proactive support of ODI continues to be limited, mainly to preventing illegal capital outflows and loss of control of state assets. Since 2003, privately-owned enterprises are officially allowed to apply for the approval of outbound investment projects. Heightened domestic competitive pressures, due to the opening of once protected industries and markets to foreign and domestic competitors, forces some Chinese firms to seek new markets abroad. Latest policy announcements indicate that the Chinese authorities are moving from a pre-investment approval procedure to a post-investment registration system. Provincial differences in implementation prevail.

Sources: Ding (2001), Guo (1984), UNCTAD (1996), Wong/Chan (2003), Wu/Chen (2001), Ye (1992), Zhang (2005). An earlier version is reproduced in Buckley and Clegg and Cross and Liu and Voss and Zheng (2007).

China's official FDI approval process and some concomitant changes to the character of Chinese ODI are presented in Table 7.2.

Even before the introduction of China's 'Open Door' policy reforms in 1978, numerous small-scale investments by Chinese SOEs could be found in major trading hubs around the world, mostly in service sectors such as international trade, transportation and financial services. After 1979, and in hand with the 'Open Door' policies, the Chinese government cautiously sought to encourage ODI as a means to better integrate the country into the global economy and to improve access to domestically scarce raw materials (Zhang, 2003). The government promoted international trade by permitting, and later encouraging, export-oriented FDI by state-owned import and export corporations. However, in the 1980s and 1990s tight centralised control of outward FDI was reimposed amid concerns that it was detrimental to national development. Outward direct investment was seen as a substitute for domestic investment (Sauvant, 2005). It was also feared that control of state property held overseas might be lost because of both the cost of supervising international projects at a distance and the inexperience of Chinese firms at competing internationally (Zhan, 1995; Ding, 2000). However, a few selected SOEs, like China International Trust and Investment Corporation (CITIC) and Shougang, were granted the freedom to expand abroad as 'experimental' MNEs (Zhang, 2003).

In the late 1980s and 1990s, it is generally acknowledged that Chinese firms internationalised mainly in pursuit of certain national and provincial economic goals and policy objectives, in particular: (i) to support the export function of state-owned manufacturers; (ii) to help stabilise the supply of domestically-scarce natural resources; and (iii) to acquire information and learning about operating abroad for the benefit of other domestic enterprises (Lu, 2002; Ye, 1992; Zhan, 1995; UNCTAD, 2006; Sauvant, 2005). State-owned enterprises also undertook FDI to meet aspects of the government's political agenda, not least in establishing and strengthening diplomatic relations with other developing countries through the building of economic links. For these reasons, research has generally stressed the importance of state engagement in the business affairs of Chinese firms, either through direct ownership of productive assets or indirectly, through various kinds of regulatory control and intervention (Sauvant, 2005). From the late 1990s onwards, however, Chinese firms are increasingly portrayed in the literature as internationalising in order to achieve other objectives, in particular (i) to improve access to foreign proprietary technology, immobile strategic assets and capabilities; (ii) to exploit new markets for products and services; and (iii) to enhance overall firm competitiveness through the diversification of business activities (e.g., Taylor, 2002; Child and Rodrigues, 2005; Pei and Wang, 2001; Deng, 2003; Deng, 2004; Zhang, 2003; Zhang, 2005; Warner, Hong and Xu, 2004; Sauvant, 2005; Beebe, 2006). Ostensibly, these motivations are attributable as much to market forces, industry dynamics and discretionary, autonomous, managerial decision-taking as to government intervention and fiat. As UNCTAD (2006) comments, state-ownership does not necessarily invoke state-directed international strategy. At the same time, however, there remains a presumption held by some that the Chinese authorities continue to exert considerable influence over the investment activities of Chinese MNEs (e.g., Deng, 2004; Deutsche Bank Research, 2006). In this somewhat paradoxical milieu, it is interesting to investigate the extent to which engagement and disengagement of various levels of government has influenced the internationalisation decisions of Chinese firms (Voss, 2007).

There is little doubt that state control over the international activities of Chinese firms has been relaxed considerably since the late 1990s. Perhaps the most prominent and clearly articulated policy has been the introduction of the 'go global', or *zou chu qu*, policy in 1999. This was subsequently formalised in China's 10th five year plan, 2001–2006, and re-emphasised in the latest 11th five year plan, 2007–2010. Its objective is to encourage ODI through various means with a view to improving the international competitiveness of domestic companies and thus strengthen the national economy (Sauvant, 2005; UNCTAD, 2006).[5] It is partly in response to marketisation of the Chinese economy and the country's World Trade Organisation (WTO) accession commitments (Sauvant, 2005), both of which have combined to heighten domestic competition, amongst other things. Accordingly, since 2001, policies towards ODI have been liberalised (mainly through the easing of investment restrictions,[6] simplification of approval procedures and relaxation of foreign exchange controls) and with indirect, 'hands-off' economic policies increasingly substituting for direct, 'hands-on' management (see also Table 7.2). To illustrate, government agencies like MOFCOM and the National Development and Reform Commission (NDRC), which were previously instrumental to the formal approval process, now purport to provide mainly advisory, information and support functions to international investors. A further important aspect is the treatment of private Chinese enterprises, which were prevented from investing abroad officially (with a few notable exceptions, like the white goods manufacturer Haier) before this restriction was lifted in 2003.

In future, it seems likely therefore that the individual investment decisions of Chinese firms will be shaped more by commercial considerations and less by political ones. The partial nature of the privatisation of SOEs may also influence ODI. In the early years of privatisation SOEs were given the opportunity to invest overseas and encouraged to do so but they were not strictly governed as for-profit enterprises. This led to a serious agency problem. Top managers in SOEs could increase their income by positioning themselves overseas as managers of the companies' foreign operations. This perverse incentive (together with round-tripping to exploit tax incentives) induced excessive ODI and may account for some of the unique patterns of China's ODI. As institutional reform proceeds, we would expect these perverse incentives to subside.[7] However, the picture is complex and the challenge for researchers is to disentangle the role of national and sub-national government from other determinants (such as demand conditions and competition) of the level and direction of Chinese ODI flow.

China's outward direct investment position[8]

When firm level and individual FDI data are aggregated in source country statistics, some issues become blurred. However, from the above account we expect that Chinese ODI will be aimed at developing countries, especially in Asia. In line with theory, we expect proximity effects to decline over time as more global strategies are developed and as investing firms become more experienced. We note that the stage of development of firms in this trajectory will slowly feed into the aggregate data. To address this, we analyse project-level data collated by SAFE to draw inferences about the behaviour of single foreign direct investments. Ecological fallacy issues are avoided by analysing MOFCOM data at an aggregate level and SAFE data at the level of the individual foreign investment project.

Trends in China's aggregate annual ODI flow

Between 1982 and 1991, ODI from China increased year on year, but only slowly and never exceeding US$1bn annually (see Figure 7.1). In addition to restrictive investment approval procedures and tight foreign exchange control, the poor competitiveness of many Chinese firms was a contributory factor. Outward investors were generally large SOEs investing in projects of national importance, typically resource-oriented ones. Between 1991 and 1993 outward investment policies were relaxed and ODI surged, only to slow again in 1994 as the government sought to cool the rate of domestic economic expansion. New project proposals were subjected to more exacting approval procedures.

After 1994, ODI flows recovered, accelerating modestly between 1995 and 1998 in parallel with further foreign exchange and trade liberalisation, growth in Chinese exports (which promoted trade-complementing FDI) and the handover of Hong Kong. In 1999, official

Figure 7.1 China's approved outward FDI flows (current prices), 1991–2005 (US$mn).

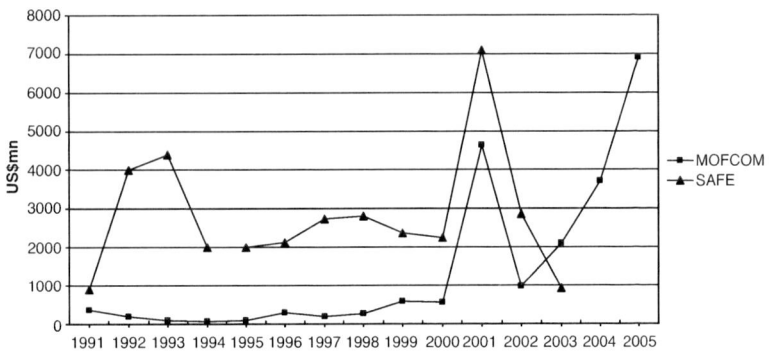

Source: MOFCOM (various years) and authors' calculations using SAFE data (no longer collected after 2003).

Chinese investment outflow again declined, partly in response to the re-imposition of foreign exchange controls and the economic slowdown of several neighbouring countries, both outcomes of the Asian Financial Crisis. This continued to 2000, after which Chinese ODI accelerated sharply. This was concomitant with the introduction of the government's formal 'go-global' (*zou chu qu*) policy initiative. At the time, this growth caused some commentators to assert that Chinese companies were on the threshold of becoming major foreign direct investors in Asia and beyond (e.g., UNCTAD, 2003). By contrast, between 2002 and 2003 levels of Chinese approved outward FDI was in decline. This mirrored trends in global FDI flows more generally, with the economic downturn in the US and in the broad global economy being contributory factors. More recently, Chinese ODI has accelerated once more: in 2006, it amounted to some US$16bn, a seven fold increase on 2004 levels (MOFCOM, 2007; NBS, 2006).

The rapid recent growth in Chinese ODI is reflected in a number of key indicators. First, the contracted value of Chinese-owned outward FDI stock (at current prices) increased from US$1.4bn in 1991 to US$73bn in 2006. By 2006, Chinese ODI was distributed across some 160 countries (MOFCOM, 2007). Second, although China's ODI stock position is still quite modest relative to industrialised country norms, it already compares favourably to a number of smaller developed economies. To illustrate, by 2004 it was greater in value terms than that of Israel and Ireland and was only slightly smaller than that of Norway and Portugal, for example (UNCTAD, 2004b). Third, between

1996 and 2003 the number of Chinese MNEs grew from 103 to 510, while the number of Chinese-owned affiliates abroad rose from 1008 in 1991 to 8259 in 2004 (MOFCOM, 2005). Fourth, the number of mainland Chinese firms among the world's top one hundred non-financial MNEs from the developing countries rose from three in 2000 to ten in 2004 (UNCTAD, 2002, 2006).

Although Chinese ODI is dominated by state-owned enterprises, since private Chinese firms were not permitted to invest abroad officially prior to 2003, at least a proportion of the recent improvement in China's ODI performance will have been due to the international expansion of firms outside of direct state-control. However, data on this development are sketchy. Estimates suggest that 12% of Chinese ODI in 2004 was undertaken by private sector firms, but the overall contribution of the private sector to the accumulated stock of Chinese ODI remains minimal, standing at around 2% in 2004 (MOFCOM, 2005). Although these data hint to the fact that private Chinese enterprise is likely to contribute increasingly to annual FDI outflows, research is needed to establish just how much of the recent expansion of Chinese ODI is attributable to this or to the relaxation of ODI controls enjoyed by state firms.

Geographic distribution

MOFCOM statistics allow us to characterise changes to the geographic distribution of Chinese outward FDI since 1990. The MOFCOM *Almanac of China's Foreign Economic Relations and Trade* (now the *China Commerce Yearbook*) reports an individual annual stock position for each host country in respect of approved Chinese FDI. These data are cumulative flow statistics based on new project approvals (but does not distinguish by ownership form or industry). We present these data in Table 7.3, using a rolling three year annual average to smoothen the irregularities commonplace in annualised FDI flow statistics. It also shows the number of investment projects made by Chinese firms per country per period so inferences can be drawn about average project value. Informal transactions that circumvent official FDI approval procedures (e.g. those associated with the round-tripping phenomenon) inevitably are excluded from the data.[9]

In the period 1990 to 1992, the majority of China's outward stock of approved FDI (almost 70% of the total value) was located in the developed countries. Indeed, the bulk of Chinese ODI was concentrated in just three countries: Australia (host to an annual average of 23.3% of the total), the USA (22.2%) and Canada (19.4%). Western European

Table 7.3 Approved Chinese ODI by host region and economy, 1990–2004 (US$ 10,000 and per cent).

	Percentage Annual Average Cumulative FDI Stock (Project Number)				
	1990–1992	1993–1995	1996–1998	1999–2001	2002–2004
TOTAL CHINESE OUTWARD FDI STOCK: US$ 10,000 (project number)	133,847.53 (1057)	176,010.77 (1765)	235,466.77 (2173)	377,761.70 (2855)	1,196,772.09 (7572)
Percentage distribution by area:					
DEVELOPED COUNTRIES	69.44 (384)	64.12 (574)	49.95 (652)	36.11 (759)	21.97 (1920)
Western Europe	2.62 (81)	2.63 (108)	2.21 (122)	1.72 (141)	4.55 (453)
European Union (15 countries)	*2.29 (71)*	*2.38 (97)*	*2.01 (110)*	*1.58 (129)*	*4.48 (437)*
Denmark	0.02 (2)	0.02 (2)	0.01 (2)	0.01 (2)	2.56 (3)
Germany	0.52 (21)	0.48 (27)	0.42 (30)	0.36 (35)	0.66 (168)
France	0.58 (8)	0.52 (12)	0.41 (14)	0.26 (16)	0.35 (56)
Italy	0.22 (6)	0.17 (6)	0.13 (6)	0.22 (9)	0.24 (34)
UK	0.33 (6)	0.33 (8)	0.29 (10)	0.22 (13)	0.24 (60)
Other Western Europe (3 countries)	*0.33 (11)*	*0.25 (11)*	*0.20 (12)*	*0.14 (12)*	*0.07 (16)*
North America	41.59 (186)	39.86 (291)	31.25 (335)	23.67 (401)	11.75 (948)
USA	22.19 (137)	18.87 (217)	15.98 (256)	13.65 (311)	8.00 (791)
Canada	19.40 (49)	20.98 (74)	15.27 (79)	10.03 (90)	3.75 (157)
Other developed countries (4 countries)	25.22 (117)	21.63 (174)	16.49 (194)	10.71 (217)	5.68 (519)
Australia	23.34 (56)	18.39 (85)	13.93 (95)	9.03 (110)	4.44 (232)
Japan	0.71 (56)	0.78 (77)	0.68 (85)	0.46 (90)	0.81 (254)
New Zealand	1.18 (5)	2.46 (11)	1.88 (14)	1.22 (16)	0.42 (29)

Table 7.3 Approved Chinese ODI by host region and economy, 1990–2004 (US$ 10,000 and per cent) – continued

	Percentage Annual Average Cumulative FDI Stock (Project Number)				
	1990–1992	1993–1995	1996–1998	1999–2001	2002–2004
DEVELOPING COUNTRIES	30.56 (673)	35.88 (1191)	50.05 (1521)	63.89 (2096)	78.03 (5652)
Africa	**4.03 (111)**	**5.18 (173)**	**11.02 (259)**	**16.07 (401)**	**8.64 (642)**
North Africa (6 countries)	*0.20 (10)*	*0.19 (16)*	*0.76 (24)*	*1.13 (43)*	*1.23 (93)*
Egypt	0.14 (3)	0.10 (3)	0.37 (5)	0.70 (15)	0.46 (31)
Morocco	0.03 (5)	0.05 (10)	0.04 (10)	0.07 (14)	0.06 (24)
Sudan	0.00 (0)	0.01 (1)	0.32 (6)	0.30 (8)	0.20 (16)
Other Africa (46 countries)	*3.83 (101)*	*4.99 (156)*	*10.27 (235)*	*14.93 (358)*	*7.41 (549)*
Zambia	0.24 (3)	0.20 (4)	0.91 (8)	2.77 (15)	1.17 (19)
South Africa	0.02 (1)	0.45 (14)	1.95 (39)	2.44 (76)	1.33 (109)
Mali	0.00 (1)	0.42 (2)	1.20 (3)	1.29 (5)	0.49 (5)
Nigeria	0.51 (11)	0.68 (18)	0.65 (21)	0.69 (27)	0.51 (62)
United Republic of Tanzania	0.15 (2)	0.19 (6)	0.69 (9)	1.02 (13)	0.36 (22)
Zimbabwe	0.19 (1)	0.14 (1)	0.88 (4)	0.85 (9)	0.30 (15)
Congo, Democratic Republic	0.00 (1)	0.00 (1)	0.12 (3)	0.64 (7)	0.27 (11)
Mauritius	0.47 (14)	0.39 (16)	0.30 (18)	0.33 (20)	0.32 (26)
Latin America & the Caribbean	**4.87 (72)**	**4.96 (121)**	**10.04 (147)**	**13.83 (207)**	**8.08 (402)**
South America (12 countries)	*3.64 (45)*	*3.19 (70)*	*8.40 (85)*	*8.89 (109)*	*3.71 (209)*
Peru	0.06 (2)	0.14 (6)	5.12 (8)	5.23 (11)	1.69 (22)
Brazil	0.83 (10)	0.72 (15)	1.38 (21)	1.78 (27)	1.07 (72)
Chile	1.60 (4)	1.24 (5)	0.93 (6)	0.55 (6)	0.21 (19)
Argentina	0.03 (6)	0.11 (10)	0.16 (13)	0.20 (18)	0.12 (28)

Table 7.3 Approved Chinese ODI by host region and economy, 1990–2004 (US$ 10,000 and per cent) – *continued*

	Percentage Annual Average Cumulative FDI Stock (Project Number)				
	1990–1992	1993–1995	1996–1998	1999–2001	2002–2004
Other Latin America & Caribbean (18 countries)	*1.23 (27)*	*1.78 (52)*	*1.64 (62)*	*4.94 (98)*	*4.37 (192)*
Mexico	0.38 (9)	0.92 (27)	0.83 (30)	3.60 (35)	1.40 (47)
British Virgin Islands	0.00 (0)	0.00 (0)	0.01 (0)	0.05 (17)	0.51 (56)
Bermuda	0.37 (2)	0.28 (2)	0.33 (3)	0.36 (8)	1.72 (12)
Cuba	0.00 (0)	0.00 (0)	0.00 (0)	0.35 (3)	0.22 (10)
Central & Eastern Europe (18 countries)	**4.17 (114)**	**5.76 (251)**	**4.85 (280)**	**4.44 (344)**	**4.92 (722)**
Russian Federation	4.09 (106)	5.43 (224)	4.14 (240)	3.09 (284)	3.93 (527)
Romania	0.00 (0)	0.00 (0)	0.07 (2)	0.34 (8)	0.25 (31)
Georgia	0.00 (0)	0.00 (0)	0.01 (1)	0.24 (2)	0.22 (5)
Asia	**16.61 (358)**	**18.71 (606)**	**22.22 (790)**	**27.87 (1090)**	**55.81 (3823)**
West Asia (Middle East) (12 countries)	*1.09 (35)*	*1.17 (47)*	*0.98 (51)*	*1.61 (67)*	*1.38 (146)*
United Arab Emirates	0.32 (12)	0.38 (16)	0.33 (19)	0.44 (25)	0.44 (80)
Yemen	0.24 (7)	0.22 (8)	0.18 (8)	0.49 (9)	0.36 (10)
Central Asia (8 countries)	*0.09 (5)*	*0.26 (19)*	*0.49 (34)*	*1.50 (75)*	*1.06 (152)*
Kazakhstan	0.01 (2)	0.08 (12)	0.16 (17)	0.80 (36)	0.51 (63)
Kyrgyzstan	0.02 (1)	0.06 (4)	0.16 (8)	0.46 (19)	0.30 (36)
Uzbekistan	0.04 (2)	0.09 (2)	0.12 (6)	0.17 (15)	0.18 (36)

Table 7.3 Approved Chinese ODI by host region and economy, 1990–2004 (US$ 10,000 and per cent) – continued

	Percentage Annual Average Cumulative FDI Stock (Project Number)				
	1990–1992	1993–1995	1996–1998	1999–2001	2002–2004
South, East and SE Asia (20 countries)	**15.42 (319)**	**17.28 (540)**	**20.74 (705)**	**24.75 (948)**	**53.38 (3526)**
Hong Kong (China SAR)	8.12 (116)	8.08 (146)	9.35 (176)	8.83 (240)	38.19 (2127)
Thailand	2.94 (76)	3.15 (120)	2.83 (135)	2.96 (146)	2.15 (247)
Korea, Republic	0.23 (2)	0.39 (9)	0.39 (17)	0.35 (23)	3.68 (75)
Macao (China SAR)	1.19 (24)	1.02 (26)	2.11 (40)	1.55 (57)	1.71 (238)
Cambodia	0.00 (0)	0.11 (4)	1.17 (21)	2.40 (47)	1.51 (65)
Indonesia	0.16 (4)	0.78 (27)	0.96 (37)	1.45 (43)	1.19 (66)
Viet Nam	0.00 (0)	0.03 (2)	0.14 (8)	0.86 (27)	0.81 (91)
Singapore	0.65 (26)	0.81 (49)	0.87 (69)	0.86 (90)	0.79 (188)
Myanmar	0.02 (1)	0.06 (4)	0.18 (11)	0.93 (19)	0.59 (39)
Mongolia	0.07 (6)	0.14 (22)	0.12 (25)	1.28 (53)	0.63 (78)
Malaysia	0.82 (21)	1.21 (51)	1.17 (71)	0.85 (80)	0.34 (106)
India	0.00 (0)	0.00 (1)	0.04 (3)	0.41 (9)	0.18 (16)
The Pacific (9 countries)	**0.88 (18)**	**1.27 (41)**	**1.92 (46)**	**1.69 (55)**	**0.58 (63)**
Papua New Guinea	0.45 (5)	0.56 (9)	1.31 (12)	1.16 (17)	0.37 (20)
Fiji	0.21 (6)	0.29 (11)	0.26 (13)	0.24 (14)	0.08 (16)

Source: Calculated from MOFCOM, *Almanac of Foreign Relations and Trade 1991–2003* and *China Commerce Yearbook 2004*.
Notes: The principal host countries of Chinese FDI are listed for each region. The total number of recipients of Chinese FDI is shown in the region heading. Regions are as per UNCTAD (2003). Countries are listed in declining rank order for the period 2002–2003.

and other developed countries received negligible amounts. Developing countries, by contrast, hosted collectively just under a third (30.5%) of China's ODI, with the South, East and Southeast Asian region receiving almost half of this amount (15.4%). Of this, Hong Kong (the fourth ranked recipient), Thailand (6th) and Macao (8th) were the main destinations, the balance being more or less evenly distributed amongst the others. The remaining share of Chinese ODI to developing countries was divided almost equally between three regions, namely Africa (4.0%), Latin America and the Caribbean (4.9%) and Central and Eastern Europe (4.8%). No individual developing country in these regions was host to more than one percentage point of Chinese outward FDI stock except the Russian Federation (4.1%) and Chile (1.6%).

The distribution of Chinese ODI by value observed in the early 1990s is at odds with aspects of the received view of developing country FDI and its development path as predicted by the stages theory. In particular, the prominence of the industrialised countries and the comparatively weak positions of developing countries as hosts to Chinese ODI, especially in Southeast Asia, Africa, South America and, notably, India, suggest that Chinese firms were generally slow to invest substantial funds in other developing countries. In respect of geographic distance, the 16 countries that physically border China attracted only 13.5% of Chinese ODI by value between 1990 and 1992.[10] This provides some evidence for the assertion that, when viewed in aggregate, Chinese ODI at this time was not influenced much by geography. Moreover, the fact that developed countries like the USA, Australia and Canada (all physically and, arguably, psychically distant from mainland China) figure so highly as hosts to approved Chinese FDI in the 1990s,[11] and that Hong Kong and Macao (both with large ethnic Chinese populations) were not major recipients, suggests that psychic distance and relational location advantages were also not key determinants. This interpretation contrasts to that of Zhan (1995), for example, who, among others, identifies ethnicity as a major determinant of the location decision of Chinese MNEs in the early 1990s. We attribute the distribution to the high degree of government involvement in the internationalisation decisions of Chinese firms.

A somewhat different picture emerges when we examine project numbers, however. Between 1990 and 1992, Australia, the USA and Canada were host to 24.2% of the investment projects made by Chinese firms, while the developing countries were host to 63.6%, with Hong Kong and Macao together accounting for 13.2% of the total. This hints at the possibility that a combination of physical proximity, cultural affinity and relational location advantages did indeed contribute to strengthening the presence of Chinese MNEs in these locations relative to others, but only when smaller scale investments are concerned. This is recognised by Fung (1996), who reports that Chinese FDI to Hong Kong in the early 1990s was largely motivated by the need to access new sources of finance for mainland operations. Besides a few large-scale investments in Hong Kong by China Resources, China Merchants International and the Bank of China, amongst others, this involved the formation of numerous shell companies – Sung (1996) estimates more than 14,000 – with minimum registered capital and limited commercial activities (Sung, 1996). Such investment is not modelled well by the stages theory. However, as Fung (1996) comments, some Chinese ODI in Hong Kong at this time was to gain early internationalisation experience in a location with a contrasting institutional setting but cultural similarities to home, a behaviour which is predicted by the 'stages' model.

Between 1992 and 2001, there was a steady, three-fold increase in the annual average value of Chinese ODI. However, this growth was distributed unevenly. Although Australia, the USA and Canada continued to attract increasing amounts of Chinese outflows (in terms of both value and number), this was outstripped by that recorded for developing countries. Contrary to expectation, perhaps, the improvement in the relative position of developing countries in Chinese ODI is not accounted for by Hong Kong SAR and Macao: the proportion of total annual approved Chinese ODI destined to these countries over this period remained confined to the narrow range of 8 to 10% and 1 to 3%, respectively. Similarly, the position of the Russian Federation changes little over this period, consistently hosting between 3 and 6% of outflow. Overall, this pattern suggests that geography, geopolitical and culture-related factors continued to play only a limited role in determining the destination of new Chinese ODI at the time. Again, this suggests that the stages theory has only limited explanatory power when applied to the internationalisation of Chinese firms prior to 2001, particularly of investments made by state-owned enterprises via the formal, approved route, with government influence a key contributory factor.[12]

Instead, the greatest growth in China's ODI position took place in Africa, and especially sub-Saharan Africa (notably Zambia, South Africa, Mali and Tanzania), Latin America and the Caribbean (especially Peru, Mexico, and Brazil) and in the South, East and Southeast Asian region generally (notably Cambodia and Indonesia). This distribution mirrors the findings of a survey on leading Chinese TNCs conducted by UNCTAD (2003). Since many of these countries at the time were characterised by comparatively high levels of political and economic risk, this distribution raises a number of interesting issues concerning the management of risk by internationalising Chinese firms. First, Chinese firms may have drawn on their home-country embeddedness (beyond those culturally-derived relational advantages) to exploit opportunities abroad in countries that industrialised country MNEs might regard as risky and where international competition levels are therefore low. Scott (2002), for example, points to the ability of Chinese-owned enterprises to manage risk as being a key source of ownership advantage (though his analysis is confined mainly to Chinese *family-owned* enterprises). Second. soft budget constraints and access to cheap capital (that is, domestic capital market imperfections) arising from high levels of state involvement in overseas projects may also have led Chinese MNEs to demonstrate a perverse attitude to risk management in comparison to industrialised country firms (Buckley, Clegg, Cross, Liu, Voss and Zheng, 2007; Antkiewicz and Whalley, 2006). Third, the conclusion by the Chinese government of bilateral investment treaties, double taxation agreements and other initiatives designed to build strong economic and diplomatic relations with developing countries will also have helped Chinese investors to mitigate certain aspects of investment risk in the countries concerned (Buckley, Clegg, Cross, Voss, Rhodes and Zheng, 2008). This is especially relevant in the case of state-directed FDI that advances the political agenda of the Chinese government: for example, when it is used to develop connections with countries ideologically or politically distant from the west, for whatever reason. In such instances, the normal commercial considerations associated with risk, psychic distance and exposure to the liabilities of foreignness, for example, will have had little bearing upon the decision-taking of Chinese firms.

Given its population, geographic proximity and developing-country status, India continues to be a notable absentee from the list of principal destinations for Chinese firms throughout the period under investigation (mirrored also in India's relatively modest position in global FDI flows generally). Also evident is continuation in the comparatively weak position of the western European countries, which attracted less than 1.7% of annual global Chinese ODI flow in the period 1999–2001, a decrease from the 2.5% or so generally observed in the 1990s. Given the relative openness of the European Union (EU) countries to inbound FDI, this is worthy of comment. First, despite the

Single European Market and other economic harmonisation initiatives, Chinese firms may have been discouraged from investing because the EU is viewed by them as comprising distinct and separate national markets, each with their own set of standards, regulations, employment laws, immigration and visa requirements, language and so forth, unlike other attractive markets such as the USA. Second, because Chinese firms are required to negotiate separately with different national and regional investment agencies in Europe, this may have served as a disincentive by comparison to investing in other large markets. In sum, there may be a perception among Chinese firms that investing in the EU is more complex and bureaucratic than investing elsewhere.

Notwithstanding the dominant position of the USA as a host, figures suggest that the distribution of Chinese ODI in recent years has begun to approximate that of developing countries more generally in that other developing countries are increasingly being targeted as investment locations by Chinese MNEs. Indeed, the widening distribution of Chinese FDI by country over the period is striking. The number of individual countries host to Chinese ODI rose from 95 in 1990, to 139 in 1996 and to 162 in 2003, by when Chinese MNEs had invested in 46 Sub-Saharan countries, 30 Latin American countries and 18 Central and Eastern European countries. While this distribution can be attributed to responses to market opportunities and other factors endogenous to the firm, another interpretation is that it is in response to the government's preference for a spatially diversified overseas production portfolio that minimises exposure to political and other risks, especially in places like Africa and West and Central Asia.

In the 2002–2004 period, when Chinese ODI continued to increase sharply, this again was mainly to the developing rather than developed countries, in terms of both value and project number. Much of this is attributable to Hong Kong SAR, which has become a major destination for Chinese investors. This suggests that geo-cultural affinity is an increasingly important driver of Chinese ODI, although Hong Kong's position as a financial centre and as a pathway for investing elsewhere is also an important locational advantage for Chinese MNEs.

Sectoral distribution

Using SAFE data, we are able to discern certain changes to the sectoral distribution of Chinese ODI. The SAFE dataset, the most detailed available on the subject, comprises approved investment project information by host country, industry and entry mode for the years

1991 to 2001 (after which project level data were no longer formally collected). Annually collected data on projects by sector reveals that the bulk of Chinese ODI by value in the early to mid 1990s was predominantly engaged in the tertiary and manufacturing sectors (see Table 7.4). Historically, Chinese FDI in services has generally involved a large number of small scale investments in trade-supporting activities by Chinese trading companies, with investments in the banking sector (notably by the Bank of China but also by CITIC and China Merchant Holdings, both in Hong Kong), insurance and construction, communication, real estate and restaurants also are significant. Many of these investments served as vanguard operations for later Chinese entrants in addition to providing important overseas trade support to firms in China. Similarly, Chinese manufacturing ODI has generally involved relatively small-scale and labour-intensive production of undifferentiated and low-value-added goods using simple product and process technologies. In more recent years, SAFE data reveal that Chinese ODI has occurred mostly in the manufacturing sector. The presence of foreign invested enterprises in China and two decades of market opening have yielded spillover benefits that have enhanced domestic and international competitiveness (Buckley, Clegg and Wang, 2002). Together with greater familiarisation with operating internationally, this is likely to have assisted in the international expansion of Chinese-owned manufacturing activity. In addition, Chinese government policy to shift international expansion away from 'one-track', trade-related activity to more diversified, 'multi-purpose' operations and the support provided to Chinese manufacturers as part of China's 'go global' policy are also key driving forces. Viewed in aggregate, the growth in Chinese manufacturing FDI in recent times is congruent with the received view of developing country ODI in that a greater propensity to invest in manufacturing activity abroad is observed over time. We note, however, that official ODI stock data published by MOFCOM suggests that the

Table 7.4 Sectoral distribution of outward Chinese FDI: 1991–2001 (per cent of total value).

	1991	1992	1993	1994	1995	1996	1997	1998	1999	2000	2001
Primary	3	43	4	5	18	34	45	49	11	9	11
Manufacturing	47	28	29	61	36	31	5	30	56	56	52
Tertiary	34	15	49	18	33	22	49	20	30	25	31
Other	16	14	18	16	13	13	1	1	3	10	6

Source: Calculated from SAFE statistics on approved FDI projects.

Box 7.1 Some observations about China's FDI data collecting agencies.

In China, data on outward FDI are collected principally by those two agencies most concerned with regulating international investment by Chinese firms, namely (i) MOFCOM, the main approval granting agency for non-financial Chinese firms, and (ii) the State Administration of Foreign Exchange (SAFE), which administers, via the banking system, foreign exchange-related matters of China's international investors. Differences exist in the FDI data reported by these two agencies, however, with SAFE generally reporting much larger values than MOFCOM/MOFTEC. Some explanations follow:

(1) Overseas investments by Chinese financial institutions require approval from the People's Bank of China and therefore fall outside of the scope of MOFTEC/MOFCOM. However, such investments are recorded by SAFE through the national balance of payments statistics reporting system.
(2) Large, State Council approved 'show-case' foreign investments by privileged Chinese state-owned enterprises (SOEs) are not registered with MOFTEC/MOFCOM, but are nevertheless captured by SAFE through the balance of payments reporting system.
(3) When bidding for large-scale natural resource exploitation projects, Chinese firms are often required to have requisite foreign exchange available as 'good faith' in advance of the project 'go ahead' and before MOFTEC/MOFCOM approval has been sought. Potential investment funds like appear in the balance of payments statistics reporting system and are recorded by SAFE.
(4) Capital fund transfers by Chinese parent firms to overseas affiliates are recorded as FDI by SAFE under the capital account, but are not registered as overseas investment by MOFTEC/MOFCOM. Reinvested earnings, intra-company loans and non-financial and private sector transactions are also absent from MOFTEC/MOFCOM statistics.
(5) Contrasting treatment by SAFE and MOFTEC/MOFTEC of different financial aspects of a large scale investment project may lead the two agencies to record in different years effectively the same instance of FDI.

> **Box 7.1** Some observations about China's FDI data collecting agencies – *continued*.
>
> In many respects, SAFE data present a more complete picture of China's outward FDI position than do that of MOFCOM/MOFTEC. Nevertheless, there are limitations with SAFE data, in particular:
>
> (1) Most non-monetary (in kind) transfers, such as those relating to equipment, raw materials, technology, know-how and intellectual property are not recorded by the banking system nor, in turn, are collected by SAFE for balance of payments reasons. However, the investment division of SAFE (which manages foreign exchange administration for Chinese outward investments) does collect this type of data on an informal basis (i.e. it is not contained in the published national balance of payments statistics or those of the International Monetary Fund).
> (2) Some of the data of SAFE will be 'inflated' by round-tripping behaviour by domestic firms seeking to benefit from investor incentives only available to foreigners.
> (3) Some outward FDI initiated or approved by local government is not reported centrally in order to circumvent the approval process.

greatest proportion of Chinese ODI has occurred in the primary sector. Taylor (2002), for example, uses MOFCOM data to report that the manufacturing sector accounted for only 11.5% of China's outward FDI in the late 1990s, compared with 19.4% for resource development and extraction, 1.8% for communications and transport, and 66.4% for other categories (see also Zhan, 1995; Chan, 1995). MOFCOM (2005) report a similar sectoral distribution of Chinese ODI stock for 2003 as follows: 6.2% in manufacturing, 19.2% resources in development and extraction, 6.1% in transportation and warehousing, 19.7% in wholesale and retail trade and 48.8% for the remaining categories (construction, business services, information technology-related sectors and other industries). It is clear from these data that investment in the extractive industries is an important contribution to Chinese ODI, especially in mining, fisheries and forestry exploitation and petroleum and natural gas exploration. However, regular reclassification and procedural revisions to the reporting of ODI by activity on the part of MOFCOM makes it difficult to draw further conclusions from a longitudinal examination of the data.

Entry mode

Literature on the internationalisation of developing country MNEs suggests that minority IJVs are the preferred mode of market entry (Wells, 1983; Yeung, 1994). One reason is that such firms seldom possess the level of proprietary technology and firm-specific know-how to necessitate internalisation via majority or full ownership (Buckley and Casson 1976; Dunning, 1993). This is also evident in the early years of Chinese ODI development: project level SAFE data reveal that, in the early 1990s, around 70% of overseas projects of Chinese firms took the IJV form (see Table 7.5). Zhan (1995) also reports that Chinese firms tended to opt for majority equity shareholdings in overseas projects, typically in the range of 40 to 70% equity participation, especially in natural resource-oriented and manufacturing-related projects. A number of explanations can be envisaged. From a governmental perspective, the formal investment approval process generally required Chinese MNEs to adopt the IJV entry mode. The Chinese authorities had become familiar with the economic gains associated with the promotion of inward FDI in the form of IJVs, the promotion of which was a cornerstone of China's 'Open Door' policy. The JV form was seen as a vehicle for promoting the inflow of foreign-owned technology, management know-how and other skills to China. The authorities were also now adept and comfortable with at administering foreign invested enterprises in China. It is likely that equivalent advantages were sought when Chinese enterprises invested abroad. Familiar cost and risk-minimising features of IJVs will also have been important to the investment approval agencies (Zhan, 1995; Taylor, 2002; Wang, 2002). From an enterprise perspective, inefficient domestic capital markets and budget constraints meant that many Chinese enterprises, including state-owned ones, often found it difficult to obtain sufficient funds to purchase overseas assets outright, compelling them to opt

Table 7.5 Entry mode in Chinese outward FDI: 1991–2001 (per cent of number of foreign affiliates).

	1991	1992	1993	1994	1995	1996	1997	1998	1999	2000	2001
Wholly owned	30	32	42	46	52	62	55	58	58	58	61
Joint Venture	70	68	58	54	48	37	45	42	42	42	39

Source: Calculated from SAFE statistics on approved FDI projects.

for the IJV alternative. The JV form also allowed Chinese MNEs to exercise a degree of control over local operations whilst avoiding outright ownership and the concomitant exposure to political and commercial risk. Chinese enterprises could tap foreign partner contributions, such as improved access to market intelligence, knowledge of the local operating environment, opportunities for reputation riding and better access to local distribution channels through the IJV (Taylor, 2002). When established with other ethnically-Chinese enterprises (in Hong Kong and elsewhere), the JV form also allowed relational assets to be optimised, reducing perceived risks and costs associated with psychic distance, especially for smaller and less experienced Chinese investors (Zhan, 1995). Mutual trust would also have been easier to establish. Thus, we see both institutional and firm-specific factors influencing the choice of IJV by Chinese firms at this time.

From the mid-1990s onwards, however, SAFE data at individual project level reveal that wholly-owned FDI projects have increasingly substituted for jointly-owned ones in the international expansion of Chinese enterprise, with 61% of overseas affiliates in approved projects taking this form in 2001 compared to 30% in 1991. We note that this contrasts somewhat with the findings of Taylor (2002), who reports much greater use of IJVs in the recent internationalisation of Chinese firms, especially in manufacturing-related activity. A number of reasons explain the more frequent use of the wholly-owned entry mode in recent years. First, more frequent approval of wholly Chinese-owned projects reflects growing confidence among the regulating authorities that managers of state-owned Chinese MNEs have become sufficiently experienced and skilled to take control of, and co-ordinate effectively, the activities of geographically-dispersed affiliates. It is also a reflection, at least in part, of the strategic importance placed on particular projects by the Chinese authorities. Theory asserts that, by internalising markets, the internationalising firm is able to reduce its dependency on independent intermediaries; militate against the threat of technology and know-how leakage; reduce the risk of opportunistic behaviour by alliance partners and allow for full appropriation of returns on investment (Buckley and Casson, 1976). Both the investment approval agencies and enterprises will have found such advantages attractive, despite the costs and risks associated with full ownership. Second, greater use of wholly-owned affiliates may reflect improved availability of investment funds. Government initiatives under the 'go global' (*zou chu qu*) policy have released capital to state-owned firms (often at below market rates) in the form of loans and improved access to hard currencies, to help them finance the outright purchase of foreign assets (Antkiewicz and Whalley, 2006). Many Chinese enterprises are also now skilled at raising investment funds on international capital markets, especially in Hong Kong (Buckley, Clegg, Cross, Liu, Voss and Zheng, 2007; Chan, 1995). Thus, many Chinese firms are no longer obligated to reduce investment cost by undertaking an IJV. Third, the growth in international market entry by acquisition will have led Chinese enterprises to establish more wholly-owned subsidiaries in foreign markets rather than jointly-owned projects.

The standard theoretical model of 'Asian ODI' suggests that China is not unusual among Asian countries in using wholly owned subsidiaries more frequently over time (Pang and Komaran, 1985; Euh and Min, 1986; Yeung, 1994). However, caution should be exercised in assuming that this mirrors improvements in the managerial capacity and competitiveness of Chinese MNEs: greater deployment of majority and wholly-owned foreign operations may also be more a function of the government's desire to retain effective control of state assets abroad and a growing confidence in its ability to do so than of purely firm-specific or market-related considerations.

Motives for Chinese outward FDI

In this section, we relate historic and emergent trends in aggregate Chinese ODI data identified above to changes in the motivations driving the internationalisation of Chinese MNEs. Dunning (1993) identifies four basic motivations that provide the impetus for foreign-owned production and are discussed below; namely, natural-resource seeking, market-seeking, efficiency-seeking and strategic asset-seeking motives.

Natural resource-seeking FDI

Backward integration to acquire or secure the supply of specific location-bound resources and commodities abroad for domestic consumption has been the predominant driver of Chinese outward FDI since the late 1970s (Taylor, 2002). More recently, China's rapid economic growth over the past decade has fuelled what some say is an almost insatiable demand for raw materials and other inputs in many sectors (Economist, 2004).[13] The dual objective of further improving the supply of natural resources from abroad while ameliorating (at a national level) exposure to political and commercial risk has been Chinese enterprises recently investing in natural resources-oriented projects across a broad range of resource-rich countries, especially in Africa and East and Central Asia (see Table 7.3). Leading recent recipients are Zambia (for copper), Peru (iron ore), and western and central Asian countries like Kazakhstan (oil exploration and extraction). Most investors are state-owned enterprises which enjoy strong support from the Chinese government in the form of direct financial assistance; the negotiation of bilateral investment treaties and trade agreements with host countries and the close inter-governmental relationships that China is now reviving across certain parts of the developing world. Exemplar companies include China Natural Petroleum Corporation (CNPC), the joint owner of a Sudanese oil production plant (together with Canadian, Malaysian and local interests), Sinopec, Shanghai Baosteel (the owner of six joint ventures in Australia, Brazil and South Africa in iron-ore mining and steel trading), Sinochem and China National Offshore Oil Corporation (CNOOC). There is some evidence to suggest that official development aid provided by China to developing countries (for example, concerning telecommunications and transportation infrastructure development, project-specific inter-governmental loans, education packages and so forth) is predicated upon market access or exploitation and extraction rights being granted to Chinese MNEs (Pan, 2006; Evans and Downs, 2006).

It has been argued that MNEs from emerging countries are most likely to invest in the industrialised countries when looking to access technology and learning (Monkiewicz, 1986; Ye, 1992; Deng, 2003). However, this may not be the case for China. Whilst knowledge-acquisition has become increasingly important to Chinese MNEs in recent years, much of Chinese ODI by value was invested in the industrialised countries primarily for natural-resource seeking reasons, especially in the early 1990s. Good examples include the investments by CITIC and Huaguang Forest Co. Ltd in timber plantations in New Zealand, CITIC's investment in forestry in the USA, CITIC and China National Nonferrous Metal Industrial Corporation's 10% (US$120mn) investment in Portland Aluminium's smelter operations in Australia. Canada is also now host to a number of timber and fisheries related Chinese investments (e.g. CITIC's investment in the Celgar pulp mill and sawmill project) (Zhang, 2003).

Market-seeking FDI

Chinese MNEs now conduct both defensive and offensive market-seeking FDI. It is axiomatic to state that China enjoys a comparative advantage in low-cost labour and labour-intensive production. Given the location-bound nature of labour, the international competitiveness of the majority of (both foreign and locally-owned) firms in China necessitates domestic production and foreign market servicing by exports. Chinese enterprises have long established overseas operations to facilitate trade. Certainly, in the early 1990s, the bulk of Chinese ODI in services was export trade-related. Chinese exporters have commonly confronted a range of tariff and non-tariff trade barriers abroad. Although China's WTO accession should see these reduced, the reverse may happen in those countries with which Chinese enjoys a large trade surplus, such as the USA. For example, the imposition of protectionist measures (or its threat) presently underpins a small but significant proportion of the recent growth in Chinese ODI to the USA, Latin America and, but less so, to Europe (Taylor, 2002), for defensive market-seeking reasons. Protectionist pressure also accounts for a significant share of Chinese ODI in 'third-party' trading countries (Taylor, 2002). Increasingly, Chinese enterprises are locating 'offshore' manufacturing plants to those countries with which the industrialised nations set few, if any, export quotas and other 'anti-dumping' measures, or they invest in countries where quota rights can be appropriated readily (Lau, 2002; Taylor, 2002; UNCTAD, 2003). This accounts for much of the recent growth in market-seeking ODI by Chinese firms in a number of countries, including, for example, Cambodia (where Chinese garment manufacturers in particular enjoy fewer quota restrictions in third markets); Mauritius (where export quota restrictions are mostly absent), Jamaica and Fiji (UNCTAD, 2003). A further illustration of defensive, market-seeking FDI is provided by the purchase in 2002 of the insolvent German television maker Schneider Electronics AG by TCL, China's second largest television and mobile-phone maker. Reportedly, this was motivated, at least in part, by TCL's desire to negate possible accusations of dumping products in Europe (CNN, 2003).

A second aspect to defensive market-seeking FDI by Chinese firms is their response to factors that combine to limit growth opportunities at home (Beede, 2006). First, China is obligated under its WTO accession terms to further open domestic markets to both imports and FDI. This has inevitably increased competitive pressures in home markets (Taylor, 2002). Second, supply-chain bottlenecks, restricted demand and fragmented national markets are now commonplace in certain sectors in China (e.g., domestic appliances and machinery and in textiles, clothing and footwear) and this has led to excess capacity. Third, greater regulatory transparency and superior distribution networks abroad means it is often easier for Chinese enterprises to develop foreign markets than domestic ones, especially for those located in the coastal provinces close to international transportation networks. For many, the challenges associated with supplying domestic markets are less in evidence abroad.

There is also growing evidence to suggest that Chinese enterprises are now investing abroad for offensive market-seeking reasons; that is, to develop new markets and raise brand awareness (UNCTAD, 2003). Although inefficiencies and lack of competitiveness of Chinese enterprise across a gamut of industries and sectors have been highlighted (e.g., Nolan, 2001; Nolan and Zhang, 2002), a growing number of Chinese enterprise are now able to compete more effectively in international markets. For them, international expansion represents a *proactive* step, with new markets being developed overseas because of attractive demand conditions. Although many Chinese companies are able to compete by selling simple, undifferentiated, mature products in low-income countries (exemplified by Chinese-owned bicycle production in Ghana and video-player sales in South-East Asia), others are increasingly able to compete in more technology-intensive sectors in both developing and developed countries by undertaking large-scale, capital-intensive, market-seeking investments. Good examples include electronics companies such as Huawei, ZTE, Konka Electronics, Skyworth Group, Changhong Electronics Group Corp, Lenovo Corporation (formerly known as Legend Corporation) and Haier, and a number of enterprises in the plastics, chemicals and pharmaceuticals sectors (UNCTAD, 2003). Chinese MNEs are now establishing sales and marketing functions in target markets to lower their dependency on intermediaries. Sinochem, for example, now has 60 foreign affiliates to develop and expand sales of chemical products in major overseas markets while Lenovo Corporation now has over twenty foreign affiliates to sell software products internationally. Typically, physical proximity to key local markets reduces transportation costs and improves access to local market knowledge and information flows to and from both consumers and suppliers. It also facilitates the adaptation of products and services to local conditions. In time, a local presence should also allow Chinese investors to be perceived as 'insiders'. This may become important should neo-protectionist trade or political tensions grow between China and host countries as negative 'country of origin' effects may be reduced. To illustrate, the private Chinese autoparts supplier, Wanxiang, purchased a number of insolvent US component manufacturers to secure access to leading car assemblers in the USA and, reportedly, to help circumvent negative connotations associated with its nationality that might have been held by unionists and other stakeholders.

A second aspect to offensive market seeking FDI is the response of Chinese firms to deepening regional economic integration in some parts of the world. For example, a number of recent Chinese investments in Mexico were made in order to benefit from preferential treatment given by the USA to Mexican imports under the terms of the North American Free Trade Association (NAFTA). Similarly, a proportion of Chinese FDI bound for Cambodia and Vietnam was stimulated by the prospect of improved access to South East Asian markets as a consequence of the ASEAN Free Trade Agreement and the Asian Investment Area. However, the relatively modest amounts of Chinese ODI hosted by the European Union points strongly to the fact that regional economic integration and large markets may be a necessary but not a sufficient condition for offensive market-seeking FDI by Chinese MNEs, for reasons already discussed.

Strategic asset seeking FDI

A variety of foreign-owned assets, both tangible and intangible, are of potential interest to Chinese enterprise. Historically, the principal intangible resource sought by Chinese MNEs was information, especially about external economic and trade conditions. In the past, Chinese MNEs have been obligated to assimilate and disseminate experience and knowledge of foreign management practices to advance the international competitiveness of Chinese enterprise more generally. Indeed, Taylor (2002) comments that China's outward FDI is an on-going quest for market information to improve domestic export performance. Nevertheless, there is some evidence to indicate that Chinese MNEs are becoming less interested in market information and operations-related knowledge and instead are looking to tap foreign knowledge of technology-intensive production and local markets (UNCTAD, 2003). To this end, Chinese enterprise are now establishing research-oriented affiliates in high-income countries to assist in the development of high technology, knowledge intensive products manufactured in China and exported via sales affiliates. In some places, like the USA and UK, this process is supported by home country efforts to attract this type of investment (Sauvant, 2005), especially in sectors that do not challenge the local manufacturing base.

A second intangible asset increasingly sought by Chinese MNEs relates to brands and complementary assets (see Table 7.6 for recent

Table 7.6 International brand acquisition by Chinese companies – some successes and attempts.

Chinese party	Foreign party	Brand	Year
China Bluestar	Drakker Holdings (Belgium)	Adisseo	2006
Haier	Maytag (USA) (aborted)	Maytag	2005
Nanjing Automobile	MG Rover (UK)	MG	2005
Lenovo	IBM PC Business (USA)	Think products (e.g. ThinkPad)	2005
Shanggong	Dürkopp Adler (Germany)	Dürkopp Adler	2004
TCL	Thomson (France), Schneider (Germany)	Schneider, RCA, Alcatel	2002, 2003
Shanghai Haixing Group	Glenoit Textile (USA)	Glenoit	2002

Source: CIBUL China M&A database.

examples). While some companies, such as Lenovo Corporation and Haier, have extended their key brands and trade names into foreign markets themselves, with some success, others have found it quicker and more effective to simply acquire established western brands and associated marketing channels. To illustrate, a key reason for the formation in 2003 of TCL-Thomson Electronics, an IJV between the French electronics firm Thomson and TCL International Holdings (the Hong Kong-listed affiliate of TCL Group), reportedly was to enable the JV to exploit the brand portfolios of the partners in Asia and North America respectively (CNN, 2003).

While the large amount of investment finance required to effect an overseas acquisition may have precluded most Chinese enterprises in the past, this is no longer the case. Sales growth in certain sectors of the Chinese economy has meant that an increasing minority of Chinese enterprises, both private and state-owned, are accumulating sufficient retained earnings to fund major capital investment projects abroad. It is also helped by the relaxation of foreign exchange controls, by the low cost of capital enjoyed by some state-owned firms and by the strength of the Renminbi, which has lowered relative investment costs in certain markets. All this means that increasing numbers of Chinese enterprises are now able to obtain the foreign currency required to make strategic-asset seeking FDI in industrialised as well as developing countries a feasible option. In the case of industrialised country target firms, this often entails the purchase of loss-making

Table 7.7 Selected acquisitions by Chinese MNEs since 2000.

Chinese party	Foreign party	Value and type	Year
China National Petroleum Corp.	PetroKaz (Canada)	US$4.18bn	2005
Lenovo	IBM's PC Business (USA)	US$1.75bn	2005
China National Offshore Oil Corp.	Repsol's Indonesian oilfields (Spain)	US$585mn	2001
Shanghai Automobile and Industrial Corp.	Ssangyong (S. Korea)	US$530mn	2004
China National Bluestar (Group) Corp.	Drakker Holdings (Belgium)	US$482mn	2006
BOE Technology	Hynix Semiconductor's flat panel display plant (Republic of Korea)	US$380mn	2002
China National Chemical Import and Export Corp.	Atlantis Holding Norway AS (Norway)	US$250mn	2002
Huaneng Power International Inc	OzGen (Australia)	US$227mn	2003
PetroChina	Devon Energy Group (Indonesia)	US$216mn	2002
BOE Technology	TPV (a PC monitor manufacturer)	US$135mn	2003
Nanjing Automobile	MG Rover (UK)	US$50mn	2005
Huayi Group (Shanghai)	Moltech Power Systems (USA)	US$20mn (est)	2002
Haixin International Group	Glenoit Fabrics (H.G.) Corp (USA)	US$14mn	2004
TCL International Holdings Ltd	Schneider Electronics (Germany)	US$8mn	2002
TCL International Holdings Ltd	Thomson (France)	A merger of TV and DVD manufacturing activity in a joint venture	2003

Source: CIBUL China M&A database.

businesses (see Tables 7.6 and 7.7 for examples). Viewed alongside the observation that many Chinese MNEs have acquired intangible and complementary assets that they have little to no prior experience of managing, this raises a question concerning the ability of some Chinese firms to generate profits from post-acquired businesses.

A third type of strategic asset sought by Chinese MNEs is improved access to capital markets. China's domestic capital market has long been inefficient and Chinese policy has generally restricted the holding of external debt by SOEs. Project finance was often difficult to obtain, therefore, especially in non-priority sectors. In the early 1990s, a number of large Chinese enterprises responded by acquiring weak corporations in Hong Kong, transforming themselves into MNEs overnight. These were used to obtain listings on the Hong Kong stock exchange with the capital secured redirected to China to fund domestic enterprise (Liu, 2001; Liu and Li, 2002; Sung, 1996). Many Chinese-owned stocks are now listed on the Heng Seng Index, including China Telecom, China Merchants Holdings, China Unicom, China Mobile (HK) Ltd., Sinopec, CNPC, China Everbright Ltd., Lenovo Group Limited (formerly known as Legend Holdings Limited) and Founder Holding International (Shi, 2000). Tax-havens such as the British Virgin Islands, the Cayman Islands and Bermuda have also been used by Chinese MNEs to obtain venture capital (Frost, 2005), to channel funds back to mainland China (and thus benefit from foreign invested enterprise status) and to circumvent restrictive outward investment approval procedures (Voss, 2007).

Efficiency-seeking FDI

When a firm internationalises for efficiency-seeking reasons, it generally does so by reorganising and rationalising established resource-based or market-oriented FDI operations (Dunning, 1993). Typically, this is done to exploit the benefits of regional economic integration and the international division of labour. Firms take advantage of different factor endowments, yet converging cultures, institutional arrangements and economic systems across a regionally integrated group of countries by supplying markets from a reduced number of intra-regional plants. In contrast to much of the FDI undertaken by industrialised country MNEs, it is unlikely that greater efficiency is currently a major driver for Chinese firms. At present, Chinese enterprise have little incentive to seek production efficiencies abroad since domestic markets provide ample supplies of relatively low-cost labour, land and other factor inputs, especially away from the coastal regions. Moreover, few Chinese companies currently have sufficient numbers of overseas operations to warrant substantial reorganisation. However, as we have seen, regional integration is beginning to shape the investment strategies of Chinese MNEs, notably within NAFTA and South East Asia, though mostly for market-related rather than efficiency-related reasons. As these international operations expand in scale and scope, efficiency-seeking FDI by Chinese MNEs is likely to become more commonplace.

Conclusions: Is Chinese ODI a special case of emerging country ODI?

This paper makes a number of contributions to our current understanding of Chinese ODI. An application of several levels of explanation using aggregate (MOFCOM) data, individual project level (SAFE) data and a review of recent studies has enabled us to provide a rich picture of the phenomenon little discussed in the literature (e.g., Deng, 2003; Taylor, 2002). We find that Chinese ODI is similar to, yet distinct from, the standard model of emerging country ODI, as Table 7.1 shows.

Our analysis of the changing geographic distribution of aggregate Chinese ODI by value suggests that geographic and psychic distance were not important determinants of larger scale Chinese investment projects in the 1990s, which were generally directed towards the industrialised countries, often for resource-seeking reasons. This is at odds with aspects of the standard model of ODI from Asian developing countries and the incremental 'stages theory' approach which predict a tendency for Chinese ODI to be associated negatively with the level of development of the host country and with increasing geographic and psychic distance (see Table 7.1). We attribute this to the significant involvement of government, both direct and indirect, in the internationalisation decisions of Chinese MNEs in the 1990s. However, we observe geographic and psychic distances to have had greater influence on the international distribution of smaller scale and more recent projects by Chinese MNEs, especially after 1999. This suggests that 'stages' model of internationalisation has greater explanatory power for more recent Chinese ODI. Today, Chinese ODI is distributed more widely to encompass a large number of developing host countries (notably in Africa and Southeast Asia) in addition to the industrialised countries, which historically have been important destinations (with the exception of Western Europe). This provides some support for the argument that the distribution of Chinese ODI is beginning to conform to patterns predicted by the received view of ODI from developing Asian economies. However, to what extent this is attributable to the gradual disengagement of government from the direct regulation and control of ODI is a subject for further research.

It is clear that increasing numbers of Chinese MNEs (mainly government owned or controlled) are now grasping opportunities arising from deregulation and liberalisation of the ODI regime by extending their international reach. They continue to pursue strategies that fulfil certain national economic and political imperatives but other motivations are also now at work. In the 1990s, improvement to the supply of natural resources was an important driver of Chinese ODI and this continues to be the case. The development of overseas market opportunities also remains an important driver. However, firm strategy appears to be shifting away from merely support of the trade function and information gathering towards market-seeking FDI that is both defensive (i.e., to circumvent obstacles to trade with import-substituting and quota-hopping FDI or in response to competitive pressures and weak market access at home) or offensive (i.e., that seeks to improve foreign market access through the establishment of sales and manufacturing subsidiaries) in orientation. We also see Chinese enterprises attempting to raise their competitiveness by undertaking strategic asset seeking FDI. Often, but not always, this is achieved with the purchase of under-performing foreign firms. The objective is to acquire hard-to-replicate assets such as advanced technology and established foreign brands and to improve access to distribution channels and sources of foreign capital. For these reasons, manufacturing activity now takes a greater share of the sectoral distribution of Chinese FDI, and wholly-owned subsidiaries are now preferred to IJVs. These findings contrast with aspects of earlier work on Chinese MNEs (e.g., Taylor, 2002; Deng, 2003) and with the notion that developing country firms generally opt for the IJV entry mode because of the cost and risk-related advantages it brings, along with opportunities for learning from partners.

There is some evidence from our analysis, therefore, to suggest that Chinese MNEs can no longer be regarded as 'apprentices' on the international stage, investing primarily in the developed countries to obtain information and to support the export function, or to learn from joint venture partners. Rather, a small but growing number of Chinese MNEs are becoming truly 'transnational', acquiring not only the confidence but the knowledge, resources and capabilities needed to coordinate international activities and compete effectively for market share in both developed and developing countries. This gives rise to an 'emergent' strategic behaviour of Chinese MNEs (see Table 7.8) which

Table 7.8 Some emergent trends in approved outward Chinese FDI.

	Historic	Emergent
Government involvement	Hands on	Hands off
Geographic distribution	Concentrated in developed countries	Dispersed among developing countries
Sectoral distribution	Services-oriented	Manufacturing-oriented
Entry mode	Joint venture	Wholly-owned
Natural resource-seeking strategy	Raw materials extraction focussed in developed countries	Raw materials and commodities, distributed more widely
Market seeking-strategy	To support the export function	Defensive (import-substituting and quota-hopping FDI) and offensive (to develop new markets)
Strategic asset-seeking	To obtain information and foreign market knowledge	To obtain foreign technology and brands and to access foreign distribution channels and capital markets

Source: The authors.

we argue is increasingly superseding 'historic' behaviour under each of Dunning's internationalisation motives.

Acknowledgements

We would like to thank three anonymous referees and Joachin Wolf for their constructive comments and insights that have greatly improved this paper as well as for the helpful comments of Hafiz Mirza on an early draft.

Notes

1 We acknowledge, of course, inherent difficulties with generalising about a disparate collection of nations like the developing countries.
2 Formerly, the Ministry of Foreign Trade and Economic Cooperation (MOFTEC) and the Ministry of Foreign Economic Relations and Trade (MOFERT). For simplification, we refer only to MOFCOM in this paper. Also, SAFE has previously been the State Administration for Exchange

Control (SAEC) and the State General Administration for Exchange Control (SGEC).
3 Throughout this paper, the term outward direct investment (ODI) encompasses Chinese investment in minority-owned as well as majority and wholly-owned overseas affiliates.
4 On the other hand, upgrading developing country firms may also be able to leapfrog obsolescent technology and to adopt state-of-the-art production and product technology because of low sunk investment costs (Vernon-Wortzel and Wortzel, 1988).
5 Although the precise mechanisms for the promotion of Chinese ODI activity remain sketchy.
6 For example, the investment value ceiling has been raised to US$30mn from US$1mn for natural resources-oriented FDI and from US$1mn to US$3mn for non-resource and non-financial FDI for projects under the control of provincial authorities (Sauvant, 2005).
7 We owe these insights to a referee who we would like to thank for his help and useful comments.
8 In Box One, we outline a number of shortcomings inherent with data from MOFCOM and SAFE. In particular, the data are for *approved* outward FDI only (typically undertaken by SOEs and large private or quasi-private Chinese firms). This excludes direct investments made by those (typically private, small and medium sized) Chinese firms using 'informal' (and often illegal) routes to international expansion beyond the government approval process. In practice, MOFCOM and SAFE data probably undervalue China's outward FDI position, but to an indeterminate extent.
9 In order to better approximate the universe, future econometric work on Chinese ODI should ideally strive to incorporate estimates of 'round-tripped' FDI, although lack of suitable data inevitably makes this a difficult task.
10 Afghanistan (76 km of border with China), Bhutan (470 km) Burma (2,185 km), Hong Kong (30 km), India (3,380 km), Kazakhstan (1,533 km), North Korea (1,416 km), Kyrgyzstan (858 km), Laos (423 km), (Macau 0.34 km), Mongolia (4,673 km), Nepal (1,236 km), Pakistan (523 km), Russia (northeast) (3,605 km), Russia (northwest) (40 km), Tajikistan (414 km), Vietnam (1,281 km). Source: The CIA World Fact Book.
11 This is a contentious point, of course. The population of both the USA and Canada comprise a significant proportion of ethnically-Chinese people as does Australia, but to a lesser extent. It is likely that the presence of a large Chinese diaspora facilitates the internationalisation of Chinese firms, but in ways not well captured by models of inter-country psychic distance.
12 It is an open question whether or not the Uppsala model is relevant to the internationalisation of smaller SOEs and private firms in China which invest outside of the formal approval process (and whose activities are thus not captured by the data reported here).
13 To illustrate, *The Economist* estimates that 40% of global coal production and 30% of global steel production was consumed by China in 2003, while the British *Independent* newspaper of 7th Sept 2006 reported that 60% of African timber production is now consumed by China.

References

Aggarwal, R. and Agmon, T., The International Success of Developing Country Firms: Role of Government Directed Comparative Advantage, *Management International Review*, 30, 2, 1990, pp. 163–180.

Ahmed, Z.U., Mohamad, O., Tan, B. and Johnson, J.P., International Risk Perceptions and Mode of Entry: A Case Study of Malaysian Multinational Firms, *Journal of Business Research*, 55, 10, 2002, pp. 805–813.

Antkiewicz, A. and Whalley, J., Recent Chinese Buyout Activities and the Implications for Global Architecture, *National Bureau of Economic Research (NBER) Working Paper* 12072, Cambridge, MA: NBER 2006.

Brewer, P.A., Operationalizing Psychic Distance: A Revised Approach, *Journal of International Marketing*, 15, 1, 2006, pp. 44–66.

Buckley, P.J. and Casson, M.C., *The Future of the Multinational Enterprise*, London: Macmillan 1976.

Buckley, P.J., Clegg, L.J. and Wang, C., The Impact of Inward FDI on the Performance of Chinese Manufacturing Firms, *Journal of International Business Studies*, 33, 4, 2002, pp. 637–656.

Buckley, P.J., Clegg, L.J., Cross, A.R., Liu, X, Voss, H. and Zheng, P., The Determinants of Chinese Outward Foreign Direct Investment, *Journal of International Business Studies*, 38, 4, 2007, pp. 499–518.

Buckley, P.J., Clegg, L.J., Cross, A.R., Voss, H., Rhodes, M.J and Zheng, P., Explaining China's Outward FDI: An iInstitutional Perspective, in Sauvant, K. et al. (eds), *The Rise of TNCs from Emerging Markets: Threat or Opportunity*, Cheltenham: Edward Elgar (forthcoming 2008).

Branstetter, L. and Lardy, N. China's Embrace of Globalization, *NBER Working Paper* 12373, Cambridge, MA: NBER July 2006.

Chan, H.L., Chinese Investments in Hong Kong: Issues and Problems, *Asian Survey*, 35, 10, 1995, pp. 941–954.

Chow, I., Holbert, N., Kelley, L. and Yu, J., *Business Strategy: An Asia-Pacific Focus*, 2nd edition, Singapore: Pearson Education South Asia Pte Ltd 2004.

CNN, *Thomson, TCL Create TV-DVD Giant*, Monday, 3 November 2003, text retrieved on 25 February 2008 from edition.cnn.com/2003/BUSINESS/11/03/tcl.thomson.reut.

Deng, P., Foreign Investment by Multinationals from Emerging Countries: The Case of China, *Journal of Leadership and Organizational Studies*, 10, 2, 2003, pp. 113–124.

Ding, X.L., Informal Privatisation through Internationalisation: The Rise of Nomenklatura Capitalism in China's Offshore Business, *British Journal of Political Science*, 30, 1, 2000, pp. 121–146.

Dow, D. and Karunaratna, A., Developing a Multidimensional Instrument to Measure Psychic Distance Stimuli, *Journal of International Business Studies*, 37, 5, 2006, pp. 578–602.

Dunning, J.H., The Eclectic (OLI) Paradigm of International Production: Past, Present and Future, *International Journal of the Economics of Business*, 8, 2, 2001, pp. 173–190.

Dunning, J.H., Van Hosel, R. and Narula, R., Third World Multinationals Revisited: New Developments and Theoretical Implications, in Dunning, J.H.

(ed.), *Globalization, trade, and foreign direct investment*, Amsterdam and Oxford: Elsevier, 1997, pp. 255–285.

Dunning, J.H., *Multinational Enterprises and the Global Economy*, Wokingham: Addison Wesley 1993.

Economist, A Hungry Dragon: Does the World Have Enough Natural Resources for China to Keep Growing at Its Present Pace?, Vol. 372, No, 8395, 2 October, 2004, pp. 12–14.

Erdener, C. and Shapiro, D.M., The Internationalisation of Chinese Family Enterprises and Dunning's Eclectic MNE Paradigm, *Management and Organisation Review*, 1, 3, 2005, pp. 411–436.

Euh, Y. and Min, S.H., Foreign Direct Investment from Developing Countries: The Case of Korean Firms, *The Developing Economies*, 24, 1986, pp. 149–168.

Evan, P.C. and Downs, E.S., Untangling China's Quest for Oil through State-backed Financial Deals, *The Brookings Institution Policy Brief*, 154, May 2006.

Frost, S., Chinese Outward Investment in Southeast Asia: How big are the Flows and what does it mean for the Region?, *Pacific Review*, 17, 3, 2005, pp. 323–340.

Fung, K.C., Mainland Chinese Investment in Hong Kong: How much, why and so what?, *Journal of Asian Business*, 12, 2, 1996, pp. 21–39.

Hennart, J.F., A Transaction Cost Theory of Equity Joint Ventures, *Strategic Management Journal*, 9, 4, 1988, pp. 361–374.

Hymer, S.H., *The International Operations of National Firms: A Study of Direct Foreign Investment*, Ph.D. dissertation, MIT, 1960, Cambridge, MA: MIT Press, 1976.

Johanson, J. and Vahlne, J.-E., The Internationalisation Process of the Firm: A Model of Knowledge Development and Increasing Foreign Market Commitments, *Journal of International Business Studies*, 8, 1, 1977, pp. 23–32.

Khan, K.M., Multinationals from the South: Emergence, Patterns and Issues, in Khan, K.M. (ed.), *Multinationals from the South*, London: Pinter 1986, pp. 1–14.

Kumar, K. and Kim, K.Y., The Korean Manufacturing Multinationals, *Journal of International Business Studies*, 15, 1, 1984, pp. 45–60.

Lall, S., The Rise of Multinationals from the Third World, *Third World Quarterly*, 5, 3, 1983, pp. 618–626.

Lau, H., Industry Evolution and Internationalisation Processes of Firms from a Newly Industrialised Economy, *Journal of Business Research*, 56, 10, 2003, pp. 847–852.

Lecraw, D.J., Outward Direct Investment by Indonesian Firms: Motivation and Effects, *Journal of International Business Studies*, 24, 3, 1993, pp. 589–600.

Liu, H., *An Empirical Research and Comparative Study of Chinese Outward FDI*, in Chinese, Shanghai: Fudan University Press 2001.

Liu, H. and Li, K., Strategic Implications of Emerging Chinese Multinationals: The Haier Case Study, *European Management Journal*, 20, 6, 2002, pp. 699–706.

Lu, T., *The International Corporation of Chinese MNCs: An Empirical study on Chinese MNCs in UK*, in Chinese, Beijing: The People's Press 2002.

MOFCOM, *Almanac of China's Foreign Economic Relations and Trade 1991–2002*, Beijing various years.

MOFCOM, *2004 Statistical Bulletin of China's Outward Foreign Direct Investment (Non Finance Part)*, Beijing: MOFCOM and National Bureau of Statistics of the People's Republic of China, 2005.

MOFCOM, *China Yearbook of Commerce*, Beijing: MOFCOM 2004.
MOFCOM, UN official: China's overseas investment to reach 60 bln USD by 2010, 11 September 2006, text retrieved on 16 January 2008 from http://english.mofcom.gov.cn/aarticle/newsrelease/commonnews/200609/20060903116084.html.
MOFCOM, Address by Ma Xiuhong, Vice Minister of MOFCOM to the seminar 'China goes global', UK Parliament, 7 March 2007, text retrieved on 21 August 2007 from http://english/mofcom/gov.cn/aarticle.
Monkiewicz, J., Multinational Enterprises of Developing Countries: Some Emerging Trends, *Management International Review*, 26, 3, 1986, pp. 67–79.
National Bureau of Statistics, *China Statistical Yearbook*, Beijing: NBS 2006.
Nolan, P., *China and the Global Economy*, New York: Palgrave 2001.
Nolan, P. and Zhang, J., *The Challenge of Globalisation for Large Chinese Firms*, UNCTAD, Discussion Papers, No. 162, 2002.
Pan, E., China, Africa, and Oil, *Council on Foreign Relations*, 12 January 2006, text retrieved on 4 September 2006 from www.cfr.org/publication/9557.
Pang, E.F. and Komaran, R.V., Singapore Multinationals, *Columbia Journal of World Business*, 20, 2, 1985, pp. 35–43.
Sauvant, K., New Sources of FDI: the BRICs. Outward FDI from Brazil, Russia, India and China, *Journal of World Investment & Trade*, 6, 5, 2005, pp. 639–709.
Scott, W.R., The Changing World of Chinese Enterprises: An Institutional Perspective, in Tsui, A.S. and Lau, C.H. (eds), *Management of Enterprises in the People's Republic of China*, Boston: Kluwer Academic Press 2002, pp. 59–78.
Shi, J.Y., *On the Development of Chinese Companies in Hong Kong*, PhD Thesis in Chinese, Shanghai: Fudan University 2000.
Shiria, S., Banks' Lending Behaviour and Firms' Corporate Financing Patterns in People's Republic of China, *Asian Development Bank Institute Research Paper Series 43*, Tokyo: ADB 2002.
Sung, Y.W., Chinese Outward Investment in Hong Kong: Trends, Prospects and Policy Implications, *OECD Development Centre Technical Papers 113*, Paris: OECD.
Tallman, S.B. and Shenkar, O., A Managerial Decision Model of International Cooperative Venture Formation, *Journal of International Business Studies*, 25, 1, 1994, pp. 91–114.
Taylor, R. Globalization Strategies of Chinese Companies: Current Developments and Future Prospects, *Asian Business and Management*, 1, 2, 2002, pp. 209–225.
UN E-Brief, *China: An Emerging FDI Outward Investor*, New York: United Nations, 4 December 2003.
UNCTAD, *Sharing Asia's Dynamism: Asian Direct Investment in the European Union*, New York and Geneva: United Nations 1996.
UNCTAD, *World Investment Report 2002: Transnational Corporations and Export Competitiveness*, New York and Geneva: United Nations 2002.
UNCTAD, *World Investment Report 2003: FDI Policies for Development, National and International Perspectives*, New York and Geneva: United Nations 2003.
UNCTAD, *World Investment Report 2004: The Shift towards Services*, New York and Geneva: United Nations 2004.
UNCTAD, *Prospects for Foreign Direct Investment and the Strategies of Transnational Corporations, 2005–2008*, New York and Geneva: United Nations 2005.

UNCTAD, *World Investment Report 2006: FDI from Developing and Transition Economies: Implications for Development*, New York and Geneva: United Nations 2006.

Vernon-Wortzel, H. and Wortzel, L.H., Globalizing Strategies for Multinationals from Developing Countries, *Columbia Journal of World Business*, 23, 1, 1988, pp. 27–36.

Voss, H, *The Foreign Direct Investment Behaviour of Chinese Firms: Does the 'New Institutional Theory' Approach offer Explanatory Power?*, Unpublished doctoral thesis, University of Leeds.

Wall, D., Outflows of Capital from China, *OECD Development Centre Technical Paper No 123*, Paris: OECD 1997.

Wang, M.Y., The Motivations behind China's Government-initiated Industrial Investment Overseas, *Pacific Affairs*, 75, 2, 2002, pp. 187–206.

Warner, M., Hong, N.S. and Xu, X., Late Development' Experience and the Evolution of Transnational Firms in the People's Republic of China, *Asia Pacific Business Review*, 10, 3/4, 2004, pp. 324–345.

Wells, L.T. Jr, The Internationalisation of Firms from Developing Countries, in Agmon, T. and Kindleberger, C.P. (eds), *Multinationals from Small Countries*, Cambridge, MA: MIT Press 1977, pp. 133–156.

Wells, L.T. Jr., *Third World Multinationals – The Rise of Foreign Direct Investment from Developing Countries*, Cambridge, MA: MIT Press 1983.

Wortzel, H.V. and Wortzel, L.H., Globalizing strategies for multinationals from developing countries, *Columbia Journal of World Business*, 23, 1, 1988, pp. 27–35.

Yang, D., *China's Offshore Investment: A Network Approach*, Cheltenham: Edward Elgar 2005.

Ye, G., Chinese Transnational Corporations, *Transnational Corporations*, 1, 2, 1992, pp. 125–133.

Yeung, H.W., The Political Economy of Transnational Corporations: A Study of the Regionalization of Singaporean Firms, *Political Geography*, 17, 4, 1998, pp. 389–416.

Yeung, H.W., Transnational Corporations from Asian Developing Countries: Their Characteristics and Competitive Edge, *Journal of Asian Business*, 10, 4, 1994, pp. 17–58.

Zhan, J.X., Transnationalization and Outward Investment: The Case of Chinese Firms, *Transnational Corporations*, 4, 3, 1995, pp. 67–100.

Zhang, K., *Going global: the why, when, where and how of Chinese companies' outward investment intentions*, Asia Pacific Foundation of Canada, 2005.

Zhang, Y, *China's Emerging Global Businesses: Political Economy and Institutional Investigations*, Basingstoke: Palgrave 2003.

Zin, R.H.M., Malaysian Reverse Investment: Trends and Strategies, *Asian Pacific Journal of Management*, 16, 3, 1999, pp. 469–496.

Section III

Foreign Direct Investment in China

8
Cultural Awareness in Knowledge Transfer to China – The Role of *Guanxi* and *Mianzi*

Peter J. Buckley, Jeremy Clegg and Hui Tan

Introduction

Cultural awareness can be understood as the degree of knowledge about the way of thinking and behaving of people from a different culture. Different contexts in politics, economics, and society have shaped people's conceptions of culture in international management (Doktor, Tung and Von Glinow, 1991; Sackmann and Phillips, 2004). Difficulties often occur between managers and subordinates of the same multinational enterprise (MNE) who are from different cultures because of basic differences in how individuals respond to one another's behaviour (Shaw, 1990). This can be further complicated by the cultural diversities and organisational complexities outside the MNE in the host country, termed task environment by Thompson (1967). Foreign firms are often disadvantaged in comparison to host firms due to gaps in understanding the host culture (Calhoun, 2002). The handling of cultural diversities inside and outside the firm can affect technology transfer (Tung, 1994) and firm performance (Darby, 1995; Li and Karakowsky, 2002; Marcoulides and Heck, 1993). Indeed, the ability to manage cultural differences is seen as an example of a firm's sustainable competitive advantage (Oliver, 1997).

Knowledge transfer has been widely regarded as the key to subsidiary survival in foreign markets (Buckley, Clegg and Tan, 2004; Inkpen, 1995). Traditional research mainly focuses on the transfer of technology and management skills (Davidson and McFetridge, 1985; Grosse, 1996). Recently, an increasing number of studies have extended this research theme onto the transfer of social knowledge and organisational culture (Bhagat, Kedia, Harveston and Triandis, 2002). We argue that the transfer of corporate norms, routines and common understandings are pivotal to successful knowledge absorption and dissemination. Knowledge transfer has been an articulated target set by the Chinese government since the opening of its vast domestic market. Success in knowledge transfer and localisation depends on the business strategy of the foreign entrant and teamwork between foreign and local partners (Buckley, Clegg and Tan, 2003). As cultural differences directly impact on behavioral management practices in the process of knowledge transfer (Inkpen, 1995; Tung, 1994), MNEs have to grasp Chinese culture in order to improve their performance.

Whilst many studies have demonstrated the benefits of being culturally literate in complex or volatile institutional environments (Boyacigiller, Kleinberg, Phillips and Sackmann, 2004; Luo and Shenkar, 2002; Shenkar, 2004), the importance of cultural awareness in the process of knowledge transfer has not been fully examined (Bhagat *et al.*, 2002; Jackson, 2001; Ofori-Dankwa and Ricks, 2000). In particular, for MNEs, ways to improve cultural awareness in managing knowledge transfer is a challenge. In this paper, this issue is addressed based on the experiences of four foreign invested firms in China. Two key issues, *guanxi* and *mianzi*, are examined in the Chinese business environment. We develop an integrated view on the interaction between internal and external stakeholders and create a framework of cultural engagement for long-term successful performance. Using knowledge transfer as the centerpiece of the empirical work, we also examine the operationalisation of *guanxi* and *mianzi* in practice.

In the following sections, the relevant literature is reviewed to identify the gaps in respect of cultural awareness with special reference to knowledge transfer to China. In accordance with Yin (1994), who recommended that case studies should first identify theoretical framework or propositions, a theoretical model is derived to explain the management of cultural awareness in knowledge transfer to China. Next, a profile of the four foreign invested firms is presented and the research methods employed are introduced. Then, the empirical findings are discussed. Finally, the contribution of this research is evaluated and areas for future study suggested.

Literature review

Cultural characteristics in China

Culture is defined as shared norms, values and assumptions (Schein, 1996). There is a large body of literature on Chinese culture (e.g., Lovett, Simmons and Kali, 1999; Luo, 1997; Tsang, 1998; Vanhonacker, 2004;

Xin and Pearce, 1996). Chinese culture is considered to be different from that of the West in many ways (Chen and Francesco, 2000; Child and Lu, 1996; Tung, 1986). Characteristics of Chinese culture, such as family orientation, *guanxi*, relational interdependence, face, favour and harmony are found to have an influence on MNE's relationship cultivation strategies (Hung, 2004; Paik and Tung, 1999).

Guanxi (personal connections) and *mianzi* (face) are the most prominent cultural characteristics that have strong implications for interpersonal and inter-organisational dynamics (e.g., Child and Lu, 1996; Tung and Worm, 2001; Xin and Pearce, 1996; Yeung and Tung, 1996). *Guanxi* is an inseparable part of the Chinese business environment. It is a fundamental web of interpersonal relations permeating Chinese societies. *Guanxi*-based business practices can reduce uncertainty, lower search and other transaction costs, provide usable resources and a sense of connectedness (Wellman, Chen and Dong, 2002). For foreign investors, *guanxi* relationships provide informal ways to reduce environmental uncertainty and opportunistic behavior (Standifird and Marshall, 2000). Foreign entrants should mount sustained efforts to build up *guanxi* to give them a competitive edge in their search for an insider position in the China business arena. *Guanxi* can be a negative asset, however, if not well managed within and between foreign and local firms (Vanhonacker, 2004). While it is vital to adopt the *guanxi* approach in their relationships with Chinese partners, foreign investors should be aware that *guanxi* alone cannot eliminate threats and competition (Fock and Woo, 1998).

Mianzi is an equally important concept in Chinese culture. It is defined as the recognition by others of an individual's social standing and position (Lockett, 1988). In Chinese culture, it is not only important to maintain good relationships but also vital to protect a person's *mianzi* or dignity and prestige. The need for *mianzi* is intrinsic to various aspects of personal and interpersonal relationship development in China. Saving *mianzi* is a shortcut by Chinese to build their network and tapping into other's social resources. Thus, *mianzi* is a key component in the dynamics of *guanxi* (Sherriff, Lorna and Stephen, 1999). Saving *mianzi* has to go hand in hand with nurturing *guanxi*. They operate on a reciprocal basis, i.e., all parties of a business relationship must show respect to, and save *mianzi* for, each other.

National culture can influence the development of trust (Doney, Cannon and Mullen, 1998; Schoorman, Mayer and Davis, 1996). In the context of China, developing *guanxi* and saving *mianzi* create trust between partners (Luo, Shenkar and Nyaw, 2002; Xin and Pearce,

1996). Due to uncertainties in the business environment and possible opportunistic behaviors of partners, trust is regarded as one of the most important managerial issues of the corporate agenda (Buckley and Casson, 1988; Inkpen and Currall, 1998; Lui and Ngo, 2004). Ellis (1996) suggests that building trust between partners in strategic alliances is one of the critical components for the long-term success of the relationship. The potential benefits of trust include reliable and open information exchange, improved coordination and less bureaucratic cost of unified governance (Ebers, 1997). Although *guanxi* is often said to be the source of sustained competitive advantage for foreign companies doing business in China (Tsang, 1998), trust has to be nurtured and maintained to reduce risks and afford better business control in unstable environmental conditions (Xin and Pearce, 1996).

Cultural awareness between partners

Harrigan (1985) argued that international alliances fail because operating managers did not make them work, not because contracts were poorly written. Tung (1994, p. 821) also found that 'a major cause for expatriate failure is the lack of human relational skills'. Based on an extensive case study of Shanghai Volkswagen and Beijing Jeep, Hoon-Halbauer (1999) examined the complex relationships between parents, between headquarters and the joint ventures and between foreign and local staff. Cultural differences are identified as one of the main roots for the complexity and conflicts of the relationships. Kogut and Singh (1988) and Brannen and Salk (2000) argued that national culture can influence the behavior of managers and contribute to potential conflicts between partners. Partners also have to consider the existence of subcultures in the same firm, based on which informal networks develop (Sackmann, 1992). Informal networks can be a base of power in parallel to formal organisational structure (Krackhardt, 1990). Thus, misunderstandings often happen between partners due to a lack of culture awareness (Inkpen and Currall, 1998). Indeed, the existence of different national cultures and subcultures (Caulkins, 2004) in organisations can have a positive or negative impact on firm performance. For example, as long as perceptions of goal congruence are maintained, local culture will contribute to improvement in organisational integration and firm performance (Fischer, Ferreira, Assmar, Redford and Harb, 2005; Wilkins and Ouchi, 1983).

Prior relationships between partners appear to negate some complexities arising from cultural differences (Park and Ungson, 1997). Partly, this can be attributed to the establishment of trust. Trust can lower transaction costs, facilitate inter-organisational relationships, and enhance manager–subordinate relationships. The establishment of trust is a potent force in overcoming the otherwise adverse reactions that employees may exhibit in reaction to decisions yielding unfavorable outcomes (Brockner et al., 1997).

In the context of China, the establishment of a positive inter-partner working relationship is critical to the venture's operation. This inter-partner relationship refers to the quality of co-operation and trust between the partners while co-managing the joint venture (JV) (Yan and Gray, 1996). As Chinese culture is heavily influenced by Taoist principles, *guanxi* and *mianzi* are regarded to have their Yin and Yang (Durlabhji, 2004). Eagerness, aggressiveness and outcome orientation (Yang) must be balanced by long-termness, coordination and people orientation (Yin) in the process of trust building. Otherwise, either side of a relationship can be responsible for trust destruction. In extreme cases, those ruthlessly pursuing their goals without regard to what others think can be accused of being 'thick face' and 'black heart' (Chu, 1992; Pheng, 1997). Foreign investors have to engage with the Chinese business environment by embracing *guanxi* and *mianzi* to establish and enhance inter-partner relationships based on trust (Luo et al., 2002), but ways to improve cultural awareness in order to facilitate knowledge transfer have not been researched.

The role of the party and the government in China

The Chinese government has long played two incompatible roles in its economy: an industry regulatory role and an ownership role in SOEs (Buckley, Clegg and Tan, 2005). Since China's transition from a central command system to a market economy, the Chinese government began to reduce its role in running business entities. The Chinese government still influences the decision making process of SOEs through its control of key resources and its power to appoint and dismiss managers (Groves, Hong, McMillan and Naughton, 1995; Martinsons, 1999). Even though less intense than previously, 'State paternalism remains a dominant feature of China's business environment' (Child and Tse, 2001, p. 17). Moreover, it retains powers to change the rules of the business system and to differentiate its policies towards firms of different categories (Child and Tse, 2001). This is exemplified in Sino-foreign joint ventures. Aiello (1991) examined the relationship between foreign and local partners of Beijing Jeep and the role of government in the control and operations of this firm. It highlights the weakness of the joint venture relationship and the rigidity of host government control.

A key problem is that both central and local governments perform regulatory and participating roles that are not always consistent with each other (Walder, 1995). Foreign investors therefore need to maintain communications with different levels of government to be well informed of the changing rules and policies. Given China's lengthy history of bureaucratic control, foreign firms have to be aware of the rules governing the interaction between foreign invested firms and the government. Foreign managers need to 'recognise systemic and/or cultural factors in their [Chinese] environment that cannot be overtly challenged' (Roehrig, 1994, p. 12). Typical Confucian values, such as respect for age and hierarchy, avoidance of conflict and the need for harmony, and protection of *mianzi* (Fang, 1999), must be taken as central to managing interactions with local and central governments. As policy outcomes and regulatory process are largely determined at local levels through bargaining between foreign investors and local government authorities (Roehrig, 1994), foreign managers may find it in their own interest to cultivate their enterprise's personal relationship with relevant Chinese officials to create a facilitating environment and to obtain an optimal result from bargaining.

Knowledge transfer to China

The bulk of the literature on knowledge transfer is focused on developed countries. Comparable levels of economic development between developed countries mean that the research is largely based on studies of knowledge transfer within organisations. In the transition economies, researchers must grapple with knowledge transfer within a setting where institutional and cultural factors play an important role in deciding corporate performance (Luo, 2002). The existing literature therefore does not relate well to knowledge transfers to transition economies that are at a lower stage of development coupled with diverse cultural and institutional differences. Among the existing studies, Tung (1994) established that societal culture was the most important determinant of success in technology transfer from industrialised to developing countries. Fabry and Zeghni (2003) argued that knowledge transfer to transition economies involved extensive cross-cultural adaptation to promote organisational learning and develop specific relationships within affiliates. However, how to manage cross-cultural adaptation has not been properly examined. In particular, little is known about the effectiveness of cross-border transfer of organisational knowledge involving dissimilar cultural contexts (Bhagat et al., 2002).

China has been the research subject in knowledge transfer in a number of studies (e.g., Buckley *et al.*, 2003; Osterloh and Frey, 2000; Si and Bruton, 1999; Tsang, 1999). Tsang (1999) argued that FDI represented the transfer of a firm's physical and organisational technologies from the home country to another country. Foreign affiliates in China are expected to undertake efficient organisational learning based on a good understanding of the manner and mindset of the local partners. Marcotte and Niosi (2000) found that tacit knowledge constitutes a substantial part of the total knowledge transferred by Canadian firms to China. The nonexplicit nature of knowledge leaves room for numerous problems of interpretation, not only at the technical and managerial level, but also at the more global level of national culture and institutions. An equity JV is the vehicle of choice for firms seeking transfer of tacit, embedded knowledge (Shenkar and Li, 1999). Overcoming cultural constraints and nurturing a sound partner relationship is vital for success of knowledge transfer (Si and Bruton, 1999). Similarly, Buckley *et al.* (2003) found that while technologies were ranked highly in knowledge seeking by local partners, knowledge of a tacit nature was more important in making the transferred technologies work efficiently. A lack of understanding of the task environment, including the surrounding society's values and mindsets, contributed to lower performance in knowledge transfer and localisation (Allaire, 1984). Clearly, it is well recognised that some types of knowledge are more difficult to transfer between firms because they are more deeply embedded, and highly dependent on broader contextual factors to operate effectively. Given the diversity and complexity of the Chinese business environment, even for explicit knowledge to be transferred and absorbed, cultural barriers have to be removed and good inter-partner relationships have to be established. Strategies to achieve this goal in the knowledge transfer process remain unexplored. We tackle this weakness in the literature by examining four cases of knowledge transfer to China.

Managing cultural awareness in China: a proposed model

Figure 8.1 represents our attempt to integrate existing literature on managing cultural awareness into a model. Previous literature has emphasised *guanxi* and to a much lesser extent, *mianzi*, as means of managing in China. Some of this literature has concentrated on relationships with external bodies and local JV partners. Other parts of it have emphasised relationships with central and local governments. A final strand concerns the management of employees. Our contribution

```
┌─────────────────────┐
│ Managing Cultural   │
│ Awareness in China  │
└──────────┬──────────┘
           │
           ▼
┌─────────────────────┐
│  Guanxi (Mianzi)    │
└──────────┬──────────┘
     ┌─────┼─────┐
     ▼     ▼     ▼
┌─────────┐ ┌──────────────┐ ┌──────────────────────────┐
│Employees│ │Local Partners│ │Central and Local Governments│
└─────────┘ └──────────────┘ └──────────────────────────┘
```

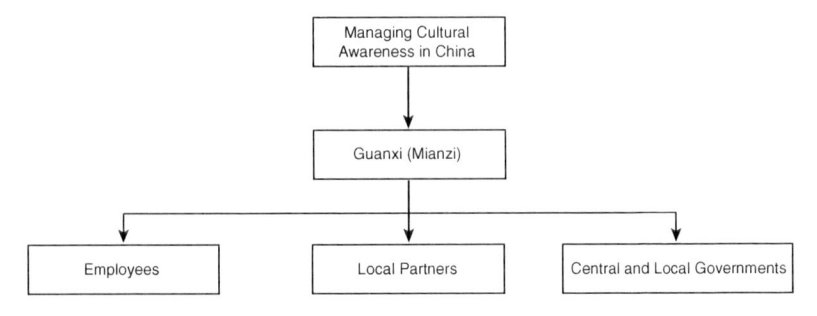

Figure 8.1 An integrated model of received thinking on managing cultural awareness in China.

is to place these literatures together in an integrated model and to go on to confront this model with empirical evidence and to refine it.

Research method

This paper is exploratory and seeks to fill an identified gap in the literature. It employs a multiple-case design (Yin, 1994) with research questions centered on the 'how' and 'why' of knowledge transfer in the emerging market of China. This approach enables us to generate new theoretical concepts grounded in case and cross-case analysis (Herriott and Firestone, 1983; Wright, 2004).

Data collection

In identifying potential research candidates, MNEs that had been operating in China for a period of at least five years were chosen (Inkpen, 1995, p. 129). Thirty-nine companies met the criteria, roughly half in each of the two industries, were contacted in order to seek permission for interviews. Twelve firms responded positively which enabled the pilot fieldwork to be conducted. As a result, four firms were identified for further research (see Table 8.1 for a profile of the four firms). As final assemblers, these firms engaged in greater knowledge transfer than the other firms. Two rounds of both open-ended and semi-structured in-depth interviews were conducted using multiple interviewees in each company. The interviewees were senior executives, including those responsible for functional units such as business planning, marketing, finance, production and human resources. Some of the top managers experienced the whole process of negotiation on establishing the foreign invested firms and attended numerous discussions on

Table 8.1 Profile of the four case companies.

Company	Year of establishment	Equity structure	Core business	Location of HQ
Shanghai Bell	1984	Belgian Bell (32%), Belgian government (8%) and Chinese government (60%). Since 2001, Alcatel 50% +1 and Chinese government 50% –1	Initially telephone exchanges only. Lately fixed and mobile networking, broadband access, intelligent optical networking etc.	Shanghai
Motorola (China)	1992	Wholly owned by Motorola	Cellular phones, network equipment, semiconductor, auto electronics and accessories	Regional HQ in Beijing but main manufacturing base in Tianjin
Beijing Jeep	1983	Beijing Automotive Works (68.85%) and American Motor Corporation (31.15%), which was acquired first by Renault Group and then by Chrysler Motor Corporation (now DaimlerChrysler Group)	Off-road vehicle production	Beijing
Shanghai VW	1984	Volkswagen AG of Germany (50%), Shanghai Automotive Industry Corporation (25%), Bank of China Shanghai Trust and Consultancy Company (15%) and China National Automotive Industry Corporation (10%)	Car production	Shanghai

facilitating knowledge transfer and localisation. The majority of the senior executives had at least ten years' employment in their respective firms, and participated in the process of knowledge transfer. Members of the knowledge transfer team, such as the training manager, operational manager, project engineer and other technical professionals, were also interviewed. As the interviewees consisted of both foreign expatriates and Chinese, the English version of the questionnaire was carefully translated into Chinese. Back translation, as suggested by Brislin (1970), was carried out to verify the content consistency between the two versions of the questionnaire.

Data coding

Interview data and field notes were coded using content analysis procedures (Lincoln and Guba, 1985; Strauss, 1987). This involved coding data into categories in line with the context of foreign cultural interaction with the host environment. These categories comprised the milestones of these companies, main technologies transferred, cultural interaction with employees, local partners, other local firms, and central and local governments. These data were then structured to address the research issues identified (Yin, 1994), including *guanxi, mianzi*, trust and other cultural characters exhibited. Emerging themes were further pursued to extract leads for understanding of managing cultural awareness in the four case companies (Figure 8.2).

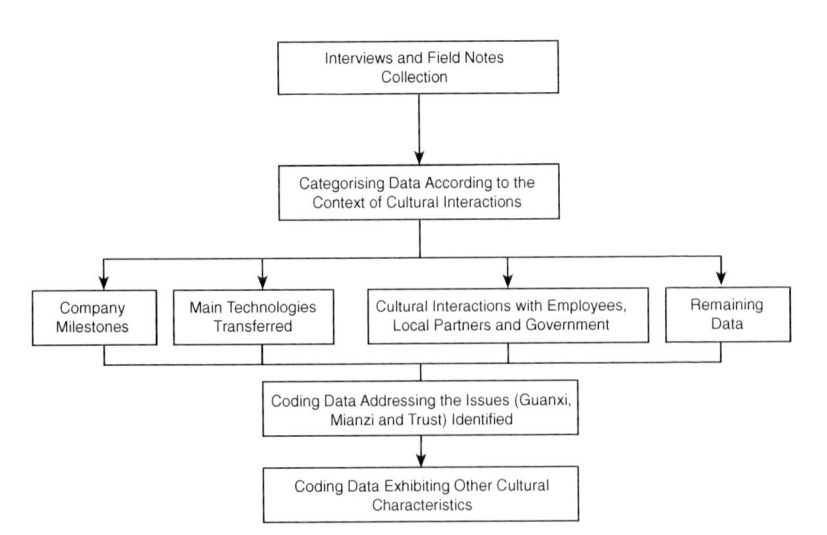

Figure 8.2 Coding data based on the context of managing cultural awareness.

Data analysis

Data analysis in this research followed closely the procedures set for interpreting qualitative data (Easterby-Smith, Thorpe and Lowe, 1991; Strauss, 1987) in general, and those for case study methodology (Yin, 1994) in particular. The interviews were analyzed to focus on the cultural dimensions in knowledge transfer. Using a 'within-case' analysis, theory was first developed by examining the context of cultural interactions in one case. Then, pattern matching (Miles and Huberman, 1984; Yin, 1994) was adopted to compare the finding from this first case with the other three. Cross referencing between interviews, and between primary data and secondary data, were carried out to establish connections among factors and further verify the validity of these data by triangulation. This constituted an emergent process in constructing grounded interpretations of the collected data (Glaser and Strauss, 1967) and elicited implications on issues relevant to the topic under research based on 'analytical generalisation' (Yin, 1994). Case write-ups were made available for circulation among leading participants to verify overall accuracy.

Findings

Our interview data suggest that the four foreign invested firms transferred knowledge to China through an episodic process of learning and utilisation. Many factors contributed to achieving better performance in this process, including culture awareness, shared mindsets, government support and long-term vision.

Cultural awareness

Cultural awareness includes the understanding of both traditional Chinese culture and the behavior of Chinese people, and more importantly, China's political system. *Guanxi* and *mianzi* are regarded as the core of Chinese culture (Child and Lu, 1996). The effective development and use of *guanxi* and respect of *mianzi* is seen as a requirement for the successful establishment of new business ventures and for the effective day-to-day management of Chinese enterprises. Alcatel Bell agreed to establish Shanghai Bell with the then Ministry of Post and Telecommunications (hereafter the 'Ministry', which was replaced by Ministry of Information Industry in 2003), though the official Chinese parent of this JV is the Post and Telecommunications Industry Corporation of China (PTIC) which was under control of the Ministry. This was a wise move for Alcatel Bell because it could guarantee the proper implementation of the JV contract and elicit substantial government support. Alcatel Bell's expatriates were also quick to realise the importance of maintaining '*guanxi*' with their Chinese partners. One piece of evidence is their understanding and cooperation in receiving hundreds of visitors annually ranging from Shanghai Bell, Shanghai Bell's suppliers and customers (i.e., local bureaus of post and telecommunications), the Ministry and other governmental officials, to Belgium in the name of inspecting new products or for attending short 'training courses'. As there was hardly any need for them to go to Belgium from a technical point of view, these sightseeing-natured visits were used as a way of rewarding employees by the Chinese partner. It was of great benefit to Alcatel Bell's *guanxi* building when judging it from a business point of view. Culturally, it was prestigious to visit the West at the invitation of a high-profile international firm which could give *mianzi* to these officials and their respective employers. Receiving these numerous Chinese delegations greatly enhanced Alcatel Bell's *guanxi*.

The other three firms also manifested a similar quality of being culturally aware in the Chinese market. For example, Motorola sent in an American Chinese as the first general manager of its China operation. It also adopted a fast track management localisation plan, put housing allocation at the core of its employee benefit system (which did not exist in any other subsidiary of the firm), and donated scholarships and financial resources to various educational establishment. Chrysler also developed a sense of cultural awareness through its interaction with Chinese partners. It transferred the then most advanced model into the JV in a response to the plea of Chinese partners, therefore giving *mianzi* to the majority local partner. This was highly appreciated by the local Chinese partners and *guanxi* between them improved significantly. While conflicts and mistrust between foreign and local employees existed due to fundamental cultural differences (Hoon-Halbauer, 1999), VW did manage to show considerable cultural awareness in its dealing with the Chinese government. It enlisted the support of the German government in persuading the Chinese government to agree to the establishment of a JV with a 50:50 equity structure in 1984; the highest equity stake up to this date. This was bolstered by a large German government grant towards training local Chinese employees. The firm was an active sponsor of major sports events, of educational institutions, and of various projects for helping the poor in inland areas of China. This was intended to establish itself as a responsible corporate citizen. Shanghai VW was the largest business project between China and Germany, receiving unparalleled attention and support from both governments – indicated by numerous personal visits of national signatories from each side. This is an excellent example of promoting *guanxi* between the two partners of the JV through the governments of the two countries. This string of facts indicates that cultural awareness should be a key component of the business strategy of MNEs entering the Chinese market.

Trust

Trust between partners is the foundation of cooperation. It comprises technical trust and personal trust (Chang and Rosenzweig, 1995). In the case of Shanghai Bell, the Belgian partner moved from suspicion to full confidence in the technical capability of their Chinese counterpart.

> The Chinese engineers in Shanghai Bell are first class. They are not inferior to any engineers in the West.
>
> (Belgian senior manager)

Due to technical capabilities of the Chinese engineers, they participated in the refining and modification of the transferred product from Alcatel Bell in accordance with Chinese circumstances. A R&D center owned by Shanghai Bell was also set up in Belgium, just neighboring Alcatel Bell. It worked on projects subcontracted by Alcatel Bell. This subsidiary also served as a product design department for Shanghai Bell.

Similar examples were available in the other three firms, e.g., the increasing contribution of Chinese engineers in Beijing Jeep in the assimilation and modification of the off-road range from Chrysler, the establishment and further expansion of R&D centers in China by both Motorola and VW. The four firms regarded highly the technical capability of Chinese engineers they employed. This reflected the great improvement in Chinese higher education since the end of the 1970s.

Personal trust was also engineered at different levels in the affiliate firm, especially among managers and engineers. Management localisation programs in Motorola and other three JVs were clear evidence of the confidence held by foreign investors in their Chinese colleagues. This was a result of numerous meetings and consultations in the process of knowledge transfer. Personal trust can also be established from a situation where equal power sharing made personal trust essential to keep the company functioning. In Shanghai VW, where the equity was shared equally by the Chinese and the German partners, each of the four members of Shanghai VW's executive committee had the power to handicap the operation of the whole company by vetoing any proposed motions. Therefore, compromises based on mutual trust and saving *mianzi* were the way to achieve the overall goals of the firm. This confirms Casson's (1991) argument that the ambiguity of control created by a certain type of ownership structure can be used to engineer trust. Even if the foreign partner's equity holding was less than 50%, it could impose far greater bargaining power in negotiation due to its advantageous position deriving from proprietary assets. The foreign partner could exercise influence by withholding knowledge transfer, changing technical criteria and withdrawing expatriates, for instance. The Chinese partner with majority control, in each case, had to make compromises in exchange for the continuous support of the foreign counterpart in providing proprietary assets. Therefore, the non-equity bargaining power enjoyed by foreign partners in the JVs made trust a more important factor in attaining efficiency of knowledge transfer and utilisation. Trust has thus extended from personal trust between foreign and local managers to inter-organisational trust between foreign and local partners.

Shared mindsets

Shared mindsets indicate that partners of a JV have a common understanding on aspects concerning the development of the firm. It is gained not only in the course of negotiation in the JV, but also after facing challenges arising from internal operational problems. Lack of a shared mindset can derail the undertaking of the agreed knowledge transfer program, pushing the whole business into crisis. This was vividly illustrated in the case of Beijing Jeep's foreign exchange shortage during 1986–1987. This incident arose from a lack of foreign exchange in the JV to pay for imported components from the foreign parent, which lead to misunderstanding and mistrust between foreign and local partners. Chrysler later refrained from sending back all its profits to its headquarters for a few years in order to help find some time in solving this issue. The Chinese side also realised the importance of communication with the foreign partner. As a result, mutual trust was created based on a shared mindset for making this JV a competitive operator in the Chinese market.

> The whole-hearted support and active participation of the American side has been the cornerstone of the success of Beijing Jeep's localization. They have been very supportive and considerate in each

stage of localization, i.e. transfer and assimilation of technology, ordering and testing of the imported equipment, quality control, upgrading and renovating of certain parts of the design and production, and so on. Members of Chrysler's transfer team have been frequent visitors to Beijing Jeep, but all of their travel cost has been paid by the American side ... They have worked very hard with us in making this joint venture competitive in a short period, which directly served their motive of entering China and the Far Eastern market.

(Senior manager, Beijing Jeep)

In Shanghai Bell, however, Belgian managers showed great flexibility and understanding from the very beginning. The marketing performance of Shanghai Bell was in a poor state in the middle of the 1980s due to cost and technical problems. Belgian managers did everything they could to push the business back on track based on their own expertise in technology and management. At the same time, they sought the sympathy and support from the host government which subsequently decided to subsidise products from Shanghai Bell. This experience, which resulted in greater cooperation to solve the problem, enabled the two sides to work together even more harmoniously since then. Similar evidence can be found in Shanghai VW where both sides shared a belief in making the Santana the best car in the Chinese market. They negotiated on the scale and speed of technology transfer and argued on the issue of quality control. However, these were conducted based on mutual trust and understanding. Shanghai VW has maintained its role of China's largest car manufacturer since its inception.

A shared mindset was also important in a wholly-owned subsidiary, but it was demonstrated in a different way. Owing to the sole control of the parent, there was an internal process in working out differences between headquarters and Chinese subsidiaries. For example, business strategies were drawn first by its China headquarters in Beijing and then revised and added to by its headquarters in the USA. Therefore, they were a product of internal coordination through constant communications. Both headquarters and local subsidiary contributed to the formation of Motorola's strategies in China.

In sum, a shared mindset is a key aspect contributing to the success of foreign invested firms in China. In essence, a shared mindset is trust between foreign and local firms. This can be achieved through active *guanxi* building and respect of the *mianzi* of each side. In this sense, relationships between firms in China can be nurtured by following the same cultural doctrines as at personal level.

Government support

Government support can decide the success of foreign invested firms in China. It proved to be the lifeblood of Shanghai Bell in the early years of operation when the firm struggled for survival and to maintain on-going knowledge transfer. This is also a factor in the recent development of Shanghai Bell. To date, Chinese governmental agencies are still the primary purchasers of Shanghai Bell's products.

> Government support is very, very important. Without government support from both countries, we can do nothing. That is partly the reason why Alcatel Bell preferred to hold minority equity in Shanghai Bell – in this way the Belgian side could get concrete local [Chinese] government support. As this project was listed as one of the key national projects, it has always enjoyed the endorsement of the Chinese government. The Ministry of Post & Telecommunications even set up a special Bureau, called System 1240 Bureau, for the development of this project ...
>
> (Senior manager, Alcatel Bell)

Government support received by Shanghai Bell from the Belgian government mainly comprised interest free loans, free training programs (technical and management) for Chinese engineers and managers, and inter-governmental co-ordination. Issues like technology transfer licenses governed by relevant European dual use agreements, which the firm could do nothing about, are examples of inter-governmental co-ordination.

Government support was cited as the chief external factor affecting knowledge transfer and utilisation in the other three firms. Unlike Shanghai Bell where both central and local governments were direct stakeholders, local governments played a key role in the establishment of these firms. Due to the size and importance of these firms, the local governments (Shanghai, Beijing and Tianjin) regarded the development of Shanghai VW, Beijing Jeep and Motorola (China), respectively, as the locomotive of local economic development. Projects to upgrade and expand these firms were made priorities of the cities, sometimes named as 'No. 1 project' in various years. Local governments in these cities also encouraged the formation of localisation communities, members of which can get access to special government funding, technical assistance and tax relief, to speed up assimilation and upgrading of the transferred products. Government procurement of their products was sometimes guaranteed for certain period. Government support of this nature ensured the allocation of much needed resources to these firms, the opening of local markets to their products and, most importantly, the provision of a high status.

> We enjoyed some special treatment from government, such as exempt of tax for the first two years and half tax rate for the following three years, special access in using foreign exchange which was very important at the beginning of this joint venture.
> (Senior manager, Shanghai VW)

To date, Chinese government support has been selective but nevertheless powerful when FDI falls into the designated priority categories of the host local governments. The importance of government support indicates that foreign investors must pay particular attention to macro-environmental factors when doing business in China (Yip, 1995).

To seek government support, foreign invested firms should endeavor to set up personal relationships with government officials and offer legitimate support to give *mianzi* to government. Relationship building with the government in China is essentially a two-way process based on effective communications. Examples of this are Shanghai Bell's technical and management training for local firms, and its repeated donations to charitable causes such as Project Hope, Shanghai VW's technical assistance to other state-owned enterprises in the automotive industry at the request of government, Beijing Jeep's donation of its products to the Beijing Municipal Government and the Military, and Motorola (China)'s free training and seminars for governmental officials of the Ministry of Post and Telecommunications. In fact, the relationship with government was so important that each of the four firms set up a department named 'Government Relations' in its China headquarters specially mandated to deal with various government organisations. Former government officials or relatives of current officials were recruited to ensure access to key government officials so that an active communication channel could be maintained. Visits by CEOs of foreign parents to China were always an opportunity to promote good relationships with the government. Therefore, high profile meetings with top government officials (such as vice premier or at least ministers) were seen as a must. Commitments from both sides regarding ambitious new investment plans and further government support were declared after meetings of this kind. These meetings, as well as other similar occasions, were often used by foreign investors to lobby the government.

As a result of these efforts, these firms were successful in creating a favorable task environment for doing business, a strengthened capability for localisation and a growing customer base in their respective markets. Good *guanxi* with the government in China also means creating a favorable operating environment by avoiding excessive government inference. This supports the argument made by Roehrig (1994). It is an important strategy for foreign invested firms to elicit favorable implementation of laws, rules, regulations, and policies from local authorities and to establish good, personal relationships with strategically-located individuals in business, government, and bureaucracy. This is because they may be able to influence the outcomes of possible future questions and disputes in favor of the enterprise.

Long-term vision

All the firms showed a common characteristic – long-term vision – in dealing with the challenges and problems in the process of knowledge transfer. For example, one senior manager of Shanghai VW repeatedly emphasised the following point.

> Our strategy is to seek long-term engagement with the Chinese market. We want to stay here long and grow along with the market expansion. Even though there may be numerous problems emerging every day, we are confident about the long-term prospect, at least not less than our Chinese partner. This has shaped our business strategy and even our mentality.

Evidence of long-term vision includes the gradual increase of the foreign equity holding in Beijing Jeep and Shanghai Bell and the reinvestment of all the profits into production and training in the initial period of their developments. Alcatel increased its equity holding from 32% to 50% plus one extra voting stock, making Shanghai Bell a majority owned subsidiary. Likewise, Chrysler increased its equity in Beijing Jeep from 31% to 42.5%. All the four firms invested new capital and reinvested earnings over several years into production expansion, demonstrating their long-term interest in the Chinese market. For example, Motorola (China) had not only invested US$ 1.2 billion of new capital in China and reinvested all its profits from its Chinese operations back into the country, but also invested an additional US$ 1.3 billion by the end of 2000. When asked about the secret of Motorola's successful operation in China, one senior manager commented very briefly, in four words: heart, mutual trust and patience.

Long-term vision may not be a characteristic enjoyed by every foreign investor, but it is a prerequisite for success in dealing with the Chinese market. This is partly due to the complications of the Chinese market where foreign investors have to learn to manage. It is also rooted in the Chinese culture which appreciates long-term engagement so that people can cultivate mutual understanding and nurture trust. This again reflects the importance of *guanxi* building in the Chinese context which has been observed at personal and inter-organisational levels and with government.

Discussion

Extension of guanxi, mianzi and trust to corporate and governmental relationships

Guanxi and *mianzi* are predominant cultural characteristics associated with inter-personal relationships in China. The experiences of the four firms indicate that these cultural characteristics are extended into relationships between business partners and with the government. From face-to-face negotiations to maintenance of the commercial relationship, foreign investors interact with the Chinese environment through people. It is therefore important to establish *guanxi* and give *mianzi* on reciprocal basis when dealing with Chinese, be they employees, managers of related firms or government officials. This will lead to the establishment of trust which can save transaction cost and reduce uncertainty (Park and Harrison, 1993). The purpose of relationship building with the Chinese environment is to nurture trust. This cannot be achieved in a short period. Instead, it is a result of long-term engagement through 'local networking' (Luo et al., 2002). Alcatel Bell's courting of Chinese partners by receiving large number of visitors, Motorola and VW's extensive training cooperation with government, and Chrysler's transfer of latest technology are examples of relationship cultivation. Relationship building with business and government in China based on *guanxi* and *mianzi* can enhance foreign investors' chance of constructing a favorable environment and strengthen their bargaining position in dealing with the government. They can also influence the decision making in government through active lobbying. In fact, the four firms all received government support of various kinds in their post-entry development as a result of their *guanxi* building.

Managing cultural awareness in China: refining the model

Based on our analysis of the four case firms, the initial model can be improved by integrating the key dimensions of relationship building in the Chinese context. It is clear that foreign investors should recognise the key role played by *guanxi* and *mianzi* in Chinese culture and seek to establish a trust-based relationship when interacting with the host environment. At the personal level, foreign investors need to establish personal as well as technical trust in Chinese employees based on active communications and respect of *mianzi*. Likewise, at the corporate level, *guanxi* building and respect of *mianzi* should be applied to seek shared mindsets, an equivalent of trust between partners. Foreign investors should also treat government as an important partner instead of a rival when operating in China. Active communication channels should be set up between foreign invested firm and government based on personal *guanxi* and personal trust. Foreign investors can use this channel to inform and lobby government. They also need to behave as a corporate citizen through subscription to various social and charitable programs supported by government. In essence, foreign investors have given government *mianzi* in participating in these activities. The purpose of this engagement is to construct an enabling environment and to seek government support. The latter can often decide the

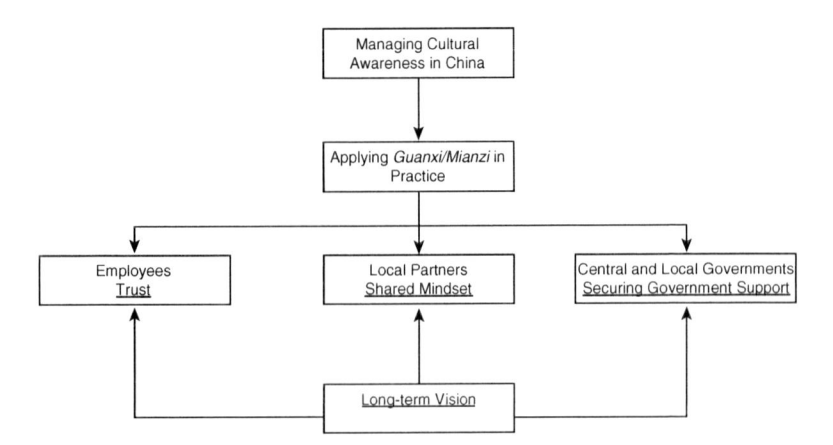

Figure 8.3 A refined model of managing cultural awareness in knowledge transfer to China.

outcome of foreign operations in China. Finally, Chinese culture appreciates trust but only when nurtured through long-term engagement. Foreign firms thus need to design their business and knowledge transfer strategies with a long-term vision (see Figure 8.3).

Conclusions

Previous studies on doing business in China examined the complexity of relationships within joint ventures and with government and cultural differences were identified as an important issue (e.g., Aiello, 1991; Hoon-Halbauer, 1999). None of them offered guidance on how to adopt the concept of cultural awareness in daily business operations. This paper examined the most prominent Chinese cultural elements, *guanxi* and *mianzi*. It contributes to knowledge by presenting an integrated approach to the handling of relationships with employees, business partners and government based on *guanxi* and *mianzi* in the context of China. Our findings suggested that foreign investors must be aware of *guanxi* and *mianzi* of the institutions they dealt with and better establish institutional connections based on personal connections with local partners and government. Foreign investors can use this channel of communications to inform and lobby local and central governments. Trust lies at the heart of the interactions between foreign investors and local stakeholders including employees, local partners and government. Shared mindset and government support can only be secured when there is trust between the parties. Therefore, the essence of relationship building and managing cultural awareness is to establish trust. This has to be achieved by long-term engagement in the context of China.

Based on our case evidence, the model of managing cultural awareness in China at three levels is proposed and refined: personal, inter-partner and with government. This model establishes the central role of trust in relationship building in China. It becomes more dynamic after integrating the long-term view in engaging the Chinese market. This is a new contribution to doing business in China.

This paper has implications for research into FDI located in transitional economies. First, cultural awareness is an issue worthy of representation in firm's business strategy. It can affect knowledge transfer and firm performance (Darby, 1995). Foreign investors need to take a comprehensive view in dealing with stakeholders in the host country based on understanding of local culture. Second, trust is at the core of relationship building at personal, corporate and governmental levels. It is more difficult to establish trust with local partners and government due to differences in business orientations and organisational culture. Cultural literacy and a long-term commitment can help in securing trust between organisations. Last, government is not always a restrictive force. If a close relationship can be set up based on personal trust and respect of *mianzi*, government support can be sought and its policy making influenced. This will create an enabling institutional environment for foreign investors.

Given the similarity of the institutional environment in other transitional markets, future research could explore ways of managing cultural awareness in these countries. In the context of China, more research is needed to look at how firms turn the bad *guanxi* to good and how to handle situations where good *guanxi* turns bad. This applies to relationships between joint venture partners and with government. As a result of the rapid changes and developments since China's accession into the World Trade Organisation, further research should also look at the changing Chinese culture as a whole: Is it leaning towards individualism? If so, what is the impact on managing cultural difference in this country? This research is limited by its small number of case companies. Surveys based on large sample investigation should be adopted to test the validity of the cultural awareness model proposed in this paper.

Acknowledgements

The authors would like to thank Professor Rosalie Tung and the referees for their constructive comments. Financial support from the Universities' China Committee in London (UCCL) and the Sino-British Fellowship Trust for conducting interviews in China is gratefully acknowledged.

References

Aiello, P. (1991) Building a joint venture in China: The case of Chrysler and the Beijing Jeep Corporation. *Journal of General Management*, 17(2): 47–64.
Allaire, Y. (1984) Theories of organizational culture. *Organization Studies*, 5(3): 193–226.
Bhagat, R.S., Kedia, B.L., Harveston, P.D. and Triandis, H.C. (2002) Cultural variations in the cross-border transfer of organizational knowledge: An integrative framework. *Academy of Management Review*, 27(2): 204–221.
Boyacigiller, N.A., Kleinberg, J., Phillips, M.E. and Sackmann, S.A. (2004) Conceptualizing culture: Elucidating the streams of research in international cross-cultural management. In B.J. Punnett and O. Shenkar (eds), *Handbook*

for International Management Research (pp. 99–167). Ann Arbor: The University of Michigan Press.

Brannen, M.Y. and Salk, J.E. (2000) Partnering across borders: Negotiating organizational culture in a German–Japanese joint venture. *Human Relations*, 53(4): 451–487.

Brislin, R. (1970) Back-translation for cross-cultural research. *Journal of Cross-Cultural Psychology*, 75: 3–9.

Brockner, J., Siegel, P.A., Daly, J.P., Tyler, T. and Martin, C. (1997) When trust matters: The moderating effect of outcome favourability. *Administrative Science Quarterly*, 42(3): 558–583.

Buckley, P.J. and Casson, M.C. (1988) A theory of co-operation in international business. In F.J. Contractor and P. Lorange (eds), *Cooperative Strategies in International Business*. Lexington, MA: Lexington Books.

Buckley, P.J., Clegg, J. and Tan, H. (2003) The art of knowledge transfer: Secondary and reverse transfer in China's telecommunications manufacturing industry. *Management International Review*, 43(2): 67–93.

Buckley, P.J., Clegg, J. and Tan, H. (2004) Knowledge transfer to China: Policy lessons from foreign invested firms. *Transnational Corporations*, 13(1): 31–72.

Buckley, P.J., Clegg, J. and Tan, H. (2005) Reform and restructuring in a Chinese state-owned enterprise: Sinotrans in the 1990s. *Management International Review*, 45(2): 147–172.

Calhoun, M.A. (2002) Unpacking liability of foreignness: Identifying culturally driven external and internal sources of liability for the foreign subsidiary. *Journal of International Management*, 8(3): 301–321.

Casson, M.C. (1991) *The Economics of Business Culture*. Oxford: Clarendon Press.

Caulkins, D. (2004) Identifying culture as a threshold of shared knowledge: A consensus analysis method. *International Journal of Cross Cultural Management*, 4(3): 317–333.

Chang, S.J. and Rosenzweig, P.M. (1995) *A Process Model of MNC Evolution: The Case of Sony Corporation in the United States* (Carnegie Bosch Institute Working Paper 95–9). Carnegie Mellon University, the United States.

Chen, Z.X. and Francesco, A.M. (2000) Employee demography, organizational commitment, and turnover intentions in China: Do cultural differences matter? *Human Relations*, 53(6): 869–887.

Child, J. and Lu, Y. (1996) Introduction: China and international enterprise. In J. Child and L. Yuan (eds), *Management Issues in China: International Enterprises*. London: Routledge.

Child, J. and Tse, D.K. (2001) China's transition and its implications for international business. *Journal of International Business Studies*, 32(1): 5–21.

Chu, C.N. (1992) *Thick Face Black Heart*. Or. AMC Publishing.

Darby, R. (1995) Developing the Euro-manager: Managing in a multicultural environment. *European Business Review*, 95(1): 13–16.

Davidson, W.H. and McFetridge, D. (1985) Key characteristics in the choice of international technology transfer mode. *Journal of International Business Studies*, 16(2): 5–21.

Doktor, R., Tung, R.L. and Von Glinow, M.A. (1991) Incorporating international dimensions in management theory building. *Academy of Management Review*, 16(2): 259–261.

Doney, P.M., Cannon, J.P. and Mullen, M.R. (1998) Understanding the influence of national culture on the development of trust. *Academy of Management Review*, 23(3): 601–620.

Durlabhji, S. (2004) The Tao of organization behavior. *Journal of Business Ethics*, 52: 401–409.

Easterby-Smith, M., Thorpe, R. and Lowe, A. (1991) *Management Research: An Introduction*. London: Sage Publication Ltd.

Ebers, M. (1997) *The Formation of Inter-organizational Networks*. Oxford: Oxford University Press.

Ellis, C. (1996) Making strategic alliances succeed, the importance of trust. *Harvard Business Review*, 8–9.

Fabry, N.H. and Zeghni, S.H. (2003) FDI in CEECs: How do Western investors survive? *Thunderbird International Business Review*, 45(2): 133–147.

Fang, T. (1999) *Chinese Business Negotiating Style*. London: Sage Publications.

Fischer, R., Ferreira, M.C., Assmar, E., Redford, P. and Harb, C. (2005) Organizational behaviour across cultures: Theoretical and methodological issues for developing multi-level frameworks involving culture. *International Journal of Cross Cultural Management*, 5(1): 27–48.

Fock, H.K.Y. and Woo, K. (1998) The China market: Strategic implications of guanxi. *Business Strategy Review*, 9(3): 33–43.

Glaser, B.G. and Strauss, A.L. (1967) *The Discovery of Grounded Theory: Strategies for Qualitative Research*. London: Weidenfeld and Nicolson.

Grosse, R. (1996) International technology transfer in services. *Journal of International Business Studies*, 27(4): 781–800.

Groves, T., Hong, Y., McMillan, J. and Naughton, B. (1995) China's evolving managerial labor market. *Journal of Political Economy*, 103: 873–892.

Harrigan, K.R. (1985) *Strategies for Joint Ventures*. Lexington, MA: Lexington Books.

Herriott, R.E. and Firestone, W.A. (1983) Multisite qualitative policy research: Optimizing description and generalizability. *Educational Researcher*, 12: 14–19.

Hoon-Halbauer, S.K. (1999) Managing relationships within Sino-foreign joint ventures. *Journal of World Business*, 34(4): 344–371.

Hung, C.F. (2004) Cultural influence on relationship cultivation strategies: Multinational companies in China. *Journal of Communication Management*, 8(3): 264–281.

Inkpen, A.C. (1995) *The Management of International Joint Ventures: An Organizational Learning Perspective*. London: Sage.

Inkpen, A.C. and Currall, S.C. (1998) The nature, antecedents, and consequences of joint venture trust. *Journal of International Management*, 4(1): 1–20.

Jackson, T. (2001). Cultural values and management ethics: A 10-nation study. *Human Relations*, 54(10): 1267–1302.

Kogut, B. and Singh, H. (1988) The effect of national culture on the choice of entry mode. *Journal of International Business Studies*, 19(3): 87–98.

Krackhardt, D. (1990) Assessing the political landscape: Structure, cognition, and power in organizations. *Administrative Science Quarterly*, 35(2): 342–369.

Li, J. and Karakowsky, L. (2002) East meets East and East meets West: The case of Sino-Japanese and Sino-West joint ventures in China. *Journal of Management Studies*, 39: 841–863.

Lincoln, Y.S. and Guba, E.G. (1985) *Naturalistic Inquiry*. London: Sage.

Lockett, M. (1988) Culture and the problems of Chinese management. *Organization Studies*, 9(4): 475–496.
Lovett, S., Simmons, L.C. and Kali, R. (1999) Guanxi versus the market: Ethics and efficiency. *Journal of International Business Studies*, 30(2): 231–247.
Lui, S.S. and Ngo, H. (2004) The role of trust and contractual safeguards on cooperation in non-equity alliance. *Journal of Management*, 30(4): 471–485.
Luo, Y. (1997) Guanxi: Principles, philosophies, and implications. *Human Systems Management*, 16(1): 43–51.
Luo, Y. (2002) Capability exploitation and building in a foreign market: Implications for multinational enterprises. *Organization Science*, 13(1): 48–63.
Luo, Y., Shenkar, O. and Nyaw, M. (2002) Mitigating liabilities of foreignness: Defensive versus offensive approaches. *Journal of International Management*, 8(3): 283–300.
Luo, Y. and Shenkar, O. (2002) An empirical inquiry of negotiation effects in cross-cultural joint ventures. *Journal of International Management*, 8(2): 141–162.
Marcotte, C. and Niosi, J. (2000) Technology transfer to China: The issues of knowledge and learning. *Journal of Technology Transfer*, 25(1): 43–57.
Marcoulides, G.A. and Heck, R.H. (1993) Organizational culture and performance: Proposing and testing a model. *Organization Science*, 4(2): 209–225.
Martinsons, M.G. (1999) Management in China after two decades of an open door policy. *Journal of Applied Management Studies*, 8(1): 119–126.
Miles, M.B. and Huberman, A.M. (1984) *Qualitative Data Analysis: A Sourcebook of New Methods*. London: Sage.
Ofori-Dankwa, J. and Ricks, D.A. (2000) Research emphases on cultural differences and/or similarities: Are we asking the right questions. *Journal of International Management*, 6(2): 173–186.
Oliver, C. (1997) Sustainable competitive advantage: Combining institutional and resource-based views. *Strategic Management Journal*, 18(9): 697–713.
Osterloh, M. and Frey, B.S. (2000) Motivation, knowledge transfer, and organizational forms. *Organization Science*, 11(5): 538–550.
Paik, Y.S. and Tung, R.L. (1999) Negotiating with East Asians: How to attain 'Win-Win' outcomes. *Management International Review*, 39(2): 103–122.
Park, H. and Harrison, J.K. (1993) Enhancing managerial cross-cultural awareness and sensitivity: Transactional analysis revisited. *Journal of Management Development*, 12(3): 20–29.
Park, S.H. and Ungson, G.R. (1997) The effect of national culture, organizational complementarity, and economic motivation on joint venture dissolution. *Academy of Management Journal*, 40(2): 279–307.
Pheng, L.S. (1997) Thick face, black heart and the marketing of construction services in China. *Marketing Intelligence & Planning*, 15(5): 221–226.
Roehrig, M.F. (1994) *Foreign Joint Ventures in Contemporary China*. New York: St Martin's Press.
Sackmann, S.A. (1992) Culture and subcultures: An analysis of organizational knowledge. *Administrative Science Quarterly*, 37(1): 140–161.
Sackmann, S.A. and Phillips, M.E. (2004) Contextual influences on culture research: Shifting assumptions for new workplace realities. *International Journal of Cross Cultural Management*, 4(3): 370–390.

Schein, E.H. (1996) Culture: The missing concept in organization studies. *Administrative Science Quarterly, 41*(2): 229–240.

Schoorman, F.D., Mayer, R.C. and Davis, J.H. (1996) Social influence, social interaction, and social psychology in the study of trust. *Academy of Management Review, 21*(2): 337–339.

Shaw, J.B. (1990) A cognitive categorization model for the study of intercultural management. *Academy of Management Review, 15*(4): 626–645.

Shenkar, O. (2004) Cultural distance revisited: Toward a more rigorous conceptualization and measurement of cultural differences. In B.J. Punnett and O. Shenkar (eds), *Handbook for International Management Research* (pp. 168–188). Ann Arbor: The University of Michigan Press.

Shenkar, O. and Li, J. (1999) Knowledge search in international cooperative ventures. *Organization Science, 10*(2): 134–143.

Sherriff, T.K., Lorna, F. and Stephen, C.Y. (1999) Managing direct selling activities in China – A cultural explanation. *Journal of Business Research, 45*(3): 257–266.

Si, S.X. and Bruton, G.D. (1999) Knowledge transfer in international joint ventures in transitional economies: The China experience. *Academy of Management Executive, 13*(1): 83–90.

Standifird, S.S. and Marshall, R.S. (2000) The transaction cost advantage of guanxi-based business practices. *Journal of World Business, 35*(1): 21–42.

Strauss, A. (1987) *Qualitative Analysis for Social Scientists.* New York: Cambridge University Press.

Thompson, J.D. (1967) *Organizations in Action.* New York: McGraw-Hill Book Company.

Tsang, E.W.K. (1998) Can guanxi be a source of sustained competitive advantage for doing business in China. *Academy of Management Executive, 12*(2): 64–73.

Tsang, E.W.K. (1999) Internationalization as a learning process: Singapore MNCs in China. *Academy of Management Executive, 13*(1): 91–101.

Tung, R.L. (1986) Corporate executives and their families in China: The need for cross-cultural understanding in business. *Columbia Journal of World Business, 21*(1): 21–26.

Tung, R.L. (1994) Human resource issues and technology transfer. *International Journal of Human Resource Management, 5*(4): 804–821.

Tung, R.L. and Worm, V. (2001) Network capitalism: The role of human resources in penetrating the China Market. *International Journal of Human Resource Management, 12*(4): 517–534.

Vanhonacker, W.R. (2004) When good guanxi turns bad. *Harvard Business Review, 82*(4): 18–20.

Walder, A. (1995) Local governments as industrial firms: An organizational analysis of China's transitional economy. *American Journal of Sociology, 101*: 263–301.

Wellman, B., Chen, W. and Dong, W. (2002) Networking guanxi. In T. Gold, D. Guthrie and D. Wank (eds), *Social Connections in China: Institutions, Culture, and the Changing Nature of Guanxi.* Cambridge: Cambridge University Press.

Wilkins, A.L. and Ouchi, W.G. (1983) Efficient cultures: Exploring the relationship between culture and organizational performance. *Administrative Science Quarterly, 28*(3): 468–481.

Wright, L.L. (2004) The need for international qualitative research. In B.J. Punnett and O. Shenkar (eds), *Handbook for International Management Research* (pp. 49–67). Ann Arbor: The University of Michigan Press.

Xin, K.R. and Pearce, J.L. (1996) Guanxi: Connections as substitutes for formal institutional support. *Academy of Management Journal, 39*: 1641–1658.

Yan, A. and Gray, B. (1996) Linking management control and interpartner relationships with performance in US-Chinese joint ventures. In J. Child and L. Yuan (eds), *Management Issues in China; International enterprises*. London: Routledge.

Yeung, I.Y.M. and Tung, R.L. (1996) Achieving business success in Confucian societies: The impact of Guanxi connections. *Organizational Dynamics, 24*(3): 54–65.

Yin, R.K. (1994) *Case Study Research: Design and Methods* (2nd ed.). London: Sage.

Yip, L. (1995). The emergence of a retail market in China. In H. Davies (ed.), *China Business: Context and Issues*. Hong Kong: Longman Asia Ltd.

9
Is the Relationship between Inward FDI and Spillover Effects Linear? An Empirical Examination of the Case of China

Peter J. Buckley, Jeremy Clegg and Chengqi Wang

Introduction

This paper finds evidence for the coexistence within Chinese manufacturing industry of both curvilinear and linear relationships between inward foreign direct investment (FDI) and the productivity of locally owned enterprises (LOEs). This complexity of spillover effects challenges the *laissez-faire* view that all inward FDI into all types of domestic industry is equally valuable in terms of productivity spillover benefits. Our findings suggest that inward FDI into China leads either to spillovers that decline beyond a critical point, or to effects that continue linearly, depending on the ownership of foreign investors and the technological characteristics of the industry concerned. Our analysis yields original insights into the complex pattern of spillover effects from FDI into China, and deeper understanding of its possible causes.

The issue of multinational enterprises' (MNEs) impact on host-country LOEs through productivity spillovers has generated considerable controversy in the existing literature. While a good number of empirical studies exist, little has been yielded by way of conclusive results on the subject. Görg and Strobl (2001) sought an explanation for the lack of congruent findings, believing that inconsistent results might be associated with underlying differences between the datasets employed.[1] We contend, however, that there are important weaknesses in the theoretical conceptualisation of the nature of the relationship between inward FDI and spillovers. The key to improved understanding is to explore the different types of relationship that can occur simultaneously and how spillover effects might vary with the nationality of foreign investors and host industry characteristics.

A drawback of the existing literature, with a few notable exceptions, is that it has largely been confined to examining linear relationships between foreign presence and LOEs' productivity. Furthermore, these studies are based on the assumption that investments from all countries are homogeneous. This paper specifically addresses the possibility that both positive and negative effects arise from the operations of MNEs of different home country origins, and that these together might lead to non-monotonicity in spillover benefits. The data employed are Chinese data for manufacturing industry for the year 1995.

Literature review

Spillover effects from inward FDI are usually evaluated as the influence of the presence of foreign-owned enterprises (FOEs) on the productivity of LOEs. According to Caves (1974), the beneficial effects of FOEs can be categorised in terms of allocative efficiency, technical efficiency and technology transfer. Allocative efficiency gains are thought to arise from pro-competitive effects.[2] Technical efficiency improvements spring from the demonstration of superior practices by FOEs. With technology transfer, the presence of FOEs furnishes local firms with access to advanced technology on favourable terms (Feinberg and Majumdar, 2001). It has generally been assumed that each of these theoretical effects is linear and positive, largely because this is the expectation for FDI between developed countries – where the host industry structure is typically technologically advanced.

A limited number of studies have considered how the relationship between foreign presence and spillover benefits might change as inward FDI rises. All suggest that the benefits come early. Perez (1997) argues that a moderate foreign presence is sufficient to generate positive spillovers, even when there is a relatively wide technological gap between the foreign and locally owned industry; advanced technology in just a few foreign affiliates is sufficient to stimulate acquisition by local firms, while foreign skills and managerial practices may also be effectively transferred, for example, via original equipment manufacturing (Hsu and Chen, 2000). The mere existence of new entry into host markets provides enough incentive for allocative efficiency gains, while technical efficiency benefits from demonstration effects require only modest foreign investment (Haddad and Harrison, 1993).

Since Caves' (1974) influential work on spillovers in Canadian and Australian manufacturing, an extensive empirical literature has emerged, bearing mixed results. Overall, the evidence for a positive relationship dominates. The greatest number of enquiries finds evidence that FDI enhances LOEs' productivity (Caves, 1974; Globerman, 1979; Liu *et al.*, 2000, Zhu and Tan, 2000). Others report negligible or inconclusive effects (e.g., Haddad and Harrison, 1993). Fewer and more recent studies find negative spillover effects on the performance of LOEs (Singh, 1992; Aitken and Harrison, 1999; Konings, 2000; Buckley *et al.*, 2002). In defence of these conflicting findings, differences between data sets and periods of measurement have been widely invoked (e.g., Görg and Strobl, 2001).

The pattern of results suggests that the assumption, going back to Caves (1974), that there is a universal positive and monotonic relationship between the level of foreign presence and local productivity underestimates the complexity of spillover effects. We argue that the dearth of conclusive findings is a strong indication that divergent spillover impacts coexist within data sets. In particular, existing studies test neither for the links between the impact of spillovers and the country of origin of the foreign investor, nor whether these links are influenced by the industry characteristics in the host country. Yet these are key dimensions in the theory of the MNE (Buckley and Casson, 1976; Dunning, 1977, 1993), which remains highly relevant to investigating spillovers.

A central plank of international business theory is that ownership advantages and the motivations for FDI vary with the nationality of the investor. MNEs with different ownership advantages, linked to country of origin, invest abroad in different industries and locations (Dunning, 1988, pp. 53–57), so producing distinctive patterns of FDI. In similar vein, Lecraw (1993) argues that the rationale and behaviour of FDI are likely to be heterogeneous across source countries because the correspondence between home and host market structures varies with investors' geographic origin. Yet the spillovers literature has ignored this reasoning. In the case of China, although certain studies (e.g., Shi, 2001) have identified the incentives for investment by MNEs with diverse technological characteristics, research has not attempted to investigate the link between differences in ownership advantages and the industry and impact of FDI on LOEs. Empirical analysis of FDI spillovers has therefore remained a context-specific issue. This is a weakness that may produce seemingly contradictory findings.

Two groups of FOEs dominate the foreign-owned sector of Chinese manufacturing industry. These are FOEs owned by overseas Chinese firms, notably from Hong Kong, Macau and Taiwan (hereafter HMT), and FOEs from all other countries (hereafter OTHER), dominated by the USA, EU and Japan. We can consider ownership advantages to fall into two main categories: technological, or knowledge-based, advantages for the production of differentiated products; and non-technological advantages, such as organisational and marketing skills suitable for standardised goods. The typically small HMT firms do not own 'strategic assets in terms of physical resources' (Kay, 1993, p. 64); what they do possess is ownership advantages in the application of standardised and mature technologies, referred to as 'appropriate technology' (Lee and Plummer, 1992; Davis, 1996) that suit labour-abundant locations (Shi, 1998). In contrast, MNEs in the OTHER group epitomise the standard qualities identified by Caves (1974). It is generally held that OTHER MNEs employ state-of-the-art technology from heavy investment in R&D to produce innovative and differentiated products.

It is reasonable to expect that these different ownership advantages will exhibit contrasting profiles in terms of spillover effects.[3] FOEs are able to compete at low marginal cost through access to their parents' ownership advantages (Aitken and Harrison, 1999), but only weak spillover benefits are envisaged from the mature or non-technological ownership advantages of HMT firms. Moreover, negative competition impacts are likely from market stealing in standardised final goods markets (in which FOEs and LOEs compete head-on in the same segments of saturated markets), or from crowding-out in factor markets. Harrison (1996) has also pointed out that market stealing by foreign investors impedes LOEs' ability to attain scale economies. This reasoning suggests that, in sectors where HMT capital is prevalent, there will be limited scope for positive spillovers, while negative effects will intensify with rising foreign presence, causing net (observed) spillover benefits to either stagnate or decline, that is, to be non-monotonic. For MNEs in the OTHER group, we should expect a linear positive relationship between foreign presence and spillovers, in line with Caves' (1974) analysis.[4]

Furthermore, in Chinese industry we would expect greater negative competition effects on LOEs' productivity from HMT firms, because of the dominance of state-owned enterprises (SOEs). State-owned firms face barriers in shedding capacity and to exit. The result is that it is not the most efficient firms that survive in such industries, leading to the persistence of depressed productivity in the locally owned sector. Declining LOE productivity is likely to accelerate with foreign presence, as SOEs are driven back up their average cost curves.

Our analysis of the literature suggests that FDI-productivity spillover benefits are the outcome of positive and potential negative effects.

Table 9.1 Interactions between positive and negative spillovers.

	Secondary effect		
	Positive	Negative	Zero
Primary effect			
Positive	1. Increasing at an increasing rate	2. Increasing at a decreasing rate	3. Increasing
Negative	4. Decreasing at an increasing rate	5. Decreasing at a decreasing rate	6. Decreasing

However, empirical work has looked only for positive or negative effects, not a combination of both, and, as a consequence, has been restricted to enquiring after a linear form in the spillover benefit relationship. In fact a family of possible combinations of primary and secondary spillover effects can be posited, and it is important to give due consideration to the possibilities in justifying a non-linear functional form, as shown in Table 9.1.[5]

In principle, the primary spillover effects of FDI may be either positive or negative, as in Table 9.1; the typical approach of studies of FDI spillovers is to look only for these primary effects. Theory suggests that all MNEs transfer ownership advantages of some description. There-fore there is a general expectation in the literature (e.g., Caves, 1974), which is borne out in empirical work (e.g., Globerman, 1979; Liu *et al.*, 2000), that the primary effects of foreign presence are positive. In circumstances where there is inward FDI with a lower technological contribution (and so little technology capable of dissemination), coupled with direct competition with domestically owned firms, foreign penetration is more likely to generate market stealing and crowding out, and so secondary effects of a negative sign. Accordingly, of cells 2, 4 and 6, we expect cell 2 to apply to HMT firms. This is on the basis that cell 4 would require that HMT firms transferred no ownership advantages but generated an accelerating negative competitive effect. Further, for cell 6 to apply, it would be necessary that HMT firms transferred little ownership advantages, while generating a linear negative competitive effect. Both cells 4 and 6 imply that LOEs are competed away by HMT firms, a scenario that is not borne out by a reality. As positive primary spillovers are anticipated from HMT firms' ownership advantages, coexisting with increasing negative competitive effects, cell 2 applies.

The prior arguments predict a linear relationship between the presence of OTHER firms and spillover benefits to LOEs. The manner in which secondary effects interact with primary effects produces a complex relationship between foreign presence and the level of spillover benefits, creating monotonicity. The higher technological complement of OTHER firms' ownership advantages is expected to produce greater technological spillover benefits, therefore strengthening the competitive power of LOEs. This argues in favour of cell 3 and against cell 1, and also against cell 5, as OTHER firms transfer a substantial technological component.

Our discussion suggests the following two hypotheses:

Hypothesis 1: The relationship between the presence of HMT firms and LOEs' productivity is curvilinear: specifically, beyond some level of foreign presence productivity spillovers begin to fall.

Hypothesis 2: The relationship between the presence of OTHER firms and LOEs' productivity is linear (and positive).

The contrasting types of ownership advantages of HMT and OTHER firms map directly to host industry characteristics, namely low- and high-technology sectors in Chinese industry, respectively. For HMT FDI, the low-technology nature of the host industry is thought to exacerbate the severity of the negative competitive impact. Under such conditions, the growth of negative spillover effects can rapidly become dominant when foreign presence increases beyond some level. In contrast, OTHER firms are more likely to produce differentiated products for the premium market segments of low-technology sectors. This would mean that the presence of OTHER MNEs is able to exert a moderate pro-competitive and demonstration effect towards LOEs.

The discussion of Table 9.1 in connection with H1 also applies *a fortiori* to H3, which refers specifically to low-technology industries. Similarly, our discussion of the table with respect to H2 applies especially strongly to H4, which also focuses on low-technology industries.

Hypothesis 3: The relationship between the presence of HMT firms and LOEs' productivity is curvilinear in low-technology industries: specifically, beyond some level of foreign presence productivity spillovers begin to fall.

Hypothesis 4: The relationship between the presence of OTHER firms and LOEs' productivity is linear (and positive) in low-technology industries.

We argue that, although HMT firms are on the whole characteristically low technology, nevertheless some of them operate in technology intensive industries, and therefore are similar to their Western counterparts. Therefore in high-technology sectors we expect the spillover effects grow linearly with the presence of HMT firms. Similarly, the ownership advantages of OTHER firms in high-technology sectors lead us to expect dominant positive spillover effects that raise LOEs' productivity, according to the theoretically positive arguments first put forward by Caves (1974) and reiterated by Feinberg and Majumdar (2001), as above.

We have already argued that for OTHER firms a linear and positive relationship should apply, on the grounds that these firms are characteristically technology intensive. By direct analogy, HMT firms that operate in high-technology industries are no different from their OTHER counterparts. Therefore only cell 3 will apply both to H5, for HMT firms, and to H6, for OTHER firms.

Hypothesis 5: The relationship between the presence of HMT firms and LOEs' productivity is linear (and positive) in high-technology industries.

Hypothesis 6: The relationship between the presence of OTHER firms and LOEs' productivity is linear (and positive) in high-technology industries.

Methodology

Following Kokko (1992) and Buckley *et al.* (2002), we assume that labour productivity of LOEs (Y), measured as value-added per worker, is a function of foreign presence (FP). Unlike previous studies where FP is typically measured at the aggregate level as the overall foreign capital share in each industry, this study disaggregates overall foreign presence into two separate measures according to the country of origin of the investors: the capital share accounted for by HMT MNEs in each industry (FP_{hmt}) and the capital share accounted for by OTHER MNEs in each industry (FP_{other}).

Our multivariate analysis includes a set of relevant control variables for Chinese LOEs that may influence labour productivity: capital intensity (*KL*), the capital labour ratio; R&D intensity (*RI*), R&D expenditure per employee; labour quality (*LQ*), the share of college graduates in total employment, which reflects human capital; and firm size (*FS*), the value of assets per firm, to capture firm size effects (Liu, 1999; Luo, 1997, 1998).

In investigating the impact of foreign presence, we should expect differences between industries with regard to the pace with which inward investment has taken place.[6] For instance, in certain industries, the rate of FDI has been constrained by government policy (i.e., restricted to some extent). In other industries FDI has been encouraged, completely without restriction. This has implications for the ability of LOEs to adjust to the entry of foreign MNEs. In liberalised industries this ability may be lower, as inward FDI is unfettered. To capture this we introduce *D*, a dummy variable, which takes a value of 1 in sectors where inward investment is encouraged by government policy, and zero otherwise (MOFTEC, 1996).[7] These control variables increase our confidence in the robustness of the findings, through adjusting for influences other than foreign presence.

The literature review suggests that we should investigate the expected non-monotonic nature of spillover effects using a curvilinear (inverted U-shape) form. Within this category, the quadratic is a function capable of capturing all the effects expected on the basis of our review, and is selected as follows:

$$Y_i = \alpha_0 + \alpha_1 (KL)_i + \alpha_2 (RI)_i + \alpha_3 (LQ)_i + \alpha_4 (FS)_i \\ + \alpha_5 (FP_{hmt})_i + \alpha_6 (FP_{hmt})_i^2 + \alpha_7 (FP_{other})_i \\ + \alpha_8 (FP_{other})_i^2 + \alpha_9 D_i + \varepsilon \qquad (1)$$

Model (1) is a single comprehensive model, and it has the following two advantages over the conventional approach, such as Liu *et al.* (2000). First, since two separate and disaggregated measures of foreign presence are employed in the same equation, the model allows for possible differential effects between the nationalities of investors. Second, the inclusion of squared terms for the foreign presence variables enables us to examine the possibility of curvilinear effects. Indeed, since a linear specification is nested in the full model, we can test for the linear as against the curvilinear specification and formally determine the better one.

Ordinary least squares (OLS) regression is employed throughout. Given that small, medium and large-sized firms or industrial branches are sampled together in our cross-sectional data set, heteroskedasticity is expected to be widespread, and this was confirmed in pre-testing. Consequently, all variance-covariance matrixes have been estimated according to White's (1980) method. In testing for curvilinearity as against linearity in the relationship between foreign presence and productivity, an *F*-test is employed to comparatively evaluate Eq. (1) with, and without, the squared terms as a restricted version of the model.

Our enquiry is based on industry-level data from the Third Industrial Census of the People's Republic of China, published by the State Statistical Bureau of China (SSB) in 1997. The Census reports data for 1995 on a cross-section of branches of Chinese industry, and is the latest and most comprehensive industrial survey published to date. There are 191 sectors in the Census (19 mining, 165 manufacturing, 7 public utilities). Because of missing data, our study includes 130 sectors.

Empirical results

Table 9.2 displays the correlation matrix and descriptive statistics for the independent variables. Of the correlations between the independent variables just one is higher than 0.50, indicating that there are no serious problems of multicollinearity. The *FP* variables show high correlations in the expected direction.

Before we proceed to present results, we first test whether the two measures of foreign presence variables, FP_{hmt} and FP_{other}, should be included simultaneously in Eq. (1). The result from the Wald test

Table 9.2 Descriptive statistics and correlation matrix for selected variables ($n = 130$).

Variables	Mean	s.d.	2	3	4	5	6	7	8
1. *KL*	3.05	2.67	0.07	0.21	0.35	−0.15	−0.03	−0.21	−0.15
2. *RI*	1016.36	1850.63		0.64	0.50	−0.26	−0.14	0.03	0.07
3. *LQ*	0.07	0.03			0.23	−0.22	−0.14	0.22	0.22
4. *FS*	0.27	0.51				−0.16	−0.01	−0.27	−0.14
5. FP_{hmt}	0.31	0.13					0.87	−0.08	−0.11
6. FP_{hmt^2}	0.11	0.10						0.02	0.03
7. FP_{other}	0.23	0.13							0.95
8. FP_{other^2}	0.07	0.07							

clearly justifies the inclusion of both FP_{hmt} and FP in the model at the 1% level of statistical significance.

We also need to examine the possibility of simultaneity between foreign presence and productivity. Theory suggests that the existence of FOEs exerts a positive effect on the performance of LOEs (Caves, 1974), but there are also reasons for believing that foreign MNEs select industries in the host country in which productivity is higher than average, and in which supernormal profits are earned.[8] In the event of a two-way relationship between foreign presence and domestic productivity, the estimation of model (1) using OLS will lead to spurious results. Thus we use the Hausman test (Hausman, 1978) to examine the issue of simultaneity, with export intensity (exports/total sales), profitability (total profit/sales), market size (sales in each sector) and the number of firms in each sector as instrumental variables.[9] We found no evidence of two-way links between our foreign presence variables and productivity, consistent with Buckley et al. (2002).

Full sample results

The first set of results estimated from model (1) is reported in Table 9.3. We first notice that the inclusion of the industry liberalisation dummy (D) in almost all the regressions makes no material difference to the size nor the significance of the coefficient of the relevant FP variable.[10] This increases our confidence in the results that we find for the FP variables, in particular that the findings do not depend on any industry-specific factors for which we are unable to account. The results in the linear specifications of model (1) (columns (1)–(3)) are that FP_{hmt} is positive and statistically significant[11] (equating to cell 3 of Table 9.1), indicating a generally positive role for HMT capital. We report the results of both the linear and curvilinear specifications of model (1) and conduct an F-test in which the linear specification (e.g., column (1)) is treated as a restricted equation of the full model (e.g., column (4)). The result suggests that the curvilinear specification fits the data better than the linear one at the 1% level of significance.[12]

The results for our preferred curvilinear specifications (columns (4)–(6)) show that FP_{hmt} is positive and statistically significant, while FP^2_{hmt} is negative and significant throughout. These results clearly point to curvilinearity in the relationship between the presence of HMT firms and LOEs' productivity (cells 2 and 4 of Table 9.1). They demonstrate that positive spillovers predominate when the level of penetration by HMT firms is low or moderate, but that past some level of foreign presence productivity spillovers begin to fall. The negative

Table 9.3 Regression results (full sample).

Dependent variable: Y (Labour productivity)	Linear (1)	Linear (2)	Linear (3)	Curvilinear (4)	Curvilinear (5)	Curvilinear (6)
Constant	−0.407 (−2.25)**	−0.459 (−1.66)*	−0.248 (−0.93)	−0.710 (−2.84)***	−0.740 (−2.39)**	−0.289 (−1.10)
KL (Capital intensity)	0.244 (11.01)***	0.245 (10.74)***	0.238 (10.36)***	0.257 (11.63)***	0.258 (11.37)***	0.246 (10.64)***
RI (R&D intensity)	0.001 (1.43)	0.000 (1.44)	0.000 (1.28)	0.001 (1.80)*	0.001 (1.77)*	0.000 (1.55)
LQ (Labour quality)	14.747 (6.78)***	11.19 (5.16)***	15.42 (6.88)***	13.898 (6.48)***	13.837 (6.33)***	14.991 (6.73)***
FS (Size)	0.067 (0.51)	0.064 (0.48)	0.025 (0.18)	0.142 (1.04)	0.139 (1.00)	0.031 (0.22)
D		0.059 (0.25)	−0.012 (−0.04)		0.038 (0.16)	−0.026 (−0.08)
FP_{hmt} (HMT capital share)	1.196 (2.11)**	1.188 (2.08)**		4.387 (3.62)**	4.378 (3.59)***	
$FP_{hmt}*D$			0.967 (1.66)*			3.361 (2.66)***
FP_{hmt}^{2}				−6.736 (−2.96)***	−6.727 (−2.94)***	
$FP_{hmt}^{2}*D$						−5.034 (−2.13)**

Table 9.3 Regression results (full sample) – continued

Dependent variable: Y (Labour productivity)	Linear		Curvilinear			
	(1)	(2)	(3)	(4)	(5)	(6)
FP_{other} (Other capital share)	0.829 (1.86)*	0.821 (1.82)*		1.181 (0.81)	1.143 (0.77)	
$FP_{other}*D$			0.233 (0.50)			−1.045 (−0.66)
FP_{other}^2				0.169 (0.07)	0.227 (0.09)	
FP_{other}^2*D						2.891 (1.08)
Number of observations	130	130	130	130	130	130
$\bar{R}^2$	0.726	0.724	0.715	0.740	0.738	0.723
F-statistics	58.016***	49.356***	47.284***	46.993***	41.438***	38.435***

Figures in parentheses are *t*-statistics (two-tailed tests); *, **, and *** denote significance at the 10, 5 and 1% levels respectively.

sign for FP^2_{hmt} means that a decreasing relationship between spillovers and foreign presence will set in when the presence of HMT firms is high, in particular that the secondary negative effect becomes the stronger. Our results thus corroborate Hypothesis 1. The finding of a curvilinear relationship is consistent with our prior discussion in the literature review. It is also broadly consistent with that of Zhou et al. (2002), who find evidence that inward FDI negatively impacts on the productivity of Chinese domestic industry. This previous study's finding appears to reflect the dominance of overseas Chinese capital in Chinese industry as a whole. Our review has suggested that the literature offers some reasons for negative competitive impacts in the form of market-stealing effects (Aitken and Harrison, 1999). Our finding here supports the argument that the industrial concentration of HMT firms' FDI (in line with their ownership advantages) in standardised goods market segments within industries means that the scope for technological spillovers is limited.

In the curvilinear specifications FP_{other} (and FP^2_{other}) fails to reach significance throughout. Therefore a linear relationship between the presence of OTHER capital and LOEs' productivity could not be established in the superior curvilinear version of our model. It appears that this result does not support Hypothesis 2.[13] A possible explanation for this result is the very low share of OTHER investment in total capital at the date of the Census. While we also notice that in two out of the three linear regressions FP_{other} is marginally significant, this is in the context of the inferior specification.

We now turn to examine further the curvilinear relationship between FP_{hmt} and Y. The point of inflection, where spillovers begin to decline, can be computed by taking the partial derivative of regression Eq. (1) with respect to foreign presence variable (FP_{hmt}) as follows:

$$\frac{\delta Y}{\delta FP_{hmt}} = \alpha_5 + 2(\alpha_6 FP_{hmt})$$

This partial derivative represents the slope of the spillover benefit curve with respect to FP_{hmt}. It implies that positive spillover effects reach a maximum at the inflection point (the critical level of foreign presence), and subsequently decline as the growth of negative effects come to dominate over positive effects with rising levels of foreign presence. Hence, by substituting the α coefficients, the inflection point can be obtained. Based on this procedure, the inflection point was found to be 0.326 (32.6%).

There are 53 industries in our sample that exceed the level of 32.6% and which are likely to experience declining spillover benefits. The distribution of industries shows that nearly 60% of industries in the sample are still below the optimum point beyond which spillover benefits begin to fall. A non-trivial minority of industries are found to exceed the crossover point in the data. This supports the view that our sample, which is drawn from the universe of Chinese domestic industries, is not constrained by range restrictions, and therefore increases our confidence in the findings.

If we try to characterise the industries where spillover benefits begin to decrease, the majority of them fall into light and low-technology industries such as 'food' and 'textiles'[14] where HMT MNEs dominate. Equipped with ownership advantages in the labour-intensive production and marketing of standardised products (Shi, 1998), it appears that HMT firms are in a strong position to outcompete LOEs, which are typically of small size and use outdated technology and management practices to produce undifferentiated, low-quality products. This discussion suggests that the source of the secondary negative spillovers is likely to be domestic market stealing effects that readily arise in mature saturated markets. Local firms are unprotected by brand loyalty and are reliant on price competitiveness alone: as a result negative primary and secondary competitive effects interact in a reinforcing manner. This links strongly to the dualistic nature of China's domestic economy, dominated by a low-technology sector producing stand-ardised goods, with a much smaller newer high-technology sector producing differentiated products.

We should at this point acknowledge that the weak ability of the Chinese statistical authorities to identify accurately the ultimate beneficial ownership of foreign investors may affect our results. We can, in particular, note the phenomenon of 'round tripping', whereby local Chinese firms direct capital to affiliates in Hong Kong, which in turn reoriginate this capital as FDI by Hong Kong firms in China. The World Bank (EIU, 1994) and other agencies estimate that this round-tripping phenomenon could account for as much as 20–30% of total FDI inflows into China (Wu, 2003). This effect could lead to 'capital stealing' from the Chinese locally owned sector. In this account, the capital base of LOEs would appear to be diminished, and the Chinese-owned sector would be deprived of growth, while the HMT-owned sector would be boosted by inflows of capital. This might contribute to the progressively decreasing impact that we have discerned.

Subsample results

The discussion in the literature review suggests that the level of technology is a potentially important means of discriminating between those host industries likely to experience different types of relationship. Accordingly, we separate those industries with 'high' and 'low' levels of technology in order to investigate more thoroughly the nature of the FDI-productivity spillovers relationship. This is done by carrying out a Chow breakpoint test. We find that there are five breakpoints at the 1% level of statistical significance.[15] We chose a breakpoint of 397.44 yuan of R&D intensity (measured as R&D expenditure in local currency per employee) where the F-statistic shows the highest value. At this point we split the sample into 'low' and 'high' technology groups. The 'low' group contains 72 industries and the 'high' group 58 industries.

Table 9.4 presents the results from re-estimation of Eq. (1) for the 'low' and 'high' technology groups separately. The liberalisation dummy (D) is now dropped, since it proved to be insignificant in all regressions throughout in the full sample. Again, we carried out F-tests for linear as against curvilinear specifications in both 'low' and 'high' groups. We found again that the curvilinear specification (column (2)) is superior to the linear specification (column (1)) in the 'low' group. However, in the 'high' group the linear specification (column (3)) is found to be preferable to the curvilinear specification (column (4)). Indeed, in column (4) no squared terms are significant, in marked contrast to the results in Table 9.3. This means that a curvilinear relationship cannot be established in the 'high' group.

In the 'low' group both FP_{hmt} and FP^2_{hmt} are correctly signed and are statistically significant, indicating a clear curvilinear relationship between FP_{hmt} and Y (cells 2 and 4 of Table 9.1). This result corroborates our Hypothesis 3. This finding is consistent with what we find for the full sample in Table 3, implying that it is the low-technology industries that dominate the overall FDI-productivity spillovers relationship in the full sample. It also suggests that market stealing effects are even stronger in low-technology sectors, in which competition is most intense, and that this negative impact may be amplified by barriers to exit by Chinese SOEs or by impediments to LOEs' exploitation of scale economies arising from foreign presence. FP_{other} is not significant in column (2), lending no support for our Hypothesis 4. We attribute this to the lack of ownership advantages held by OTHER firms suitable for standardised goods industries.

Table 9.4 Regression results (subsamples).

Dependent variable: Y (Labour productivity)	Low-technology group Linear (1)	Low-technology group Curvilinear (2)	High-technology group Linear (3)	High-technology group Curvilinear (4)
Constant	0.329 (2.68)***	−0.014 (−0.07)	−1.785 (−4.94)***	−1.256 (−3.81)***
KL (Capital intensity)	0.209 (14.10)***	0.204 (14.14)***	0.365 (7.64)***	0.377 (6.87)***
RJ (R&D intensity)	−0.001 (−1.34)	−0.000 (−1.42)	0.000 (1.37)	0.001 (1.86)*
LQ (Labour quality)	8.296 (4.42)***	8.499 (4.56)***	16.048 (4.79)***	13.344 (4.24)***
FS (Size)	−0.322 (−0.88)	0.448 (0.97)	0.120 (0.65)	−0.003 (−0.14)
FP_{hmt} (HMT capital share)	0.691 (2.12)**	2.342 (3.02)***	5.635 (3.09)***	6.739 (1.19)
FP^2_{hmt}		−3.625 (−2.39)**		−2.88 (−0.93)
FP_{other} (OTHER capital share)	0.281 (0.89)	1.432 (1.36)	2.600 (3.04)***	6.116 (4.40)***
FP^2_{other}		−1.696 (−0.81)		−0.001 (−0.62)
Number of observations	72	72	58	58
$\bar{R}^2$	0.839	0.851	0.700	0.762
F-statistic	62.915***	51.507***	23.207***	23.798***

Figures in parentheses are t-statistics (two-tailed tests); *, ** and *** denote significance at the 10, 5 and 1% levels, respectively.

In respect of the 'high' group the coefficients on both FP_{hmt} and FP_{other} are positive and statistically significant in our preferred linear specification (column (3)), supporting both Hypotheses 5 and 6. This linear profile might be generated by a situation in high-technology industries in which negative spillovers either are absent or are more or less invariant with the level of technology and the ownership of foreign investors (over the range observed in our data) while positive spillovers are rising. The positive sign for both FP_{hmt} and FP_{other} tells us that the primary spillover benefits of the two types of capital in high-technology industries are positive and increase linearly with rising foreign presence (cell 3 of Table 9.1). Both FP_{hmt}^2 and FP_{other}^2 in column (4) are statistically insignificant, suggesting the absence of negative secondary effects in the high-technology group. One interpretation is that in high-technology sectors FOEs tend not to compete head to head with LOEs, therefore dramatically reducing the scope for market stealing effects.

The finding of a significant role for HMT capital in the high-technology sectors merits further discussion. It suggests that, in high-technology industries, the home country origin of the foreign investor is of little consequence. Although it is true that, in 1995, Chinese inward FDI was dominated by HMT capital concentrated in low-technology sectors such as food and textiles, there was nevertheless a sizeable presence of HMT firms in high-technology industries such as electronics.

The regressions include a number of theoretically important control variables. Two of these variables, KL and LQ, perform as expected, promoting LOEs' productivity. RI, however, fails to reach significance at the level of 5% in any of the regressions, even in the 'high' group. This is, at first, a little puzzling, given the theoretically important role of R&D intensity in promoting the absorptive capacity of local firms, especially in terms of contributing to LOEs' learning activities. One of the causes of this unexpected result may be imperfections in the data used to create this variable. The R&D data in the Census refer only to expenditure by large and medium-sized SOEs: that is, they exclude other domestic firms such as collectively owned enterprises.[16] For the greatest number of LOEs (those that are not SOEs) research expenditure is either negligible or zero. As the absolute level of R&D expenditure in Chinese domestic industry is very low, a clear relationship with productivity cannot be established. FS is correctly signed in most regressions but fails to reach significance in all the regressions.

Conclusions

The current literature shows mixed evidence for spillover effects, and our results make a contribution to understanding why this might be: spillovers are very complex and may have a non-monotonic relationship with foreign presence. We have reviewed a number of leading, but disparate, studies on spillovers, and have argued that the root of the problem is the pervasiveness of a curvilinear relationship between FDI and spillover effects to LOEs.

In our study we find that the impact, and the form that this takes, of inward FDI on Chinese domestic industry depends on the nationality of investors. A key finding is that the relationship between HMT capital and LOEs' productivity is curvilinear: that is, past some level of penetration, the spillover benefits begin to fall. Our finding contrasts markedly with the majority of earlier work. The finding of a curvilinear relationship signals the existence of increasing negative spillover effects counteracting the primary positive ones, reflecting the nature of the ownership advantages of the foreign investors. In the full sample, because of the relatively small presence of MNEs from OTHER countries, no relationship, either linear or curvilinear, could be established between the presence of OTHER capital and LOEs' productivity using our preferred curvilinear model.

In order to discern more accurately the nature of the relationships, the data were further segmented by the level of technology of the domestic industries. We find that the curvilinear relationship between HMT capital and LOEs' productivity holds only for the low-technology sectors, not the high-technology sectors. This finding agrees with research that has found Chinese manufacturing industries to be dominated by low-technology sectors. We have inferred that the decreasing spillovers result from the effects of market stealing, and from the low-technology nature of the industries, combined with the low technological contribution of HMT firms. We have found OTHER capital to exhibit a significant linear relationship with local Chinese productivity in high-technology sectors, from which we are able to infer the existence of primary positive spillover effects.

We find that there are benefits to disaggregating the data used to identify the relationship between inward FDI and spillover effects, in order to reveal relationships that up until now have remained hidden. In this paper we have demonstrated that it is necessary to break down inward FDI by foreign ownership, as this makes a significant improvement over previous findings. The two categories of foreign capital that we employ are clearly vindicated. We have also found that analysis by technological intensity of the host industry is fully justified. This disaggregated approach has enabled us to gain clearer insights into the complex mechanisms though which FDI spillover effects are generated in LOEs.

In anchoring the findings of this study in the larger literature, some of its limitations must be acknowledged. First, the absence of panel data is a limitation. Panel data would allow us to explore the dynamic dimension of spillover effects, which is particularly important in the Chinese context of rapid change. It would also facilitate addressing the issue of simultaneity of foreign presence and productivity, by controlling industry and firm effects (Smarzynska, 2002). Second, it is recognised that Chinese statistics are not of the quality of a developed country. This results in missing data and thus produces lower statistical significance. The general problems of Chinese statistics are recognised to be those of overstatement of output (Rawski and Xiao, 2001). If the input of foreign capital is correctly measured but output is inflated, this would tend to bias our findings towards positive spillover effects, rather than towards the declining effects that we identify for HMT capital. This study also suggests an extension of the research agenda on spillovers in China to take account of geographic proximity between FOEs and LOEs. This argues for conducting further research on a regional or provincial basis.

The findings of this paper have implications for the importance of domestic industrial reform, and for policy towards inward FDI. Declining spillover benefits in Chinese-owned industry point to the persistent problems of SOE reform in China. Our results suggest that long-run barriers to exit faced by SOEs have underlain the declining spillover benefits experienced by Chinese LOEs in the face of competition from HMT firms, as these barriers prevent the operation of the pro-competitive spillover mechanisms.

Our finding for the complexity of spillover effects challenges the *laissez-faire* view that advocates the unmanaged inflow of FDI as an optimal policy prescription for the development of Chinese industry. It is now the case that limiting further growth in FDI from HMT firms in liberalised industries is circumscribed by China's accession to the WTO. While it is contrary to the principles of non-discrimination to legislate against investment from specific nationalities, adjusting the level of encouragement given to foreign investors in high-technology sectors through legislation on an industry-by-industry basis is feasible, in order that LOEs benefit from spillovers. In coming to these conclusions it might seem that our findings advocate retrospective action, but this is not necessary. High foreign penetration is concentrated in China's eastern region, while the interior and west remain at very low levels of foreign presence, for all nationalities. Our findings suggest that the Chinese government should not promote high inward FDI in low-technology industries (associated with HMT firms), in which negative primary and secondary spillovers to local firms are most likely, unless Chinese reform includes progress in allowing SOEs to exit their respective industries. This line of argument suggests that the suitability of FDI penetration should be monitored on an industrial basis as inward FDI expands in China. On the other hand, inward FDI of whatever home origin should be encouraged in high-technology industries for the spillover benefits they confer.

Acknowledgements

We thank three anonymous referees and the *JIBS* Departmental Editor, Professor José Manuel Campa, for their very constructive comments on our earlier versions of this manuscript.

Notes

1. The effect of productivity spillovers appears to be higher in cross-sectional studies than in panel data studies (Görg and Strobl, 2001).
2. In Caves' (1974) scheme, only the competitive effect may exert either a positive or negative impact on spillovers, with the precise effect depending on industrial conditions. For instance, the survival of the most efficient LOEs, given low barriers to exit, is one of the theoretically positive mechanisms. The majority of studies support a positive effect of competition on LOEs' productivity (Blomström, 1986; Wang and Blomström, 1992).
3. The appropriability 'problem' identified by Hymer (1960) and by Magee (1977) suggests that spillover benefits to rival LOEs will bear the signature of the foreign investor's technological advantages.
4. Smarzynska (2002) argues that market-oriented FDI generates more spillovers than export-oriented FDI. It is widely accepted that OTHER FDI is market-oriented and HMT FDI is more export-oriented (e.g., Buckley et al., 2002). This lends further support to our argument for a linear relationship between OTHER FDI and LOEs' productivity.
5. The authors would like to thank an anonymous reviewer for suggesting this analysis.
6. The authors are grateful to an anonymous reviewer for pointing this out.
7. Editions of the *Orientation Directory of Industries for FDI* record the progress of laws and regulations relevant to specific sectors to comply with the State plan for national economic growth (Luo, 2000). Prior to 1978 inward FDI was prohibited. From 1978 to 1986 FDI was promoted in all but certain

sensitive sectors (e.g., electricity, railways and financial services), but only in joint venture form. Controls on the numbers of foreign investors and ownership restrictions were then removed from 1987, with the exception of sectors of strategic importance (e.g., final assembly of transportation equipment, post and telecommunications network operation, power generation, aerospace and defence).
8 Shaver (1998) argues that failure to control for selection of industry may lead to biased results. Admittedly, this selection problem can be better addressed with panel data.
9 As is widely recognised in the literature, the fundamental problem with any instrumental variable is the difficulty of finding good instruments. There are no perfect instruments, and therefore caution must be exercised when interpreting results.
10 This lack of perceptible impact may be partly caused by the exclusion of all but seven FDI-restricted industries from the regressions on the grounds of incomplete data. After excluding these typically sensitive industries, for which the government is unwilling to divulge full information, fewer industries that are FDI restricted are left in our sample. The insignificance of the dummy variable suggests that the selection of sensitive industries by the government has been appropriate, with no locally owned industry suffering deleterious impacts through inadequate protection from inward FDI.
11 Most existing studies employ capital share to proxy foreign presence (FP). Following Blomström and Persson (1983), we also tried foreign employment share and found that this made no material difference to the results.
12 The F-test is a formal way to compare the linear with the curvilinear specification in the context of our model. Indeed, the existence of the significant FP_{hmt}^2 term alone is sufficient to reject the linear specification.
13 The primary objective of this paper is to examine the form of the relationship between foreign presence and LOEs' productivity. The key element of Hypothesis 2 is linearity rather than the sign of the relationship. Therefore, though FP_{other} has a positive sign, Hypothesis 2 is rejected.
14 According to Buckley et al. (2002), HMT firms' FDI is concentrated in light industries. Their capital shares in these industries are as follows (with OTHER capital penetration in brackets for comparison): other food processing, 0.211 (0.136); cake and sugar confectionery, 0.211 (0.127); soft drinks, 0.186 (0.128); knitting, 0.225 (0.076); other textile products, 0.278 (0.138); clothes, 0.239 (0.098); toys, 0.397 (0.058); household chemical products, 0.072 (0.254); fishing equipment and associated materials, 0.273 (0.091); rubber tyres, 0.077 (0.17); household plastic groceries, 0.268 (0.077).
15 The five breakpoints are very tightly clustered, and the choice of any of them makes very little difference to the size of the two subsamples. This also means that the selection of more than two subsamples is not feasible. We therefore chose the point with the highest significance.
16 The evidence is that SOEs conduct the over-whelming majority of R&D in Chinese-owned industry.

References

Aitken, B.J. and Harrison, A.E. (1999) 'Do domestic firms benefit from direct foreign investment? Evidence from Venezuela', *The American Economic Review* 89(3): 605–618.

Blomström, M. (1986) 'Foreign investment and productivity efficiency: the case of Mexico', *Journal of Industrial Economics* 35(1): 97–110.

Blomström, M. and Persson, H. (1983) 'Foreign investment and spillover efficiency in an underdeveloped economy: evidence from the Mexican manufacturing industry', *World Development* 11(6): 493–501.

Buckley, P.J. and Casson, M. (1976) *The Future of Multinational Enterprise*, Macmillan: London.

Buckley, P.J., Clegg, J. and Wang, C. (2002) 'The impact of inward FDI on the performance of Chinese manufacturing firms', *Journal of International Business Studies* 33(4): 637–655.

Caves, R.E. (1974) 'Multinational firms, competition and productivity in host country markets', *Economica* 41(162): 176–193.

Davis, H. (1996) 'High IQ and low technology: Hong Kong's *Key to Success*', *Long Range Planning* 29(5): 684–690.

Dunning, J.H. (1977) 'Trade, Location of Economic Activity and the Multinational Enterprise: A Search for an Eclectic Approach', in B. Ohlin, P.-O. Hesselborn and P.M. Wijkman (eds) *The International Allocation of Economic Activity*, Macmillan: London, pp. 395–418.

Dunning, J.H. (1988) *Explaining International Production*, HarperCollins: London.

Dunning, J.H. (1993) *Multinational Enterprises and the Global Economy*, Addison-Wesley: Wokingham, Berks.

Economic Intelligence Unit (1994) 'Making sense of Chinese statistics', World Bank, 2 May 1994, pp: 5–6.

Feinberg, S.E. and Majumdar, K.S. (2001) 'Technology spillovers and foreign direct investment in the Indian pharmaceutical industry', *Journal of International Business Studies* 32(3): 421–437.

Globerman, S. (1979) 'Foreign direct investment and 'Spil-lover' efficiency benefits in Canadian manufacturing industries', *Canadian Journal of Economics* 12(1): 42–56.

Görg, H. and Strobl, E. (2001) 'Multinational companies and productivity spillovers: a meta-analysis', *The Economic Journal* 111(475): F723–F739.

Haddad, M. and Harrison, A. (1993) 'Are there positive spillovers from direct foreign investment? Evidence from panel data for Morocco', *Journal of Development Economics* 42(1): 51–74.

Harrison, A. (1996) 'Determinants and Consequences of Foreign Investment in Three Developing Countries', in M. Robers and J. Tybout (eds) *Industrial Evolution in Developing Countries: Micro Patterns of Turnover, Productivity, and Market Structure*, Oxford University Press: Oxford, pp. 163–186.

Hausman, J.A. (1978) 'Specification tests in econometrics', *Econometrics* 46(6): 1251–1271.

Hsu, M. and Chen, B. (2000) 'Labor productivity of small and large manufacturing firms: the case of Taiwan', *Contemporary Economic Policy* 18(3): 270–283.

Hymer, S. (1960) 'The international operations of national firms: a study of direct foreign investment', PhD Dissertation, Massachusetts Institute of Technology, Cambridge, MA (published by MIT Press, 1976).

Kay, J. (1993) *Foundations of Corporate Success*, Oxford University Press: Oxford.

Kokko, A. (1992) *Foreign Direct Investment, Host Country Characteristics and Spillovers*, Stockholm School of Economics: Stockholm.

Konings, J. (2000) 'The effects of foreign direct investment on domestic firms: evidence from firm level panel data in emerging economies', Discussion Paper No. 2586, Centre for Economic Policy Research, London.

Lecraw, D.J. (1993) 'Outward direct investment by Indonesian firms: motivation and effects', *Journal of International Business Studies* **24**(3): 589–600.

Lee, K. and Plummer, M.G. (1992) 'Competitive advantages, two-way foreign investment, and capital accumulation in Korea', *Asian Economic Journal* **6**(1): 93–114.

Liu, X. (1999) 'Comparative Productivity of Foreign and Local Firms in Chinese Industry', paper presented at the 26th Annual Conference of the Academy of International Business United Kingdom Chapter, University of Strathclyde, Glasgow, Conference proceedings.

Liu, X., Siler, P., Wang, C. and Wei, Y. (2000) 'Productivity spillovers from foreign direct investment: evidence from UK industry level panel data', *Journal of International Business Studies* **31**(3): 407–425.

Luo, Y. (1997) 'Performance implications of international strategy: an empirical study of foreign-invested enterprises in China', *Group and Organization Management* **22**(1): 87–116.

Luo, Y. (1998) 'Industry attractiveness, firm competence, and international investment performance in a transitional economy', *Bulletin of Economic Research* **50**(1): 73–82.

Luo, Y. (2000) *Multinational Corporations in China: Benefiting from Structural Transformation*, Copenhagen Business School Press: Copenhagen.

Magee, S.P. (1977) 'Multinational corporations, the industry technology cycle and development', *Journal of World Trade Law* **2**(4): 297–321.

MOFTEC (1996) *Regulations Towards Foreign Direct Investment*, Social Science Publishing House: Beijing.

Perez, T. (1997) 'Multinational enterprises and technological spillovers: an evolutionary model', *Journal of Evolutionary Economics* **7**(2): 169–192.

Rawski, G.T. and Xiao, W. (2001) 'Roundtable on Chinese economic statistics introduction', *China Economic Review* **12**(4): 298–302.

Shaver, M.J. (1998) 'Accounting for endogeneity when assessing strategy performance: does entry mode choice affect FDI survival', *Management Science* **44**(4): 571–585.

Shi, Y. (1998) 'Technological assets and the strategy of foreign firms to enter the China market', *Journal of International Marketing and Marketing Research* **23**(3): 129–138.

Shi, Y. (2001) 'Technological capabilities and international production strategy of firms: the case of foreign direct investment in China', *Journal of World Business* **36**(2): 184–204.

Singh, R. (1992) 'Government introduced price distortion and growth, evidence from twenty nine developing countries', *Public Choice* **73**(1): 83–99.

Smarzynska, B.K. (2002) 'Does foreign direct investment increase the productivity of domestic firms? In search of spillovers through backward linkages', World Bank Policy Research Working Paper 2923, October.

Wang, Y. and Blomström, M. (1992) 'Foreign investment and technology transfer: a simple model', *European Economic Review* **36**(1): 137–155.

White, H. (1980) 'A heteroscedasticity consistent covariance matrix estimator and a direct test for heteroscedasticity', *Econometrica* **48**(4): 817–838.

Wu, F. (2003) 'Chinese economic statistics – Caveat Emptor', *Post-Communist Economies* **15**(1): 127–145.

Zhou, D., Li, S. and Tse, D. (2002) 'The impact of FDI on the productivity of domestic firms: the case of China', *International Business Review* **11**(4): 465–484.

Zhu, G. and Tan, K.Y. (2000) 'Foreign direct investment and labor productivity: new evidence from China as the host', *Thunderbird International Business Review* **42**(5): 507–528.

10
Inward FDI and Host Country Productivity: Evidence from China's Electronics Industry

Peter J. Buckley, Jeremy Clegg and Chengqi Wang

Introduction

There has been a great deal of research examining whether foreign affiliates exhibit higher levels of productivity than local firms (see, for example, Aitken and Harrison, 1999). The premise for this is that the firm-specific assets of transnational corporations (TNCs) increase productivity in FDI-receiving firms (Egger and Pfaffermayr, 2001). If this is the case, one would expect FDI to enhance overall industry performance as measured, for example, by labour productivity through this direct effect on foreign affiliate performance. Empirical research supports the view that firms with foreign equity participation outperform firms that are entirely locally-owned (see, for example, Blomström and Sjöholm, 1999).

A second source of impact from FDI on the performance of host country industry is that the presence of TNCs generates spillovers to other firms (Caves, 1974). Recently, research has focused on the question of the existence of such spillover effects from foreign to locally-owned firms in the form of increased productivity. These are known as productivity or technological spillovers (Kokko, 1996; Aitken and Harrison, 1999; Buckley *et al.*, 2002). Studies in this vein investigate the extent to which the presence of technologically-advanced foreign affiliates stimulates growth in the performance of local firms. To date, most studies find that spillovers benefit the productivity of local firms. However, little attention has been given to the investigation of the conditions under which spillovers might be large, non-existent or indeed negative.

In this article we pursue the idea that the overall productivity effects of FDI may neither be as uniform, nor as high, as many studies suggest. In examining the productivity impacts of foreign ownership in China's electronics industry, we address two questions. First, do the productivity spillover effects tend to diminish over time, following the establishment of foreign affiliates? Second, does FDI affect all market segments within an industry, or only certain segments? The article is therefore an advance on those existing studies that use China's data for a number of industries taken as a whole (see for example, Liu *et al.*, 2000; Buckley *et al.*, 2002). Such studies simply search for the presence of spillover effects at the industry level at a snapshot in time. Such an approach may mask the true relationship between inward FDI and host country productivity growth. A further distinctive feature of this article is that it examines the impact of inward FDI on overall productivity, that is to say the combined productivity of local and foreign-owned firms, whilst explicitly controlling for industry specific effects. The previous literature typically focuses on either the impact of FDI on GDP growth or on domestic firms alone.

China's electronics industry produces a wide range of household appliances, from refrigerators, air conditioning, cleaning, ventilating and heating appliances to kitchen, cosmetic and health care equipment, and a variety of accessories. China's open door policy (since 1978) has prioritised the securing of inward FDI as a means for upgrading domestic manufacturing capabilities. Judged simply in terms of the volume of inward FDI, the industry under study represents a success. Today, AT&T, Hewlett Packard, Hitachi, IBM, NEC, Olivetti, Philips, Samsung, Siemens, Toshiba, amongst others, have made substantial investments in China. At the same time, China's electronics industry has experienced dramatic growth. Our data show that, from 1996 to 2001, FDI in this industry has increased by a factor of 2.53, to come to account for more than 30% of the industry's total capital. Both sales revenue and industrial exports have grown over three fold. Exports of electronics goods reached $70 billion in 2001, accounting for 24.3% of China's total exports in 2001, compared with 14.2% in 1996. In view of this profile, China's electronics industry offers an ideal opportunity to conduct a micro-level investigation of the FDI-productivity relationship and its development.

This article proceeds as follows: section II briefly reviews the literature on FDI and productivity. Section III presents the methodology and data. The empirical results are presented in section IV and are discussed in section V. The last section offers conclusions.

Literature review

Firm-specific intangible assets, such as technological know-how, marketing and management skills, favourable relationships with suppliers and customers, and reputation, have played a dominant role in the conventional theory of FDI. John H. Dunning's eclectic paradigm (Dunning, 1981, 1988) combines ownership, internalisation and location advantages to explain the existence and growth of TNCs. The paradigm posits that all three conditions must be satisfied for potential investing firms to find FDI worthwhile.

The same argument can be put in another way. For FDI to occur, all that is required is for TNCs to be more efficient than their indigenous counterparts when operating in the same location. It follows that the ownership advantages of foreign affiliates should lead to relatively higher performance than their indigenous counterparts (Wang et al., 2002). The notion of this productivity differential, in effect, underlies the specialised literature on the industrial 'catch up' that occurs as a result of FDI (Perez, 1997). This provides the basis for the general hypothesis that FDI generates host country productivity growth (Driffield, 2001).

The above argument concerns the direct effects of FDI, i.e., the productivity growth contributed by foreign affiliates themselves. A further body of studies has arisen that focuses on the productivity spillover benefits associated with the presence of such affiliates. Positive spillovers arise when the productivity of locally-owned firms is enhanced through access to the leading-edge technologies employed by foreign affiliates (Feinberg and Majumdar, 2001). This access is not associated with a transaction (either in an external or internal market), and therefore the resulting locally-owned firms' productivity growth is an external or spillover benefit.

More recently, a number of theoretical reasons for negative spillover effects have been put forward. The key argument is that at greater levels of foreign presence, negative effects start to become apparent, and may begin to counteract the positive effects on local firms' productivity. Foreign affiliates may be able to draw demand away from their local counterparts through the introduction of new differentiated products and through process innovation leading to price reductions. As a result, the productivity of local firms might fall owing to a 'market stealing' effect (Aitken and Harrison, 1999).

The identification of negative effects also opens up the possibility that net positive spillover effects may diminish over the duration of foreign affiliates' operations. The dynamics of this process might be as follows. In the initial period when foreign affiliates are rare and just beginning operations, spillovers would be of small absolute magnitude. Locally-owned firms growing within a closed economy typically have weak technological capabilities. Local firms' capabilities are insufficient to enable them to appreciate the value of externally-generated knowledge, and restrict their ability to absorb the potential spillovers created by foreign affiliates. In these circumstances it is possible that that limited positive spillovers might occur through 'demonstration effects' and 'contagion effects', but not through pro-competitive effects. This is because locally-owned firms are concentrated in the standardised segments of industries that foreign affiliates avoid.

With the passage of time, foreign affiliates become more fully integrated into host countries' business networks, as their localisation rates rise and they establish links with local suppliers. Foreign affiliates' superior technological, marketing and management skills become more familiar to locally-owned firms and, as a result, those local firms with rising technological capacity have greater opportunities to absorb spillovers. At some point, however, the amount that local firms can learn from foreign affiliates will decrease. This occurs as the steady state of technological flow from parent firms to their foreign affiliates takes over from the initial transfer of technological stock. Accordingly, the scope for positive spillover effects from assimilating foreign technology diminishes. However, competitive effects may become more important. The incentives to locally-owned firms to become more efficient rises through competition, as they move into the same market segments as foreign affiliates. Eventually, it can be foreseen that spillover effects become exhausted, and any positive impact of foreign presence on host country productivity becomes indiscernible.

This last point may be one explanation for the prevalence of studies that report negligible or inconclusive effects of foreign presence (e.g., Aitken and Harrison, 1999; Haddad and Harrison, 1991). If so, we might take this prevalence as an indication that spillovers vary over time, and that it is quite reasonable to expect the magnitude of spillovers to change with the length of time that foreign affiliates have been operating in a host country. Further, inconclusive results could be generated by the concurrence of such a decline in positive spillovers and the appearance of spillovers with opposite effect.

A further and little researched dimension to spillover effects is the speed with which foreign presence is built up. T. Perez (1997) points out a theoretically inverse link between the magnitude of spillover benefits and the speed of foreign penetration. When locally-owned firms, even those with a relatively small technological gap behind foreign affiliates, face rapidly increasing foreign penetration, they may be driven out of the market.

More complex distributional effects may also exist. It can be argued that positive spillovers favour certain groups of local firms. Foreign entry into a host market increases the intensity of competition and forces domestic firms to become more efficient (Kokko, 1996). But the scope for such spillover benefits will vary. M. Blomström and F. Sjöholm (1999) argue that there are more significant spillover benefits to non-exporting than exporting firms, on the grounds that export oriented firms already face competition from the international market. The ability of local firms to absorb foreign know-how is also critical to spillover benefits. This capacity depends on firms' technological competence (Liu *et al.*, 2000). Local firms with high competence are expected to benefit more from spillovers. Furthermore, competence is associated with the type of ownership of local firms. Empirical work suggests that industries dominated by state ownership are less able to benefit from the presence of foreign affiliates, and therefore reap fewer spillover benefits compared to industries in which private ownership is more pronounced.

If we look at the literature, the evidence for positive spillovers from FDI predominates (Caves, 1974; Globerman, 1979; Liu *et al.*, 2000; Zhu and Tan, 2000). It has also been found that positive spillovers are highest in those industries in which the technology gap is small, thus allowing local firms to benefit from their technologically advanced foreign counterparts (Kokko, 1996).

A number of recent studies, however, have identified negligible spillovers (Haddad and Harrison, 1991) or negative spillovers (Singh, 1992; Aitken and Harrison, 1999). More recent research on Chinese data shows that State-owned enterprises can experience negative spillover effects, while collectively owned enterprises benefit from foreign presence (Buckley *et al.*, 2002). This wide variation in findings suggests that positive spillover effects are by no means guaranteed, and that their presence depends on extraneous economic and technological factors (Sjöholm, 1999).

This article seeks to explore whether the strength of host country productivity benefits reported for China's manufacturing industry as a whole can be supported by data at the sub-sector level for one industry – electronics – using a panel of data covering four years. This study fills a gap in knowledge concerning the existence of sub-sector-specific effects and the possibility that productivity benefits from FDI decline over time. Both are notably under-researched questions.

Methodology and data

A simple model is employed to investigate the impact of FDI on the productivity of China's electronics industry, both locally and foreign-owned, along with appropriate controls. The model is as follows:

$$LP_{ij} = C + \beta_1 KL_{ij} + \beta_2 INT_{ij} + \beta_3 LQ_{ij} + \beta_4 FS_{ij} + \beta_5 FP_{ij} + \varepsilon_{ij} \qquad (1)$$

Following the practice of existing studies, we assume that value-added per worker (*LP*) in a sub-sector of China's electronics industry, is a function of foreign presence (*FP*), represented by the foreign equity share in each sub-sector. We expect that FP exerts a positive and significant impact on LP.

Our multivariate analysis includes a set of control variables that may influence labour productivity: the capital labour ratio (*KL*), which is constructed to control for capital intensity; intangible assets per employee (*INT*) serves as a proxy for the stock of knowledge accumulated by firms from past R&D investment in the form of technological competence; labour quality (*LQ*) measures by the share of engineers and managers in total employment; and fixed assets per worker (*FS*) captures firm scale economies. These variables increase our confidence in the robustness of the findings through controlling for influences other than foreign presence. All variables are in logarithmic form, and ordinary least squares (*OLS*) is employed throughout.

Previous studies have typically estimated some variant of equation (1) using a cross section of industries. These studies are unable to control for differences in productivity between industries that might be correlated with, but not caused by, foreign presence. If foreign affiliates locate in more productive industries, then a positive association between the foreign capital share and productivity will be found even if no spillovers take place (Aitken and Harrison, 1999). If so, it is likely that the results will tend to overstate the true positive impact of foreign capital participation. To avoid this problem, we estimate equation (1) using a panel data set within a single industry. The panel nature of our data allows us to track the same industry over time. Hence we are able to allow for other time-invariant industry specific effects, such as infrastructure and technological opportunity. Data are not available with which to investigate these effects econometrically; nevertheless these factors may affect the level of productivity. Investigating at the sub-sectoral level enables us to control for the potential endogeneity of foreign ownership and overall productivity within the industry (Aitken and Harrison, 1999).

Panel data estimation, however, does not allow us to observe whether and to what extent the magnitude of spillover effects changes over time. To do so is an important objective of this article, and therefore cross-sectional estimations are also conducted to investigate this. We examine the effect of FDI on the level of domestic labour productivity for every year and also on the growth of productivity over the period of study. The growth specification is included because it is deemed to be a way to avoid the casuality problem at the micro-level[1] (Sjöholm, 1999).

The data employed for estimation in this study are from the *Yearbook of China's Electronics Industry*, for the years 1996, 1998, 2000 and 2001. Industry-level data are preferred because there is more variation in the FDI variable. In the *Yearbooks*, the electronics industry is divided into nine categories: (1) radar; (2) communications equipment; (3) broadcasting and TV; (4) computers; (5) components; (6) measurement equipment; (7) special equipment; (8) household electronic appliances; and (9) other electronic devices. These categories are then divided into 47 sub-sectors. Due to data imperfections, our sample consists of 41 sub-sectors for the years 1996, 1998, 2000 and 2001, yielding a total of 164 observations in the form of a panel.

Table 10.1 shows that labour productivity in the electronics industry as a whole in 2001 was about 2.5 times that of 1996, while the foreign capital share remained almost unchanged. *Prima facie*, this might indicate that productivity growth over the period might not, at least in the largest measure, be attributable to the direct impact of foreign capital participation.

Further information on the share of foreign capital in each sub-sector is detailed in Table 10.2. As is evident from the table, foreign capital accounted for a varying percentage of the total in different sub-sectors. For instance, in 2001 the foreign capital share was a mere 1.6% in 'electronic heating equipment'; whereas it amounted to 99.4% in the 'calculator' sub-sector.

While the overall foreign capital share remained almost unchanged over the period, the distribution of the foreign capital share changed considerably, i.e., there has been significant variation in the data. The share decreased by 98% in 'electronic heating equipment', while there was almost a 21-fold increase in 'wire transmission equipment'. From 1996 to 2002, in about half of the sub-sectors (21) the foreign capital share rose, and declined in the other half. The sub-sectors with the

Table 10.1 Summary (Observations = 41) statistics.

Items	1996 Mean	1996 S.D.	1998 Mean	1998 S.D.	2000 Mean	2000 S.D.	2001 Mean	2001 S.D.	2001/1996 Mean
Labour productivity	3.95	4.83	5.30	5.26	8.99	6.63	9.80	7.45	2.45
Capital-labour ratio	6.71	4.33	9.82	6.67	13.37	10.87	13.25	11.77	2.01
Intangible assets per worker	1.01	0.99	1.22	.04	0.45	0.98	1.52	1.19	1.50
Employment share of engineers & managers	0.25	0.09	0.26	0.11	0.29	0.12	0.29	0.12	1.16
Fixed assets per firm	4007	4885	6794	8933	11566	14745	10147	11571	2.53
Foreign capital share	0.32	0.19	0.34	0.27	0.26	0.22	0.33	0.27	1.03

Source: authors.

Table 10.2 The foreign capital share of China's electronics industry 1996–2001, per cent.[a]

Category	1996	1998	2000	2001/2001	1996
I. Communication Equipment	26.13	32.27	19.99	35.21	1.35
1. Wire transmission equipment	1.59	24.34	20.73	33.07	20.80
2. Wireless transmission equipment	13.93	31.99	15.84	16.48	1.18
3. Exchange equipment	34.87	25.04	18.59	16.55	0.47
4. Wire communication terminal equipment	38.60	37.67	28.48	33.18	0.86
5. Wireless communication terminal equipment	24.73	36.77	21.68	62.73	2.54
6. Other communication equipment	20.38	19.38	8.83	23.51	1.15
II. Broadcast and TV	30.36	33.18	42.44	36.47	1.20
7. Broadcast and TV equipment	2.08	3.24	2.07	2.99	1.44
8. TV sets	26.73	29.45	41.17	35.34	1.32
9. Radio and recorders	36.31	36.10	48.17	55.83	1.54
10. Video	46.16	49.40	41.19	27.17	0.59
11. Other broadcast and TV products	18.06	20.71	21.54	21.46	1.19
III. Computers	35.99	27.21	20.84	23.84	0.66
12. Complete computer	18.18	12.06	15.93	22.51	1.24
13. Computer exterior equipment	56.94	43.34	34.22	38.97	0.68
14. Computing requisite accessories	20.27	10.16	3.86	6.31	0.31
15. Software	20.72	15.64	1.22	1.99	0.10
16. Calculators	22.24	42.99	88.69	99.39	4.45
17. Other computer products	71.02	65.24	59.57	63.85	0.90
IV. Electronics Components	24.31	31.56	32.71	33.83	1.39
18. Electronic micro-electrical machines	33.02	23.95	31.18	34.10	1.03
19. Electronic electrical wires and cables	11.13	13.54	16.82	18.25	1.64
20. Electronic storage batteries	4.26	29.33	7.52	31.41	7.38
21. Electronic dry batteries	85.64	85.08	77.67	71.04	0.83
22. Electronic components	24.66	33.49	36.79	38.78	1.57

Table 10.2 The foreign capital share of China's electronics industry 1996–2001, per cent).[a] – continued

	Category	1996	1998	2000	2001/2001	1996
	23. Electronic component special materials	37.90	40.49	35.48	38.50	1.02
	24. Other electronic component products	32.24	39.79	21.68	14.82	0.46
V.	Electronic Measuring Equipment	11.29	11.03	8.76	10.84	0.96
	25. Electronic measuring instruments	6.33	7.04	5.29	10.47	1.65
	26. Other electronic measuring instruments	23.11	22.12	14.87	11.19	0.48
VI.	Electronic Special Equipment	23.25	20.03	19.51	26.57	1.14
	27. Electronic special equipment	29.60	28.80	29.68	22.98	0.78
	28. Electronic industrial moulds and gear	21.37	21.21	21.04	23.88	1.12
	29. Other electronic equipment	19.98	16.98	13.88	28.65	1.43
VII.	Household Electronic Appliances	47.40	36.43	21.30	33.11	0.70
	30. Refrigerators	49.19	1.50	14.32	24.04	0.49
	31. Electrical fans and air conditioners	60.12	67.92	2.92	24.23	0.40
	32. Electronic heating equipment	85.39	63.86	2.36	1.60	0.02
	33. Electronic toys	27.29	33.64	56.68	70.97	2.60
	34. Other household electronic appliances	35.88	46.43	42.53	58.61	1.63
	35. Other	30.92	26.64	13.46	11.89	0.39
VIII.	Electronic Devices	29.67	32.57	32.88	32.08	0.91
	36. Bulbs	57.26	54.95	23.78	50.35	0.88
	37. Electrical vacuum valve devices	29.51	36.03	37.81	33.60	1.14
	38. Semi-conductor devices	16.12	16.18	20.60	3.46	0.21
	39. Integrated circuits	36.57	40.84	15.78	29.27	0.80
	40. Electronic device materials manufacture	30.69	26.98	22.91	21.02	0.68
	41. Other electronic device products	40.72	15.57	7.58	32.98	0.81

Source: authors

[a] The foreign capital shares for eight aggregate sub-sectors are calculated as the sales-weighted arithmetic average.

Table 10.3 Labour productivity of China's electronics industry, 1996–2001.[a]

Category	1996	1998	2000	2001
I. Communication equipment	8.63	43.01	17.48	22.64
II. Broadcast and TV	2.61	33.35	52.69	9.94
III. Computers	4.93	16.55	13.54	15.45
IV. Electronics components	1.86	8.90	5.80	8.13
V. Electronic measuring equipment	1.09	5.84	3.42	4.74
VI. Electronic special equipment	1.63	7.81	4.42	14.21
VII. Household electronic appliances	2.60	19.36	9.13	10.76
VIII. Electronic devices	3.61	17.76	10.20	7.58

Source: authors.
[a] The remarkable fluctuations over the years are due to a number of external and internal factors. For example, the dramatic drop of productivity in 2000 over 1998 may be related to the lagged effects of the Asian crisis. Other factors include industrial restructuring, large scale redundancy in State-owned enterprises, price fluctuations and the entry of large foreign TNCs.

greatest increase in foreign capital share include 'distributed communication equipment', 'broadcast and TV equipment', 'electronics components and electronic special equipment'. Each of these are sub-sectors with particularly high growth worldwide.

Table 10.3 shows that 'communications equipment', 'broadcast and TV' and 'computers' enjoyed the highest levels of productivity. These sub-sectors are also those with heavy foreign investment, as indicated in Table 10.2. While the overall picture conveyed by Table 10.2 suggests a generally high penetration by foreign capital, these three sub-sectors support the view that FDI does gravitate towards the more productive sub-sectors (Aitken and Harrison, 1999).[2]

Results

We first pooled data on the 41 sub-sectors over four years and then estimated results from equation (1). These are presented in Table 10.4. Column (1) shows that the FP variable carries a rather large, statistically significant coefficient, suggesting that firms in sub-sectors with more foreign capital are significantly more productive than those in sub-sectors with a smaller foreign presence. The point estimate, 0.20, suggests that a 10% increase in foreign capital share is associated with a 2% growth in overall productivity. This result is in accordance with studies by R. Caves (1974), S. Globerman (1979) and X. Liu et al. (2000), each of which finds evidence of spillovers that increase local firms' labour productivity. It also accords with studies on China (Zhu and Tan, 2000; Buckley et al., 2002).

This result, however, should be treated with some caution since the estimation does not control for sub-sector-specific productivity differences in employing a specification that is closest in spirit to earlier cross-section studies. Since the apparent effect of productivity spillovers tends to be higher when cross-sectional data are employed (Görg and Strobl, 2001), we therefore re-estimate equation (1) while controlling for sub-sector-specific productivity differences by including sub-sector dummies. The results are presented in column (2) of Table 10.4. By comparing the two adjusted R-squares, one can see that explanatory power is significantly increased when sub-sector dummies are included in the equation.[3]

In column (2), the coefficient on the FP variable registers the correct positive sign but fails to reach significance, indicating that the positive effect is not robust. The apparent spillover benefits of FDI in our results vanish when industry-specific productivity differences are controlled. This suggests, *prima facie*, that the positive effects of foreign presence

Table 10.4 The impact of FDI on productivity[a] (Pooled estimation for 1996, 1998, 2000 and 2001).

Dependent variable: LP (Value-added per worker)	(1)	(2)
C	−0.07 (−0.13)	
KL (Capital-labour ratio)	0.26 (2.61)***	0.23 (1.86)*
INT (Intangible assets per worker)	0.04 (0.82)	0.058 (1.23)
FS (Fixed assets per firm)	0.31 (4.72)***	0.36 (3.68)***
FP (Foreign capital share)	0.20 (3.33)***	0.11 (1.60)
Industry dummies	No	Yes
R-square adjusted	0.48	0.64
F-statistic	31.71***	83.89***
Number of observations	164	164

Source: authors.
[a] Figures in parentheses are t statistics (two-tailed tests); *, **, and *** denote significance at the 10%, 5% and 1% levels, respectively.

measured in previous studies may, to some extent, be attributable to the tendency of TNCs to concentrate in more productive industries. An overview of the data in Tables 10.2 and 10.3 accords with the view that foreign affiliates cluster in above-average productivity industries.

One possible explanation for the lack of robustness in the FDI–productivity relationship is that spillovers may diminish over time, leading to insignificant results from panel data. A second possibility is that FDI presence may positively affect only a selection of sub-sectors. As discussed in section II, FDI may be important in certain sub-sectors, but not in others. To investigate these possibilities, the remaining part of this section first examines whether or not there is a pattern of diminishing spillovers over time. Then we break the full sample into sub-samples based on: (1) export intensity; (2) intangible assets intensity; and (3) State capital share, to see whether spillovers benefits only pertain to local firms in certain types of industry.

Table 10.5 shows the results from cross-sectional estimations of equation (1) for each individual year.[4] The FP variable is positive and statistically significant in the 1996 and 1998 estimations, though the magnitudes of both coefficient and level of significance slightly decreased. However, we should note that the FP variable becomes insignificant in the regressions for 2000 and 2001. This appears to signal a declining trend in the impact of FDI spillover effects in the China's electronics industry within the period under consideration, though these effects are nevertheless significant in the growth form in column (5).

Surprisingly, the capital intensity variable (KL) fails to reach significance as expected in all but the regression for 2000, thereby performing inconsistently and contrary to standard results. From this we might surmise that capital intensity is a less important determinant of labour productivity in China's electronics industry, perhaps on account of the labour intensive nature of this broad industry compared with developed countries. Two further factors may explain this insignificance. First, China's electronics enterprises have been under so-called 'asset restructuring'. This involves a substantial re-allocation of assets between firms under different ownership and between different sub-sectors within the industry to improve overall industrial efficiency. The outcome is a change in the distribution of assets between sub-sectors, causing some degree of mismatch between capital intensity and productivity. The effect may be to wash out the significance of the variable. Second,

Table 10.5 The impact of FDI on productivity[a] (Cross-sectional estimations).

Dependent. Variable: LP (Value-added per worker)	Level estimation				Growth estimation 1996–2001
	1996	1998	2000	2001	
	(1)	(2)	(3)	(4)	(5)
C	2.10	−0.04	−2.02	0.96	0.82
	(1.89)*	(−0.03)	(−1.54)	(0.91)	(6.14)***
KL (Capital-labour ratio)	0.10	0.01	0.69	−0.09	0.06
	(0.32)	(0.08)	(2.69)***	(−0.78)	(0.56)
INT (Intangible assets per worker)	−0.01	−0.05	−0.08	0.29	0.11
	(−0.13)	(−0.36)	(−1.74)*	(3.83)***	(1.18)
LQ (Employment share of engineers and managers)	1.52	1.24	0.20	0.52	0.62
	(4.63)***	(3.98)***	(0.46)	(1.36)	(2.65)***
FS (Fixed assets per firm)	0.20	0.44	0.28	0.27	0.13
	(1.62)	(3.43)***	(2.58)***	(3.20)***	(1.04)
FP (Foreign capital share)	0.49	0.45	−0.10	0.24	0.26
	(4.89)***	(3.23)***	(−0.71)	(1.66)	(3.38)***
R-square adjusted	0.60	0.45	0.63	0.47	0.44
F-statistic.	12.92***	7.64***	14.79***	8.17***	7.21***
Number of observations	41	41	41	41	41
Heteroscedasticity (F-statistic)[b]	(2.52)**	(2.00)*	(4.85)***	(4.09)***	(1.56)
Functional form (F-statistic)[c]	(0.85)	(0.49)	(5.68)*	(0.02)	(0.98)

Source: authors.
[a] Figures in parentheses are t statistics (two-tailed tests); *, **, and *** denote significance at the 10%, 5% and 1% levels, respectively.
[b] White test (Cross term).
[c] Ramsey RESET tests are based on the squares of the fitted values (one term).

the relatively small number of observations may contribute to this insignificance. As shown in Tables 10.4 and 10.6, the capital intensity variable is more often significant when the number of observations increases.

Over time, *INT* changes from insignificant to significant, while *LQ* shows quite the reverse movement – changing from significant to insignificant. Taking a broader view of learning activities, *INT* and *LQ* might be acting as proxies for different aspects of the technological capability of China's firms.[5] The significance of *LQ* in the 1996 and 1998 regressions could be construed as an indication that labour quality was the primary variable capturing the knowledge complement of domestic firms. However, the 2001 regression shows that by the end of the period *INT* has come to dominate. This pattern of results suggests that there may have been an increase in the role played by intangible assets in domestic productivity.[6] The firm size effect variable, *FS*, registers the correct sign and is statistically significant in all regressions. This suggests that industry sub-sectors populated by larger firms are more likely to achieve higher levels of productivity. This result also implies that most firms are smaller than the size of the most efficient firm in the industry, and that scale economies are available to them in the event that they grow.

Table 10.6 displays the results for the sub-samples. The first two columns show that those sectors in which firms are local-market oriented, the coefficient for foreign presence is positive and statistically significant at the 5% level. On the other hand, export oriented sectors experience no significant productivity benefits from foreign investment. This finding agrees with Blomström and Sjöholm (1999), who have suggested that inward FDI confers little additional benefit on sectors that are already exposed to international competition by exporting to the international markets.

Contrary to expectation, the results in columns (3) and (4) show that the *FP* variable does not attain statistical significance in either the high or low intangible assets per worker sub samples. This may reflect the generally low absolute importance of intangible capital in China's industry, a characteristic that may share common roots with the widespread labour intensity. Taken together with the negative signs in earlier regressions in Table 10.5, the performance of *INT* seems poor and unstable. This could either be an outcome of poor data quality, as Chinese firms have only recently started to calculate and report intangible assets. The problem of errors might also be compounded by lumpiness, caused by the absolutely low values in the data.

Table 10.6 The FDI impact and industry characteristics[a] (Pooled estimation for sub-samples over 1996, 1998, 2000 and 2001)

Dep. Var.:	Exports/Sales		Int. assets intensity		State capital share	
LP (Value-added per worker)	High (1)	Low (2)	High (3)	Low (4)	High (5)	Low (6)
KL (Capital-labour ratio)	0.11 (0.44)	0.51 (2.98)***	0.29 (1.74)*	0.32 (1.42)	0.47 (2.49)***	0.24 (1.25)
INT (Intangible assets per worker)	0.06 (0.94)	0.05 (0.59)	0.25 (2.33)**	−0.03 (−0.46)	0.05 (0.57)	0.06 (0.77)
LQ (Employment share of engineers and managers)	0.20 (0.53)	0.94 (3.60)***	2.57 (4.92)***	0.39 (1.64)*	2.09 (4.63)***	0.26 (1.16)
FS (Fixed assets per firm)	0.45 (2.51)***	−0.01 (−0.06)	−0.02 (−0.15)	0.23 (1.59)	−0.01 (−0.10)	0.15 (1.13)
FP (Foreign capital share)	−0.16 (−0.79)	0.16 (2.17)**	0.11 (1.20)	0.09 (0.88)	0.15 (1.79)*	0.08 (0.78)
R-square adjusted	0.57	0.68	0.71	0.66	0.67	0.63
F-statistic	34.17***	47.80***	55.79***	43.61***	48.53***	39.77***
Number of observations	84	80	84	80	84	80

Source: authors.

[a]Figures in parentheses are t statistics (two-tailed tests); *, **, and *** denote significance at the 10%, 5% and 1% levels respectively.

The third pair of sub-samples (columns 5 and 6) concerns the impact of State ownership on the FDI-productivity relationship. The results suggest that the effect of foreign presence on labour productivity is statistically significant only in sub-sectors in which the State capital share is large. At first sight, this result appears to conflict with the results of P. Buckley *et al.* (2002), who found that State-dominated sub-sectors in manufacturing experienced negative spillover effects. However, the purpose of the present study is to employ a more detailed unit of analysis – the single industry rather than the whole of manufacturing, and this might be expected to alter the findings. This point is taken up in the discussion section.

Discussion

Here we reflect further on some possible explanations for the unexpectedly weak role that has apparently been played by foreign affiliates in the electronics industry. First, the considerable FDI into China's electronics industry might not have been accompanied by a commensurate amount of technology transfer via FDI. In support of this, a number of studies – not specific to the electronics industry – have pointed out that there has been a lack of technology transfer via FDI into China (e.g., Chen and Zhang, 1995; Lan and Young, 1996). A possible factor behind this, and one that might be expected to influence a technology-intensive industry such as electronics, is weak intellectual property protection in China. This may discourage the transfer of all but the labour-intensive stages of production to China, and act as a disincentive to TNC's from undertaking significant technological development in the host country. The insignificant contribution of foreign affiliates to overall domestic productivity might therefore be a result of limited opportunities for technological spillovers.

A second explanation relates to the nature of the relationship between spillover effects and foreign ownership. The very high share of foreign capital may be responsible for the unexpected findings. At greater levels of foreign presence, the market share of local firms may be cannibalised, so raising their costs of production and resulting in a 'crowding out' effect. In such a situation, negative spillover effects can arise that counteract the existing positive effects, so resulting in a decline in overall spillover benefits (Buckley *et al.*, 2003).

Third, in this article we address the bias-evident in much empirical work-towards finding a positive impact for FDI on host country productivity. Our results suggest that TNCs are attracted to higher productivity sub-sectors. We control for this effect, but the implication is that much of the prior literature may have over-estimated the impact of FDI on host country productivity. Consequently, our results stand in stronger contrast with the existing body of work and appear more unexpected than perhaps they should be.

A fourth consideration is that other factors that determine productivity may overshadow the role of FDI. For instance, despite policy efforts to foster the transfer of technology via FDI, Chinese firms may be primarily absorbing technology through imports of technology embodied in physical capital assets. A good reason for believing this is that the Government of China implemented preferential policies encouraging imports of advanced technology in the electronics industry, as a means of localising high technology. In certain circumstances, the Government allowed machinery and equipment incorporating advanced technologies to be imported duty free. Product and process technologies imported in this way may have played a primary role in developing new electronics products and in improving the performance and quality of China's electronics industry. This inference is in line with the emerging literature on the link between international trade and international technological spillovers.

Fifth, the results in Table 10.5 point to a diminution of spillovers over time following the establishment of foreign affiliates in sub-sectors of the electronics industry. However, it is easy to see how a snapshot of the years 1996 or 1998 could lead researchers to believe in the existence of a strong positive and continuing relationship between foreign presence and host country productivity. Equally, the growth regression for 1996–2001 suggests the same strong relationship. However, snapshots of 2000 and 2001 would produce the opposite conclusion. These regressions make the point powerfully that the date of measurement can determine the results obtained. This may help to account for the large amount of mixed findings in the literature in studies that rely on data for just one year. But our results also indicate that a dynamic structure may exist in the relationship between foreign presence and host country productivity, which is as yet very inadequately explored. This may account for the weak effect of the foreign capital share in the last two years of our sample, and points the way for future research.

The positive relationship between State ownership and domestic industrial productivity is at variance with previous research. This article concerns one industry as opposed to the whole of the manufacturing sector. It is therefore necessary to consider the special conditions that might apply to the electronics industry. First, it is a fast changing industry and this may profoundly modify the nature of the relationship between inward FDI, high State ownership and productivity. Second, a very different performance outcome is likely where inward FDI takes the form of joint ventures with successful State-owned firms, rather than competition against State-owned firms. A large number of high-technology foreign affiliates, e.g., the local affiliates of Motorola (China) are joint ventures with State-owned enterprises. These close and productive partnerships may be responsible for a sort of 'crowding in' effect. Such affiliates are also often highly export oriented, and are responsible for high levels of intra-group exports.

The breaking of the data into sub-samples reveals and supports some of the above discussion. We have seen that the impact of inward FDI on host country productivity is significant only for certain groups of firms, not all. The pattern of significance gives some idea of why this might be. As prior research suggests, export oriented sub-sectors experience insignificant gains from foreign capital presence. Experience of exporting points to the existence of a learning effect for local firms, and this learning appears to pre-empt that which might otherwise be conferred by inward FDI. This gives some support to the notion that learning via independent technology imports and via foreign presence are substitutes. It also indicates that the learning is of a 'one shot' nature. A given gap in knowledge between foreign and local firms, once closed, exhausts the potential for significant spillover effects. If so, it provides some supporting evidence that host country productivity gains via learning from FDI, even when they are initially present, should be expected to diminish over time.

Conclusions

Using a small panel of China's electronics industry subsectors, we find partial support for the view that inward FDI has promoted overall productivity growth over the period 1996 to 2001. However, we also find some support for our argument that the impact of FDI on host country industry performance diminishes over time. Our evidence suggests that the productivity gains from FDI were significant for certain (but not all) groups of firms in China's electronics industry. This suggests that spillovers benefits do not flow automatically from FDI, but are contingent upon other factors. This article also provides some evidence to caution that sub-sector-specific productivity effects associated with, but not caused by, foreign presence exist. TNCs do appear to concentrate in more productive sub-sectors within China's electronics industry. This suggests the possibility that prior research has been biased in favour of finding stronger impacts on host country productivity. Our research also suggests that the date of measurement in cross-sectional research can be critical, and misleading if generalisation is sought, when making inferences about the relationship between inward FDI and host country productivity.

We must acknowledge the limitations of our study. In particular, it should be noted that some factors that influence productivity have not been controlled for. These include variables such as R&D and imports, for which data are unavailable at this level of disaggregation. As our data are drawn from those collected by the Ministry of the Electronics Industry, unlike the industrial census data published by the State Statistical Bureau of China, the productivity of foreign and domestically owned firms is not separately identified. While this would have been desirable, the investigation in this article has been constructed to make optimal use of the data that are available for the host country industry.

The fact that the impact of FDI on overall productivity is so sensitive to the set of sub-sectors that are selected suggests caution in inferring the existence of spillovers without first adequately controlling for industry-specific characteristics. Recent studies of spillovers from FDI suggest that such effects may be significant, but that they are not guaranteed, automatic, or free. The effects may depend to a large extent on the host country, in particular on host country industry characteristics and on the policy environment in which TNCs operate.

There are a number of policy implications that arise from our findings. First, foreign capital participation in China's industries, and sub-sectors, with low levels of exports is likely to be especially beneficial for productivity growth in China, and should be encouraged. A caveat here is that the industry concerned should be one in which export potential exists. Second, the import of technology by local firms, outside an equity relationship with TNCs, may well be an effective means to raise productivity in China, especially where there are no long-term benefits from foreign capital participation or where TNCs express little interest in investing in an industry.

Third, and linked to the previous point, joint ventures between foreign affiliates and China's State-owned enterprises, for which we find evidence of beneficial effects, may offer a more long lasting route to learning than stand-alone foreign affiliates.[7] The significance of the FP variable for sub-sectors in which the State capital share is high may be a sign that joint ventures between foreign affiliates and state-owned firms can be a productive one under certain industrial conditions, as in this case. As our data show, the electronics industry is dynamic, and in these circumstances benefits are thought to arise from establishing a learning network within China linked to TNCs' international operations. It can be argued that, once linked into the international network of foreign firms, state-owned enterprises enjoy an extended opportunity to benefit from learning and knowledge transfer. In high technology industries, foreign affiliates frequently operate a learning network, both globally and locally, into which state-owned enterprises have the potential to be embedded (Buckley *et al.*, 2002). This embeddedness can include joint R&D. With regard to the long term impact on host country productivity, such inward FDI might offer a significant and sustained positive impact. We can contrast this with the time-limited benefits from foreign affiliates operating in China, where foreign firms exploit an existing technological advantage created outside the host country, with little or no local linkages.

Notes

1 The drawback of a levels specification is that the direction of causality between FDI and productivity is not clear, since it is likely that foreign affiliates may locate in above-average productivity industries. Although our data constitute a panel, there are observations only for four years. This period is not long enough to allow us to test causality between overall productivity and FDI. However, employing Chinese manufacturing industry data, Buckley *et al.* (2002) found that causality runs as expected from FDI to growth rather than the other way around.
2 This justifies our procedure of controlling for differences in productivity between sub-sectors.
3 The sub-sector dummy variable itself also serves to eliminate a potential source of omitted-variable bias.
4 Where heteroscedasticity exists, variance-covariance matrices have been estimated according to White's (1980) method. Ramsey RESET tests indicate that all models suffer no specification error.
5 The correlation coefficient between the two variables is very small.
6 Although the quality of this variable is suspect, as discussed later.
7 Joint ventures between the primary affiliates of TNCs and State-owned enterprises are to be distinguished from primary affiliates that are international joint ventures, as used to be legally required in most of China's industry. The type of joint ventures referred to here are entirely voluntary, and are expected to be superior in terms of knowledge transfer and spillover benefits.

References

Aitken, Brian and Ann. E. Harrison (1999) 'Does domestic firms benefit from direct foreign investment? Evidence from Venezula', *The American Economic Review*, 89(3), pp. 605–618.

Blomström, M. and F. Sjöholm (1999) 'Technology transfer and spillovers: Does local participation with multinationals matter?', *European Economic Review*, 43, pp. 915–923.

Buckley, J. Peter, Jeremy Clegg and Hui Tan (2003) 'The Art of knowledge transfer: Secondary and reverse transfer in China's telecommunications manufacturing industry', *Management International Review*, 43, Special Issue, 2, pp. 67–93.

Buckley, J. Peter, Jeremy Clegg and Chengqi Wang (2002) 'The impact of inward FDI on the performance of China's manufacturing firms', *Journal of International Business Studies*, 33(4), pp. 637–655.

Buckley, J. Peter, Jeremy Clegg and Chengqi Wang (2003) 'Is the relationship between inward FDI and spillovers linear? An empirical examination of the case of China', paper presented at the *29th Annual Conference of European Academy of International Business*, Copenhagen, 11–13 December 2003, mimeo.

Caves, E. Richard (1974) 'Multinational firms, competition and productivity in host country markets', *Economica*, 41, pp. 176–193.

Chen Chung, Lawrence Chang and Yimin Zhang (1995) 'The role of foreign direct investment in China's post-1978 economic development', *World Development*, 23 (4), pp. 691–703.

Driffield, Nigel (2001) 'The impact of domestic productivity of inward investment in the UK', *The Manchester School*, 69(1), pp. 103–119.

Dunning, John H. (1981) *International Production and Multinational Enterprise*, (London: George Allen & Unwin).

Dunning, John H. (1988) *Explaining International Production*. London: George Allen & Unwin.

Egger, Peter and Michael Pfaffermayr (2001) 'A note on labour productivity and foreign inward direct investment', *Applied Economics Letters*, 8, pp. 229–232.

Feinberg, S. and S.K. Majumdar (2001). 'Technology spillovers and foreign direct investment in the Indian pharmaceutical industry', *Journal of International Business Studies*, 32(3), pp. 421–437.

Globerman, S. (1979) 'Foreign direct investment and 'spillover' efficiency benefits in Canadian manufacturing industries', *Canadian Journal of Economics*, 12, pp. 42–56.

Görg, Holger and Eric Strobl (2001) 'Multinational companies and productivity spillovers: a meta-analysis', *The Economic Journal*, 111 (November), pp. 723–739.

Haddad, M. and A. Harrison (1991) Are there dynamic externalities from direct foreign investment? Evidence for Morocco, Industry and Energy Department Working Article No. 48, Washington, D.C., The World Bank, pp. 1–28. mimeo.

Kokko, Ari (1996) 'Productivity spillovers from competition between local firms and foreign affiliates', *Journal of International Development*, 8, pp. 517–530.

Lan, Ping and Stephen Young (1996) 'Foreign direct investment and technology transfer: a case-study of foreign direct investment in north China', *Transnational Corporations*, 5(1), pp. 57–83.

Liu, Xiaming, Pamela Siler, Chengqi Wang and Yingqi Wei (2000) 'Productivity spillovers from foreign direct investment: evidence from UK industry level panel data', *Journal of International Business Studies*, 31(3), pp. 407–425.

Perez, T. (1997) 'Multinational enterprises and technological spillovers: an evolutionary model', *Journal of Evolutionary Economics*, 7, pp. 169–192.

Singh, R. (1992) 'Government introduced price distortion and growth, evidence from twenty nine developing countries', *Public Choice*, 73, pp. 83–99.

Sjöholm, Fredrik (1999) 'Technology gap, competition and spillovers from direct foreign investment: evidence from establishment data', *The Journal of Development Studies*, 36(1), pp. 53–73.

Wang, Chengqi, Pamela Siler and Xiaming Liu (2002) 'The relative economic performance of foreign subsidiaries in UK manufacturing', *Applied Economics*, 34, pp. 1885–1892.

White, H. (1980) 'A heteroscedasticity consistent covariance matrix estimator and a direct test for heteroscedasticity', *Econometrica*, 48, pp. 817–838.

Zhu, G. and K.Y. Tan (2000) 'Foreign direct investment and labour productivity: new evidence from China as the host', *Thunderbird International Business Review*, 42(5), pp. 507–528.

11
China's Inward Foreign Direct Investment Success: Southeast Asia in the Shadow of the Dragon

Peter J. Buckley, Jeremy Clegg, Adam Cross and Hui Tan

Introduction

A key aspect of the success of globalisation is the emergence of the People's Republic of China as a major player in the world economy. This paper explores not only the success of China as a location for foreign direct investment (FDI) but also examines some negative externalities of this success for neighbouring countries of Southeast Asia, in particular those of the Association of South East Asian Nations (ASEAN).[1] Much has been written on the character of inward FDI to China (Child and Lu, 1996; Wei and Liu, 2001) and, particularly following its accession to the World Trade Organisation (WTO) in December 2001, the determinants of FDI and its effect on the domestic economy, in terms of, for example, growth (Buckley, Clegg, Wang and Cross, 2002) and productivity (Liu, Parker, Vaidya and Wei, 2001). Other work assesses the implications of China's WTO accession for world merchandise trade flows (e.g., Lardy, 2002; Ianchovichina, Martin and Fukase, 2000; Ianchovichina and Martin, 2001). However, with the notable exception of a report by the ASEAN-China Expert Group on Economic Cooperation (ACEGEC, 2001), much less has been written on how multinational enterprises (MNEs) might adjust investment strategies in response to opportunities arising from China's deepening integration into the global economic system post-WTO and what the consequences of this might be for developing countries like those of Southeast Asia as FDI recipients.

China's growing prominence in the regional and global economy comes at a time when many Southeast Asian nations are themselves striving to augment stocks of FDI to help reinvigorate faltering economic growth in the wake of the Asian economic crisis of 1997. Since the inception of its 'Open Door' policy in 1978, China has been successful in capturing an increasing and substantial proportion of global FDI; its share of world FDI stock (estimated using accumulated flow data) grew from 1% in 1980 to stand at just over 6% by 2002 (UNCTAD, 2003). When it entered the WTO, China was already host to the world's fifth largest FDI stock by country, a position which rises to second with the inclusion of Hong Kong Special Administrative Region (SAR). Over the same period, the performance of the Southeast Asian countries in this respect was steady; collectively they hosted around 4% of world FDI stock in 2001, a position not dissimilar to that of China (UNCTAD, 2001). However, since the Asian crisis, China has successfully out-stripped the Southeast Asian countries, individually and collectively, in terms of the share of annual global FDI flow attracted (see Table 11.1). The share of China and the Southeast Asian countries in global FDI flow all weakened in the final years of the 1990s, due in part to the effects of the Asian crisis. However, the decline in China's share was far less dramatic, dropping from 9.3% of annual world FDI flow in 1997 to 2.7% in 2000, compared with 6.4 to 0.7% for the ASEAN countries over the same period. Moreover, the decline in China's position in global investment flows is negated entirely when Hong Kong's rising status after the hand-over in 1997 is factored in (see Table 11.1). A resurgence of FDI flow to the region began in 2000, but, again, China's position improved more quickly than its Southeast Asian neighbors. China's share of world FDI flow rose to just over 8% in 2002 (or 10.2% with the inclusion of data for Hong Kong SAR) compared to 2.1% collectively for the ASEAN countries (UNCTAD, 2003).

For much of their recent histories, China and the Southeast Asian countries have followed a similar economic development model with regard to FDI. In general, they have all promoted high levels of foreign ownership in export-oriented, low-value added mass manufacturing, using combinations of relatively high tariff and non-tariff barriers to restrict imports and special trade regimes (typically liberal duty exemptions on inputs) to encourage exports (Lemoine, 2000). China and Southeast Asia may therefore be rival locations for certain types of FDI. In this paper, we review the literature on China's increasingly progressive policies towards FDI in recent times and against this map the concomitant effect on inward investment by source country, investment motive, sectoral trends, entry method and geographic distribution. Our aim is to assess whether or not China was a rival to the Southeast Asian economies as an investment location prior to WTO accession. We then consider how China's accession might impact its investment climate

Table 11.1 FDI inflows, by host region and economy, 1990–2001 (US$m and percentage).

Host region/economy	1990–1995 (annual average)	1996	1997	1998	1999	2000	2001
World	225,321	386,140	478,082	694,457	1,088,263	1,491,934	735,146
South, East and Southeast Asia	44,564	87,843	96,338	86,252	99,990	131,123	94,365
China	19,360	40,180	44,237	43,751	40,319	40,772	46,846
Share of world total	8.6%	10.4%	9.3%	6.3%	3.7%	2.7%	6.4%
S, E and SE Asia total	43.4%	45.7%	45.9%	50.7%	40.3%	31.1%	49.6%
Hong Kong, China	4,859	10,460	11,368	14,770	24,596	61,938	22,834
Share of world total	2.2%	2.7%	2.4%	2.1%	2.3%	4.2%	3.1%
S, E and SE Asia total	10.9%	11.9%	11.8%	17.1%	24.6%	47.2%	24.2%
Brunei	102	654	702	573	596	600	244
Cambodia	80	586	-15	230	214	179	113
Indonesia	2,135	6,194	4,677	-356	-2,745	-4,550	-3,277
Laos	33	128	86	45	52	34	24
Malaysia	4,655	7,296	6,324	2,714	3,895	3,788	554
Myanmar	180	310	387	314	253	255	123
Philippines	1,028	1,520	1,249	1,752	578	1,241	1,792
Singapore	5,782	8,608	10,746	6,389	11,803	5,407	8,609
Thailand	1,990	2,271	3,626	5,143	3,561	2,813	3,759
Vietnam	947	1,803	2,587	1,700	1,484	1,289	1,300
ASEAN-10	16,932	29,370	30,369	18,504	19,691	11,056	13,241
Share of world total	7.5%	7.6%	6.4%	2.7%	1.8%	0.7%	1.8%
S, E and SE Asia total	38.0%	33.4%	31.5%	21.5%	19.7%	8.4%	14.0%

Source: UNCTAD (2002).

relative to the Southeast Asian economies. We do this under two generic scenarios; one, that China is willing and able to comply with the conditions of WTO accession and two, that compliance is partial. This review is used to draw some tentative conclusions on whether or not China will have a magnetic, neutral or benign effect on the future spatial distribution of MNE-owned production in East and Southeast Asia. Some policy recommendations for the Southeast Asian countries are presented in light of this analysis.

Patterns of FDI in China

The degree to which China's WTO accession might impinge on patterns of Southeast Asian FDI depends largely on, firstly, whether or not China and Southeast Asia are substitute hosts for certain types of FDI and, secondly, how China's locational advantages might change after accession relative to Southeast Asia. To explore the first point, it is important to distinguish between two types of direct investment by motivation; namely labour-intensive, export-oriented (henceforth export platform) FDI and technology-intensive, market-seeking FDI. The former universally concerns manufacturing and is driven by cost pressures while the latter can be in both services and manufacturing and is driven by revenue-generation pressures. We disregard natural-resource seeking motives (insofar as the data allow) as the location-bound nature of many resource-based factor inputs makes it unlikely that Southeast Asia and China have been or will be substitute hosts for this type of activity.

The character of inward investment to China prior to WTO accession suggests strongly that China and Southeast Asia were not substitute investment hosts to this point. This is because the primary source of this investment was overseas Chinese capital. Table 11.2 presents four distinct phases in the evolution of China's FDI policy direction and investment climate prior to WTO accession, against which we characterise the investment responses of foreign firms. (For more detail, especially on the early periods, see Cross and Tan, 2004; OECD, 2000; Wei and Liu, 2001). Over much of the pre-WTO period, China's investment policy had two parallel strands. The first sought to boost domestic productivity and output by attracting export-oriented FDI to Special Export Zones (SEZs) and other opened areas, mostly in the easternmost provinces, to generate foreign exchange, expand currency reserves and to finance imports of capital goods and production inputs. The second strand sought to shelter inefficient and vulnerable local firms (in which

Table 11.2 FDI Policy in China and some resulting inward investment trends (1979–1999).

PHASE AND POLICY MOTIVATION:

Experimental Period (1979 to 1983)

To attract greater inward FDI, especially from overseas Chinese, as one of the 'four modernisations', and to learn from the experiences of the opened areas.

Main Policy Developments
- ✓ A series of laws on joint ventures (JVs) permitted FDI, define equity JVs and set out the fiscal arrangements concerning foreign invested enterprises (FIEs).
- ✓ Creation of four Special Economic Zones (SEZs), with special investment incentives, at Shenzen, Zhuhai, Shantou and Xiamen in Guangdong and Fujian provinces, along with greater economic autonomy for these two provinces.
- ✓ Duty exemptions for imports of intermediate inputs used in the production of exports.
- ✓ Highly constrained access to domestic markets granted to foreign investors.
- ✓ Ministry of Foreign Economic Relations and Trade (MOFERT) created, responsible for FDI, trade and other foreign economic affairs.

Investment character and strategic motivation
- ✓ Mostly speculative investment in real estate (hotels and apartment buildings).
- ✓ Some small-scale, export-oriented FDI in labour intensive industries manufacturing industries such as footwear, clothing, toys, and electrical appliances.
- ✓ Hong Kong and Taiwan ROC are main source countries.

Gradual Development Period (1984 to 1991)

To build upon the success of the first SEZs and to divert FDI away from real-estate and into technology intensive, export-oriented and infrastructure-related sectors.

Main Policy Developments
- ✓ Law for the Encouragement of Foreign Investment promulgated (1986) and implementing regulations announced (1987).
- ✓ Continued loosening of investment restrictions, mostly in sectors with few domestic firms (e.g. tourism and hotels) and where foreign capital and technology was sought (e.g. oil exploration).
- ✓ Hainan Island and 14 coastal cities across ten provinces opened to FDI in 1984.
- ✓ Preferential income tax arrangements for FIEs granted in 1984.
- ✓ The Yangtze River (Changjiang) Delta, the Pearl River (Zhujiang) Delta and South Fujian area become Open Export Zones (OEZs) in 1985, followed in 1987 by Shandong and East Liaoning Peninsulars.
- ✓ Shanghai's Pudong New Area opened in 1989, a flagship SEZ.

Table 11.2 FDI Policy in China and some resulting inward investment trends (1979–1999) – *continued*

	Investment character and strategic motivation ✓ Initially some resource-oriented FDI in extractive industries, but a general shift in FDI towards export-oriented and technology intensive manufacturing industries occurs across the period. ✓ Around half of FDI by value is in hotel construction and real estate. ✓ Hong Kong and Taiwanese investment predominate, but investments from USA and Japan are increasingly common. ✓ Equity JVs (51% of contracted value of FDI in 1991), co-operative JVs (18%), wholly foreign-owned enterprises (WFOEs) (31%).
Peak Period (1992 to 1993) The imperative of Deng Xiaoping to accelerate economic reform and to develop new export industries.	Main Policy Developments ✓ Foreign firms allowed to sell more to China's domestic market. ✓ Some FDI approvals conditional on achievement of certain policy goals. Special investment incentives available in preferred sectors. ✓ New sectors opened up experimentally to foreign investment (e.g., domestic retail trade, finance, tourism, shipping, resource development). ✓ FDI remains tightly controlled by state policy, though approval of smaller projects now devolved to provincial and municipal government. Thousands of new SEZs spring up as a result. ✓ Market entry remains regulated through as performance requirements, local sourcing requirements, location restrictions, forced JV establishment. ✓ Further opening of 28 cities and 8 regions in the Yangtze River Delta area. Investment character and strategic motivation ✓ Around 60% of inward FDI flows into highly export-oriented and technology intensive industrial sectors, especially in the coastal provinces, but market-seeking motives beginning to grow in importance. ✓ Slowdown in FDI from the Triad regions. ✓ Equity JVs (49% of contracted value of FDI in 1993), Co-operative JVs (23%), WFOEs (27%).

Table 11.2 FDI Policy in China and some resulting inward investment trends (1979–1999) – *continued*

Adjustment Period (1994 to 1999)	
To adjust the industrial structure of FDI and to provide national treatment for foreign investors reductions.	Main Policy Developments ✓ The State Council decides to categorise sectors into those in which FDI was 'encouraged', 'restricted' or 'forbidden'. The former (typically export-oriented, technology intensive or import substituting investment) benefit from tariff exemptions and fiscal reductions. ✓ Duties re-imposed in 1995 on imported machinery, equipment, parts and other materials by FIEs (but repealed in 1997 for FDI in 'encouraged' sectors). ✓ Domestic market access continues to be constrained, to shelter inefficient and vulnerable state-owned enterprises from international competition, using similar policy instruments as before. ✓ These highly selective special investment regimes are gradually abandoned for more nationwide implementation of open policies towards end of period. Investment character and strategic motivation ✓ Market-seeking gradually becomes the dominant investment motivation with resource-seeking in relative decline. ✓ FDI is more capital-intensive, and FIE production is directed more to China's domestic market than on export markets, although FIEs still make a decisive contribution to export-intensive activity. ✓ Growth in FDI from USA, Japan and EU towards end of period. ✓ Equity JVs (32% of contracted value of FDI in 1999), Co-operative JVs (17%), WFOEs (51%).

Sources: Cross and Tan (2003), UNCTAD World Investment Report (various issues), Graham and Wada (2001), Wei and Liu (2001), Lemoine (2000).

the State typically held a full or partial equity stake) by severely limiting domestic market access to foreign firms with devices like performance requirements, location restrictions and entry mode constraints. Later, as the capacity of foreign invested enterprises (FIEs) to absorb foreign capital and technology became clear and because such firms were demonstrably more efficient than local incumbents, tight centralised control was slowly relaxed. Investment approval decisions and FIE-related matters were progressively devolved to the provinces and municipalities, investment (and particularly sectoral) restrictions were eased and larger geographic areas were opened, though still confined mostly to the coastal regions. Viewed in retrospect, each policy phase represents a cautious, pragmatic and staged opening of China's economy to foreign, and especially ethic Chinese, investors. As Thomsen (1999) comments, this is in stark contrast to the Southeast Asian countries, whose FDI policy has often been determined by events rather than shaping them.

Data on the aggregate value of realised cumulative FDI (Figure 11.1) reveals that each liberalisation phase in China gave fresh impetus to FDI inflows.[2] Despite some volatility in global supply, FDI flows to China surged in the early 1990s, especially in manufacturing, in response to open political commitment to market-oriented reform, strong domestic growth, and the continued creation of SEZs and other investor benefits. The mid-1990s saw a deceleration in this inflow, however, as other developing countries in Latin America, Eastern Europe and Southeast Asia competed more effectively as FDI hosts and as internal policy served as a brake. In particular, the introduction of national treatment in 1995 brought with it import duties and other investment disincentives. A further deceleration in FDI inflow occurred between 1998 and 1999 (see Figure 11.1 and Table 11.1), which coincided with a slowdown in economic growth in China and the Asian crisis; China's share of global FDI flow dropped from 10.4% in 1996 to 2.7% in 2000. Nevertheless, China's role in the investment strategy of MNEs seems unaffected over this period – a fourfold increase in inward FDI to Hong Kong (by value) between 1998 and 2000 is at least partly indicative of investment funds being 'parked on the doorstep' of mainland China by foreign firms in anticipation of emerging opportunities

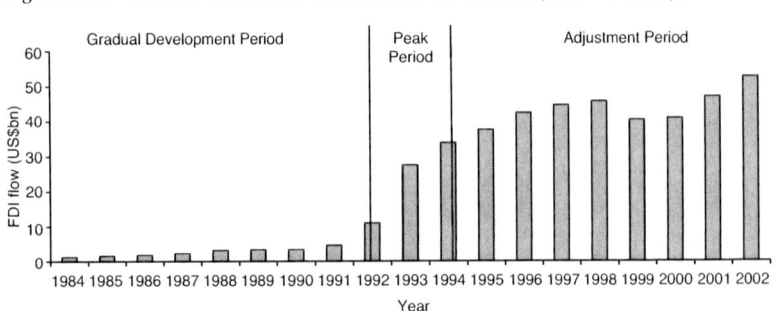

Figure 11.1 Annual inflows of utilised FDI into China (1984 to 2002).

Note: data for 1984 are accumulated stock of FDI since 1979.
Source: China Statistical Yearbook (various issues).

post-WTO (although Hong Kong's role as a tax haven and round-tripping hub will also have had a part to play).

Investment motivation

Table 11.3 shows that in 1998 just under 60% of the contracted value of China's FDI stock and the bulk of individual investments was in manufacturing sectors (followed by real estate at around 24%) (China Statistical Yearbook, 1999). Of the former, an estimated 50% (by value) was in labour-intensive manufacturing, while technology-intensive manufacturing accounted for around 27% and capital-intensive manufacturing, 23% (OECD, 2000). Graham and Wada (2001) estimate that, overall, some 60% of FDI inflow in the mid-1990s was to highly export-intensive industrial sectors in China. Access to low cost labour was clearly a key investment motive at this time. However, Graham and Wada go on to report a distinct shift in the late 1990s towards market-oriented FDI, in sectors in which China had no revealed comparative advantage. This was driven by domestic market expansion and improved market access for foreigners (Lemoine, 2000). Similarly,

Table 11.3 Contracted FDI in China by sectors at the end of 1998.

Sector	Number of Projects	Share (%)	Contracted value (US$bn)	Share (%)
Manufacturing	249,352	73.0	365,547	59.6
Real estate	33,877	9.9	149,977	24.4
Distribution	21,279	6.2	36,929	6.0
• wholesale, retailing, catering	17,558	5.1	21,960	3.6
• transport, warehousing and telecommunications	3,721	1.1	14,969	2.4
Construction	8,826	2.6	11,860	3.1
Agriculture, forestry, animal husbandry and fishing	9,534	2.8	19,827	1.8
Scientific research and technical services	2,410	0.7	1,874	0.3
Education, broadcasting, film and TV	1,317	0.4	2,040	0.3
Healthcare, sports and social welfare	999	0.3	4,618	0.8
Other sectors	13,944	4.1	23,045	3.8
Total	341,538	100	613,717	100

Source: China Statistical Yearbook (1999).

UNCTAD (2001) note that inward Chinese FDI had become more capital and technology-intensive by this time, an observation confirmed by Li, Qian, Lam and Wang (2000) in a study of FDI in China's electronics industry. Of course, it is no coincidence that market-seeking investment increased in hand with more capital and technology-intensive investment. The local adaptation of products and processes to suit particular market needs and the establishment of miniature replica-type production plants in China equipped in much the same way as equivalent plants elsewhere are two explanations.

Investment source

Indications are strong that the propensity to shift towards market-oriented investment in China differed by source country. Table 11.4 shows that Hong Kong and Taiwanese firms together accounted for the bulk (60.1%) of the accumulated FDI stock in China between 1983 and 1998 (OECD, 2000). This is followed by firms from Japan (8.3%), the U.S.A. (8.1%), Western Europe (6.7%) and the ASEAN-5 (6.2%).[3] Moreover, the geographic distribution of ethnic Chinese-owned investors in China closely reflects the ancestral homeland of the migrant source country population. Hence, Fujian province has been generally favored by Taiwanese firms, and Guangdong province by firms from Hong Kong and Macao. Such firms enjoy transaction cost-related ownership advantages in these places relative to other investor nationalities because of geographic proximity, cultural convergence and familial

Table 11.4 Accumulated FDI stock in China, by home country and region (1995 constant prices and %).

	1979–91	1983–90	1991–95	1996–98	1983–98
Total FDI stock (US$m)		24,528	118,086	126,119	268,733
Source country and region (% share)					
Hong Kong	62.0	58.5	58.8	45.2	52.4
Taiwan	n/a	1.1	9.8	7.3	7.9
ASEAN 5	n/a	1.5	5.1	8.1	6.2
Japan	14.0	13.7	6.9	8.6	8.3
USA	10.0	12.1	7.4	8.0	8.1
Western Europe	n/a	6.6	4.5	8.7	6.7

Sources: OECD (2000); Lamoine (2000).
Note: ASEAN 5 = Singapore, Thailand, Philippines, Malaysia and Indonesia.

ties. However, the combined share of Hong Kong and Taiwan in utilised FDI in China dropped to 43.7% in 2000, while the share of the U.S.A. and Western Europe (led by France and the U.K.) rose to 10.8% and 11.2%, respectively.[4] Japan's position weakened slightly to 7.2%, and ASEAN-5 recorded a small increase, to 7.0% (two thirds of which was from Singapore). Overall, these changes suggest that firms from the Triad countries had raised their level of equity participation appreciably in China in the two years prior to WTO accession. Moreover, while Hong Kong and Taiwanese firms invested mostly in export-processing activities in China, it was Western European and Japanese companies that were now making more capital-intensive investment, mainly to supply goods and services to China's domestic market; U.S. firms are thought to fall somewhere in between (Graham and Wada, 2001; UNCTAD, 2001; Lemoine, 2000).

Investment form

Until 1993, the equity joint venture was the preferred entry mode for China, accounting for just under half of all contracted amounts of FDI (OECD, 2000). However, after the mid-1990s, wholly-foreign owned enterprises were increasingly favoured; in 1999 just over half (51%) of the contracted value of FDI took this form, mostly as greenfield operations (OECD, 2000). Graham and Wada (2001) note that the average size of individual investments also began to rise in 1999, which they attribute to a growing preponderance of larger-scale Japanese, U.S. and E.U. investments compared to smaller individual investments from Hong Kong, Taiwan and other Newly Industrialising Countries.

Geographic distribution

In general, FDI has been concentrated in just four coastal provinces of China: (in descending order of FDI value) Guangdong, Jiangsu, Fujian and Shanghai (Lemoine, 2000). For the period 1983 to 1998, the eastern provinces together absorbed 87.8% of total FDI inflows, with 8.9% going to the central provinces, and less than 4% to the western provinces. But since the mid-1990s, FDI has become more evenly distributed between the eastern provinces. For example, the share of Guangdong province in total FDI inflows dropped from 46% in the 1980s to 28% in the 1990s, while other coastal provinces and the central provinces recorded an upward share. One interpretation is that more recent investors to China are less drawn to Guangdong and Fujian provinces than earlier ones (probably because they benefit less from transaction cost-related ownership advantages), and that a more even distribution of FDI in China is now underway.

To summarise, then, we see a general transformation in the character of inward FDI in China in the few years immediately prior to WTO accession. In very broad terms, a greater proportion of investment by developed country firms (notably from the Triad countries) which is of a larger scale, is more capital-intensive and is more market-oriented, has made steady inroads on the substantial stock of smaller scale, labor-intensive and export-oriented investments of Hong Kong and Taiwanese firms since the 1980s. This distinct shift in the character of inward FDI to China began in the Adjustment Period (1994–1999, see Table 11.2) when a significant number of large investments by Western MNEs joined the much larger number of small investments originated from overseas Chinese sources. Furthermore, wholly-owned foreign operations supplanted equity joint ventures as the preferred means of entry, and FDI progressively, albeit slowly, began to penetrate regions beyond the coastal provinces. For the first time since the Second World War, the general pattern and character of FDI in China has begun to converge with that of the developed countries (Buckley and Clegg, 1998).

Rivalry between China and Southeast Asia for FDI prior to WTO accession

This description suggests strongly that, before the mid 1990s, China and Southeast Asia were unlikely to have been rivals as hosts for export-platform FDI. As we see, in China this type of FDI is characterised by certain ownership advantages derived from transaction cost benefits peculiar mainly to Hong Kong and Taiwanese investors in particular geographic contexts. Although ethnic Chinese firms from these source countries also invest in Southeast Asia, they are much less prominent (Thomsen, 1999), as their ownership-specific advantages are much reduced in contexts outside of mainland China. Up until the late 1990s, therefore, the opening of China probably *increased* the global supply of export-platform FDI; that is, opening had an FDI *creating* effect. This included significant amounts of 'round-tripping', whereby domestic investment was transformed into FDI by being routed through Hong Kong and Macao back to China to benefit from positive discrimination afforded to foreigners. WTO accession, with its provision for national treatment, should remove this artificial incentive. Moreover, several authors (such as Tan, 1999; Cheong, 2000; and

Palanca, 2001) hold that the emergence of China as an FDI host has not crowded out regional FDI *in general*, and that WTO accession offers little threat of this in the future. Data on the share of China and Southeast Asia in total investment flow underscores this view (see Table 11.1). As China's annual share of global FDI rose from around 8% in the early 1990s to just over 10% by 1996, so too did that of Southeast Asia, if only slightly. The magnitude of the growth in China's share, and that of Southeast Asia, was matched by a drop in FDI share for the industrialised countries and a positive change in world FDI flows, from which both China and Southeast Asia benefited, perhaps in a noncompetitive way. Closer examination of the data, however, reveals some evidence of crowding out in the late 1990s. As we have already noted, after 1997, and despite rising total values, China and Southeast Asia's annual share of global FDI flow both decreased, reflecting worsening investment climates in the region compared to elsewhere. However, the rate of decline was much faster for the Southeast Asian countries. This decline is accentuated if we consider Hong Kong and China together in the regional context. In the mid-1990s, Southeast Asia consistently received almost a third of the annual investment flow to South, East and Southeast Asia; by 2000 this figure stood at just 8.4%. Over the same period, China and Hong Kong's combined share rose from just over 57% to almost 79%. Notwithstanding the tax haven position of Hong Kong it seems likely that investment allocated at the *regional level* by MNEs (and perhaps at the global level) was indeed being preferentially diverted towards China and Hong Kong in the few years prior to WTO accession. The correlation between the rise in market-seeking FDI by developed country firms in China from 1997 onwards, and the decrease in overall FDI in Southeast Asia, is suggestive that a proportion of China's FDI growth was at the expense of market-seeking manufacturing FDI in Southeast Asia. Moreover, this trend may not be confined to the Triad countries as an FDI source. In 1997, China overtook Malaysia to become Singapore's principal FDI destination, and by 2000 Singapore held the fifth largest stock of cumulative FDI in China (around 5% of the total) notably in labour intensive manufacturing (Heng, 2001). Some intra-Southeast Asian FDI flows may also have been diverted to China at this time.

Rivalry between China and Southeast Asia for FDI after WTO accession

In order to ascertain whether or not rivalry between China and Southeast Asia as investment locations will grow following China's

Table 11.5 China's WTO accession obligations and commitments.

- The average bound tariff level for all industrial goods will be reduced to 9.4% by 2005 from the current 24.6%, with a wide range of detailed commitments to lower tariffs on other products. Some tariff reductions will be immediate, and others phased. All will be complete by 2005.
- The average tariff level for ASEAN products will be reduced by 34% to 47% by 2005, faster than the average reduction.
- Rules on Trade-Related Investment Measures (TRIMs) will be observed immediately on entry. Almost all administrative examination and approval procedures for the import of goods (such as quotas, licenses and other non-tariff quantitative restrictions) will be abolished. Many quotas were eliminated on accession; most of the remainder to be eliminated by 2003 and entirely phased out by 2005. The following devices were eliminated immediately on entry:
  o local content requirements,
  o technology transfer requirements and offsets as a condition for investment,
  o export performance and trade balancing requirements.
- Intellectual Property Rights – China agreed to implement TRIPS immediately on entry. Requirements that Chinese partners to a JV gain ownership of trade secrets after a certain number of years are removed.
- Trading Rights (the right to import and establish distribution networks) for foreign companies will be eliminated by 2003. Coverage is comprehensive, and includes commission agents' services, wholesaling, retailing, franchising, sales away from a fixed location, and related activities like inventory management, after sales service, repair and maintenance services, with foreign ownership allowed, up to 49%.
- All tariffs on information technology equipment and computers will be removed by 2005, by participation in the WTO Information Technology Agreement.
- Liberalisation of telecommunications, allowing the provision of telephony services by foreign firms across any distance within two to six years; foreign investment allowed up to 49% in all services, and 50% for value-added and paging services.
- Liberalisation of financial services by 2005, opening markets in banking, insurance, securities, fund management and other sectors. Licenses are to be granted on prudential criteria alone, and not on economic-needs tests or numeric bases.
- Domestic market access and foreign ownership (majority or up to 49% foreign equity share) is now permitted in sectors such as travel and tourism and audio-visual materials.
- Support for state-owned and state-invested enterprises. China has agreed that WTO rules will apply to firms in which the state has an equity interest. Such firms are required to buy and sell on a commercial basis, such as quality and price. Trade between SOEs and foreign firms will be permitted. Government procurement systems will become more transparent.

Source: ACEGEC (2001); Nolan (2001).

accession to the WTO, it is necessary to examine how this event might reconfigure China's locational advantages relative to Southeast Asia. China became committed to implementing a comprehensive package of market liberalisation measures on entering the WTO (see Table 11.5). Simply put, China is obligated to open and further liberalise many of its markets, providing foreign firms with greater access to domestic markets and levelling the playing field for foreign and domestic business, either immediately or through a phased implementation, to be completed by 2005.

As with past periods of policy reform, China's membership of the WTO is likely to provide fresh impetus to FDI inflows. In particular, the elimination of severe controls on distribution in China should enhance market access and increase substantially the incentive to make new and sequential market-oriented investments across many sectors. Also, new investment opportunities are likely to arise in sectors previously closed or highly restricted to foreign firms, especially in telecommunications services, wholesaling and retailing, logistics, financial services, travel and tourism, and audiovisual-related activity. But the interactions are complex, and the outcome – for China as well as for the Southeast Asian countries – is far from clear.

First, given China's already prominent position in global investment flow, it is unlikely that accession to the WTO will bring about any dramatic change to China's *external* economic relations in this regard (Cross and Tan, 2004). Instead, the major and most immediate changes are likely to be *internal*. These could concern not only its economy, but its social fabric and political order as well. If China's authorities do decide to comply fully with its accession commitments, then China will almost certainly experience several simultaneous 'shocks'. Nolan (2001, p. 925) characterises these shocks as arising from:

- normal restructuring, as a consequence of rapidly intensifying competition, especially from overseas;
- having to compete on a global level playing field with a highly concentrated global business system;
- the IT revolution and modern production systems on employment;
- the drastic impact of the global media revolution upon Chinese culture;
- for its people's self-esteem, should China fail to establish a collection of powerful indigenous corporations;

- dealing with the dominance of foreign-owned corporations, especially those from the USA.

Painful short-term restructuring of previously sheltered state-owned enterprises brought about by sharply heightened competitive pressure from abroad could adjust employment away from the state-owned sector in a manner that nascent foreign and domestic owned private sectors could find difficult to absorb. At the same time, the ability of China's institutions to provide and abide by a framework of international law and to make the fundamental and wide-ranging systemic adjustments necessitated may well prove limited. Chang (2001) and others are doubtful that the ability or will exists in China to balance rapid market liberalisation after accession against equally rapid social cost hikes and societal tensions. Given these challenges, instead of reduced government intervention in foreign trade and investment, the enhancement of intellectual property rights, and the modernisation of China's administrative and legal systems and practices, all agreed under WTO (that is, full compliance), what might occur instead is a heightening of bureaucratic and technical barriers to investment (cf. Japan in the 1970s), patchy implementation of WTO obligations, and on-going arbitrariness amongst local government agencies and the judiciary (that is, partial compliance). Partial compliance would provide new and established foreign investors with their own 'shock' – that investment barriers remain high and that accession fails to make Chinese investments any more profitable.

The implications of China's WTO accession for Southeast Asia

Three possible generic outcomes concerning FDI patterns in East and Southeast Asia can be envisaged following China's accession to the WTO. The first is the *magnetic effect* argument. This asserts that accession will strengthen China's locational advantages for FDI relative to the Southeast Asian countries. Firms would respond by (i) switching 'footloose' foreign owned operations in the region to China; (ii) diverting investment funds intended for existing operations in Southeast Asia to China; and (iii), direct new investments to the region towards China. The second is the *neutral effect* argument. This asserts that, once the euphoria surrounding China's entry has waned, regional investment flows will readjust to produce a distribution of FDI across the region equivalent to that of the mid 1990s, before the Asian crisis. The third is the *benign effect* argument. This asserts that, should China attract greater shares of regional and global FDI flows, the Southeast Asian countries will be able to 'ride on the back' of this success, through greater trade and investment, so neutralising any detrimental effects to their own economic development that might otherwise occur. The outcome observed depends greatly upon China's willingness and ability to comply with its accession commitments and, if it does, whether or not it can make the profound structural and institutional adjustments necessitated. The growth of the Chinese economy brought on by greater integration with the regional and global economy could provide a huge stimulus to income effects which have the potential to benefit the whole of East Asia (including Southeast Asia and Japan) while the relative attractiveness of China as an investment location creates a potential substitution effect which threatens to reduce FDI in the East Asian region. Nevertheless, the extent to which China will rival Southeast Asia as a host for export platform and market-seeking FDI activity after joining the WTO remains an open question. Let us now explore some of the issues.

With regard to the export platform FDI, China's full compliance with its WTO obligations will bring about a reduction in tariffs and other non-tariff barriers to trade. This will help foreign firms to serve China's market by exporting from other nearby production locations rather than from production bases *within* China (Nolan, 2001). Accession and compliance may therefore have the effect of *strengthening* the position of neighbouring countries, including Southeast Asian countries, as hosts for export-platform manufacturing FDI oriented towards serving the China market. Naturally, this effect would be accentuated if China's investment climate worsens after accession, because of growing political or social instability or rising factor input costs, for example. However, if China is unable to fully comply with its accession conditions, and if barriers to trade do rise (especially non-tariff barriers) in order to protect Chinese industry or for other economic or political imperatives, then the incentive for MNEs to continue with import-substituting strategies in China will be strong. With regard to market-seeking FDI, full compliance should create many new business opportunities for foreign firms, especially in those services sectors where market access is being granted for the first time. Given the inseparability of production and consumption for many services, the propensity for service MNEs to undertake FDI is likely to rise as they achieve market access. However, investment in new manufacturing capacity (i.e., greenfield projects) may not grow as fast as in services.

There is much over-capacity in many goods markets in China where structural weaknesses have stifled demand. However, full compliance could see many of these weaknesses diminish as greater competitive pressures raise efficiencies, as export-led economic growth accelerates, and as inward investors themselves provide a spur to domestic demand.

This account points to the fact that accession and the extent of compliance could reconfigure China's investment climate relative to those of Southeast Asia which, in turn, may lead to further adjustment in regional FDI flow patterns. The degree to which intra- and extra-Southeast Asian FDI inflows might be displaced to China depends greatly on factors such as relative market growth projections, cost structures of location-bound factor inputs for production, and overall location attractiveness of China and individual Southeast Asian countries after China's WTO accession. We now consider each of these in turn.

Market growth projections

Ianchovichina and Martin (2001), working for the World Bank, use a conservative static model to predict that the removal of barriers to Chinese imports following WTO membership will bring about a 2.2% rise in China's income as exports grow (by at least 6.8% under one scenario), especially in textiles and clothing. This figure may even be understated as dynamic considerations like the positive effect of accession on wages, economic efficiency and investment in China are discounted. On the other hand, the authors predict a gloomier outlook for the Southeast Asian countries. Although Singapore, Thailand, Malaysia and Indonesia in particular benefited in the 1990s by exporting to China and that this may accelerate (by 3 to 14% depending on the economy) as aggregate demand in China rises, it is predicted that such increases will be insufficient to compensate for export sales lost to China in third markets, especially in textiles, apparel and electronics. Consequently, a modest 0.1% decline in income for the Southeast Asian countries is forecast, with the exception of Singapore, which shows a small rise of 0.9%. Providing the reform process is not derailed, accession should accelerate economic growth in China. This in turn should stimulate both new market-seeking investments and sequential investments by foreign incumbents already active in the China market. Concomitantly, and with some exceptions, the relative market attractiveness of the Southeast Asian countries will probably decline in general terms. This may have the effect of reducing the propensity for foreign firms to undertake market-seeking FDI in these countries relative to China.

Location attractiveness

Recent surveys allow us to comment on the relative attractiveness of China, Hong Kong and the ASEAN-5 countries as inward investment hosts. Table 11.6 presents data from the IMD (2001) Annual Executive Opinion Survey of current and expected competitiveness conditions for 47 host countries. China is ranked 29th overall as an investment location in the period 1998–99, a position bettered only by Singapore and Malaysia among the ASEAN-5 (the other five Southeast Asian countries being excluded from the survey). As a production location, China has many advantages relative to Southeast Asia. Perhaps most obvious is its abundant pool of low cost labor. Despite certain shortages, especially in middle management, there are in general sufficient numbers of workers skilled at most stages of the value chain to satisfy the current needs of the majority of investors, even in more capital-intensive and knowledge-intensive sectors. China has also developed stocks of technological capability in several sectors, notably in electronics, due in part to its economic isolation in recent decades and to the spill-over effects of FDI. This stock is now being augmented by China's rapidly modernising educational system, overseas educated returnees and FIE training and development programs. China's technical and transport infrastructures have also been upgraded considerably in recent years, especially in the eastern provinces. New foreign investment in services, distribution and logistics sectors following accession could help to further drive down manufacturing costs. The unevenness

Table 11.6 Location attractiveness rankings for China, Hong Kong and the ASEAN-5.

	Manufacturing	R&D	Service and Management	Overall ranking
China (PRC)	39	40	45	33
Hong Kong	6	16	10	6
Singapore	1	3	3	2
Thailand	42	42	40	38
Malaysia	28	35	32	29
Indonesia	48	49	48	49
Philippines	36	37	35	40

Note: data not available for Brunei, Cambodia, Laos, Myanmar and Vietnam.
Source: IMD (2001).

of China's development means that the underdeveloped northern and western provinces will continue to offer many equivalent benefits to foreign investors, certainly in respect of labour, should manufacturing costs rise in the coastal provinces after accession. By contrast, several Southeast Asian countries are reported to have labour shortages and rising labour and land costs (Yean, 1998).

The IMD survey also presents data on the FDI regimes and transactions costs of doing business in the region (see Tables 11.7 and 11.8). In terms of its FDI regime, China scores lower than each of the ASEAN-5 countries except Indonesia, faring particularly badly on the availability of local capital and foreign ownership of domestic firms. However, full compliance to the WTO should bring about considerable improvement in these areas, and in others such as equal treatment and national protectionism. In terms of transaction costs, China's overall assessment compares favourably with the ASEAN-5 countries, bettered only by Singapore and Malaysia. While China scores poorly on bureaucracy and levels of corruption, its business environment in general seems to be no worse than that of the ASEAN-5 countries (with the obvious exception of Singapore), and is in some respects better. Importantly, unlike the smaller Southeast Asian economies, many foreign firms will view China's large market potential as sufficiently adequate compensation for the comparatively high transaction costs experienced there.

A measure recently invoked by UNCTAD (2002) reinforces the view that China has a generally more favourable investment climate compared to Southeast Asian countries (see Table 11.9). UNCTAD (2002) calculate the Inward FDI Performance Index as an approximate measure of a nation's relative performance in attracting FDI, allowing for economic size. For China, this index rose from 0.9 to 1.2 between the periods 1988–90 and 1998–2000; an improvement in its 'revealed competitive advantage' for FDI, and an indication perhaps of the country's resilience to the Asian crisis and its causes. However, the index declines for each Southeast Asian country except Vietnam over the same period, indicating a reduction in the attractiveness of the Southeast Asian countries relative to China, especially in market-related aspects. This may be due to the consequences of the Asian crisis, or an indication perhaps of more serious structural economic deficiencies.

Other surveys of MNEs also reveal optimism among the international business community that China's relative position as an investment location will be sustained. UNCTAD (2001) cites a recent

Table 11.7 Survey results of the FDI regimes in China and the ASEAN-5 countries.

	Local capital market	Acquisition of control	Equal treatment	Employment of foreigners	National protectionism	Investment protection	Image of country	Overall assessment
	A	B	C	D	E	F	G	H
China (PRC)	4.5	4.6	7.5	6.0	5.4	7.3	7.4	5.49
Hong Kong	9.1	9.0	9.0	6.3	8.1	7.0	7.3	8.21
Singapore	8.0	7.9	8.8	7.8	8.2	7.7	8.4	7.99
Thailand	7.5	5.9	7.4	5.6	6.3	7.1	5.6	5.99
Malaysia	6.4	5.4	7.2	6.5	6.0	7.9	6.2	5.59
Indonesia	7.5	6.0	6.1	5.7	4.6	5.8	2.0	5.19
Philippines	8.0	5.9	7.3	6.0	4.3	7.4	2.6	6.37

Notes: i) survey results are scaled from 0 (least favourable for FDI) to 10 (most favourable) for each item.
  ii) data not available for Brunei, Cambodia, Laos, Myanmar and Vietnam.
(A) Access to local capital is restricted for foreign investors (0) / is not restricted (10)
(B) Foreign investors are not (0) / are free (10) acquire control in a domestic company
(C) Foreign investors are not (0) / are (10) treated equally to domestic firms
(D) Immigration laws prevent (0) / do not (10) prevent your company from employing foreign labour
(E) National protectionism does (0) / does not prevent (10) foreign products and services from being imported
(F) Investment protection schemes are not available (0) / are available (10) for most foreign partner countries
(G) Image of the country abroad hinders (0) / supports (10) the development of business
(H) Average assessment according to criteria A to G (unweighted)
Source: IMD (2002), after Dunning (2001, p. 266 to 267).

Table 11.8 Transaction cost-related barriers to FDI in China and the ASEAN-5 countries.

	Cultural barriers A	Government competence B	Legal framework C	Transparency D	Bureaucracy E	Corruption F	Protection of IP G	Distribution systems H	Infrastructure I	Labour regulations J	Overall assessment K
China (PRC)	5.7	4.9	5.6	4.7	2.9	2.6	5.0	5.4	5.3	4.3	5.11
Hong Kong	8.1	4.9	7.6	5.6	5.2	7.0	6.4	8.8	8.1	8.1	7.22
Singapore	7.9	8.8	8.5	7.3	7.5	8.8	7.8	9.3	9.0	8.4	8.47
Thailand	8.2	4.7	5.0	4.4	3.5	2.8	4.9	6.9	6.0	6.4	4.89
Malaysia	7.4	5.4	6.6	5.0	4.6	4.5	6.2	8.0	7.2	6.7	5.96
Indonesia	5.8	2.2	2.4	2.4	2.8	1.0	2.5	3.6	2.3	4.0	3.34
Philippines	7.8	3.1	3.3	3.9	2.0	1.5	3.7	3.2	2.8	3.6	4.47

Notes: i) survey results are scaled from 0 (least favourable for FDI) to 10 (most favourable for FDI) for each items.
ii) data not available for Brunei, Cambodia, Laos, Myanmar and Vietnam.
(A) National culture is closed (0) / is open to foreign influence (10)
(B) Government decisions are not (0) / are effectively implemented (10)
(C) The legal framework is (0) / is not (10) detrimental to your country's competitiveness
(D) The government does not (0) / does communicate its policy intentions clearly (10)
(E) Bureaucracy does (0) / does not (10) hinder business development
(F) Bribery and corruption exist (0) / does not exist in the public sphere (10)
(G) Patent and copyright protection is not (0) / is (0) enforced in your country
(H) The distribution infrastructure of goods and services is generally inefficient (0) / efficient (10)
(I) Infrastructure maintenance and development is not (0) / is adequately planned and financed (10)
(J) Labour regulations are too restrictive (0) / are flexible enough (10)
(K) Mean of score for items A to J (unweighted)
Source: IMD (2002), after Dunning (2001, p. 266 to 267).

Table 11.9 UNCTAD FDI performance and potential indexes for China and SE Asian countries.

	FDI Performance Index				FDI Potential Index			
	Value		Rank		Score (0–1)		Rank	
	1988–1990	1998–2000	1988–1990	1998–2000	1988–1990	1998–2000	1988–1990	1998–2000
China	0.9	1.2	61	47	0.234	0.251	59	84
Hong Kong, China	5.4	5.9	4	2	0.441	0.589	21	13
Brunei	0.0	0.1	125	128	0.315	0.424	35	33
Cambodia	n/a	n/a	n/a	n/a	n/a	n/a	n/a	n/a
Indonesia	0.8	−0.6	63	138	0.203	0.189	73	110
Laos	n/a	n/a	n/a	n/a	n/a	n/a	n/a	n/a
Malaysia	4.4	1.2	8	44	0.252	0.368	52	40
Myanmar	1.9	0.6	36	82	0.067	0.083	138	139
Philippines	1.7	0.6	39	89	0.139	0.265	111	78
Singapore	13.8	2.2	1	18	0.470	0.641	16	3
Thailand	2.6	1.3	25	41	0.235	0.298	57	61
Vietnam	1.0	2.0	53	20	0.134	0.277	115	71

The FDI Performance Index is the ratio of a country's share in global FDI flows to its share in global GDP The FDI Potential Index is the unweighted average of the normalised values of GDP growth rate; per capita GDP; share of exports in GDP; telephone lines per 1000 inhabitants; commercial energy use per capita; share of R&D expenditure in gross national income; share of tertiary students in population; and country risk.
Source: UNCTAD (2002).

survey of 3,000 regional headquarters and representative offices of MNEs situated in Hong Kong. Some 45% of respondents reported that they planned to increase their investment in mainland China, and 93% predicted that the investment climate there would be 'favourable' or 'very favourable' through to 2005. Bartels and Freeman (2000) report similar findings in their 1999 survey of 31 retail-oriented MNEs with regional headquarters in Singapore, 71% of whom indicate that 'greater China' was given 'high' or 'highest' priority by the parent firm as a business location. More recently, UNCTAD (2002) highlight two studies by the Japan Bank for International Cooperation (JBIC) and JETRO that hint at the growing importance of China in Japanese investment strategy. Of 469 respondent Japanese manufacturing firms surveyed by JBIC in 2002, over half (57%) find China more attractive than the ASEAN-5 as an investment location. The JETRO survey revealed that 21% of the 645 respondent Japanese MNEs were planning to relocate production to China following WTO accession, mostly from Japan itself (92 firms), but also from Hong Kong (13 firms) and the ASEAN-5 (11 firms).

Two final and interrelated observations also bear upon China's position as a future rival to the Southeast Asian countries as an investment location. First, there is ample absorptive capacity in China for FDI. FDI stock on a per capita basis remains comparatively low in China (U.S. $348 in 2002), well below that of Hong Kong and Singapore (U.S. $59,296 and U.S. $27,866 respectively), but also below that of Malaysia (U.S. $2,493) and Thailand (U.S. $454). The uneven sectoral and geographic distribution of FDI in China means that much geographic and economic space is untouched by it, particularly in the northern and western provinces where many SOEs are located. Second, strategic-asset FDI in China (that is, mergers and acquisitions involving Chinese SOEs and foreign firms) has been highly restricted by the regulatory regime and underdeveloped stock markets. However, regulatory changes following WTO membership, embodied in the State Council's 10th five-year plan, should lead to the removal of many of these obstacles. Providing political opposition is also quelled, this should generate significant inflows of FDI in the medium term as performing SOEs are partially or totally sold-off. This could see strategic asset-seeking FDI surge to the northern and western regions of China, despite the relatively under-developed physical and technical infrastructures there.

China's role as a regional driver

China currently enjoys the powerful combination of a large, low cost and educated labour pool, strong demand potential and at least a favourable investment climate relative to the Southeast Asian countries. As long as social and political cohesion is preserved (by no means a guarantee), China's full compliance to its accession terms should lead to a rise in domestic demand, better market access for foreign firms and an improvement in its investment climate relative to the Southeast Asian countries. WTO accession could therefore further strengthen China's position as a rival host for global and regional FDI flows in the future. While a good proportion of future FDI flow to China will be 'new' (that is, China's further opening could continue to have an FDI-creating effect), it is important for policy-makers in the region to recognise that an indeterminate yet potentially significant amount could be displaced from intra-Southeast Asian FDI, or from initial and sequential FDI made by the Triad countries in Southeast Asia. The greatest competitive effect is likely to be on higher value-added market-oriented FDI, which is already accelerating following accession, especially from the Triad countries. Certain structural impediments currently prevent this from happening in many, if not most, of the Southeast Asian countries. The most immediate surge in China's inward FDI is expected in those services-related sectors being opened for the first time. However, as domestic demand in China expands, more manufacturing-based FDI should also be attracted, particularly from developed country firms undertaking increasingly more capital and technology-intensive production. Some foreign and domestically owned production in Southeast Asia may also migrate to China, as its investment climate improves relative to current production locations. Both Singapore – already a major investor in China – and Malaysia have recently registered increased outward FDI flows in labour-intensive manufacturing as production costs rise at home, and a growing proportion of this may soon be directed to China. Likely candidates would be those more 'footloose' export-oriented manufacturing operations with relatively few backward and forward linkages to local suppliers and other parties. These are presently commonplace in Southeast Asia, especially in textiles and garment production and some in types of electronics manufacturing. The coastal provinces of China are likely to exert the more immediate pull effects on export-platform FDI in Southeast Asia. However, as wage and non-wage related production costs here rise, then greater pressure should be felt from China's central and western provinces, as transport and technical infrastructures are further improved and as economic development is boosted by the acquisition of SOEs by foreign investors. The provinces of Sichuan, Hunan and Henan are strong candidates for the next wave of inward FDI to China, for cost-oriented as well as market-seeking motives. Nevertheless, coastal locations such as Beijing, Shanghai, Zhejiang and Hebei will retain their appeal for many foreign investors, for obvious reasons.

Should China have a magnetic effect on patterns of regional FDI, this could have significant implications for each of the Southeast Asian countries, though to varying degrees and for different reasons. Of course, a certain level of market-seeking FDI will always be maintained in the Southeast Asian region, irrespective of developments in China. For example, MNEs will continue to support and establish subsidiaries in individual Southeast Asian countries, to complement their import function with sales, marketing, and distribution activities. But this is relatively low-value added activity, and generates few spill-overs and other benefits for the host economy compared to more capital intensive investment. Moreover, for some Southeast Asian countries, such as Brunei, Myanmar and Indonesia, FDI is mostly natural resource-oriented, notably in the oil and gas extraction and support industries. It is unlikely that China is, or will be, a magnet for FDI in these sectors. In this regard, China's influence on regional FDI flows will be least felt by more resource-oriented economies. However, if China does prove able to attract a greater proportion of regionally allocated market seeking FDI in services and manufacturing, this will impact most those Southeast Asian countries which themselves have relatively small markets in terms of, for example, population (such as Brunei, Laos and Singapore) or purchasing power (such as Myanmar and Vietnam). Larger Southeast Asian countries like Malaysia, Thailand and the Philippines should continue to attract market-seeking FDI, but whether this is in capital and technology-intensive sectors may be open to question. Currently, the FDI stock of these countries exhibits a strong source country affiliation, with a preponderance of European, and especially British-owned, FDI in Malaysia and American investment in the Philippines and Thailand. Should these source countries continue to direct their investment in China to levels typically found in developed host countries, then this may be at the expense of at least some sequential FDI in Southeast Asia. What is more, some of these Southeast Asian countries may experience divestment, as 'footloose' foreign and domestically-owned production relocates to China.

Of course, several Southeast Asian countries should benefit directly from market opening in China. An obvious candidate is Singapore, whose firms have expertise in a variety of service-related sectors such as education, construction, engineering consultancy, business services, transport and logistics. Certain language and cultural similarities should enhance the competitive advantage of Southeast Asian firms in China compared to their U.S. and European counterparts. Nevertheless, although intra-Southeast Asian FDI is not significant in terms of world flows, it is important to some ASEAN economies. For example, the newer ASEAN members – Cambodia, Laos, Myanmar and Vietnam – only attract relatively small amounts of FDI in absolute terms (although often large as a proportion of GDP), but their principal source tends to be fellow Southeast Asian countries, particularly Singapore. If China's opening does displace intra-Southeast Asian FDI, and especially Singapore-sourced FDI, these countries could suffer economically. Indonesia and Malaysia, which also host large amounts of Singaporean FDI, could be similarly affected.

Alternative policy responses for Southeast Asia

MNEs are incentivised to withstand global competition by strengthening their ownership advantages across all markets in which they operate. It is important therefore that each Southeast Asian country provides competitive immobile assets to complement the mobile assets of MNEs if they are to counter any rivalry effects from China as an investment location after WTO. On a unilateral level, this means continued proactive national policies to enhance the quality of the workforce, infrastructure, supply networks, institutions and so forth. Deficiencies in the respective investment climates also need to be tackled. As we have seen, transaction costs in Southeast Asia are often on a par with those in China, while several nations lack an economic base of comparable size that would enable investing MNEs to offset transaction costs against revenue streams. Investment promotion measures targeted at particular industries (in which the host country has an actual or potential competitive advantage) or source countries (with existing trade or historic connections) will also continue to be important policy instruments. Southeast Asian countries could also compete individually with China as a production site by depreciating their currencies and cutting production costs. However this is an untenable solution given the high social costs and lower living standards that would follow. The countries could also realign their economies to become more resource-oriented, supplying agriculture and minerals, not only to a growing China, but also the wider region. However, economic rigidities and under-investment in several of the Southeast Asian economies will be a constraint to this, at least in the short term. Nevertheless, those countries with a common border to China – Laos, Myanmar and Vietnam – should improve their transport and communications infrastructure with both China and the rest of Southeast Asia in order to benefit as conduits for the rise in China-Southeast Asian trade flows that should follow accession.

Although such unilateral initiatives may go some way to offsetting China's improving situation as a host economy, the real gains to Southeast Asia will come by replacing deteriorating *individual* locational advantages relative to China with a superior *regional* one. Consequently, the ASEAN Free Trade Agreement (AFTA) or the Asian Investment Area (AIA), or both, should form at least part of the policy solution. For two reasons, more concerted effort is needed to coordinate and harmonise investment regulations and regimes across Southeast Asia. First, this would help to negate unilateral 'beggar thy neighbor' policies, in which individual Southeast Asian countries 'race to the bottom' by attempting to out-compete each other with improved investment conditions under WTO rules. Second, coordination could facilitate an improved division of labour across Southeast Asia. This would permit Southeast Asian and outsider firms to allocate resources regionally according to the comparative advantage of member states, in much the same way that MNEs are beginning to do now in China. Both Southeast Asian and non-Southeast Asian MNEs would be better able to rationalise existing production across the region, and to generate greater economies of scale and other efficiencies as a result. Opportunities for intra-industry specialisation would provide a boost to the investment climate of Southeast Asia as a whole, especially for efficiency-seeking FDI. Thus labour-intensive manufacturing may be encouraged in low cost countries like Myanmar and Vietnam, while high-end, capital-intensive manufacturing could continue to be sited in Singapore, for example. At the same time, a workable AFTA would also create a single market of sufficient size to begin to counter that of China for market-seeking FDI. It could also help to stimulate outward investment in Southeast Asia by Chinese enterprises, which themselves will soon be under growing competitive pressure to develop foreign markets following accession. Indeed, this process is already underway, with the Philippines, Malaysia and Thailand beginning to attract Chinese FDI in resource-based sectors such as agriculture, chemicals, paper and rubber (ACEGEC, 2001). Southeast Asia is a net investor in China, however, which means that investment cooperation both within Southeast Asia, and between Southeast Asia and China, may be directed more to protecting Southeast Asian investors in China and improving the conditions for Southeast Asian firms there than *vice versa*. If so, any further deepening of economic integration within Southeast Asia could be impeded. However, if implemented, greater regional integration in the form of AFTA and the AIA should provide fresh stimulus to both intra- and extra-Southeast Asian FDI, and could go some way towards offsetting China's growing economic weight in the region.

Conclusion

This paper shows that the impact of global FDI goes beyond host and source countries. The rise of China as a major location for world FDI can be counted as a success for the globalisation of the world economy. However, even such spectacular successes can have negative consequences in the interdependent global economy. The success of China poses particular policy challenges for Southeast Asia. In order to counter the growing economic weight of China in East and Southeast Asia, and as individual member states will be limited by what they can accomplish alone, the Southeast Asian countries should act in concert to enhance the attractiveness of the region as an investment location relative to China. Greater regional integration (in the form of AFTA or the AIA) will be an important, if not crucial, element of the policy solution. Whilst the income effect of China's growth should stimulate the economies of Southeast Asia, there is also likely to be a substitution effect such that China attracts FDI and other economic activities away from the Southeast Asian region. The balance of these effects needs further detailed investigation.

Acknowledgement

The authors are grateful to the Sino-British Fellowship Trust for its financial support of our data collection in China.

Notes

1 ASEAN comprises Indonesia, Malaysia, Philippines, Singapore and Thailand (ASEAN-5), plus Brunei, Cambodia, Laos, Myanmar (Burma) and Vietnam (the latter four collectively being the 'newer ASEAN' countries). For longevity purposes, we refer to them collectively as the Southeast Asian countries.
2 We acknowledge fully the inherent inadequacies of the China Statistical Yearbook and other official Chinese data sources. It is widely accepted that much FDI in China is illusory and that actual total inflow is significantly lower than that reported. Over-valued foreign contributions and 'round tripping' of FDI via Hong-Kong and other intermediaries to avoid certain investment restrictions inflated the figures. Broadman and Sun (1997) estimate

that such shortcomings inflated China's 1994 FDI inflow figures by as much as 37%.
3 Firms from Macao and Taiwan are also major investors. However, as Taiwanese investment was prohibited in China before 1990 an unquantifiable proportion was routed through intermediary countries, notably Hong Kong, thus boosting its contribution to FDI flows by source.
4 The Cayman Islands and the British Virgin Islands are significant sources, but as they are not the ultimate home country of FDI, they are disregarded in this discussion.

References

ACEGEC (ASEAN-China Expert Group on Economic Cooperation) (2001) *Forging closer ASEAN-China economic relations in the Twenty-First century*, October, Manila.
Bartels, F.L. and Freeman, N.J. (2000) Multinational firms and FDI in South East Asia: Post crisis changes in the manufacturing sector. *ASEAN Economic Bulletin*, 17 (3), pp. 324–341.
Broadman, H.G. and Sun, X. (1997) The distribution of foreign direct investment in China. *Policy Research Working Paper* No. 1720, China and Mongolia Department, World Bank.
Buckley, P.J. and Clegg, J. (1998) Transatlantic foreign direct investment flows, in G. Boyd (Ed), *The struggle for world markets: Competition and cooperation between NAFTA and the European Union*, pp. 155–176, Cheltenham: Edward Elgar.
Buckley, P.J., Clegg, J., Wang, C. and Cross, A. (2002) Foreign direct investment, regional differences and economic growth: Panel data evidence from China. *Transnational Corporations*, 11(1), pp. 1–28.
Chang, G.G. (2001) *The coming collapse of China*, London: Century Random House.
Cheong, Y.R. (2000) The impact of China's entrance to the WTO on neighboring East Asian economies. *China Economic Review*, 11, pp. 419–422.
Child, J. & Lu, Y. (eds) (1996) *Management issues in China: International enterprises*, London: Routledge.
China Statistical Yearbook (1999) Beijing: China Statistical Press.
Cross, A. and Tan, H. (2004) The impact of China's WTO accession on FDI in East and South East Asia: Trends and prospects, in F.L. Bartels and N.J. Freeman (eds), *The Future of Foreign Investment in South East Asia*, London: RoutledgeCurzon.
Graham, E.M. and Wada, E. (2001) Foreign direct investment in China: Effects on growth and economic importance, forthcoming in P. Drysdale (Ed), *Achieving High Growth: Experience of Transitional Economies in East Asia*, Oxford: Oxford University Press.
Heng, T.M. (2001) National report: Singapore, in ACEGEC (ASEAN-China Expert Group on Economic Cooperation) (2001), *Forging Closer ASEAN-China Economic Relations in the Twenty-First Century*, October 2001.
IMD (1999) *World Competitiveness Yearbook 1999*, Lausanne: IMD.
IMD (2001) *World Competitiveness Yearbook 2001*, Lausanne: IMD.
IMD (2002) *World Competitiveness Yearbook 2002*, Lausanne: IMD.

Ianchovichina, E. and Martin, W. (2001) Trade liberalization in China's accession to the World Trade Organization, World Bank, June 2001.

Ianchovichina, E., Martin, W. and Fukase, E. (2000) Assessing the implications of merchandise trade liberalization in China's accession to WTO, World Bank, June 2000.

Lardy, N.R. (2002) *Integrating China into the Global Economy*, Washington D.C.: Brookings Institution Press.

Lemoine, F. (2000) FDI and the opening up of China's economy, Centre D'Etedes Prospectives et D' Information Internationales (CEPII), *Working paper* No. 00–11, June 2000.

Li, J., Qian, G., Lam, K. and Wang, D. (2000) Breaking into China: Strategic considerations for multinational corporations, *Long Range Planning*, 33 (5), pp. 673–687.

Liu, X., Parker, D., Vaidya, K. and Wei, Y. (2001) Impact of foreign direct investment on productivity in China's electronics industry, *International Business Review*, 10 (4), pp. 421–439.

Nolan, P. (2001) *China and the Global Business Revolution*, Basingstoke: Palgrave.

OECD (2000) Main determinants and impacts of foreign direct investment on China's economy, Directorate for Financial, Fiscal and Enterprise Affairs, *Working Papers on International Investment*, 2000/4.

Palanca, E.H. (2001) China's economic growth: Implications to the ASEAN (An integrative report), Philippine APEC Study Centre Network (PASCN), *Discussion paper* No. 2001–01.

Tan, R. (1999) Foreign direct investment flows to and from China, Philippine APEC Study Centre Network (PASCN), *Discussion paper* No. 1999–21.

Thomsen, J. (1999) South East Asia: The role of foreign direct investment policies in development, OECD Directorate for Financial, Fiscal and Enterprise Affairs, *Working Papers on International Investment*, 1999/1.

UNCTAD (2001) *World Investment Report 2001: Promoting Linkages*, Geneva: United Nations.

UNCTAD (2002) *World Investment Report 2002: Transnational Corporations and Export Competitiveness*, Geneva: United Nations.

UNCTAD (2003) *World investment report 2003: FDI Policies for Development – National and International Perspectives*, Geneva: United Nations.

Wei, Y. and Liu, X. (2001) *Foreign Direct Investment in China: Determinants and Impact*, Cheltenham: Edward Elgar.

Yean, T. S. (1998) Competition and cooperation for foreign direct investment: An ASEAN perspective. *Asia-Pacific Development Journal*, 5 (1), pp. 9–36.

12
The Impact of Inward Foreign Direct Investment on the Nature and Intensity of Chinese Manufacturing Exports

Chengqi Wang, Peter J. Buckley, Jeremy Clegg and Mario Kafouros

1. Introduction

The contribution of transnational corporations (TNCs) to exports from developing countries has long been a point of debate. Host countries often complain that TNCs export too little, and the findings in some studies support these arguments. For example, Lall and Mohammad (1983) found that TNCs performed rather poorly in generating exports from India. However, other empirical studies have suggested the opposite, showing that inward foreign direct investment (FDI) was export-oriented and raised the level of exports from host economies (O'Sullivan, 1993; Blake and Pain, 1994; Cabral, 1995). Research on the role of inward FDI in improving Chinese export performance has been a more recent addition to the literature. Many studies found evidence of a generally positive and significant role for inward FDI in promoting the expansion of Chinese exports (Buckley, Clegg and Wang, 2002; Sun, 1999, 2001; Zhang and Song, 2000).

What remains unclear, however, is the mechanism through which FDI creates or encourages Chinese exports; the rise in Chinese exports could result either directly from the export activities of foreign affiliates[1] or from the expansion of exports by domestically-owned firms. This study contributes to this stream of research by shedding some light on the ways in which inward FDI has impacted on Chinese export expansion and upgrading.

The question at issue is the nature and structure of the relationship between inward FDI and Chinese exports. Firstly, we examine the extent to which the growth of Chinese exports is attributable to inward FDI. Secondly, we assess whether FDI has contributed to the changing structure of Chinese exports. The expansion of Chinese exports is taking place alongside a shift in the composition of exported goods, namely, an increasing share of capital- and technology-intensive goods (and a relative decline of traditional labour-intensive goods). There has not been much research on this issue. Thirdly, we examine the country-of-origin effects. Depending on the origin of the parent company, foreign affiliates in China are perceived as either 'local market-oriented' or 'export-oriented'. A survey by De Beule *et al.* (2001) showed that the affiliates of 'overseas' Chinese firms in Guangdong province sold a substantially larger share of its output abroad than western TNCs. The affiliates of European TNCs exported less than 30% of their sales, while the average in Guangdong province was approximately 50%. This study examines whether (and to what extent) these country-of-origin effects are present in more recent data.

The rest of this article proceeds as follows. Section 2 outlines the theoretical framework. We then present the model specification and the data in section 3. The empirical results and discussion are given in sections 4 and 5. Concluding remarks are offered in the last section.

Conceptual framework

One of the challenges currently facing applied research is how to investigate the theoretical predictions regarding the impact which the movement of factors of production (and the export of factor services) via TNCs' operations has on the patterns of the host economy' trade. In this regard, the recent experience of China offers a valuable case for examining how developing countries are able to realise their export potential when factors and services are internationally mobile. The substantial differences in factors endowments between China and developed countries are the principal drivers of the export of technology, management skills and headquarter services in the form of FDI from developed countries to China, which, according to theory, could stimulate exports from the labour-abundant host. Dunning (1998) argued that the relationship between trade and FDI was conditional on the motivation of the FDI in question. Market-seeking FDI can displace exports from the home to the host country, while efficiency-seeking FDI will increase the volume of trade (Gray, 1998; Kojima, 1978; Buckley, 1983). Theory therefore suggests that FDI plays an important role in reallocating global economic resources and stimulating productive capabilities.

Foreign affiliates are usually considered as better placed to serve international markets than their host country counterparts since they are usually better informed about international market conditions and benefit from access to international marketing and distribution networks of their parent companies. Moreover, TNCs are often larger than local firms and have managerial, entrepreneurial and financial resources to afford the high fixed costs associated with export activities (Blomström and Kokko, 1998). Hence, inward FDI should positively impact on the volume of exports from China. Thus, our first hypothesis is:

Hypothesis 1: Inward FDI has raised the volume of exports from China.

Foreign affiliates may directly enhance the exports of local firms in the host economy through the provision of competitive assets (UNCTAD, 2002), but may also indirectly create external effects that enhance the export prospects of local firms (Rhee and Belot, 1990). Such externalities may arise, for example, through the formation of linkages where local firms are engaged as suppliers and subcontractors to TNCs. These linkages provide channels through which knowledge about technologies and foreign market conditions can be transmitted. In addition, local firms may learn how to succeed in foreign markets by imitating TNCs. In the case of Sino-foreign joint ventures, marketing knowledge and know-how might be transferred back to the Chinese parent company. TNCs may also train local employees in export management and foreign market knowledge, and local firms can acquire this knowledge through hiring these employees of TNCs. These arguments are empirically supported by Aitken *et al.* (1994) for Mexico and by Kokko *et al.* (1997) for Uruguay. This forms the basis of our hypothesis 2:

Hypothesis 2: Inward FDI has raised the volume of exports by domestically-owned firms.

The first two hypotheses are concerned with the general impact of FDI on exports. Next, we investigate the specific nature of the impact that arises from China's current stage of development and its comparative advantage. As China is abundant in labour, it is expected that the dominant motive of incoming TNCs is to use it as a production base for labour-intensive goods. Thus, our third hypothesis is:

Hypothesis 3: The impact of inward FDI on Chinese exports is stronger for labour-intensive goods than for capital- and technology-intensive goods.

A notable feature of inward FDI in China is that investing countries can be divided into two distinct groups: 'overseas' Chinese, including

Hong Kong (China) and Macao (China), and 'western' countries (primarily, the European Union, Japan and the United States).[2] TNCs from overseas Chinese and those from developed countries have different types of technological advantages (Yeung, 1994; Shi, 1998; Luo, 1999). Western TNCs' knowledge assets are typically in proprietary state-of-the-art product and process innovations, generated by extensive investment in R&D (Buckley and Casson, 1976). In contrast, overseas Chinese TNCs are relatively small and less innovation-intensive. Their primary knowledge assets are skills of using standardised technology and experience in organising labour-intensive production. Much of these have been generated through export-oriented production conducted during the take-off period of the development of their home economies (Shi, 1998).

These differences in ownership advantages are expected to influence the motivations of the two groups of investors. Market-seeking is the prime motivation for FDI by western TNCs in developing countries with large domestic markets (Shi, 1998). TNCs from overseas Chinese typically originate from newly-industrialised economies (NIEs) which are export-oriented. The ownership advantages of overseas Chinese TNCs – in combination with the availability of cheap labour and land in the host economy – allows them to reduce production costs. The main motive for FDI by overseas Chinese TNCs is therefore likely to be efficiency-seeking. These TNCs relocate export-oriented industries out of their home economies to take advantage of cheaper immobile factors abroad in order to pursue export expansion. This line of argument suggests that overseas Chinese TNCs contribute more to China's exports than their western counterparts. This is the basis for hypothesis 4:

Hypothesis 4: *The contribution of overseas Chinese FDI to Chinese exports is greater than that of western FDI.*

Data and model specification

The econometric analysis was conducted using aggregate data obtained from various issues of *the China Statistical Yearbook* and *the China Foreign Economic Statistical Yearbook*. Table 12.1 presents the figures for annual exports and inward FDI for the period under consideration. It is clear that the rapid increase in the volume of exports from China was accompanied by an increasing share of exports by foreign affiliates. Partly as a result of the priority given to the development of new export industries in China, a substantial share of FDI flows has been in industries that are highly export-intensive. Wei (1995, 1996) concluded that almost all of the growth of Chinese exports since 1992 could be directly or indirectly attributed to foreign affiliates' activity. The growth of exports by domestically-owned firms has been relatively slow but still substantial in absolute terms. Total exports by these firms in 2002 were worth $156 billion, seven times the value of 1983.

Although many of the world's largest TNCs have established operations in China, a large share of the realised investment has originated from smaller investors within the Asian developing region. Table 12.1 shows that over the period under consideration, 47% of the accumulated FDI came from Hong Kong (China) and Macao (China).[3] Since 1996, a growing proportion of inward FDI has come from other sources, such as the European Union, Japan and the United States. Nevertheless, in terms of accumulated investment, China's inward FDI

Table 12.1 Exports and inward FDI of China, 1983–2002 (Millions of dollars).

Years	Export Total	Domestic firms	Foreign firms (the share in per cent)	FDI Total	Hong Kong and Macau (China)	Japan	United States	EU
1983	22 226	21 896	330 (1.49)	636	378	97	52	41
1984	26 139	26 070	69 (0.26)	1 258	748	225	256	148
1985	27 350	27 053	297 (1.08)	1 661	956	315	357	168
1986	30 942	30 360	582 (1.88)	1 874	1 132	201	315	130
1987	39 437	38 229	1 208 (3.06)	2 314	1 597	219	263	53
1988	47 516	45 060	2 456 (5.17)	3 194	2 095	515	236	157
1989	52 538	47 625	4 913 (9.35)	3 392	2 077	356	284	188
1990	62 091	54 277	7 814 (12.6)	3 487	2 214	503	456	147
1991	71 843	59 796	12 047 (16.8)	4 366	2 487	533	323	246
1992	84 940	67 584	17 356 (20.4)	11 007	7 709	710	510	243
1993	91 763	66 526	25 237 (27.5)	27 515	19 516	1 324	2 060	671
1994	121 006	86 293	34 713 (28.7)	33 767	20 170	2 075	2 490	1 876
1995	148 780	101 904	46 876 (31.5)	37 521	20 500	3 108	3 083	2 239
1996	151 048	89 538	61 510 (40.7)	41 725	21 257	3 679	3 443	3 002
1997	182 792	107 893	74 899 (41.0)	45 257	21 027	4 326	3 239	4 439
1998	183 712	102 750	80 962 (44.1)	45 463	18 930	3 400	3 898	4 309
1999	194 930	106 302	88 628 (45.5)	40 319	16 673	2 973	4 220	4 797
2000	249 210	129 769	119 441 (47.9)	40 720	15 847	2 916	4 383	4 673
2001	266 152	132 932	133 218 (50.1)	46 850	17 038	4 348	4 433	4 182
2002	325 600	155 615	169 985 (52.2)	52 943	18 329	4 190	5 424	3 909
Total				445 070	210 710	36 010	39 780	35 610

Source: authors' calculations from *Almanac of China's Economy* and *China Statistical Yearbook*, various issues.

is still dominated by Asian developing economies. FDI from developing Asia typically consists of fairly small scale, labour-intensive projects, often concentrated in the processing of imported inputs for re-exports.

The composition of China's exports has also experienced a significant transformation over the period. Table 12.2 shows that the share of capital- and technology-intensive goods in Chinese exports has more than doubled, from 19.6% in 1983 to 43.7% in 2002. UNCTAD (2002) reported that all of China's 10 principal exported goods in 2000 (accounting for 42% of the total) were products exhibiting rapid growth in world trade. All of these findings are consistent with the common perception that inward FDI has been important for China, but more research on the precise nature of this relationship is necessary.

Following previous studies (Sun, 2001; Zhang and Song, 2000), we model the level of exports as a function of FDI, domestic investment,

Table 12.2 Export structure of China, 1983–2002 (Millions of dollars).

Year	Labour intensive goods	Capital and technology intensive goods (% of total)
1983	8 169	2 472 (19.6)
1984	9 751	2 857 (20.1)
1985	7 979	2 130 (15.8)
1986	10 804	2,827 (14.4)
1987	14 843	3 976 (15.2)
1988	18 757	5 666 (17.1)
1989	21 652	7 075 (18.9)
1990	25 262	9 318 (20.2)
1991	31 076	10 967 (19.7)
1992	50 369	17 567 (25.9)
1993	55 173	19 905 (26.5)
1994	73 155	28 131 (27.8)
1995	86 788	40 501 (31.8)
1996	84 922	44 189 (34.2)
1997	104 836	53 927 (34.0)
1998	102 610	60 550 (37.1)
1999	105 800	69 200 (39.6)
2000	129 050	94 700 (38.0)
2001	131 530	108 270 (40.7)
2002	154 779	142 301 (43.7)*(1)*

Source: Authors' calculations from *China Statistical Yearbook, China Foreign Economic Statistical Yearbook* and *China Almanac of Foreign Economy and Trade*, various issues. In this study, capital or technology intensive goods comprise 'chemicals and related products' and 'mechanical and transport equipment'.

the exchange rate and the economic performance of the host country (as proxied by the level or growth of GDP). The following theoretical arguments underpin the selection of these variables. Domestic investment allows local firms to upgrade their technological capabilities and improve efficiency. As a result, they are better able to compete in international markets. Indeed, studies of the determinants of exports confirm that domestic investment is a significant predictor of export performance (Zhang and Song, 2000). Exports are also affected by exchange rates. A depreciation of the country's currency tends to increase its export earnings.[4] GDP (and its growth) is also an important determinant of export performance as it represents the overall performance of the economy (Zhang and Song, 2000). The model can be written as follows:[5]

$$LogEX_t = \alpha_0 + \alpha_1 LogFDI_{t-1} + \alpha_2 LogR_{t-} \qquad (1)$$

where EX is the value of exports, FDI is the 'utilised FDI'[6], R is the exchange rate, expressed as the Renminbi (RMB) yuan price of foreign exchange.[7] We estimate the model by OLS. The value of exports (EX) is deflated by a retail price index (as there is no other appropriate deflator). A similar approach has been used in other studies (e.g. Pain and Wakelin, 1998; Sun, 2001; Zhang and Song, 2000; Zhang, 1995). The real effective exchange rate (REER) is used as the exchange rate variable. The data on REER were obtained from the IMF. We expect the coefficients on $LogFDI_{t-1}$ and $LogR_{t-1}$ to have positive signs.

Of particular interest is the coefficient of $LogFDI_{t-1}$, as this indicates the elasticity of exports with respect to inward FDI (of the previous year). The use of lagged dependent variables in examining the impact of FDI on export performance has long been established (e.g. Orr, 1991). The first-order lag structure is also adopted for the exchange rate variable ($LogR_{t-1}$) to take into account the time taken for demand to respond to price changes in international markets. The time variable (*TIME*) is included in order to capture the time trend. To assess the impact of FDI on exports by domestically-owned firms, the model in equation (1) is estimated using exports by domestically-owned firms, denoted as $EX(D)_t$, as the dependent variable (Table 12.3).

Two further variations of the model in equation (1) are estimated to examine the nature of the relationship. First, the model is estimated by separating the data for the dependent variable into two groups: exports of labour-intensive goods and those of capital-intensive goods (Table 12.4). Second, the model is estimated by separating the data for FDI by country of origin (Table 12.5).

Empirical results

The results of the estimations are presented in Tables 12.3–12.5.[8] Column (1) in Table 12.3 shows that the coefficient on the FDI variable is positive and statistically significant, confirming the contribution of FDI to China's overall export expansion in the period under study. The result shows that a 1% increase in FDI leads to a 0.2% growth in exports in the following year. This finding is consistent with H1. It is also consistent with Thoburn (1997), Sun (1999, 2001) and Zhang and Song (2000), which found evidence of a positive role for foreign TNCs in promoting China's export growth.

The variable $LogFDI_{t-1}$ is also significant in column (2), which presents the estimation of the model with exports from domestically-own firms as the dependent variable. This result confirms the existence of externalities. It is also in line with the findings by Buckley *et al.* (2002), Kokko *et al.* (1997) and Aitken *et al.* (1994).

The significant results for the exchange rate variable ($LogR_{t-1}$) confirm that a depreciation of the RMB yuan promotes the growth of exports. These results are also consistent with Wang (1993), Wu (1994) and Zhang (2001), which provide accounts of the contribution of the exchange rate policy to export growth in China. Table 12.3 shows that the price responsiveness of exports by domestically-owned firms appears greater than the average for all Chinese exports.

Table 12.4 shows the impact of FDI on exports of different categories of goods, namely exports of labour-intensive goods, denoted by $EX(L)_t$, and exports of capital-intensive goods, denoted by $EX(C)_t$. Although it would have been better to examine the impact that FDI

Table 12.3 FDI and Chinese export performance, 1983–2002.

Dep. variable	$LogEX_t$ (1)	$LogEX(D)_t$ (2)
Constant	5.613 (36.31)	6.058(38.26)***
$LogFDI_{t-1}$	0.196(4.06)***	0.179(3.62)***
$LogEX(F)_{t-1}$	–	–
$LogR_{t-1}$	0.369(3.15)***	0.532(4.44)***
TIME	0.132(8.62)***	0.087(5.56)***
R^2 – adj	0.99	0.98
D.W.	1.95	2.34

Source: Authors' analysis.
Figures in parentheses are t statistics (two-tailed tests); *, **, and *** denote significance at the 10%, 5% and 1% levels respectively.

Table 12.4 FDI and Chinese export performance by category of exported goods, 1983–2002.

Dep. variable	$LogEX\ (L)_t$ (1)	$LogEX\ (C)_t$ (2)
Constant	4.756(18.37)***	2.850(9.96)***
$LogFDI_{t-1}$	0.220(2.73)***	0.152(1.71)*
$LogR_{t-1}$	0.711(3.63)***	0.426(1.96)*
TIME	0.135(5.27)***	0.236(8.32)***
$R^2 - adj$	0.98	0.98
D.W.	1.16	1.01

Source: Authors' analysis.
Figures in parentheses are t statistics (two-tailed tests); *, **, and *** denote significance at the 10%, 5% and 1% levels respectively.

in labour-intensive industries had on labour-intensive exports (rather than the effect of total FDI on labour-intensive exports), this was not possible in our case as the data were not available.

The aggregate FDI is shown to have a positive and significant impact on both groups of Chinese exports. What is interesting, however, is the difference between the coefficients; the size of the coefficient (and the level of significance) of the FDI variable is greater for the labour-intensive group than the capital-intensive group. Thus, the results provide support for hypothesis 3.

Table 12.5 presents the results of the estimation in which FDI is separated by home economy. The coefficient of FDI is positive and statistically significant for all home economy groups.

Table 12.5 FDI and Chinese exports by major source countries, 1983–2002.

	Dependent variable: exports by China ($LogEX_t$)		
FDI origin	Hong Kong and Macau (China)	United States	EU
Constant	5.624(36.77)***	6.125(70.91)***	6.377(46.27)***
$LogFDI_{t-1}$	0.180(3.77)***	0.220(5.45)***	0.165(3.50)***
$LogR_{t-1}$	0.449(4.05)***	0.710(9.09)***	0.825(7.56)***
TIME	0.146(11.14)***	0.125(9.84)**	0.129(7.08)***
$R^2 - adj$	0.99	0.98	0.99
D.W.	2.04	2.24	1.83

Source: Authors' analysis.
1. Figures in parentheses are t statistics (two-tailed tests); *, **, and *** denote significance at the 10%, 5% and 1% levels respectively.

Since the dependent variable used in the analysis is aggregate exports from China, the results do not allow us to say whether the positive impact of FDI from western economies on exports is due to their affiliates' exports or through spillover effects that stimulate exports from domestically-owned firms. But the impact of FDI from western countries on Chinese exports is no less than the impact of FDI by overseas Chinese firms. Hence, hypothesis 4 is not supported by the data.

Discussion

The results show that foreign affiliates in China appear to be acting as a platform for exports, which is in line with the findings in Zhao and Zhu (2000). The location advantages of China are likely to centre on the exploitation of cheap labour and land. Inward FDI realises export potential of the economy through transferring either entire production processes or labour-intensive and less technology-intensive segments of high technology industries (Lee, 1992). Further investigation is required to understand better which intangible assets are being transferred and through what mechanisms.

It is noted that the exchange rate has a larger coefficient for labour-intensive goods than for capital and technology-intensive goods. This is to be expected as labour-intensive export goods are likely to be more standardised, competing in foreign markets on price rather than on quality. Consequently, they are more sensitive to changes in the price caused by exchange rate movements. This explanation can also account for the findings presented in Table 12.3 that the exchange rate has a greater impact on exports by domestically-owned firms, since they are exporting more standardised goods than the affiliates of TNCs.

In contrast with previous findings that European Union and United States affiliates in China were mostly local market-oriented operations, we found (by using more recent data) that their impact on Chinese exports were comparable to those of FDI from Hong Kong (China) and Macao (China). This finding may be explained by two possible factors. First, the export-oriented approach of western TNCs might have taken longer to implement, perhaps because TNCs under pressure to satisfy local content requirements (Bjorkman and Osland, 1998) have not found many local subcontractors and suppliers with capabilities to meet their quality requirements. Second, those TNCs that entered the country primarily for servicing the local market might have changed their strategy to focus more on exports following intensifying competition and local market saturation in China.

Finally, the results concerning Hong Kong (China) and Macao (China) in Table 12.5 are in line with the findings in De Beule *et al.* (2001). It is likely that investment from Hong Kong (China) and Macau (China) in mainland China is undertaken to establish labour-intensive operations on imported intermediate goods for re-export.

Conclusion

We found that inward FDI exerted a considerable effect on overall Chinese export expansion. This export expansion comprises the growth of exports by foreign affiliates as well as those by domestic firms that have benefited from externalities associated with the presence of foreign affiliates. We also found that the impact of inward FDI on Chinese exports was stronger for labour-intensive goods than for capital-intensive goods. This finding is consistent with the observation that while there is an increasing share of capital-intensive goods in exports, China's exports of manufactures still consist mainly of products with low value-added and a low level of technology (e.g., textiles, garments, shoes and low-value electronics and machinery).

We also examined whether there are differences in the impact of FDI on Chinese exports by the investors' home economy. We found that the differences were insubstantial. The dominant view in the past was that western TNCs that invest in China were primarily domestic market-oriented (in contrast with overseas Chinese FDI), and had been little concerned with exports. The more recent data used this study indicate that this has changed.

The findings also have implications for Chinese policy towards the encouragement of inward FDI and the promotion of exports. The results show that FDI had a more marked impact on the exports of labour-intensive goods than the export of capital-intensive goods. This reflects China's current comparative advantage, and signals the potential for the development of China's exports in more capital-intensive activities. TNCs are increasingly locating research and development in China. This is likely to result in the gradual rise of the impact of inward FDI on exports of goods in this category.

The study has also shown that the policy of the Government of China to allow the exchange rate to depreciate stimulated Chinese exports. This policy was criticised abroad for rendering Chinese goods 'too cheap'. However, the findings suggest that this policy has been important to China's export performance. With the accession of China to the World Trade Organisation, the Government of China has lost discretion to discriminate between national and foreign firms. Our results suggest that this loss will have lesser impact than might have been expected from earlier studies. In fact, whatever the home economy of the investors, inward FDI is found to stimulate Chinese exports. Hence, from the perspective of export promotion, FDI from all economies should be equally welcomed.

Notes

1 In China, foreign affiliates are often referred to as foreign-invested enterprises or FIEs.
2 The use of the term 'overseas' Chinese to refer to firms based in Hong Kong and Macao is, in some sense, a misnomer since these two territories are part of China. However, the business communities in these territories are quite distinct from their mainland counterparts and so are the regulations governing them. Therefore, they are treated as 'overseas' firms in this study.
3 The dominance of Hong Kong (China), however, may be overstated for two reasons. First, some of the investments may have been 'round-tripping' investments: i.e., domestic Chinese investment re-routed through Chinese affiliates in Hong Kong so that they are able to enjoy the special tax breaks and incentives FDI into China receives. Second, some FDI listed as originating from Hong Kong is in reality from Taiwan Province of China that is placed into China via their affiliates in Hong Kong.
4 During the period under study (1983–2002), the Chinese currency depreciated significantly from $1=RMB 1.98 yuan in 1983 to $1=RMB8.27 yuan in 2002. The REER of Chinese currency fell from 285.16 in 1983 to 121.37 in 2002. The Chinese authorities have stated that in managing the RMB exchange rate, priority must be given to encouraging export.
5 Following Zhang and Song (2000) and Sun (2001), we sought to avoid the problem of omitted variables by including lagged domestic investment and GDP growth. In almost all preliminary regressions, GDP growth had no effect on exports, while domestic investment was usually insignificant and often wrongly signed. In view of this, and suspected collinearity with the FDI variable, these two variables were removed from the equation. Possible reasons for the poor performance of the domestic investment variable include the extreme variability in the data: the average growth rate from 1983–2002 was 13.7%, with a low of 6.5% in 1989 climbing to 25.0% in 1991, 35.1% in 1992 and 47.8% in 1993. Another possible explanation is that the bulk of domestic investment went to the infrastructure sector, which may be only weakly linked to export activities.
6 Utilised FDI is the official term given to investment actually made. This is to be distinguished from the value of investment for which permission has been granted by the Chinese authorities.
7 A rise in this variable represents a depreciation in the foreign exchange value of the Chinese currency, and therefore a fall in the foreign currency price of Chinese exports.
8 As indicated by adjusted R^2 and D.W. statistics, most of the regressions fit the data well. All our calculated d values but one (column (5) in Table 12.3) lie

well between du (0.998) and $4 - du$ (2.324) at the usual 5% level of significance, Therefore, there appears to be no general problem of autocorrelation.

References

Aitken, Brian, Gordon H. Hanson and Ann Harrison (1994) 'Spillovers, foreign direct investment, and export performance', *NBER Working Paper*, No. 4967, National Bureau of Economic Research.

De Beule, Filip, Daniel van den Bulcke and Luodan Xu (2001) 'Foreign invested enterprises in Guangdong Province, China: survey results'. Paper presented at the 27th Annual Conference of the European International Business Academy, 2001, ESCP-EAP-Paris, December.

Blake, Andrew P. and Nigel Pain (1994) 'Investigating structural change in UK export performance: the role of innovation and direct investment', *NIESR Discussion Paper*, 71.

Blomström, Magnus and Ari Kokko (1998) 'Multinational corporations and spillovers', *Journal of Economic Surveys*, 12(2), pp. 1–31.

Bjorkman, Ingmar and Gregory E. Osland (1998) 'Multinational corporations in China: responding to government pressures', *Long Range Planning*, 31(3), pp. 436–445.

Buckley, Peter J. (1983) 'Macroeconomic versus international business approach to direct foreign investment: a comment on Kojima's approach', *Hitotsubashi Journal of Economics*, 24(1), pp. 95–100.

Buckley, Peter J. and Mark C. Casson (1976) *The Future of Multinational Enterprise* (London: Macmillan).

Buckley, Peter J., Clegg, Jeremy and Wang, Chengqi (2002) 'The impact of inward FDI on the performance of Chinese manufacturing firms', *Journal of International Business Studies*, 33(4), pp. 637–655.

Cabral, S. (1995) 'Comparative export behaviour of foreign and domestic firms in Portugal', *Banco de Portugal Economic Bulletin*, March, pp. 69–78.

Dunning, John H. (1998) 'The European internal market program and inbound foreign direct investment', in John H. Dunning, ed., *Globalization, Trade and Foreign Direct Investment* (Oxford: Elsevier).

Gray, Peter H. (1998) 'International trade and foreign direct investment: the interface', in John H. Dunning, ed., *Globalization, Trade and Foreign Direct Investment* (Oxford: Elsevier).

Kokko, Ari, Ruben Tansini and Mario Zejan (1997) 'Trade regimes and spillover effects of FDI: evidence from Uruguay' (Stockholm School of Economics, Stockholm), mimeo.

Kojima, Kiyoshi (1978) *Direct Foreign Investment, A Japanese Model of Multinational Business Operations* (New York: Praeger).

Lall, Sanjaya and Sharif Mohammed (1983). 'Foreign ownership and export performance in the large corporate sector in India', *Journal of Development Studies*, 20(1), pp. 56–67.

Lee, C.H. (1992) 'Direct foreign investment, structural adjustment, and international division of labor: a dynamic macroeconomic theory of direct foreign investment', *Hitotsubashi Journal of Economics*, 31, pp. 61–72.

Luo, Yadong (1999) 'Dimensions of knowledge: comparing Asian and Western TNCs in China', *Asia Pacific Journal of Management*, 16, pp. 75–93.

Orr, J. (1991) 'The trade balance effects of foreign direct investment in U.S. manufacturing', *Federal Reserve Bank of New York Quarterly Review*, 16, pp. 63–76.

O'Sullivan, Patrick J. (1993) 'An assessment of Ireland's export-led growth strategy via foreign direct investment: 1960–80', *Weltwirtschaftliches Archiv*, 129, pp. 139–158.

Pain, Nigel and Katharine Wakelin (1998) 'Export performance and the role of foreign direct investment', *The Manchester School Supplement*, pp. 62–88.

Rhee, Yung Whee and Therese Belot (1990) 'Export catalysts in low-income countries', *World Bank Discussion Papers*, 72, (Washington, D.C.: World Bank).

Shi, Yizhen (1998) 'Technological assets and the strategy of foreign firms to enter the China market', *Journal of International Marketing and Marketing Research*, 23(3), pp. 129–138.

The State Statistical Bureau (SSB) (1996) *The Data for Third Industrial Census of China* (Beijing: China Statistical Press).

The State Statistical Bureau (SSB) (2002) *The Annual Report of Chinese Industry* (Beijing: China Statistical Press).

Sun, Haishun (1999) 'Impact of FDI on the foreign trade of China', *Journal of the Asia Pacific Economy*, 4 (2), pp. 317–339.

Sun, Haishun (2001) 'Foreign direct investment and regional export performance in China', *Journal of Regional Science*, 41(2), pp. 317–336.

Thoburn, John (1997) 'Enterprise reform, domestic competition and export competition', *Journal of the Asia Pacific Economy*, 2(2), pp. 166–177.

UNCTAD (2002) *World Investment Report* (New York and Geneva: United Nations).

Wang, H. (1993) *China's Exports Since 1979* (New York: St. Martin's Press).

Wei, Shang-Jin (1995) 'The Open Door policy and the China's rapid growth: evidence from city-level data', in Takatoshi Ito and Anne Krueger, eds., *Growth Theories in Light of the East Asian Experience* (Chicago: University of Chicago Press).

Wei, Shang-Jin (1996) 'Foreign direct investment in China: sources and consequences', in Takatoshi Ito and Anne Krueger, eds., *Financial Deregulation and Integration in East Asia* (Chicago: University of Chicago Press).

Wu, S. (1994) 'Exchange rate policies and its contribution to export growth in China, 1978–1992', *Research Paper*, Centre for Development Economics, William College.

Yeung, Henry Wai-Chung (1994) 'Transnational corporations from Asian developing countries: their characteristics and competitive edge', *Journal of Asian Business*, 10(4), pp. 17–58.

Zhang, Honglin K. and Song, Shunfeng (2000) 'Promoting exports: the role of inward FDI in China', *China Economic Review*, 11, pp. 385–396.

Zhang, Zhaoyong (1995) 'International trade and foreign direct investment: further evidence from China', *Asian Economic Journal*, 9(2), pp. 153–167.

Zhao, Hongxin and Zhu, Gangti (2000) 'Locational factors and country of origin difference: an empirical analysis', *Multinational Business Review*, 8(1), pp. 60–73.

13
The Impact of Foreign Direct Investment on the Productivity of China's Automotive Industry

Peter J. Buckley, Jeremy Clegg, Ping Zheng, Pamela A. Siler and Gianluigi Giorgioni

Introduction

There is increasing interest in the impact of foreign direct investment (FDI) on host country productivity. However, contradictory empirical results have been obtained from a number of previous studies. Kokko *et al.* (1994, 1996), Egger and Pfaffermayr (2001), Blomström and Persson (1983), and Bertschek (1995), for example, found evidence of a significant positive effect of FDI on spillovers. Haddad and Harrison (1993), Girma *et al.* (2001), Kholdy (1995), Globerman (1979), and Veugelers and Houte (1990), however, found insignificant, or negative impacts in their empirical results. Interestingly, Aitken and Harrison (1999), Zukowska-Gagelmann (2000), and Djankov and Hoekman (2000) obtained a complicated pattern of mixed results in their respective studies. This paper adds to this important field of research by examining the impact of FDI on China's automotive industrial productivity using a panel data set.

The automotive industry is chosen for several reasons. First, the automotive industry is one of the six key industries[1] in China. It has expanded rapidly over the reform years and typically accounts for a large and increasing share of industrial production, output, exports, and employment. In 1999, total sales of China's auto-industry were about US$ 38 billion, accounting for nearly 4% of the country's GDP. In 1998, seven million employees worked in the auto-industry, accounting for 3.3% of the total Chinese urban workforce (Harwit, 2001). The automotive industry, particularly in industrialised countries, is a focus of attention due to its major contribution to GDP and employment (Irandoust, 1999). Historically, in the USA, Japan, and South Korea, automotive exports have been an important element of foreign trade. Further, the development of China's automotive industry has been driven by both domestic policy and foreign economic participation. Through studying this sector it is possible to investigate issues both of industrialisation in general, and the impact of technology transfer in particular (Harwit, 1995). It is also important to note that there has been a significant amount of FDI in the Chinese automotive industry. By the end of 2000, the cumulative 'actually used' FDI[2] in the automotive industry reached US$ 45.4 billion; accounting for 13% of total realised FDI in China. Moreover, China is also one of the largest automobile markets in the world and has become the most important destination for FDI by automobile multinational enterprises (MNEs), especially since China's entry into the World Trade Organisation (WTO).

WTO entry, however, has forced China's automotive industry to face fierce international competition. As Sit and Liu (2000) point out, China's entry into the WTO has two effects on China's automotive industry: one is the gradual reduction of tariffs on imported automobiles and components and the other is the further opening of the industry to FDI. With increasing inflows of FDI into the industry, it is essential to improve our understanding of the effects of FDI on the productivity of the industry.

The rest of the paper is organised as follows. Section 2 provides a background on FDI in the Chinese automotive industry. Section 3 discusses the theoretical framework and reviews the relevant literature. Section 4 focuses on the empirical analysis, discussing the model, data, and methodology. Section 5 presents the empirical results and the last section summarises the key conclusions and policy implications.

FDI in China's automotive industry

According to the Chinese Automotive Industry Yearbook (1999), the development of China's automotive industry after 1949, when the People's Republic of China was established, can be split into three different phases. The period 1949–65 can be termed the early 'starting stage'. The 'growing up stage' can be thought of as the time period 1966–80. From 1981 onwards China's automotive industry has been in a 'rapidly developing stage'.

Since the 1950s, the Chinese government has made several attempts to introduce Soviet-style structures and methods in order to achieve the goal of industrialisation. China's automotive industry originated with the founding of the First Automotive Works (FAW) in

Changchun, Jilin province, which is now the largest state-owned automaker in China. In July 1953, China and the Soviet Union reached an agreement to introduce Soviet automotive technology and assembly lines to produce medium trucks with a projected capacity of 30,000 units. China's first truck was produced by FAW in 1956, marking the birth of China's automotive industry. The Nanjing Automotive Works were set up in March 1958, Beijing Automotive Works in June of the same year, Jinan Automotive Works in April 1960, and Shanghai Automotive works in October 1960. The Chinese automotive industry then had five production bases and 104 plants, including one vehicle assembler, one motor engine maker, sixteen repair plants, and eighteen motor and motorcycle parts producers. In 1965, 40,542 units of automotive vehicles were produced, of which only 133 were cars (see Table 13.1), accounting for 0.3% of total output.

China's automotive industry advanced in the second 'growing up' stage. In March 1966, Sichuan Automotive Works was set up in Chongqing, Sichuan province. In April 1967, Second Automotive Works (SAW) was set up in Shiyan, Hubei province, which was later renamed Dongfeng Automotive Corporation in 1992. In March 1978, Shannxi Automotive Works was set up in Xi'an. Moreover, three new firms emerged as important automotive vehicle production sites in Tianjin, Shenyang, and Wuhan. During this period, most of the provinces and autonomous regions, and even the cities of China set up local automotive production. By 1980, the number of automotive enterprises had risen to 2,379 – consisting of 56 vehicle manufacturers, 129 repair plants, 24 motorcycle makers, 33 motor engine makers and 2,076 parts producers. In 1980, 222,288 units of automotive vehicles were produced, of which 135,500 were trucks and 5,418 were cars (see Table 13.1), accounting for 61% and 2.4% of the total output respectively.

However, owing to the absence of competition, all production units ran at low levels of productivity and efficiency. Central planning also created a further problem of restricted product scope in terms of limited product lines. The result was a fragmented production system with severe overcapacity in auto production nation-wide, characterised by production at levels below minimum efficient scale in each province.

The opening up of China's economy brought unprecedented opportunities and challenges for its automotive industry. Domestic demand for cars (initially dominated by demand from the government sector for official use) rose rapidly in the 1980s. However, China's vehicle

Table 13.1 China's automotive industry 1955–1999.
Volume in Units

Year	Output Total	Output Car	Import Total	Import Car	Export Total	Export Car
1955	61	0				
1956	1654	0	56466	4067	0	
1957	7904	0	(1953–57)	(1953–57)	(1953–57)	
1958	16000	57				
1959	19601	101	68157	3048	1317	
1960	22574	98	(1958–62)	(1958–62)	(1958–62)	
1961	3589	5				
1962	9740	11				
1963	20579	11	18549	4266	2695	
1964	28062	100	(1963–65)	(1963–65)	(1963–65)	
1965	40542	133				
1966	55861	302				
1967	20381	144	41200	949	5952	
1968	25100	279	(1966–70)	(1966–70)	(1966–70)	
1969	53100	163				
1970	87166	196				
1971	111022	562				
1972	108227	661				
1973	116193	1130	97863	2317	21267	
1974	104771	1508	(1971–75)	(1971–75)	(1971–75)	
1975	139800	1819				
1976	135200	2611				
1977	125400	2330	141926	20292	4449	
1978	149062	2640	(1976–80)	(1976–80)	(1976–80)	
1979	185700	4152				
1980	222288	5418				
1981	175645	3428	41575	1401	726	
1982	196304	4030	16077	1101	238	
1983	239886	6046	25156	5806	1892	
1984	316367	6010	88743	21651	2919	
1985	443377	5207	353992	105775	1659	
1986	372753	12297	150052	48276	4179	
1987	472538	29865	67182	30536	6129	
1988	646951	36798	99233	57433	9159	
1989	586936	28820	85554	45000	2676	6
1990	509242	42409	65430	34063	4431	73
1991	708820	81055	98454	54009	4108	789
1992	1061721	162725	210087	115641	6375	914
1993	1296778	229697	310099	180717	11116	2866
1994	1353368	250333	283060	169995	18648	784
1995	1452697	325461	158115	129176	17747	1413
1996	1474905	391099	75863	57942	15112	635
1997	1582628	487695	49039	32019	14868	1073
1998	1629026	507861	40216	18016	13627	653
1999	1829396	566265	35192	19953	10095	326

Source: Chinese Automotive Industry Yearbook 1999, 2000.

producers were truck makers rather than car makers. The car industry was a minor part of vehicle production during the first three decades of China's socialist economy and was unable to meet the increasing demand for cars. Since the early 1980s, Chinese car imports have increased dramatically (see Table 13.1).

The Chinese government began to encourage FDI in auto production by setting up joint ventures with auto producing MNEs. Several major projects were established between 1984 and 2002. The first was between the Beijing Automotive Works and Chrysler of the United States (in 1984). The second was between the Shanghai Automotive Industry Corporation and Volkswagen of Germany (in 1985). The third was between the Guangzhou Automotive Company and Peugeot of France (in 1985), which was taken over by Honda of Japan, who established Guangzhou Honda with Guangzhou Automotive Company in 1998. The fourth was between the FAW and Volkswagen-Audi (in 1991). The fifth was between the Beijing Automotive Works and Hyundai of Korea (in 2002). The sixth and last was between the Tianjin Automotive Industry Corporation and Toyota of Japan (in 2002).

These joint ventures started production by assembling cars with parts and individual components imported from foreign makers. Import substitution helped to reduce the foreign exchange burden of imported finished cars. Moreover, the introduction of market competition placed increasing pressure on manufacturing operations and development, as indigenous Chinese owned firms sought to improve their technological capability and industrial competitiveness, first at home, and then in the international market. The automotive industry is both capital and technology intensive, and so joint ventures became a channel for attracting foreign investment and for obtaining modern manufacturing technology and modern management techniques. MNEs are part of an integrated international production system, and through FDI attempt to acquire greater access to markets and resources in host countries. Rapid economic growth and a large population assured a ready market for automotive products in China.

China's automotive industry continued to develop strongly during the third 'rapidly developing stage', since the introduction of Sino-foreign joint ventures. China produced 1.83 million automotive vehicles in 1999 (see Table 13.1), which placed China in the top ten automotive vehicle producers in the world according to the OICA[3] (China Automotive Industry Yearbook, 2000).

The industry now consists of foreign firms, centrally planned state-owned firms, locally planned state-owned firms, township and private firms. By the end of 2000, more than 600 foreign firms had set up in China's automotive industry from more than 20 countries. Cumulative contracted FDI amounted to US$ 52.9 billion, while actually used FDI reached US$45.4 billion (Chinese Automotive Industry Yearbook, 2000), which is 13% of the total actually used FDI in China. The major sources of foreign investment are from the US, Germany, Japan, France, Italy, South Korea, and the UK.

Despite heavy foreign investment and the market discipline of WTO entry, many industry experts argue that major structural and technological weaknesses continue to exist in the Chinese automotive industry. Sinclair (2005), for example, reports on the fragmented nature of both the auto manufacturing and components sub-sectors of the industry, with small scale producers scattered throughout the country operating below capacity. He also points to the continuing culture of protectionism, with local component suppliers favoured by local assembly firms, despite their inferior quality and higher price. Harwit (2001) agrees with this assessment, emphasising that the drive for quick utilisation of domestically produced parts has impeded the production of quality domestic vehicles. He (Harwit, 2001, p. 655) summarises the situation, noting that while China has built a 'significant vehicle production system' its 'price and quality' problems leave it vulnerable in a post-WTO environment.

Theoretical framework and literature review

The aggregate impact of FDI on a host country's productivity is often de-composed into two types of effects: direct and indirect effects. The direct effect of inward FDI refers to its impact on the productivity of FDI-recipient firms, while the indirect effect refers to the impact of foreign firms' presence on the productivity of indigenous firms i.e., productivity spillovers from foreign to indigenous firms. This paper is somewhat unusual in that it focuses on one industrial sector and the combined direct and indirect effects of FDI inflows on that sector. The policy interest of the paper is in whether the Chinese government's encouragement of foreign investment into the automotive sector has raised the overall productivity and international competitiveness of the industry. The limitations of a data set based on sub-sectors of the industry also prevents us from separating direct and indirect effects empirically, which in practice, as noted below, can become blurred. Nevertheless it is useful to briefly explore the various types of impacts on host country productivity that can be attributed to FDI.

Direct productivity benefits occur when the proportion of industrial output produced by foreign firms or FDI-receiving firms increases, assuming that foreign firms are more productive on average than indigenous firms. MNEs must have monopolistic or ownership advantages that allow them to overcome the higher costs associated with production abroad (Hymer, 1976). They may have higher productivity than indigenous firms because of their superior technological knowledge, access to international networks and superior management structures (Girma *et al.*, 2001). MNEs may also exhibit higher levels of productivity than their domestic counterparts, due to a number of other factors: employees with greater skills and training; more machinery and equipment per worker; and greater technical efficiency. Most studies, which have focused on the productivity differences between foreign and indigenous firms in developing countries, have concluded that foreign firm are superior in this respect. Willmore (1994) reported that foreign firms in Brazil typically have higher levels of labour productivity compared to indigenous firms of a similar size operating in the same industry. Using detailed Indonesian data, Blomström and Sjöholm (1999) found labour productivity to be higher in establishments with foreign equity compared to purely domestically owned firms, with the latter benefitting from spillovers from FDI. With respect to China, Zhou *et al.* (2002) concluded that the productivity of foreign firms is significantly higher than that of indigenous firms.

While the direct productivity benefits of FDI can be predicted to be positive, particularly when hosts are developing countries, there is much more controversy surrounding the direction of indirect benefits. Indirect benefits occur when the superior technology and manufacturing methods of foreign firms 'spillover' to indigenous firms increasing their productivity and competitiveness. Kinoshita (1998) decomposes spillover effects from FDI into four categories: the demonstration-imitation effect, the competition effect, the foreign linkage effect, and the training effect.

The demonstration-imitation effect arises from differences in the levels of technology between foreign and indigenous firms. Foreign firms with more advanced technologies enter a local market and introduce newer technologies to the industry. Through direct contact with foreign affiliates, indigenous firms can watch and imitate the way foreigners operate and can therefore become more productive. The competition effect arises from the additional competition created by MNEs. Because competition in the domestic market is increased, indigenous firms have to perform more efficiently and increase their innovative activity to maintain their market position (Bertschek, 1995). This type of spillover generally occurs at the intra-industry level. While not a concern of this particular study, inter-industry spillovers may also occur through backward and forward linkages when foreign affiliates enter into transactions with local suppliers and customers. Finally a training effect may be present. MNEs might be only able to transfer superior technology to their foreign affiliates after having trained local workers. The training may be provided by foreign joint venture partners, foreign buyers or suppliers. Indigenous firms may also train their own workers to increase product quality in order to cope with foreign competition. In addition spillovers might also occur through labour turnover from foreign to indigenous firms. However, this type of spillover may not materialise if there is very little labour mobility between foreign and indigenous firms (Fosfuri et al., 2001).

A number of empirical studies, using both case study and econometric techniques, have confirmed the existence of positive indirect productivity benefits from FDI. For example, in an early study Caves (1974) tested several hypotheses concerning the effects of FDI on domestically-owned firms in Canada and Australia competing with foreign subsidiaries. He found foreign subsidiaries to be an effective force in reducing the excess profits of domestic competitors and improving allocative efficiency. His evidence also was consistent with a speedier transfer of technology in industries more populated by foreign subsidiaries. Positive indirect benefits have also been identified in cases where the host country is a developing economy. Blomström and Persson (1983) and Kokko (1994) found positive spillover effects in manufacturing sectors in Mexico. Fan's (1999) results for China reveal that the behaviour of indigenous firms is critical in determining the impact of FDI on their total factor productivity. The TFP growth of collective firms[4] was positively related to FDI, while that of state-owned firms[5] was negatively related to FDI inflows to China.

As previously noted, the indirect benefits of FDI have not always been found to be positive. Kholdy (1995) found no evidence of spillover benefits in several host developing countries with a significant FDI presence in manufacturing. For developing countries especially, it is argued that positive spillovers may not materialise if the technology gap between foreign and indigenous firms is too large. Haddad and Harrison (1993) studied the effects of foreign presence on indigenous firms' productivity in Moroccan manufacturing and suggested that large technology gaps were inhibiting spillovers. In contrast, the model of Wang and Blomström (1992) predict a positive relationship between the degree of spillovers from FDI and the size of the technology gap between foreign and indigenous firms; the larger the gap the stronger the possibilities for catch-up. In his study of intra-industry spillovers from FDI in Uruguayan manufacturing plants, Kokko et al. (1996) found a positive and statistically significant spillover effect only in indigenous plants with moderate technology gaps relative to foreign firms, pointing to the existence of firm-specific differences in the ability to absorb spillovers from foreign firms. Cohen and Levinthal (1989) and Kinoshita (2000) suggested that the contradictory empirical findings might imply that the incidence of productivity spillovers requires the indigenous firms to possess the ability to absorb advanced technology from foreign firms.

A high presence of foreign firms may also have a negative impact if foreign firms take the best workers from indigenous firms, leaving them with low wage and less productive employees. There is also a possibility that the competition effect may be harmful to a host economy when indigenous firms are not efficient enough to compete with foreign firms. Indigenous firms may in fact become less competitive and eventually may be displaced by foreign firms (Cantwell, 1995). Globerman (1979) uncovered evidence of negative productivity spillovers in his study of Canadian manufacturing plants. He found there was a negative relationship between FDI and indigenous firm labour productivity, and pointed out that any positive spillovers might be offset by the negative impact of more fierce competition arising from the presence of foreign firm. The finding supports the argument that negative effects from foreign firms might overshadow positive spillovers (Buckley and Casson, 1991).

A number of studies have focused on the combined direct and indirect impacts of FDI on host country industrial productivity. Girma et al. (2001) drew mixed conclusions for UK manufacturing, finding a positive impact overall, but with little or no productivity spillovers to indigenous firms. Conclusions were also mixed for those studies focusing on developing countries as hosts; Zukowska-Gagelmann (2000) for Poland; Djankov and Hoekman (2000) for the Czech enterprises; and Aitken and Harrison (1999) for Venzuela. All of these studies suggest that a higher presence of foreign firms raises aggregate industrial productivity, even if the affect on indigenous firms is negative. In the case of Venzuela the overall impact balancing direct and indirect effects was quite small. Table 13.2 provides a summary of previous studies on the impact of FDI on the productivity of host countries.

Table 13.2 Summary of previous studies on FDI productivity.

Studies	Countries/Industry	Data/Econometric Technique	Results: The Effects of FDI Inflows on Host Country's Productivity
Caves (1974)	Canada and Australia Manufacturing sectors Uruguayan Manufacturing sector	Industry-level (1965–67 Canada; 1962, 1966 Australia)	Lagged FDI positively affected value-added per worker in indigenous firms while changes in FDI had a negative impact
Kokko et al. (1996)	Austria Manufacturing sectors	Plant-level (1988) OLS	Positive and significant in the sub-sample of plants with moderate technology gaps vis-à-vis foreign firms
Egger and Pfaffermayr (2001)	UK Manufacturing sector	Panel data (1981–94) FES	General and labour-augmenting productivity improving
Girma et al. (2001)	Poland Manufacturing sector	Firm-level Panel data (1991–1996)	Higher productivity of foreign firms raise aggregate productivity but on average no productivity spillovers to indigenous firms
Zukowska-Gagelmann (2000)	Czech Republic	Firm-level (1993–97) OLS	A higher foreign presence in an industry affects indigenous firms negatively while positive impact on performance of the whole domestic industry including foreign firms
Djankov and Hoekman (2000)	Mexico Manufacturing sectors	Firm-level (1992–96) OLS, RES	Positive on TFP growth of FDI recipient firms but negative on firms that do not have foreign partnerships
Kokko (1994)	Mexico Manufacturing sectors	Industry-level (1970) OLS, 3SLS	Positive spillovers from competition between indigenous firms and foreign affiliates but excludes suspected 'enclaves'

Table 13.2 Summary of previous studies on FDI productivity – continued

Studies	Countries/Industry	Data/Econometric Technique	Results: The Effects of FDI Inflows on Host Country's Productivity
Blomström and Persson (1983)	Mexico, Brazil, Chile, Singapore, and Zambia Manufacturing sector	Industry-level (1970) OLS	Positive spillovers of technical efficiency between indigenous plants and the foreign participation of various industries
Kholdy (1995)	Morocco Manufacturing sector	Industry-level (1970–90) Causality test	No evidence of spillover efficiency as defined by higher labour productivity and capital formation in the host developing countries merely as a result of the presence of FDI
Haddad and Harrison (1993)	Venezuela industry	Firm-level (1985–89)	The dispersion of productivity is smaller in the sectors with more foreign firms. No evidence of FDI accelerated productivity growth or technology spillovers in indigenous firms
Aitken and Harrison (1999)	Canada Manufacturing sectors	Plant-level Panel data (1979–89, excluding 1980), OLS	Positive on small FDI recipient plants but negative on indigenous plants, the net impact of FDI is quite small
Globerman (1979)	China Manufacturing sectors	Plant-level (1972)	Negative relationship between FDI and indigenous firm labour productivity because of any positive spillovers may be offset by the negative impact of greater competition
Zhou et al. (2002)		firm-level (1992–95) SAS, REG	Indigenous firms in regions that attract more FDI or have a longer history of FDI tend to have higher productivity while indigenous firms in industries that have more FDI or have a longer history of FDI tend to have lower productivity

In this study of the Chinese automotive industry, the focus will be on the total impact of FDI on labour productivity. While a knowledge of direct and indirect impacts may be useful in interpreting the empirical results, the key issue for government policy towards inward investment is its effect on the productivity and competitiveness of the industry as a whole. Also while the bulk of the literature treats direct and indirect impacts as if they could be separated empirically, in the automotive industry in particular, they are increasingly blurred. Many of the so-called indirect effects are transmitted through contractual means or even equity arrangements with foreign affiliates.

Model, data and methodology

The available data allow us to estimate the aggregate impact of FDI on the productivity of China's automotive industry. Following a number of previous studies (Caves, 1974; Globerman, 1979; Blomström and Persson, 1983; Kokko, 1994; Gorg and Strobl, 2002), we estimate a model of the production function with labour productivity as the dependent variable. Our objective is to determine the impact of foreign presence on output per worker when other important influences on labour productivity are accounted for. An alternative measure of productivity, total factor productivity, is often used (e.g., Egger and Pfaffermayr, 2001), with some arguing that the combined impact of labour and capital productivity is a superior measure. However, we employ the labour productivity measure for two reasons: (1) we want our results to be comparable to similar studies; and (2) we also want to isolate the effects of increased capital intensity on labour productivity. Traditional models of economic growth predict that capital accumulation will raise the level of output per worker, up to a point of diminishing returns. We want to see if this point of diminishing returns has been reached given the current development stage of the Chinese automotive industry. The model of the production function to be estimated is given in equation (1) below:

(1) LP = f (CI, FS, LQ, RFI, RIN, TO)

Where LP (Labour Productivity) is the ratio of industry value-added to the annual average number of staff and workers in the sub-sectors of China's automotive industry.

CI (Capital Intensity) is the ratio of the net value of fixed assets to the annual average number of staff and workers. The more machinery and equipment used by each employee, the higher level of firm automation and the higher the expected productivity. Capital intensity represents an important control variable in studies of FDI impacts. As Egger and Pfaffermayr (2001) note, investment by foreign firms leads to increases in the domestic stock of capital and enhanced production capacity. In order to isolate the productivity effects associated with firm-specific assets in FDI-receiving firms and their spillovers to other firms, it is important to control for the more traditional productivity enhancing effects of investment generally.

FS (Firm Size) is the ratio of the value of gross industrial output to the number of firms. Firm size represents the economies of scale variable, which has been particular important in some sectors of the automotive industry. According to production theory, as average firm size increases, unit costs will decrease leading to higher productivity.

LQ (Labour Quality) is the ratio of the number of technical staff to the annual average number of staff and workers in each industry sub-sector. Labour quality indicates the level of skill or education of labour force. The use of the number of technical staff offers a more direct measure of the average skill/education level of the labour force than the often-used proxy of primary and secondary school enrolment, since there is a time lag between school enrolment and entry into labour force. Improvements in labour force quality can be expected to lead to increases in productivity.

RFI (Foreign Investment) is the ratio of foreign investment to total capital. As mentioned above, FDI not only transfers capital but also transfer new technologies, managerial skills, and advanced production functions. Therefore, the greater are the foreign investment inflows, the higher productivity will be. This variable is lagged by one-year to avoid any bi-directional effects where efficient and therefore competitive sub-sectors of the automotive industry might attract inward FDI.

RIN (Innovation) is the ratio of innovation investment to total investment. Innovation represents the new methods, ideas, or products introduced into either the market or production process. A higher amount of innovation investment is expected to lead to higher productivity. It should be noted that labour quality (LQ) and innovation investment variables may be positively related in that a high level of labour quality is necessary if a strong R&D capacity is to develop. The two variables in so far that they represent the technological capabilities of the domestic economy, may also indicate something about the ability of domestic firms to absorb the technical knowledge of foreign firms.

TO (Turnover of Working Capital) is the number of the times working capital is turned over in a year. Faster rates of turnover should lead to higher productivity as current assets of the firm, such as inventories of raw materials or finished goods are converted into cash inflows.

All of the monetary variables are measured at 1995 constant prices. It is predicted that all of the explanatory variables will positively influence labour productivity in China's automotive industry. To test the model for China's automotive industry, a panel data set is employed at sub-sector level. The time period considered is the five years from 1995 to 1999. Data are from China Automotive Industry Yearbook 1996–2000, in which China's automotive industry is divided into five subsectors: Auto-manufacturing, Auto-assembling, Motor-manufacturing, Vehicle-engines, and Vehicle-parts (see Table 13.3).

In order to measure directly the impact of the explanatory variables on the dependent variable in terms of elasticity, the variables in the equation (1) can be rewritten in logarithmic form:

(2) $LLP_{it} = \beta_1 LCI_{it} + \beta_2 LFS_{it} + \beta_3 LLQ_{it} + \beta_4 LRFI_{it-1} + \beta_5 LRIN_{it} + \beta_6 LTO_{it} + v_{it}$

where L indicates logged values; i and t denote the sub-sectors of the industry and time, respectively; v_{it} is a composite term including both the intercept and the stochastic error term. The coefficients β_1, β_2, β_3, β_4, β_5, β_6 indicate the percent change in LP associated with a given percent change in CI, FS, LQ, RFI, RIN, and TO, respectively.

There are three statistical models used to estimate panel data sets: a pooled ordinary least squares model (POLS), a fixed effects model (FES), and a random effects model (RES). The models differ mainly in their assumptions concerning the intercepts and error terms. In estimating equation (2), both the POLS model and the FES model are employed. The RES model cannot be used in this study because the number of parameters exceeds the number of cross-sections, represented by the five sub sectors of the Chinese automotive industry. The Likelihood ratio (LR) test is applied to identify the better statistical model between POLS and FES. A value of LR that is significantly different from zero means that the FES estimation is preferable to the POLS estimation.

Empirical results

The empirical results obtained from the POLS and FES models are summarised in Table 13.4. As the table shows, the large and statistically

Table 13.3 China's automotive industry by sub-sector 1995–1999.

Variable	Sub-sector	1995	1996	1997	1998	1999
CI	Auto-manufacturing	4.5742558	6.2688892	9.0959735	9.8805414	14.893051
	Auto-assembling	2.2602812	3.2361879	3.7553854	4.3146843	5.764928
	Motor-manufacturing	3.8767455	5.0499728	6.1212909	8.303593	9.3519668
	Vehicle engine	3.1400503	4.6611794	5.1773525	5.8902539	9.6964367
	Vehicle parts	2.526449	3.2333535	3.8417525	4.8889233	6.1122707
FS	Auto-manufacturing	83746.984	96589.787	121157.57	131322.49	145319.65
	Auto-assembling	3026.7597	3615.4192	3907.7794	4717.6914	4645.0495
	Motor-manufacturing	35180.33	36673.331	37632.993	54353.931	62051.336
	Vehicle engine	13907.115	13158.032	15532.519	18129.143	23138.373
	Vehicle parts	2240.3232	2570.2637	3112.1928	3524.4005	4288.4156
LQ	Auto-manufacturing	0.0927242	0.0898452	0.0923135	0.0863653	0.0940836
	Auto-assembling	0.0842533	0.0839291	0.0844614	0.0836696	0.0952829
	Motor-manufacturing	0.0824712	0.0804882	0.0818508	0.0899097	0.0906366
	Vehicle engine	0.1089765	0.1043297	0.1075615	0.0990893	0.0953243
	Vehicle parts	0.07589	0.0811157	0.0811973	0.0848694	0.0933093
RFI	Auto-manufacturing	0.0383161	0.0068772	0.0194796	0.0161251	0.0176689
	Auto-assembling	0.005667	0.0026935	0.0019939	0.0043458	0.0027547
	Motor-manufacturing	0.0211781	0.0071269	0.0074143	0.0012396	0.0012174
	Vehicle engine	0.0338106	0.0103632	0.0077037	0.0043399	0.0025812
	Vehicle parts	0.0291625	0.029391	0.0177283	0.0109579	0.0081942
RIN	Auto-manufacturing	0.3606092	0.4207747	0.4417124	0.5803921	0.582734
	Auto-assembling	0.5765195	0.4207262	0.4367979	0.4211837	0.3146838
	Motor-manufacturing	0.6294588	0.5110032	0.3691246	0.5434328	0.5318273
	Vehicle engine	0.8203023	0.6749895	0.6897452	0.6387712	0.9461698
	Vehicle parts	0.7167057	0.70505	0.6000557	0.6247178	0.6391674
TO	Auto-manufacturing	1.34	1.42	1.18	1.11	1.33
	Auto-assembling	1.15	1.15	1.11	1.21	1.27
	Motor-manufacturing	2.3	1.77	1.64	1.18	1.39
	Vehicle engine	1.13	0.98	0.88	0.73	0.84
	Vehicle parts	1.17	1.01	1.08	1.02	1.06

Source: China Automotive Industry Yearbook 1996–2000, computed by the authors.

Table 13.4 Results of panel data estimations, 1995–1999.

	POLS	FES
LCI	0.8722	0.6180
	(0.2055)***	(0.2685)**
LFS	0.0287	0.8768
	(0.0593)	(0.4700)*
LLQ	–0.5505	–0.9274
	(0.6611)	(0.5581)
LRFI$_{(-1)}$	0.0185	0.1127
	(0.0494)	(0.0545)*
LRIN	0.3604	–0.3476
	(0.2417)	(0.2086)
LTO	1.3763	0.9595
	(0.3453)***	(0.2866)***
C	7.2500	–1.4040
	(1.7918)***	(4.4784)
Adjusted R^2	0.8933	0.9667
NT	20	20
Test	LR = 17.20***	

Notes: 1 Standard errors are in parentheses.
2 *** significant at 1%, **significant at 5%, *significant at 10%

significant LR value favours the FES model over the POLS model. The remaining discussion therefore focuses on the results of the FES estimation.

The results from the FES model show that LCI, LFS, LRFI$_{(-1)}$, and LTO are positive as expected and statistically significant at different levels, while LLQ and LRIN are negative but insignificant. The coefficient for LCI is positive and statistically significant at the 5% level, indicating that capital intensity positively affects labour productivity in China's automotive industry. The results suggest that capital accumulation continues to be important at the current stage of development of China's industry. The magnitude of LCI reveals that a 1% increase in capital intensity will raise labour productivity by 0.62%. The LFS variable is positive and statistically significant at the 10% level. This result implies that firm size does affect productivity positively, supporting the presence of scale economies. The magnitude of LFS indicates that a 1% firm size increase would result in a 0.88% increase in labour productivity. The coefficient for the foreign investment variable, LRFI$_{(-1)}$ again is positive and statistically significant at the 10% level, which suggests that FDI lagged by one year positively affects labour productivity in China's automotive industry. The magnitude of LRFI$_{(-1)}$ is not high, however, with a 1% increase in LRFI$_{(-1)}$ raising labour productivity by 0.11%. The result suggests only a weak transfer of know-how from foreign firms to their indigenous counterparts in sub sectors of China's auto industry, although this suggestion should be viewed with caution given the limitations of our dataset. The result however, is consistent with statements from industry experts (see section 2) who argue that a culture of protectionism existing in the industry prevents needed changes in practices and technology. The LTO variable is also positive and statistical significant at the 1% level as expected, with a 1% increase in the annual turnover of working capital leading to a 0.96% increase in productivity. This result is consistent with that expected.

Surprisingly however, LLQ and LRIN are found to be negative, though insignificant with respect to labour productivity. The results imply that labour quality and innovation are not important determinants of labour productivity in China's automotive industry. In interpreting these results, it is important to consider the stage of economic development currently attained in the Chinese industry. While China is industrialising rapidly, with a rapid rate of capital accumulation, in many industries competitiveness is still driven by the advantages of an abundant labour supply. In contrast, the importance of variables such as labour quality and innovative investment may be more important at a latter stage of development, which is driven by the accumulation and utilisation of knowledge assets. Our study covers only a five year period, so the factors influencing the productivity and competitiveness of the industry and even the type of foreign investment attracted to the industry may change over time.

The results are in accord with previous papers that suggest FDI has a positive impact on the productivity of host economies and suggests that the government should continue to promote FDI in the Chinese automotive industry. However while the FDI variable is significant, it is not the most influential factor (significant at 10% level) and efforts to increase the capital intensity of the industry, average firm size and working capital turnover should also be encouraged. The results also show that at the current stage of its development, innovative investment (as opposed to basic manufacturing investment) and improvements in labour quality are not important determinants of productivity growth in China's automotive industry. This is not however to suggest that they will not become more important as the industry matures. Such innovation investment as there has been in China may be incremental, merely tailoring existing products and methods to a new market and production environment. At least in the component sub-sector, Sinclair (2005, p. 48) notes that Chinese auto component manufacturers have been slow to invest in real product development, although they are 'adept at making prototypes based on blue-prints or physical samples'.

Conclusions

This paper has focused on the impact of FDI inflows on aggregate automotive industrial productivity in China's automotive industry using a panel data set consisting of five sub-sectors over the five years from 1995 to 1999. It has thus contributed to the empirical evidence concerning the impact of foreign presence on host economies that are developing countries through a unique approach focusing on a particular sector. An important finding is that inward FDI plays a positive role in raising labour productivity in one of China's key sectors, supporting the theory of FDI, which predicts that MNEs transfer not only capital but also advanced technologies and managerial skills. The results imply that government policies to attract foreign investment have resulted in productivity benefits.

However the results also indicate that the Chinese government cannot rely solely on FDI to improve the productivity and competitiveness of the automotive industry. In fact capital intensity, firm size and the quick turnover of working capital are equally if not more important at this stage of the industry's development. These findings are consistent with reports from industry experts on the continuing fragmentation and over-capacity in certain sectors of the industry: automanufacturers and component suppliers. Certainly our results indicate that sub-sectors of the industry could benefit in terms of productivity growth through an increase in average firm size to achieve scale economies.

While China's automotive industry has undergone rapid development since the opening up of China's economy, further structural and technological changes need to take place for it to be internationally competitive. Our estimates of the effect of inward FDI on the labour productivity of China's automotive industry suggest that the Chinese government should continue to attract FDI inflows into the industry. However in order to ensure that the industry, and particularly indigenous firms in the industry, realise the full benefits of FDI, the culture of protectionism needs to be addressed. The auto parts and components sub-sector seems to be particularly vulnerable to import competition in the post-WTO environment, as auto assemblers can no longer be pressured into buying Chinese parts for their vehicles. In this sub-sector particularly consolidation should be an important priority. If domestic firms are to survive, they need to take advantage of the demonstration and competitive effects which foreign firms in the sub-sector can offer.

Notes

1. Six key industries in China are automotive, electronics and telecommunications, electric appliances, power station equipment, chemicals, and steel.
2. The term of 'actually used FDI' means that FDI has been realised or 'utilised' in China, which is the term used in Chinese official statistics by the Chinese government as opposed to merely contracted or pledged FDI.
3. International Organisation of Automobile Manufacturers.
4. Collective firms are formally owned by local governments at the urban and rural levels and include township and village enterprises.
5. State-owned firms are formally owned by all of the people but are controlled by central, provincial or local governments.

References

Aitken, B.J. and Harrison, A.E., Do Domestic Firms Benefit from Direct Foreign Investment? Evidence from Venezuela, *The American Economic Review*, 89, 3, 1999, pp. 605–618.

Bertschek, I., Product and Process Innovation as a Response to Increasing Imports and Foreign Direct Investment, *The Journal of Industrial Economics*, 43, 4, 1995, pp. 341–357.

Blomström, M. and Persson, H., Foreign Investment and Spillover Efficiency in an Underdeveloped Economy: Evidence in the Mexican Manufacturing Industry, *World Development*, 11, 6, 1983, pp. 493–501.

Blomström, M. and Sjöholm, F., Technology Transfer and Spillovers: Does Local Participation with Multinationals Matter?, *European Economic Review*, 43, 4, 1999, pp. 915–923.

Buckley, P.J. and Casson, M., Multinational Enterprises in Less-Developed Countries: Cultural and Economic Interactions, in Buckley, P.J. and Clegg, L.J. (eds), *Multinational Enterprises in Less-Developed Countries*, London: Macmillan 1991.

Cantwell, J., The Globalisation of Technology: What Remains of the Product Cycle Model?, *Cambridge Journal of Economics*, 19, 1, 1995, pp. 155–174.

Caves, R.E., Multinational Firms, Competition, and Productivity in Host-Country Markets, *Economica*, 41, 162, 1974, pp. 176–193.

Chinese Automotive Technology Research Centre (ed.), *Chinese Automotive Industry Yearbook*, various issues.

Cohen, W.M. and Levinthal, D.A., Innovation and Learning: The Two Faces of R&D, *The Economic Journal*, 99, 397, 1989, pp. 569–596.

Djankov, S. and Hoekman, B., Foreign Investment and Productivity Growth in Czech Enterprises, *The World Bank Economic Review*, 14, 1, 2000, pp. 49–64.

Egger, P. and Pfaffermary, M., A Note on Labour Productivity and Foreign Inward Direct Investment, *Applied Economics Letters*, 8, 4, 2001, pp. 229–232.

Fan, X., How Spillovers from FDI Differ between China's State and Collective Firms, *Moct-Most*, 9, 1, 1999, pp. 35–48.

Fosfuri, A., Motta, M. and Ronde, T., Foreign Direct Investment and Spillovers through Workers' Mobility, *Journal of International Economics*, 53, 1, 2001, pp. 205–222.

Girrna, S., Greenaway, D. and Wakelin, K., Who Benefits from Foreign Direct Investment in the UK?, *Scottish Journal of Political Economy*, 48, 2, 2001, pp. 119–133.

Globerman, S., Foreign Direct Investment and 'Spillover' Efficiency Benefits in Canadian Manufacturing Industries, *The Canadian Journal of Economics*, 12, 1979, pp. 42–56.

Gorg, H. and Strobl, E., Multinational Companies and Indigenous Development: An Empirical Analysis, *European Economic Review*, 46, 7, 2002, pp. 1305–1322.

Haddad, M. and Harrison, A., Are there Positive Spillovers from Direct Foreign Investment? Evidence from Panel Data for Morocco, *Journal of Development Economics*, 42, 1, 1993, pp. 51–74.

Harwit, E., *China's Automobile Industry: Policies, Problems, and Prospects*, Armonk, New York: M.E. Sharpe 1995.

Harwit, E., The Impact of WTO Membership on the Automobile Industry in China, *The China Quarterly*, 167, 2001, pp. 655–670.

Hymer, S., *The International Operation of National Firms: A Study of Direct Foreign Investment*, Cambridge, Massachusetts: MIT Press 1976.

Irandoust, M., Market Structure and Market Shares in the Car Industry, *Japan and the World Economy*, 11, 4, 1999, pp. 531–544.

Kholdy, S., Causality Between Foreign Investment and Spillover Efficiency, *Applied Economics*, 27, 8, 1995, pp. 745–749.

Kinoshita, Y., Technology Spillovers through Foreign Direct Investment, *Working Papers 139*, Prague: CERGE-EI 1998.

Kinoshita, Y., R&D and Technology Spillovers via FDI: Innovation and Absorptive Capacity, *Working Papers 163*, Prague: CERGE-EI 2000.

Kokko, A., Technology, Market Characteristics, and Spillovers, *Journal of Development Economics*, 43, 2, 1994, pp. 279–293.

Kokko, A., Tansini, R. and Zejan, MC., Local Technological Capability and Productivity Spillovers from FDI in the Uruguayan Manufacturing Sector, *The Journal of Development Studies*, 32, 4, 1996, pp. 602–611.

Sinclair, J., Under the Hood, *The China Business Review*, 32, 2, pp. 46–51.

Sit, V.F.S. and Liu, W., Restructuring and Spatial Change of China's Auto Industry under Institutional Reform and Globalization, *Annals of the Association of American Geographers*, 90, 4, 2000, pp. 653–673.

Veugelers, R. and Vanden Houte, P., Domestic R&D in the Presence of Multinational Enterprises, *International Journal of Industrial Organisation*, 8, 1, 1990, pp. 1–15.

Wang, J. and Blomström, M., Foreign Investment and Technology Transfer: A Simple Model, *European Economic Review*, 36, 1, 1992, pp. 137–155.

Willmore, L., The Comparative Performance of Foreign and Domestic Firms in Brazil, in Lall, S. and Dunning, J. (eds), *Transnational Corporations and Economic Development*, London, New York: Routledge 1993, pp. 251–272.

Zhou, D., Li, S. and Tse, D., The Impact of FDI on the Productivity of Domestic Firms: The Case of China, *International Business Review*, 11, 4, 2002, pp. 465–484.

Zukowska-Gagelmann, K., Productivity Spillovers from Foreign Direct Investment in Poland, *Economic Systems*, 24, 3, 2000, pp. 223–256.

14
The Impact of Foreign Ownership, Local Ownership and Industry Characteristics on Spillover Benefits from Foreign Direct Investment in China

Peter J. Buckley, Chengqi Wang and Jeremy Clegg

Introduction

The past two decades have witnessed a striking transformation in the Chinese economy: from a centrally planned to an essentially market-oriented system, and away from an inward-orientated industrialisation strategy to 'open-door' policies aimed at integration with the global economy. Accompanying the progressive marketisation and internationalisation of the economy in this period, has been an unprecedented expansion in inward foreign direct investment (FDI) into China by multinational enterprises (MNEs). Indeed, in 2003 China overtook the USA and became the largest recipient of FDI (United Nations Conference on Trade and Development (UNCTAD), 2004). This growth in inward FDI is widely believed to be a key component of China's economic miracle. However, simply measuring the direct effects of inward FDI on Chinese industrial productivity will underestimate the overall contribution of foreign investment if spillover effects are significant (Buckwalter, 1995; Murphy, 1992; O'Malley, 1994). Therefore this study examines the spillover effects that arise from FDI in Chinese manufacturing.

There is little controversy within existing theoretical research on the causes of spillovers, but a considerable amount of debate within empirical work to date, largely because the evidence on spillovers remains stubbornly inconclusive (Blomström and Kokko, 1998). Part of the problem may be that existing studies typically treat foreign affiliates (FAs), of whatever home origin, and locally owned enterprises (LOEs), of whatever type of domestic ownership, as a whole. They also pay no regard to the characteristics of the industry in which these firms operate. Such studies, therefore, look at the aggregate impact of overall inward FDI on all LOEs, across all manufacturing industries. More recent research (e.g., Buckley, Clegg and Wang, 2005) has started to unpack these overall results, to allow for relationships within the aggregate data that can vary with category of foreign investors and by group of local spillover recipients.

In a commentary article on the perspective paper of Meyer (2004) and Ramamurti (2004) calls for future research in the area of spillovers to follow Buckley, Clegg, and Wang (2002) and Gillespie, Riddle, Sayre, and Sturges (1999) in investigating the impact of diasporas on economic development in poor countries. By way of a response, this study aims to offer a step forward in breaking down the general relationship between FDI and LOEs' performance. We group the whole of Chinese manufacturing into labour-intensive and technology-intensive industries; FAs into those originating in Hong Kong, Macau and Taiwan (hereafter, HMT) versus those originating from western countries; and the LOEs recipients of spillovers into state-owned enterprises (SOEs) and other LOEs (OLOEs). These classifications form the basic analytical framework of this study.

These distinctions are particularly crucial in the context of China. First, it is generally agreed that China's comparative advantage is its relatively low labour costs compared with developed countries and with other emerging economies (Cheng and Kwan, 2000). This has been a leading motive for MNEs to invest in labour-intensive activities in China (Fung, Lau and Lee, 2002). Second, the two major groups of foreign investors in China – firms from HMT and from western countries – differ enormously, in terms of both motivation and investment behaviour (Huang, 2004). This contrast means that FAs in these two ownership groups can be expected to impact differently on LOEs. Third, SOEs and OLOEs are two very heterogeneous ownership types dominating Chinese manufacturing industry. They diverge substantially in many respects. These include the structure of property rights, technological capability, learning incentives and government support, among others (Wang, 2003). These dissimilarities suggest that the two types of firms may have different absorptive capacities, and furthermore that these will vary by industry. Therefore, the richness and diversity of FDI into China, and of its potential impacts, provides a unique opportunity to explore the complexity of FDI spillovers, within the environment of an economy undergoing transition.

In this paper, we pursue the idea that the spillover effects of FDI may be not as uniform as many studies suggest. In examining the productivity impacts of foreign ownership on China's domestic industry, the paper is marked out from existing studies in the following three respects. First, by allowing the results to vary between labour- and technology-intensive industries, we expect to see the extent to which spillover effects vary with industrial technology intensity. Second, we employ alternative measures of foreign presence, and use these to investigate more deeply the influence of the source of FDI. This procedure enables us to distinguish effects that are specific to the type of country of foreign ownership, and to compare these with the overall effects of foreign ownership. Third, we allow the results to vary with respect to different types of domestic ownership. So doing enables us to observe the distribution of spillovers between differently owned LOEs. Fourth and most important, we combine the above three dimensions by organising the groups of foreign and locally owned firms within different industry categories. This systematic approach provides an opportunity to uncover 'who benefits from whom' in which types of Chinese manufacturing industry. It is this task that constitutes the central aim of this study.

If significant between-group effects are captured through the above procedures, it would imply that studies conducted only at aggregate level are deficient. It is quite possible that in aggregate analysis 'good' and 'bad' nations, industries and ownerships of LOEs may offset one another, leading to the washing out of important effects. We expect that our breakdown will reveal sub-relationships in the data that up to now have remained hidden within the aggregate relationships reported in most studies. In this way, we aim to complement and deepen the state of knowledge on spillover effects in Chinese industry, which in the main has been confined to general conclusions.

Section 2 sets the theoretical scene, together with a brief review of the relevant empirical literature. A description of the variables, the models adopted and data employed, follows in Section 3. Section 4 discusses the econometric results, while Section 5 concludes.

Literature review

Theory of spillovers

The theory of spillovers associated with inward FDI is well established, and little controversy remains. It is generally agreed that spillovers are generated by non-market transactions involving foreign MNEs' resources, in particular when knowledge is spread to local host country competitors without a contractual relationship (Meyer, 2004). Spillovers are reflected in improved productivity, or other benefits, in LOEs (Buckley et al., 2005). Görg and Greenaway (2002) mention imitation, the acquisition of skills, competition and exports as channels through which developing host countries may achieve productivity gains via intra-industry spillovers.

Despite general agreement over the theoretical basis and mechanisms of spillovers, to date theorists have not gone so far as to explore fully when precisely these spillovers might be large, small and non-existent (Caves, 1999). However, there are good reasons for believing that spillovers should be large for certain groups of LOEs in particular industries, and, that these further link to the country group of FAs. These hypotheses can only be tested by breaking down the aggregate data.

Spillovers in labour- and technology-intensive industries

Conventional theory on MNEs and FDI suggests that knowledge-based assets constitute the firm-specific advantages owned by MNEs, that these motivate investment across borders. Accordingly, Markusen (1995) notes that MNEs can be identified with a high ratio of intangible assets to market value. In industries characterised with rapidly changing technologies these assets are likely to be related to new products and processes. In line with these arguments, mainstream theoretical perspectives, such as the OLI paradigm (Dunning, 1993) suggests that MNEs operate predominantly in technology-intensive industries.

The emergence of MNEs in non-R&D intensive industries in recent years however (since the 1980s) has lead to recognition that an absolute advantage, for instance in technology or product differentiation, is not always the crucial factor driving FDI (Giddy and Young, 1982). Labour-intensive industries are a good example of those in which MNEs' competitiveness may spring from marketing skills or organisational advantages. These non-technological assets are capable of underpinning the exploitation of comparative advantages in host countries (Luo, 1999). The possession of ownership advantages of this type, taken together with favourable location-specific factors abroad, may enable even small and low-technology firms to undertake FDI (Giddy and Young, 1982). This view is corroborated by evidence on the dramatic growth in FDI from Japan in the 1970s, and the emergence of MNEs from newly developed Asian economies, such as Hong Kong and Taiwan.

However, it is within host countries' technology intensive industries that we observe a concentration of conventionally technologically advanced MNEs. This is the origin of the view that LOEs in high-technology industries are more prone to benefit from FDI technological spillovers than their counterparts in labour-intensive industries. Indeed, numerous studies find that technology plays a key role in generating spillovers in the form of improved productivity. This accounts for the interchangeable use of the terms 'productivity' and 'technology' spillover in much of the literature (Kokko, 1992). Notwithstanding the link between the use of technology and spillover benefits, there are reasons to expect a larger technology gap between FAs and LOEs in technology-intensive industries than in labour-intensive industries. The larger this gap, then the less likely are spillovers to materialise from MNEs' presence (Perez, 1997).

It follows that the scope for large spillovers should be smaller in labour-intensive industries than in technology-intensive industries. Yet LOEs in labour-intensive industries should still gain from the presence of foreign firms. The technology gap between FAs and LOEs should be smaller in labour-intensive industries than in technology-intensive industries. According to many studies this smaller technology gap should facilitate spillovers. In traditional industries, MNEs are more likely to base their competitiveness on organisational skills and marketing skills, such as experience in organising labour-intensive production and the ability to specialise across international borders. Even so, it remains to be tested whether or not non-technology-related spillovers are indeed smaller than technology-related spillovers.

Spillovers and home origin of FDI

The above-hypothesised relationships may vary depending on the source country of FDI. This assertion has its basis in Dunning's eclectic paradigm (Dunning, 1988, 1993). The Paradigm posits that the pattern of FDI varies with the country of origin of the investing firm. MNEs in a particular country often possess some specific advantages emanating from the nature of their domestic market (Tatoglu and Glaister, 1998). Lecraw (1993) argues that the rationale for, and behaviour of, FDI should be heterogeneous across source countries because the degree of similarity between home and host market structures tends to differ with investors' geographic origins. In his 'single diamond' view, Porter (1990) alleges that the strong global competitiveness generated by the core competences of a MNE, results from the characteristics of the

MNE's home base. The technological profile of an innovative affiliate will reflect the distinctive specialised technological capacities of its parent's home country.

A salient feature of inward FDI in China is that the investing countries can be identified in two distinct groups: overseas Chinese (Hong Kong, Macau and Taiwan, hereafter, HMT) and western countries (notably, the USA, European Union and Japan). It is argued that investors from these two sources possess different types of ownership advantages and business strategies, leading to heterogeneity in investment behaviour; for instance, in respect of the scale of investment, the extent of cooperative operation, productivity, and in the ability to transfer technology (Huang, 2004). MNEs from western countries have state-of-the-art technology from heavy investment in R&D. This confers ownership advantages that enable them to compete successfully in technology-intensive industries with other firms in the t market (Buckley *et al.*, 2002). This contrasts with HMT MNEs whose ownership advantages are thought to lie in skills of using standard technology and in experience of organising labour-intensive production for re-export (Shi, 1998). We therefore expect that HMT firms are more competitive in labour rather than in technology-intensive industries.

We argue that the contrasting technological capabilities and business strategies of these two groups of FAs are key determinants of spillovers. Furthermore, the effects of country of origin on spillovers might manifest themselves differentially across industries, possibly linked to the incidence of LOEs of contrasting ownership. With their state-of-the-art technology and local market-orientation, there is greater scope for western MNEs to generate technological spillovers to LOEs in technology-intensive industries of Chinese manufacturing (Buckley *et al.*, 2002). On the other hand, the nature of the ownership advantages of HMT firms, and their industrial concentration within the standardised goods market segments of industries, suggests that the generation of any technological spillovers should be less *pro rata* than for western capital, or slower in its realisation. Yet it is perfectly possible that HMT firms generate more non-technology-related spillovers. Based on data for Lithuania, Smarzynska (2002) finds that productivity spillover effects are larger when foreign investors are domestic market, rather than export, oriented. It would be interesting to see if this finding also holds true for China, where western and HMT affiliates are typically identified, respectively as local market- and export-oriented.

Spillovers and its distributional effects among LOEs

The literature suggests that the extent of spillovers depends on the actions of both foreign and locally owned firms, and is not quasi-automatic (Meyer, 2004). The magnitude of spillover benefits that LOEs can derive from foreign presence depends largely on their own technological capabilities and initiatives (Liu, Siler, Wang and Wei, 2000). Thus, spillover benefits materialise if LOEs develop capabilities to decode, interpret and apply knowledge (Meyer, 2004). When domestic competitors cannot reverse engineer and profitably adapt MNEs' core technologies, they are unable to appropriate benefits from FDI spillovers. Therefore, positive spillovers are expected to only be available to LOEs that have developed superior absorptive capacity. This implies that aggregate studies may underestimate the true significance of such effects (Görg and Strobl, 2001). The perspective of absorptive capacity implies that future researchers should move beyond merely seeking a straightforward and direct nexus between foreign presence and LOEs' productivity, and begin investigating the 'black box' that contains the acknowledged, but unobserved, mediators of the relationship.

In terms of ownership, the potential beneficiaries of inward FDI in local Chinese industry broadly comprise SOEs and OLOEs. The latter include collectively and privately owned enterprises, among others. It is well recognised that differences in the structure of property rights between SOEs and OLOEs cause them to behave differently, leading to the underperformance of SOEs (Fan, 1998; Perotti, Sun and Zou, 1999). While SOEs are the technologically better equipped of the two, OLOEs are more agile and responsive to profit opportunities, making them competitive, especially in the market for labour-intensive goods. By identifying SOEs and OLOEs separately we are be able to explore the FDI-spillovers relationship within differing institutional settings, and therefore gain insights specifically into the Chinese context. This level of detail is expected to yield both conceptual richness and policy relevance.

The above discussion leads to the following hypotheses:

Hypothesis 1. The magnitude of the effect of overall foreign capital on the performance of LOEs is greater in technology-intensive industries than in labour-intensive industries.

Hypothesis 2. The magnitude of the effect of HTM capital is greater than that of the effect of western capital in labour-intensive industries on (a) all domestic firms; (b) SOEs; (c) OLOEs.

Hypothesis 3. The magnitude of the effect of western capital is greater than that of the effect of HTM capital in technology-intensive industries on (a) all domestic firms; (b) SOEs; (c) OLOEs.

Hypothesis 4. The magnitude of spillovers absorbed by OLOEs is greater than that of spillovers by SOEs in labour-intensive industries.

Hypothesis 5. The magnitude of spillovers absorbed by SOEs is greater than that of spillovers by OLOEs in technology-intensive industries.

Hypothesis 6. The magnitude of spillovers absorbed by OLOEs from HMT capital is greater than that of spillovers by SOEs from the same source in labour-intensive industries.

Hypothesis 7. The magnitude of spillovers absorbed by SOEs from western capital is greater than that of spillovers absorbed by OLOEs from the same source in technology intensive industries.

Data and methodology

We follow the standard approach prevailing in the study of spillovers, in which an augmented Cobb-Douglas production function is implemented (e.g., Aitken and Harrison, 1999). In this function, the output of LOEs is assumed to be a function of inputs, which include measures of foreign presence in the host industry and other regressors as controls. We interpret the coefficient estimates on the foreign presence regressor as evidence in support of spillovers from inward FDI to domestic firms' output.

$$Y_{d,s,ol} = C + \beta_1 K_{d,s,ol} + \beta_2 L_{d,s,ol} + \beta_3 INTERM_{d,s,ol} + \beta_4 MGT_{d,s,ol} + \beta_5 SFARE_{d,s,ol} + \beta_6 SIZE_{d,s,ol} + \beta_7 FP_{(i-1)} + \varepsilon_i (i = overall, htm, w), \quad (1)$$

where d denotes domestic, s SOEs and ol other LOEs. Y is sales by LOEs and FP represents the level of presence of FAs, proxied by the share of foreign capital input in host industry. Görg and Strobl (2001) suggest that it is preferable to use alternative measures, rather than a single measure of foreign presence, when evaluating spillover effects. Following Buckley et al. (2002), we measure FP in three dimensions in this study: the capital share accounted for by all FAs in each industry ($FP_{overall}$); the capital share accounted for by FAs originating from HMT in each industry (FP_{hmt}); the capital share accounted for by FAs originating from western countries in each industry (FP_w). For all

FP variables, a one-year lag is adopted to allow time for spillover effects to become observable. The adoption of a lag structure for the FDI variable ($FP_{(i-1)}$) also helps to address the question of causality with respect to spillovers (Haskel, Pereira and Slaughter, 2002). We expect that FP_i exerts a positive and significant impact on sales by LOEs (Y).

K and L are routine capital and labour, proxied by total received capital and total number of employees in each industry; INTERM is intermediate inputs, proxied by the difference between total sales and value-added in each industry; *MGT, SFARE* and SIZE variables are management input, sales promotion input, and firm size economies of scale proxied by, respectively, management cost per employee, sales fare per worker, and net fixed assets per firm, by industry. Combined with the selection of *FP* variables, according to theory these control variables account for total factor productivity. The employment of these control variables increases our confidence in the robustness of the findings, through controlling for influences other than foreign presence.

In Eq. (1), the data are transformed into natural logarithms, therefore Eq. (1) should be taken as being linear in the logarithmic data. Ordinary least squares (OLS) regression is employed throughout. The model is estimated for different categories of locally owned firms, with data aggregated across firms at the three-digit industry level. Given that small-, medium-, and large-sized firms, and industrial branches, are sampled together in our cross-sectional dataset, heteroscedasticity is expected to be widespread, and this was confirmed in preliminary specifications. Consequently, where the White-based *F*-statistic showed below the 5% level of significance, all variance-covariance matrices have been estimated according to White's (1980) method.

Eq. (1) is a multi-equation model, and therefore forms the basis for the estimation of several regressions. This allows our investigation to explore variation by industry, by nationality of the foreign investor, and by ownership of LOEs, so corresponding to each of the hypotheses set out in Section 2.

Our empirical analysis is based on the Annual Industrial Report of China for 2001, compiled by the State Statistical Bureau of the People's Republic of China. Industry data is preferred because spillovers are commonly hypothesised to arise along industry or regional lines (Haskel *et al.*, 2002). In addition, there is considerable variation in the foreign presence variable at the industry level. There are 196 industries altogether, but our sample is reduced to 158 industries. This is because this study must be restricted on theoretical grounds to include only those industries where free entry and exit exist, in order to avoid biased results. Industries for which data are imperfect are also excluded.

In carrying out the empirical analysis, we divide the full sample into two sub-samples of equal size, according to the level of capital–labour ratio. The low capital–labour ratio group is labelled as 'labour-intensive industries' and the high capital–labour group as 'technology-intensive industries', with each consisting of 79 industries. The significant F test statistic of 90.366 justifies this classification of labour- versus technology-intensive industries at the 1% level of significance. This classification forms the basis of our analysis, as it allows us to examine the extent to which the magnitude of spillovers relates to the nature of industries under study. Indeed, all our hypotheses in Section 2 are set out against categories of industries.

Results

Table 14.1 displays the correlation matrix and descriptive statistics for the main independent and dependant variables. As can be seen, most of the correlations are small, accounting for little common variance, and therefore are not of present concern. The high correlation between K_d and L_d demonstrates the high capital–labour substitution effect within Chinese industry.

Tables 14.2–14.4 report results estimated from the various regressions originating from Model (1). As indicated by the adjusted R squared and Ramsey tests, the augmented Cobb–Douglas production function fits the data very well. The F statistics reveal that the null hypothesis that the regression coefficients are jointly equal to zero can be rejected at the 1% level for all regressions. This compares favourably to other spillover studies employing the same approach. Considering that this

Table 14.1 Descriptive statistics and correlation matrix for selected variables.

Variables	Mean	S.D.	2	3	4	5	6	7	8	9	10
1. K_d	3.70	1.54	0.93	0.26	0.48	−0.32	−0.38	0.23	0.96	0.94	0.84
2. L_d	2.37	1.41		−0.01	0.29	−0.28	−0.33	0.25	0.94	0.83	0.89
3. MGT	−0.25	0.50			0.52	0.18	−0.01	−0.31	0.19	0.44	−0.05
4. $Size$	−1.08	1.08				−0.31	−0.21	−0.07	0.40	0.57	0.13
5. $FP_{overall}$	−1.53	1.04					0.24	0.32	−0.19	−0.28	−0.05
6. FP_{lunt}	−1.29	0.64						−0.62	−0.33	−0.41	−0.20
7. FP_w	−1.06	0.56							0.26	0.14	0.28
8. Y_d	4.87	1.47								0.91	0.89
9. Y_s	3.63	1.84									0.69
10. Y_{ol}	4.23	1.33									

is a cross-sectional study, the models perform quite well. Because the coefficients for *INTERM* and *SFARE* are consistently insignificant throughout almost all the regressions, these two variables are dropped in the presentation of the results.

The estimation of Eq. (1) for the full sample, without any distinction by ownership of LOEs, is reported in Table 14.2. The results in regressions (2.1) and (2.4) show that overall foreign presence ($FP_{overall}$) has a positive and statistically significant impact on sales by LOEs in both labour- and technology-intensive industries. However, the coefficient for $FP_{overall}$ is larger for the technology-intensive industries than for the labour-intensive industries, with a higher level of statistical

Table 14.2 Regression results.

Y_d	All LOEs in labour-intensive industries ($N = 79$)		
	(2.1)	(2.2)	(2.3)
C	2.623 (16.45)***	2.718 (15.15)***	2.596 (14.57)***
K	0.424 (3.23)***	0.307 (2.61)***	0.347 (2.78)***
L	0.484 (3.53)***	0.614 (4.93)***	0.548 (3.99)***
MGT	−0.194 (−2.29)**	−0.123 (−1.40)	−0.277 (−2.67)***
Size	0.351 (4.52)***	0.352 (4.20)***	0.344 (4.01)***
$FP_{overall}$	0.121 (2.01)**		
FP_{hmt}		0.084 (8.80)***	
FP_w			0.054 (1.56)
Adjusted R^2	0.977	0.978	0.975
F-value	673.202***	698.387***	611.32***
White test (cross term)	(2.969)***	(0.550)	(1.523)
Ramsey RESET (one term)	(0.185)	(0.044)	(0.073)

Y_d	All LOEs in technology-intensive industries ($N = 79$)		
	(2.4)	(2.5)	(2.6)
C	3.255 (10.21)***	3.459 (9.94)***	3.529 (11.06)***
K	0.137 (1.00)	−0.072 (−0.49)	−0.023 (−0.08)*
L	0.808 (6.09)***	0.979 (6.82)***	0.904 (6.14)***
MGT	0.148 (1.42)	0.354 (2.93)***	0.255 (1.91)*
SIZE	0.379 (4.27)***	0.354 (3.96)***	0.379 (4.98)***
$FP_{overall}$	0.170 (4.76)***		
FP_{hmt}		0.025 (0.42)	
FP_w			0.136 (1.90)*
Adjusted R^2	0.950	0.937	0.940
F-value	299.825***	231.88***	245.978***
White test (cross term)	1.340	1.225	1.491
Ramsey RESET (one term)	0.071	1.030	0.025

Notes: (1) Figures in parentheses are *t* statistics (two-tailed tests); *, **, and *** denote significance at the 10%, 5% and 1% levels, respectively. (2) Log likelihood ratio values are shown in Ramsey RESET.

significance. In order to formally evaluate the difference between the magnitudes of the coefficients for $FP_{overall}$ in both regressions, the data for the two groups of industries were pooled, and a dummy variable test was conducted. The test confirms that although $FP_{overall}$ is significant in both models, the difference in the size of the coefficients is indeed statistically significant. Our results thus lend support to our Hypothesis 1. From this we can infer that it is not simply the presence of FAs that generate spillovers, but also the technology intensity of these foreign firms. This finding supports the view that it is the low-cost access to leading-edge technologies of foreign firms that has produced a productivity-enhancing effect on LOEs (Feinberg and

Table 14.3 Regression results for SOEs.

Y_s	SOEs in labour-intensive industries (N = 79)		
	(3.1)	(3.2)	(3.3)
C	2.705 (13.42)***	2.748 (13.51)***	2.646 (13.19)***
K	0.289 (3.84)***	0.265 (3.59)***	0.283 (3.74)***
L	0.646 (7.60)***	0.678 (8.10)***	0.638 (7.37)***
MGT	0.362 (4.16)***	0.403 (4.55)***	0.355 (3.65)***
SIZE	0.601 (5.82)***	0.610 (5.82)***	0.599 (5.91)**
$FP_{overall}$	0.065 (1.33)		
FP_{hmt}		0.066 (1.26)	
FP_w			0.019 (0.47)
Adjusted R^2	0.969	0.972	0.969
F-value	491.3604***	512.52***	476.477***
White test (cross term)	1.10	1.15	1.31
Ramsey RESET (one term)	0.11	0.26	0.34

Y_s	SOEs in technology-intensive industries (N = 79)		
	(3.4)	(3.5)	(3.6)
C	2.597 (9.55)***	2.421 (7.59)***	2.729 (11.21)***
K	0.333 (2.93)***	0.259 (2.10)**	0.284 (2.36)**
L	0.627 (5.53)***	0.669 (5.39)***	0.631 (5.21)***
MGT	0.350 (2.27)**	0.493 (2.97)***	0.433 (2.58)***
SIZE	0.403 (5.14)***	0.360 (4.73)***	0.403 (6.70)***
$FP_{overall}$	0.154 (3.75)***		
FP_{hmt}		−0.045 (−0.66)	
FP_w			0.204 (2.91)***
Adjusted R^2	0.964	0.957	0.962
F-value	420.487***	351.14***	398.93***
White test (cross term)	1.534	2.490***	1.99**
Ramsey RESET (one term)	0.107	1.177	0.125

Notes: (1) Figures in parentheses are *t* statistics (two-tailed tests); *, **, and *** denote significance at the 10%, 5% and 1% levels, respectively. (2) Log likelihood ratio values are shown in Ramsey RESET.

Majumdar, 2001). The difference that we observe may result from adjustment costs being higher in more labour-intensive, low-technology industries. The organisational ownership advantages of FAs may stimulate the adoption of new organisational structures in LOEs, but this process is likely to require radical (rather than incremental) organisational change, as radical change is frequently required in the case of firms in newly liberalised economies.

Breaking down the data further by ownership of foreign- and locally owned firms, however, reveals sub-relationships that up until now have remained hidden in the aggregate relationship. Focusing on labour-intensive industries alone, we find that FP_{hmt} is significant in regressions

Table 14.4 Regression results for OLOEs.

Y_{ol}	OLOEs in labour-intensive industries (N = 79)		
	(4.1)	(4.2)	(4.3)
C	3.279 (11.75)***	3.317 (14.47)***	3.224 (12.61)***
K	0.049 (0.76)	0.038 (0.78)	0.054 (0.868)
L	0.903 (13.93)***	0.916 (18.36)***	0.894 (13.95)***
MGT	0.193 (2.30)**	0.194 (2.46)**	0.156 (1.74)*
SIZE	0.419 (3.39)***	0.416 (3.57)***	0.409 (3.32)***
$FP_{overall}$	0.083 (3.71)***		
FP_{hmt}		0.054 (5.03)***	
FP_w			0.023 (0.58)
Adjusted R^2	0.975	0.979	0.976
F-value	611.144***	714.877***	613.97***
White test (cross term)	2.365***	1.545	3.242***
Ramsey RESET (one term)	0.007	0.028	0.205

Y_{ol}	OLOEs in technology-intensive industries (N = 79)		
	(4.4)	(4.5)	(4.6)
C	3.879 (11.11)***	3.732 (10.79)***	3.779 (10.21)***
K	0.053 (0.40)	0.039 (0.30)	0.041 (0.32)
L	0.892 (8.37)***	0.899 (8.33)***	0.896 (8.41)***
MGT	0.054 (0.69)	0.096 (1.17)	0.092 (1.15)
SIZE	0.710 (6.08)***	0.684 (5.93)***	0.689 (5.83)***
$FP_{overall}$	0.029 (0.71)		
FP_{hmt}		−0.020 (−0.41)	
FP_w			0.014 (0.19)
Adjusted R^2	0.951	0.945	
F-value	266.48***	236.74***	
White test (cross term)	3.614***	2.811***	2.625
Ramsey RESET (one term)	1.591	1.658	1.804

Notes: (1) Figures in parentheses are t statistics (two-tailed tests); *, **, and *** denote significance at the 10%, 5% and 1% levels, respectively. (2) Log likelihood ratio values are shown in Ramsey RESET.

(2.2) and (4.2) in Tables 14.2 and 14.4, respectively, but not in regression (3.2) in Table 14.3. These results contrast with the insignificant FP_W in regressions (2.3), (3.3) and (4.3) in the same panel of these tables. These results indicate that the positive spillover effects in labour intensive industries are more closely associated with the presence of firms from HMT rather than western countries. This finding substantiates our Hypothesis 2(a and c), but not (b).

These findings signal that spillover effects may be neither as uniform, nor as high, as many studies suggest when data are disaggregated. The assumed superiority of technology in FAs seems to matter less when these firms operate in labour-intensive industries. In these industries, foreign firms' advantages, such as the ability to adapt mature technologies to more labour-intensive contexts, and to local raw materials and marketing skills that enable the delivery of timely and uniform quality products to western markets, are more likely to be a source of spillovers. HMT firms, which are built on these types of advantage (Wells, 1993), therefore, appear to demonstrate a greater impact on LOEs than their western counterparts. In addition, there are reasons to expect a smaller technology gap between foreign and local firms in labour-intensive industries than in technology intensive industries, and this should facilitate spillovers (Perez, 1997).

Turning to technology-intensive industries, we found that the significance of FP_{hmt} no longer holds, as shown in (2.5), (3.5) and (4.5) in Tables 14.2–14.4 throughout. In contrast, FP_W becomes significant in (2.6), (3.6), though not in (4.6). These results suggest that compared with HMT firms, western affiliates in technology-intensive industries generate more spillovers to LOEs in general, and to SOEs in particular, but not to OLOEs. Our Hypotheses 3(a) and (b) are supported, but (c) is not. Again, the distribution of spillovers appears to hinge on the nature of the ownership advantages of foreign firms and of the industries involved. The ownership of non-technology-related advantages leads HMT firms to generate limited spillovers in technology-intensive industries, compared with technologically advanced western firms. These mirror our findings for the labour-intensive industries. It is particularly worth noting, however, that FP_W is significant in (3.6), consistent with Buckley, Clegg, and Wang (2006) in which it is found that Chinese SOEs have particularly benefited from joint ventures with foreign (western) affiliates in (technology-intensive) Chinese electronics industry. The insignificant FP_W coefficient in (4.6) also suggests that relatively large-sized western firms do not interact with smaller LOEs in technology-intensive industries. A possible reason is that they operate within different market segments of the industry.

We now focus on how spillovers are associated with the different ownership categories of LOEs, as shown in Tables 14.3 and 14.4. It emerged that $FP_{overall}$ is statistically insignificant in (3.1) but significant in (4.1). These results suggest that in China's labour-intensive industries OLOEs benefit more from the presence of FAs as a whole than SOEs, providing strong support for Hypothesis 4. While it may be correct to attribute the limited spillovers enjoyed by SOEs to their generally low level of competitiveness, absorptive capability and motivation to learn as compared with OLOEs (Buckley et al., 2002), there is industry specific reason. As pointed out above, the ownership advantages of FAs in labour-intensive industries are characteristically organisational in nature. This coincides with the typical weakness of Chinese SOEs: intrinsic rigidity in governance structure inherited from the central planning regime. In comparative terms, SOEs' advantages lie more in technology and less in organisation. The mismatch of ownership advantages between FAs and SOEs provides a good reason why SOEs are less likely to benefit from foreign presence in labour-intensive industries.

A different story, however, emerges in technology-intensive industries, as shown in the bottom section of Tables 14.3 and 14.4. Overall foreign presence ($FP_{overall}$) is significant in regressions (3.4), but not in (4.4), implying that SOEs reap greater spillover benefits than OLOEs in technology intensive industries. Our data thus substantiate Hypothesis 5. Although Chinese SOEs have long been criticised for weaknesses such as low a motivation to learn, they are nevertheless technologically better equipped than OLOEs, conducting the bulk of R&D in Chinese-owned industry. This advantage in technology mitigates their organisational weaknesses, enabling SOEs to better exploit new technological opportunities generated by FDI. This result might also signal a positive role for international joint ventures between western MNEs and Chinese SOEs in capital and technology intensive industries, benefiting the Chinese parent and its affiliates. A large number of high-technology western MNEs hold joint ventures with SOEs (for example, Volkswagen (China), and the local secondary affiliates of Motorola (China)). These close and highly productive partnerships may be responsible for a sort of 'crowding in' effect.

It is arguable that SOEs benefit from foreign presence not by virtue of being state-owned, but by virtue of being higher technology firms, and by increasingly being forced to compete with MNEs, in their home and foreign markets. We cannot, therefore, conclude that China and, by extension, other countries in economic transition, should pursue a policy of delaying on-going reform programmes in their state-owned sectors. Rather, China along with countries that share a similar legacy, should actively pursue the introduction of policies to develop the competitive technological capabilities of all domestic firms, including those in private ownership, in order that these domestically owned firms can maximise their opportunities to learn from, and to emulate, technologically advanced foreign firms.

In this analysis, we must not overlook the role of the government, in particular, its special relationship with SOEs. Developing and transition economies are typically characterised by high levels of government involvement in business, in the form of both ownership and regulation (Peng, 2000). The Chinese government has long favoured international joint ventures, between foreign and Chinese firms in China, over wholly owned foreign operations. This preference is an outcome of the government's desire to maximise the direct and indirect benefits of foreign firms' presence. Foreign investors have been encouraged to participate in the restructuring process of SOEs, and to transfer modern technology and management skills directly to the joint venture, and indirectly to parent and related Chinese firms. As part of the implementation of this policy, the Chinese government has been able to introduce strong foreign firms, especially western firms, through a selection and matchmaking process, to be the joint venture partners of carefully chosen Chinese firms.

The findings of this study are consistent with earlier studies which suggest that joint venture partnership with a multinational enterprise is an effective means of transferring modern practices to the Chinese firm (Guthrie, 2005). This route amounts to a kind of 'inward' internationalisation (Child and Rodrigues, 2005). Recent years have seen a growing number of multinational enterprises from developing countries investing abroad in order to acquire assets, such as technology and managerial competencies, which are not available in their own country. This strategy is aimed at alleviating these firms' competitive disadvantages. Such 'asset-augmenting' FDI can help latecomer firms to catch up with their developed country rivals (United Nations Conference on Trade and Development (UNCTAD), 2006). Our results suggest that 'inward' internationalisation is another effective route to strengthening the competitive advantages of developing country firms.

Both SOEs and OLOEs seem to benefit from the presence of HMT affiliates (FP_{hmt}) in labour-intensive industries, as shown in (3.2) and

(4.2) of Tables 14.3 and 14.4, though FP_{hmt} in the regression (3.2) fails to reach significance. These results underscore the concentration of HMT capital in labour-intensive industries, and which confers greater spillover benefits to OLOEs than to SOEs. This finding corroborates Hypothesis 6. The result for SOEs, though insignificant, contrasts sharply with Buckley *et al.* (2002), which employed data on China for 1995 and revealed a negative link between SOEs' productivity and the presence of HMT affiliates. The explanation may lie in the progressive Chinese reform process, which (since the early 1980s) has resulted in the bankruptcy and exit of numerous inefficient Chinese SOEs in labour-intensive industries. The SOEs that survive are the more competitive firms with superior absorptive capacity, and so better able to benefit from spillovers from HMT firms.

Western capital (FP_w) yields greater positive spillovers for SOEs than OLOEs in technology intensive industries, according to regressions (3.6) and (4.6). Thus, Hypothesis 7 receives substantial support. This differential impact on LOEs' productivity highlights western affiliates' ownership advantages in proprietary technology, which is best suited to the more technologically advanced firms and sectors. The interaction between western firms and SOEs can be said to produce a 'crowding in' effect in the form of improved performance in SOEs. In contrast, the mismatch between the ownership advantage of western firms and the abilities of OLOEs limits the scope for spillover benefits (Table 14.5).

Table 14.5 Hypotheses and the estimated results.

Hypotheses	Regressions	Support (S)/Not support (N) Hypotheses
H1	(2.1), (2.4)	S
H2 (a)	(2.2), (2.3)	S
(b)	(3.2), (3.3)	N
(c)	(4.2), (4.3)	S
H3 (a)	(2.5), (2.6)	S
(b)	(3.5), (3.6)	S
(c)	(4.5), (4.6)	N
H4	(3.1), (4.1)	S
H5	(3.4), (4.4)	S
H6	(3.2), (4.2)	S
H7	(3.6), (4.6)	S

Conclusions

Governments of developing and transition economies pay special attention to the impact of FDI, using this as a criterion for measuring the success of their FDI policy. Such governments often favour inward FDI in technology-intensive industries over labour-intensive industries, believing that this will bring in new technologies and know-how and therefore more spillovers to enhance the competitiveness of LOEs. In this paper, we leave aside the issue of whether this perception is true, and instead test whether the magnitude of spillovers is associated with the degree of technology (labour) intensity of the host industry involved.

Overall, we find evidence consistent with the existence of greater positive spillovers from inward FDI in technology-intensive compared with labour-intensive industries. This finding agrees broadly with the conventional hypothesis that FDI by MNEs is based on technological ownership advantages. It also justifies the policies of governments of developing countries, such as China, which have in recent years offered generous incentives packages to attract foreign investors to high-technology industries.

Our study confirms that distinguishing between different categories of foreign investor, as theory predicts, is an essential step in analysing the impact of inward FDI. We find that HMT affiliates generate more spillovers to LOEs than western affiliates in labour-intensive industries. In marked contrast, in technology-intensive industries, the presence of western affiliates exerts a larger impact on the performance of LOEs than does that of HMT affiliates. From these findings we conclude that foreign affiliates' technology intensity is a key driver of LOEs' growth.

The procedure of drawing a clear distinction between different categories of ownership in domestically owned Chinese firms is also supported by our results. We find that in general both SOEs and OLOEs seem to benefit more from inward FDI in technology-intensive industries than in labour-intensive industries. Our results indicate, however, that SOEs benefit from the presence of HMT affiliates in labour-intensive industries, and from the presence of western affiliates in technology-intensive industries. In contrast, OLOEs seem only to benefit from the presence of HMT affiliates in labour-intensive industries.

In terms of methodology, our study represents a step forward in understanding the determinants of spillovers from inward FDI. New insight has been gained from the breaking down of industries into labour- and technology-intensive groups, of foreign ownership into

HMT and western categories, and of locally owned firms into SOEs and OLOEs. The paper presents a clue as to the true diversity of issues that arise within the complex area of spillovers.

There are some policy implications that arise with regard to the use of FDI as a tool for economic development in developing and transition economies. Transition economies often have in common a history of central planning, either with the support of the Soviet Union, or at least of history of imitating the Soviet system. The legacy of this is that these economies have an existing industrial structure from which to move towards a market-driven economy. This contrasts markedly with the position of developing countries in general, which do not have the benefit even of established staple industries, or educational and technological infrastructure. Therefore, developing countries in this mould do not have to confront issues related to SOEs when designing policies toward inward FDI, e.g., of having to take into account the possible negative impacts of multinational firms on the domestic sector, and of how to avoid these. When China designed its policy towards FDI, it had in mind the effects FDI would have on its then less competitive SOEs; the policy response was to recast SOEs as a major conduit for foreign technology to enter the Chinese economy, notably through joint ventures. The implications of the findings of this study for developing countries are that they should strive to achieve at least some minimum level of domestic industrial technological capability, and of technical education. Also, the governments of developing countries need to look at the ways in which initially disadvantaged domestic firms can be helped to acquire the necessary assets to offset their disadvantages. This might be through a close association with foreign firms, in something approximating 'inward internationalisation' as a means of asset augmentation.

The wider policy implications of our discussion for developing countries in general, and non-transition economies in particular, can be summarised as dependant upon pre-existing industrial structure and its ownership. Like China, quite a few developing countries, such as Vietnam and Laos, in South East Asia, are going through transition to market economy. It is interesting to ask whether 'transition' imparts anything additional to any topic related to development. The Chinese experience of encouraging inward foreign direct investment and foreign equity participation in SOEs' restructuring process has proven very successful for China. The governments of many developing countries have some scope to build up domestic technological capability, to improve the performance of domestically owned firms through, for example, strengthening the links between state research institutions and universities and firms. A case in point is that of Korea, which promoted the growth and development of large Chaebol through supporting state research and research in other institutions. Our discussion suggests that non-transitional developing countries, without the inheritance of state-owned enterprises, can nevertheless implement a beneficial policy of inward FDI, if they give some attention to the requisite infrastructures. Given this, foreign equity ownership in local firms that are either underperforming, or that have the potential to perform better, may yield the industrial capability gains that the transition economies have enjoyed.

References

Aitken, B. and Harrison, A.E. (1999) Do domestic firms benefit from direct foreign investment? Evidence from Venezuela. *The American Economic Review*, 89(3), 605–618.

Buckley, P.J., Clegg, J. and Wang, C. (2002) The impacts of FDI on the performance of Chinese manufacturing firms. *Journal of International Business Studies*, 33(4), 637–655.

Buckley, P.J., Clegg, J. and Wang, C. (2005) The relationship between inward foreign direct investment and the performance of domestically-owned Chinese manufacturing industry. *Multinational Business Review*, 12(3), 23–40.

Buckley, P.J., Clegg, J. and Wang, C. (2006) Inward foreign direct investment and host country productivity: Evidence from Chinese electronics industry. *Transnational Corporations* (forthcoming).

Buckwalter, D.W. (1995) Spatial inequality, foreign direct investment, and economic transition in Bulgaria. *The Professional Geographer*, 47, 288–298.

Blomström, M. and Kokko, A. (1998) Multinational corporations and spillovers. *Journal of Economic Survey*, 12(3), 247–277.

Caves, E.R. (1999) Spillovers from multinationals in developing countries: The mechanisms at work. In *William Davidson Institute conference on 'the impact of foreign investment on emerging markets'*, School of Business Administration, University of Michigan, USA, 18–19 June.

Cheng, L.K. and Kwan, Y.K. (2000) What are the determinants of location of foreign direct investment? The Chinese experience? *Journal of International Economics*, 51(2), 379–400.

Child, J. and Rodrigues, B.S. (2005) The internationalization of Chinese firms: A case for theoretical extension. *Management and Organization Review*, 1(3), 381–410.

Dunning, J.H. (1988) *Explaining International Production*. Boston, MA: Unwin Hyman.

Dunning, J.H. (1993) *Globalization of Business*. London and New York: Routledge.

Fan, G. (1998) Development of the non-state sector and reform of state enterprises in China. *China in the New Millennium*. Cato Press.

Feinberg, S.E. and Majumdar, K.S. (2001) Technology spillovers and foreign direct investment in the Indian pharmaceutical industry. *Journal of International Business Studies*, 32(3), 421–437.
Fung, K.C., Lau, L.J. and Lee, J. (2002) *US Direct Investment in China*. Washington, DC: AEI Press.
Giddy, H.I. and Young, S. (1982) Conventional theory and unconventional multinationals: Do new forms of multinational enterprise require new theories? in A. Rugman (ed.), *New Theories of the Multinational Enterprise*. London: Croom Helm.
Gillespie, K., Riddle, L., Sayre, E. and Sturges, D. (1999) Diaspora interest in homeland investment. *Journal of International Business Studies*, 30(3), 623–634.
Görg, H. and Greenaway, D. (2002) *Do Domestic Firms Really Benefit from Foreign Direct Investment?* CEPR Discussion Paper No. 3485. London: Centre for Economic Policy Research.
Görg, H. and Strobl, E. (2001) Multinational companies and productivity spillovers: A meta-Analysis. *The Economic Journal*, 111(November), 723–739.
Guthrie, D. (2005) Organizational learning and productivity: State structure and foreign investment in the rise of Chinese corporation. *Management and Organization Review*, 1, 165–195.
Haskel, E.J., Pereira, C.S. and Slaughter, J.M. (2002) *Does Foreign Direct Investment Boost the Productivity of Domestic Firms?* Working Paper No. 452, ISSN 1473-0278, Department of Economics, Queen Mary, University of London.
Huang, T., Jr. (2004) Spillovers from Taiwan, Hong Kopng, and Macau investment and from other foreign investment in Chinese industries. *Contemporary Economic Policy*, 22(1), 13–25.
Kokko, A. (1992) *Foreign Direct Investment, Host Country Characteristics and Spillovers*. Stockholm: Stockholm School of Economics.
Lecraw, D.J. (1993) Outward direct investment by Indonesian firms: Motivation and effects. *Journal of International Business Studies*, 24(3), 589–600.
Liu, X., Siler, P., Wang, C. and Wei, Y. (2000) Productivity spillovers from foreign direct investment: Evidence from UK industry level panel data. *Journal of International Business Studies*, 31(3), 407–425.
Luo, Y. (1999) Dimensions of knowledge: Comparing Asian and Western MNEs in China. *Asia Pacific Journal of Management*, 16, 75–93.
Markusen, J.R. (1995) The boundaries of multinational enterprises and the theory of international trade. *Journal of Economic Perspectives*, 9, 169–189.
Meyer, E.K. (2004) Perspectives on multinational enterprises in emerging economies. *Journal of International Business Studies*, 35(4), 259–276.
Murphy, A.B. (1992) Western investment in East-Central Europe: Emerging patterns and implications for state stability. *The Professional Geographer*, 44, 249–259.
O'Malley, E. (1994) The impact of transnational corporation in the Republic of Ireland. In P. Dicken and M. Quevit (eds), *Transnational Corporations and European Regional Restructuring*. Utrecht: NGS.
Peng, M.W. (2000) *Business Strategies in Transition Economies*. Thousand Oaks, CA: Sage.
Perez, T. (1997) Multinational enterprises and technological spillovers: An evolutionary model. *Journal of Evolutionary Economics*, 7, 169–192.

Perotti, E., Sun, L. and Zou, L. (1999) State-owned versus township and village enterprises in China. *Comparative Economic Studies, 41*, 1–20.

Porter, M.E. (1990) *The Competitive Advantage of Nations*. New York: Free Press and Macmillan.

Ramamurti, R. (2004) Developing countries and MNEs: Extending and enriching the research agenda. *Journal of International Business Studies, 35*(4), 277–283.

Shi, Y. (1998) Technological assets and the strategy of foreign firms to enter the China market. *Journal of International Marketing and Marketing Research, 23*(3), 129–138.

Smarzynska, B.K. (2002) *Does Foreign Direct Investment Increase the Productivity of Domestic Firms? In Search of Spillovers Through Backward Linkages*. World Bank Policy Research Working Paper 2923, October 2002.

Tatoglu, E. and Glaister, K. (1998) An analysis of motives for Western FDI in Turkey. *International Business Review, 7*(2), 203–230.

United Nations Conference on Trade and Development (UNCTAD) (2004) *World Investment Report*. New York and Geneva: United Nations.

United Nations Conference on Trade and Development (UNCTAD) (2006) *World Investment Report*. New York and Geneva: United Nations.

Wang, C. (2003) The relative economic and technical performance of foreign subsidiaries in Chinese manufacturing industry. *Journal of Asian Business, 19*(2), 55–67.

Wells, L. (1993) Mobile exporters: New foreign investors in East Asia. In K.A. Froot (ed.), *Foreign Direct Investment*. Chicago: University of Chicago Press.

White, H. (1980) A heteroscedasticity consistent covariance matrix estimator and a direct test for heteroscedasticity. *Econometrica, 48*, 817–838.

15
Organisation and Action in a Chinese State-owned Service Intermediary: The Case of Sinotrans

Peter J. Buckley, Jeremy Clegg and Hui Tan

Introduction

The purpose of this paper is to analyse the organisational changes in Sinotrans, a Chinese state-owned service intermediary. In so doing, the paper tests a series of propositions derived from the Parsons and Thompson approach to administrative theory (Parsons, 1960; Thompson, 1967). The paper is unique in that it explores a single longitudinal case of a state-owned enterprise (SOE) in a transitional market setting, utilising a synoptic approach derived from a classic source of organisational analysis.

Organisational changes in Sinotrans

Established in 1950, Sinotrans is the largest firm in China's logistics industry. Sinotrans has subsidiaries in every province and major cities throughout China. These firms had been under the management of Sinotrans for more than three decades. It was only in 1988 that they passed into the hands of local bureaus of the Ministry of Foreign Trade and Economic Cooperation (MOFTEC) following the reform of China's foreign trade management system. Although Sinotrans headquarters still maintained superficial operational control, local MOFTEC bureaus retained the right to appoint managers and jointly controlled equity in these subsidiaries (see Figure 15.1). The general managers of Sinotrans and its subsidiaries were normally key members of the Party committee, and sometimes the Party secretaries of the relevant branches. The Party, through its various branches, discussed and decided on managerial appointments within the subsidiaries as well as in the headquarters.

As a state-owned firm, the ownership of Sinotrans subsidiaries ultimately belonged to MOFTEC, which delegated the right to 'jointly

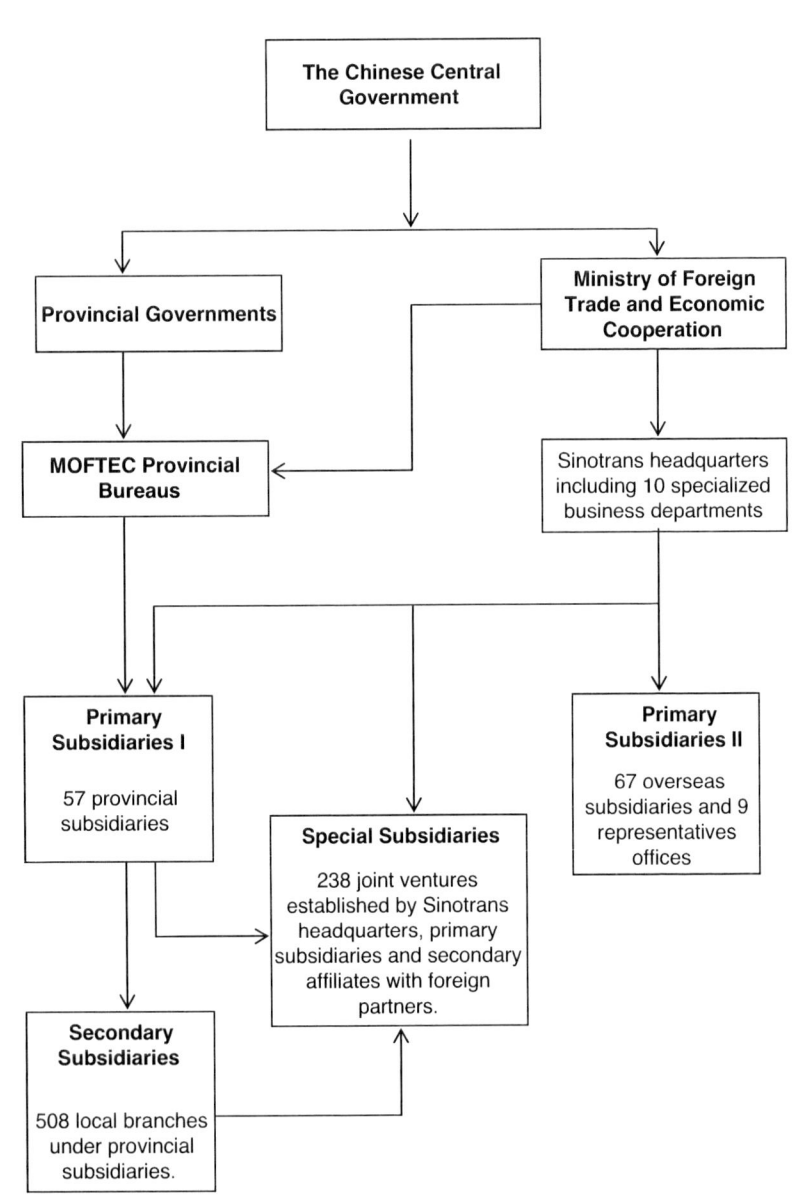

Figure 15.1 The organisational structure of Sinotrans before reorganization (1996).

manage' the equity of subsidiaries to Sinotrans headquarters and MOFTEC local bureaus. This is a reflection of the key role of local MOFTEC bureaus in feeding the subsidiaries of Sinotrans with business opportunities after the liberalisation of the industry in 1984. There was no clear division of equity share between the local bureaus and Sinotrans headquarters, leaving them to seek consensus over this issue. With managers sheltered by the local MOFTEC bureaus, the subsidiaries of Sinotrans behaved more in tune with local interests rather than with the strategy of Sinotrans' headquarters. Due to deviations of interest between the central and local governments (Kynge, 2002), the joint ownership of the Sinotrans subsidiaries and the right of local government to appoint managers created a joint venture type scenario where the deterioration of trust between 'partners' further damaged the network and central coordination on which firms in this industry rely to survive. The integration of Sinotrans was seriously handicapped, and internal competition between subsidiaries of different localities was common. Failure to address this joint venture type problem between the 'partners' led to strategic and operational constraints for business development in the period up to 1997. So, the redefinition of the relationship between Sinotrans and the government did not just stop at the central government, but extended to provincial and city levels. In 1996, MOFTEC issued an official document entitled 'Notice on Strengthening the Group Based Management of Sinotrans' (MOFTEC, 1996). This document ordered the handover of 57 local foreign trade transportation firms, then under the administration of local MOFTEC, bureaus in 30 provinces, to Sinotrans headquartered in Beijing.

After regaining these firms in 1997 through the same administrative means as it had lost them, Sinotrans changed the internal relationship between headquarters and subsidiaries from a loose, administrative relationship into an equity-based one. Having taken complete ownership and control over all the subsidiaries, Sinotrans then carried out a company-wide programme of restructuring, including the restructuring of management. Establishing just one subsidiary in each province resulted in a streamlined management structure. Competition between local subsidiaries and duplication of investment was stopped. As part of this restructuring, the 57 firms Sinotrans acquired from the local bureaus were merged into 40 provincial primary subsidiaries. Each of these manages a number of secondary subsidiaries. The new organisational structure of Sinotrans is shown in Figure 15.2.

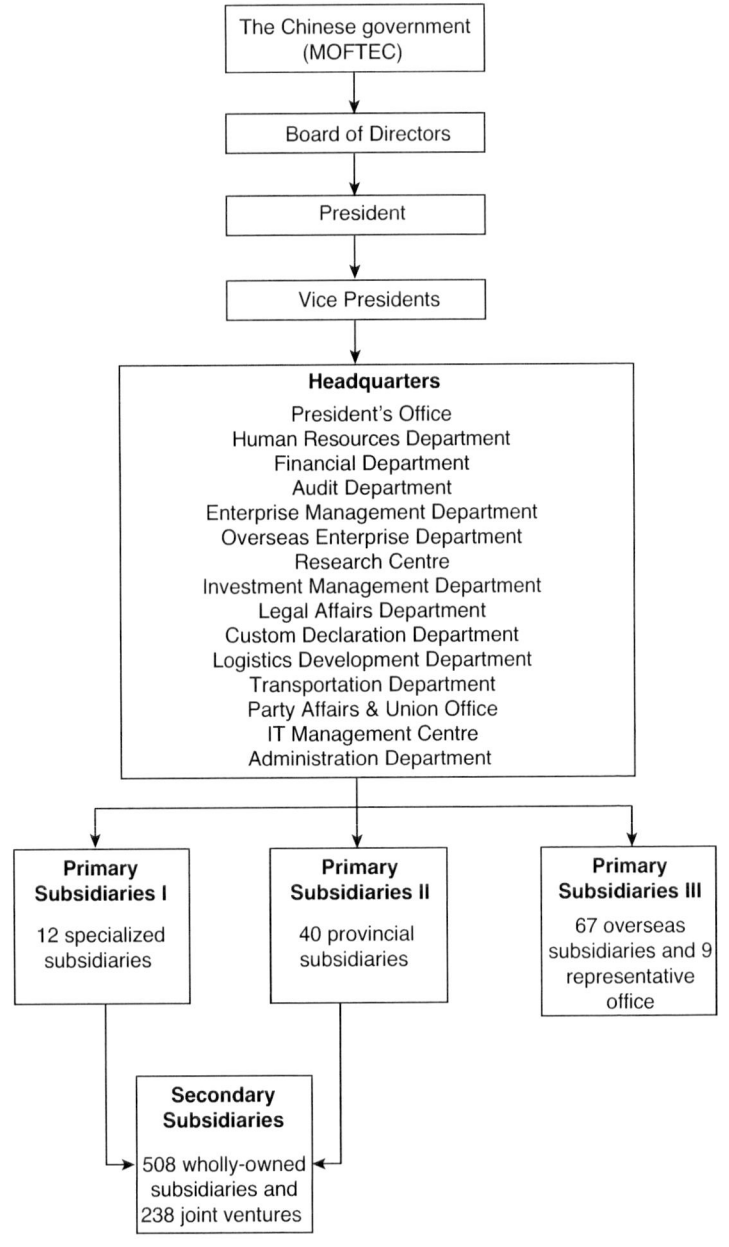

```
                    ┌─────────────────────────┐
                    │  The Chinese government │
                    │       (MOFTEC)          │
                    └───────────┬─────────────┘
                                ▼
                    ┌─────────────────────────┐
                    │   Board of Directors    │
                    └───────────┬─────────────┘
                                ▼
                    ┌─────────────────────────┐
                    │        President        │
                    └───────────┬─────────────┘
                                ▼
                    ┌─────────────────────────┐
                    │     Vice Presidents     │
                    └───────────┬─────────────┘
                                ▼
┌───────────────────────────────────────────────────────────┐
│                       Headquarters                        │
│                    President's Office                     │
│                 Human Resources Department                │
│                    Financial Department                   │
│                     Audit Department                      │
│              Enterprise Management Department             │
│               Overseas Enterprise Department              │
│                      Research Centre                      │
│              Investment Management Department             │
│                  Legal Affairs Department                 │
│                Custom Declaration Department              │
│               Logistics Development Department            │
│                  Transportation Department                │
│                 Party Affairs & Union Office              │
│                     IT Management Centre                  │
│                  Administration Department                │
└───────┬────────────────────┬─────────────────────┬────────┘
        ▼                    ▼                     ▼
┌───────────────┐    ┌───────────────┐    ┌─────────────────┐
│   Primary     │    │   Primary     │    │    Primary      │
│ Subsidiaries I│    │Subsidiaries II│    │ Subsidiaries III│
│               │    │               │    │   67 overseas   │
│12 specialized │    │ 40 provincial │    │subsidiaries and 9│
│ subsidiaries  │    │  subsidiaries │    │  representative │
│               │    │               │    │     office      │
└───────┬───────┘    └───────┬───────┘    └─────────────────┘
        │                    │
        │    ┌───────────────────────┐
        │    │      Secondary        │
        │    │     Subsidiaries      │
        └──▶ │ 508 wholly-owned      │ ◀──┘
             │ subsidiaries and      │
             │  238 joint ventures   │
             └───────────────────────┘
```

Figure 15.2 The organisational structure of Sinotrans after reorganisation (1997).

Theoretical background

The theoretical background of this paper derives from Thompson's influential 1967 book *Organisations in Action*. A series of propositions derived from this book are tested on the empirical primary and secondary data on Sinotrans. The key features of this approach are set out below together with the operational context of Sinotrans, a SOE undergoing radical change as part of China's reform process.

Thompson identified three key levels of responsibility and control in organisations, following Parsons (1960). First, every organisation contains a suborganisation whose problems centre round the effective performance of its technical function. Second, the managerial level services the technical sub-organisation by mediating between it and those who use its products and procuring the resources necessary for carrying out the technical function. The managerial level thus controls or administers the technical sub-organisation. The institutional level of the organisation concerns the interaction between the organisation and its environment. As Thompson (1967, p. 11) says 'In terms of 'formal' controls, an organisation may be relatively independent: but in terms of the meaning of the functions performed by the organisation and hence its 'rights' to command resources and to subject its customers to discipline, it is never wholly independent'. This is, of course, particularly true in the case of a SOE.

Following Thompson, we take the firm to be an organisation that is an 'open system subject to the criteria of rationality' (Thompson, 1967, p. 11) in that the processes within the organisation are significantly affected by the organisation's environment. This key factor of environmental uncertainty looms large in the analysis of Sinotrans. Changing institutional control and ownership, demand variation, changes in the competitive environment and regulation are key sources of external uncertainty. The role of government as both owner and regulator add extra degrees of uncertainty. Thompson (1967) distinguishes between open and closed system strategies. In a closed system, the organisation devises its strategies as if it were an island separated completely from exogenous influences. An open system strategy attempts to incorporate selectively the most important exogenous influences on the organisation. This is equivalent to a strategy of internalisation of external influences (Williamson, 1975; Buckley and Casson, 1976). Thus, an open system with rationality is the basis of the contingency theory of organisations of which Thompson is a founder.

Thompson (1967) offered typologies distinguishing organisations on the basis of the technologies they used. Sinotrans, as a logistics company, is a clear example of a 'mediating technology' defined by Thompson (1967, p. 11) as 'Linking clients or customers who are, or wish to be, independent'. Examples include banks, insurance firms, telephone companies and the post office. 'Mediating technology requires operating in standardised ways and extensively, e.g., with multiple clients or customers distributed in time and space' (Thompson, 1967, p. 16). In other words, it requires the creation of an integrated network. 'Standardization makes possible the operation of the mediating technology over time and through space by assuring each segment of the organization that other segments are operating in comparable ways. It is in such situations that the bureaucratic techniques of categorization and impersonal application of rules have been most beneficial' (Thompson, 1967, p. 17, after Weber, 1947, quote p. 15, and Merton, 1957). The issue of space is crucial to a logistics company, whose duties are to transport goods and provide services to spatially dispersed clients. The changing role of intra-regional, inter-regional and international operation proves crucial in the analysis of organisational change in Sinotrans.

Recent work using Thompson's framework includes Kamps and Polos (1999), Nutt (2002), Terwiesch *et al.* (2002), Schilling and Sheensma (2002), Feldman and Rafaeli (2002) and Tan (2002). Kamps and Polos (1999, p. 1800) report 'the feeling that Thompson's theory still has much to offer to contemporary scholars'. Nutt (2002) finds Thompson's prescriptions to be good predictors of success in strategic decision in the US and Canadian contexts. However, the fact that Thompson's framework is over 30 years old means that his propositions have to be amended in the light of more recent theoretical development and changes in the business environment. Consequently our research involves reinterpretation of Thompson's basic theory in the light of concepts deriving from transaction cost economics (Williamson, 1975; Buckley and Casson, 1976), the resource-based view of the firm (Penrose, 1959; Grant, 1991), strategies of risk diversification (Koopmans, 1957; Grubel, 1968; Buckley and Carter, 1999), principal-agent theory (Jensen and Meckling, 1976) and the introduction of the role of corporate culture (Schein, 1992). Our final theoretical construct concerns the 'active agent' (Wu, 1989). It is important in this analysis to separate the roles of (central) government as owner, government as regulator, local (provincial) Government and the managers of Sinotrans. The active agent has often been identified with the entrepreneur (Casson, 1982) but in the institutional context of China, it is necessary to specify carefully who is taking decisions, who holds the power and legitimacy to endorse those decisions, and who chooses the decision makers. Rent-seeking behaviours on the part of individuals and groups can therefore be identified.

A major (probably *the* major) concern of Thompson's analysis is the attempt by organisations to reduce uncertainty. Indeed Kamps and Polos (1999, p. 1776) entitle their formalisation of Thompson's propositions as 'Reducing Uncertainty'. They see Thompson as providing a unifying perspective on open and closed systems thinking in organisation theory centring on the reduction of uncertainty deriving largely from the organisation's environment. Much of organisational action is thus explained by the need to reduce the impact of uncertainty, for example by buffering (building warehouses or storages) to seal off the organisation's technical or operational core from environmental uncertainty. We should note, in passing, that a service company cannot store its output and that temporal buffering is simply ruled out for a logistics company such as Sinotrans.

Thompson's (1967, p. 159) statement is clear – 'Uncertainty appears as the fundamental problem for complex organizations, and coping with uncertainty is the essence of the administrative process'. Koopmans (1957, pp. 162–163) distinguishes two forms of uncertainty:

> In a rough and intuitive judgment the secondary uncertainty arising from a lack of communication, that is from one decision maker having no way to find out the concurrent decisions and plans made by others (or merely knowing suitable aggregate measures of such decisions or plans) is quantitatively at least as important as the primary uncertainty arising from random acts of nature and unpredictable changes in consumers' preferences.

On this reading, Sinotrans is faced with not only primary uncertainty arising from changes in demand and supply, technology and natural conditions, but also the severe secondary uncertainty of decisions and plans made in particular by government bodies. It is thus secondary uncertainty with which we as analysts as well as the management of Sinotrans are principally concerned. We should note however, following Meyer, Tsui and Hinings (1993), that organisational adaptation is not driven by a single variable but by a combination of conditions that give rise to a complex structural response.

Our conceptual framework thus focuses on the interplay between technical/managerial and institutional levels of analysis, on the implementation of a mediating technology under conditions of extreme environmental uncertainty, on spatial issues and on the identification of the active agents and their decisions over time. We derive propositions directly from this theoretical structure.

The institutional environment – reform of SOEs in China

This paper is innovative in that it places the actions of the managers centrally as active agents. This is a radical departure from Thompson's framework that subsumes managerial action within an assumption of rationality-driven organisational decision making, akin to Adam Smith's 'invisible hand' (Smith, 1776). The Chinese government since 1997 has ostensibly delegated responsibility for the operation and financial performance of Sinotrans to its managers whilst retaining state ownership and party control of the appointment of Sinotrans' top managers. As a logistics company – an intermediary between many other organisations and with national and international customers – Sinotrans is constrained to implement a highly centralised operation to match its mediating technology. This conflicts with Government rhetoric of decentralisation. In addition, local Provincial governments retain substantial ownership and influence over Sinotrans' subsidiaries. This local influence and control could impede central coordination and the efficient operation of the firm. The context in which the managers of Sinotrans operate is subject to exogenous influences which they attempt to mitigate, and this results in short-term decision making, which may appear contradictory to the overarching long-term goals of the organisation.

Research methods

Due to the lack of prior research on organisational change in China's service sector SOEs, a longitudinal single-case study approach has been chosen to conduct this research (Yin, 1994). There are obvious limitations on findings drawn from a single case analysis. However, this approach allows in-depth analysis of the complex issues inherent in the research topic, enabling 'The researcher to peep behind the formal aspects of organisation settings' (Bryman, 1989). It is especially useful when the research subject is still ongoing, or 'live' in business terms. Evidence from a single case analysis can serve well in 'analytic generalisation' (Yin, 1994).

Data collection

This research comprised three phases of data collection. The first phase, from October 2000 to June 2001, involved collecting secondary data from documents, such as annual reports, newsletters, strategic reports and press articles, the company history of Sinotrans' first 40 years of operation (Sinotrans, 1990) and the company website. Many of these materials were obtained through close contact established by the researchers with managers in Sinotrans. This preliminary information collection enabled the authors to identify the key issues for the research, forming a basis for the design of the semi-structured questionnaire.

The second phase, to collect primary data, was carried out in June and July 2001 in the headquarters of Sinotrans in Beijing. Sixteen in-depth interviews were conducted with seven managers, of which six were either general managers or deputy general managers of five functional departments of Sinotrans: Finance, Human Resource Management, Investment, Overseas Enterprises Management, and the Research Centre. All the interviewees are employees of at least five years' standing, with most of them having over 12 years' service. They all have experienced the recent organisational change in Sinotrans, and have been directly involved in strategy formulation and implementation regarding the establishment of the new management model in Sinotrans. Apart from their knowledge and views on the question asked, the interviewees were encouraged to elaborate on the process and complexities of the organisational changes experienced inside Sinotrans. They were also invited to verify the information provided by prior interviewees and clarify issues subject to contradiction and confusion. Participation in the interviews was voluntary, and the anonymity of the respondents guaranteed.

The third phase of data collection occurred after July 2001. The authors have maintained frequent information exchange with managers in Sinotrans through post, email and telephone. Our informants not only include managers (former interviewees) at the headquarters, but also four managers drawn from its provincial subsidiaries. This was to fill in any gaps identified after the field visit, to clarify conflicting information and to incorporate data on issues we ignored during interviews in the previous stages. More important, the telephone interviews with the four managers at Sinotrans' subsidiaries enabled us to understand the views on organisational change from the perspective of its subsidiaries.

Interview data and field notes were recorded using the 'critical incident' approach suggested by Erlandson *et al.* (1993, p. 103). This involved recording data on the milestones of Sinotrans' development and the key dimensions of the organisational change at Sinotrans in the 1990s, such as the changing government policy towards the service industry in which Sinotrans engages, the repeated changes in control relationship between the central government and Sinotrans, and between Sinotrans and its subsidiaries, and the steps that Sinotrans has taken in pushing for organisational change. These data were then structured to address the research topic. Emerging themes were further pursued to extract leads for understanding the change process in Sinotrans.

Table 15.1 Data collection matrix.

Phase	Collection method	Data collected
First Phase	Desk research	Secondary data such as company annual reports, newsletters, press articles, and relevant company information contained in company website and previous researchers' publications.
Second Phase	16 in-depth interviews	Facts in respect of organisational change before and in the 1990s; change process in various functional departments as well as in subsidiaries; comments and insights regarding triggers of change, interest groups, relationship between Sinotrans and central and local governments, and ways of exercising control for efficiency and central coordination in Sinotrans; verifying data given by other interviewees and filling gaps.
Third Phase	Further data collection	Frequent exchange of information with former interviewees at the headquarters to fill gaps, to clarify conflicting data and to incorporate data on previously ignored issues. Interviews with four managers at Sinotrans' provincial subsidiaries were conducted through telephone which enabled us to understand the perspective of these subsidiaries on organisational change in Sinotrans.

Table 15.2 Milestones of organisational changes in Sinotrans.

Year	Organisational Changes
1950	Founded as a regulator and monopoly in freight forwarding, chartering and foreign trade related transportation.
1984	Competition introduced into the above industries.
1986	Sinotrans rendering up its governmental function to be a full business operator.
1988	The power to appoint subsidiary managers transferred to local MOFTEC bureaus. Sinotrans headquarters and these bureaus began to share ownership over these subsidiaries while the former maintained operational control.
1996	MOFTEC issued notice transferring the ownership of subsidiaries back to Sinotrans.
1997	Having taken back the ownership of subsidiaries, Sinotrans headquarters restructuring started with the establishment of a new Board of Directors.
1998–1999	Restructuring of subsidiaries.

Data analysis

The data analysis in this research has followed closely the procedures set for interpreting qualitative data (Easterby-Smith, Thorpe and Lowe 1991; Strauss, 1987) in general, and those for case study methodology (Yin, 1994) in particular. The interviews were analysed individually to identify issues relating to organisational change and the transformation of the management model in Sinotrans. Then, cross-referencing between interviews, and between primary data and secondary data, was carried out to establish connections among factors and to verify the validity of these data by triangulation. This constituted an emergent process in constructing grounded interpretations of the collected data and elicited implications on issues relevant to the topic under research based on 'analytical generalisation' (Yin, 1994). Case write-ups were made available for circulation among leading participants to verify overall accuracy.

Findings

Prior to 1997, Sinotrans oscillated between centralising influences from its core technology and central government influence, and decentralisation, imposed by powerful provincial authorities, which had hire and fire control over managers in its subsidiaries. The objectives of different managers (servicing different masters) could conflict. Sinotrans has to be understood in the context of SOE reform in China. Steinfeld (1998, p. 73) describes SOE reform in China as a 'deeply intertwined property-rights and governance problem'. Uncertain property rights give rise to uncertain decision-making rights. The outcome of decisions is clouded by distorted information (on profits, for example) which feed back as incorrect signals for the next round of resource allocation. The incentive problem that this creates for managers (and others) leads to rent-seeking in the form of shirking and salary/benefit maximisation at the expense of the enterprise. Top-down strategies of corporatisation do not necessarily correct these problems in the absence of clear incentives aligned with the organisation's goals. Transaction costs in SOEs are high compared with other forms of enterprise (Child, 1994) and continue to distort prices, to pervert incentives and impede progress. The propositions below seek to examine the role of managers within Sinotrans faced with this unpromising scenario.

Managers in Sinotrans thus have faced step changes in their environment as market forces are introduced into the SOE environment. As Fligstein and Daube (1989, pp. 82–83) point out, the 'discipline of the market', viewed in neoclassical economic models, is in fact attenuated in time and severity. For large firms particularly, a safety net of market power, control over resources, diversification and political leverage prevents the translation of less-than-optimal performance into the firm's extinction. In other words, sufficient slack exists in organisations that a range of action is consistent with survival (Thompson, 1967; Leibenstein, 1976). As we shall see, the piecemeal introduction of market discipline was a threat to Sinotrans, and its environment was also complicated by continued Governmental interference. Its attempts to achieve control over resources and diversification are documented below, whilst its market power was eroded by liberalisation. The factors that attenuate the severity of the discipline of the market thus worked in different directions over the period of our analysis.

Our approach to this case is longitudinal and we take as an arbitrary dividing line the year 1996 when ownership of the subsidiaries were transferred back from local MOFTECs to Sinotrans (Table 15.1). This change is one of many that occurred in the period of study (1950–1999) but it allows us a benchmark to analyse 'before and after' changes using our framework. In consequence, the timing of changes as they impacted on the management of Sinotrans will be 'fuzzy' and this will be pointed out in the detailed analysis that follows.

Propositions and evidence

This section confronts the relevant propositions, drawn from Thompson (1967) with evidence from Sinotrans. The propositions follow Thompson and the choice of propositions is determined only by relevance (e.g., all those relevant to non-intermediary technology are omitted) and availability of evidence.[1]

The organisational imperatives in Sinotrans

Proposition 1. Under norms of rationality, organisations seek to seal off their core technologies from environmental influences.

The role of managers in Sinotrans is called into focus by this proposition. Our evidence suggests that they attempted to protect the functional/technical core of the firm (the logistics operation) in the face of 'political interference' from the government (as owner), provincial governments (as owners) and from the Communist Party (The Party). Their independence is compromised by the fact that the managers are appointed by these external bodies. This is an indication that 'norms of rationality', which is a fundamental building block of Thompson's framework, are critical to the context of SOEs, which are subject to constant and constantly changing interference from their immediate environment. We therefore expect that sealing off core technologies is consequently much more difficult than in the base case of capitalistic enterprise.

In the 1990s, extensive liberalisation policies and measures were adopted by the central government to gradually remove entry restrictions for local and foreign operators. Facing competition from established local rivals and the prospect of trouble-free entry by foreign investors after China's accession to the WTO, Sinotrans was squeezed into a position where its survival wholly depended on its own competitiveness.

> Competition is heating up, which threatens our position [in this industry]. There are over several thousand legally registered firms nationally in our (freight forwarding and goods transportation) business, and there are more unregistered ones doing the same job. Sinotrans has done well due to its large scale and a national network. However, this will not continue if we do not upgrade our technical hardware and software and reform the management system. (One senior manager).

This comment illustrates the importance of protecting the technical 'core' for the top management of Sinotrans and also illustrates the importance of the management system. This is not say that this protection of the technical core is costless. Innovation is inhibited by the absolute necessity to buffer the core whilst going along with government and Party directives. The following quote perfectly illustrates this element of the strategy implemented by Sinotrans managers.

> The corporate culture here must connect with the strategy of this firm. However, everybody wants to play safe instead of innovation and change. (One senior manager)

The dynamics of this situation illustrate that the mangers in Sinotrans have had to add competition to the set of variables that they consider. Before 1997, they were acting rationally in ignoring the issue of protection of the technical core as if it were not under threat. Now, the context has changed and the managers are now also threatened by competition. In both cases, they are acting 'rationally' but their decisions have been changed radically by changing circumstances. Opening the 'black box' of the firm and exposing the behaviours of the active agents focuses on the impact of the external environment on real changes in managerial decision making.

Proposition 2. Under norms of rationality, organisations seek to buffer environmental influences by surrounding their technical cores with input and output components.

This proposition points us in the direction of examining vertical integration both backward and forward in order to reduce the uncertainty faced by the organisation (i.e. to 'close the system'). Theory suggests that managers will integrate operations until the cost of using the market is lower than that of further integration (Buckley and Casson, 1976). The interesting questions in the context of SOEs are how far internalisation is over- or under-utilised and secondly whether distortions are introduced into this expansion path by government control. There is evidence of excessive backward integration (whose costs exceeded those of the market) in the period of first liberalisation of markets because this expansion route was the only one legally available (due to government restrictions on some domestic line of business), e.g., Sinotrans' establishing of its own deep sea fleet in the last two decades. The Chinese government allowed limited competition in the sea transportation sector following its economic reform program in 1984. While challenged by COSCO and other sea fleet operators in its own freight forwarding business, Sinotrans expanded into sea transportation, enhancing its position in freight forwarding with improved certainty and capacity of cargo shipping. By the end of 2000, Sinotrans has built up a sea fleet of more than 2 million tons in aggregate deadweight. The type of forward integration was restricted to bringing into the compass of the firm predominantly routine activities, rather than those that involve interaction with the final market and the customer. This is perhaps understandable as Sinotrans, in common with other SOEs, lacked the human resource in management and marketing, i.e. the soft skills that enable firms to compete most effectively in markets. Therefore, until the middle of the 1980s, forward integration was limited, with little emphasis on customers in the form of marketing, promotion and quality assurance. This aspect of forward integration only began to improve markedly after 1997.

Proposition 3. Under norms of rationality, organisations seek to smooth out input and output transactions.

Input and output transactions can be smoothed by hoarding resources against contingencies and by attempting to secure a diversity of future businesses. Managers in Sinotrans faced government-imposed radical organisational change at unknown points of time. They had an incentive to secure resources to ensure the technical core against such 'interference'. Securing a cushion of resources offered insurance to the managers against technical task failure. Managers in Sinotrans did not have the power to diversify until the reforms of 1984, but they extended their spatial reach by province and internationally in their core areas of business. In so far as provincial trade is not fully covariant across provinces, spatial diversification ameliorates uncertainty in two ways, by tapping new business and by seeking business that is not entirely co-cyclical.

After 50 years of development, Sinotrans evolved to become a logistics service provider with a global network, 'Boasting 3,000 trucks, 160 standard and refrigerated warehouses, 75 ships, 77 railway sidings, and 15 train-loading port terminals' (Gates, 2001). It transports cargoes by sea, rail, air and land, providing chartering, liner services, ship management, freight forwarding, air courier services, container leasing, storage and warehousing, and distribution. Sinotrans has 52 domestic subsidiaries, 238 domestic joint ventures, and nine representative offices and 67 subsidiaries overseas, employing some 47,000 staff. The total assets of Sinotrans in 1999 were about RMB 22 billion yuan (approximately US$2.6 billion).

In terms of output transactions, SOE managers attempted to raise revenue by diversifying into areas that improved cash flow even in unrelated businesses. This effect was very pronounced when restrictions on diversification were lifted at the beginning of the 1990s.

> Sinotrans diversified into multiple businesses during 1988–95, such as real estate, international economic cooperation, stock market investment, restaurants, tourism, and even forestry (it bought a big forestry operation in New Zealand). The majority of these businesses were loss-making due to a lack of industry related knowledge. In its hey day, there were over 1000 projects undertaken in the diversified business areas with a total investment of several hundred million US dollars. Sinotrans withdrew from most of these businesses, because it realized that it was capable of making money only in its traditional core areas. There are still about 200 such projects in existence. However, Sinotrans employed specialists to manage these businesses. It now extends into the financial services, insurance (Taikang Life, one of a handful of big insurance companies in China) and banking (it is the second largest shareholder of China Merchant Bank). But, Sinotrans mainly concentrates in its core business of freight agency and forwarding, with heavy investment into warehousing, IT networks, ports and so on. (One senior manager)

Thus, Sinotrans was transformed into a diversified business operator, with interests ranging from insurance, banking, real estate, manufacturing in addition to its core business.

On the input side, Sinotrans was faced with financing large lumpy cost items such as ships. In the absence of a smoothly functioning capital market it was constrained to use internal sources of funds and to seek government guarantees for soft loans from the banks. This emphasised the firm's dependence on government officials and further reinforced its diversification strategy. As the pace of marketisation increased, Sinotrans was driven back to concentrate on its core business and to dispose of its unrelated activities.

Proposition 4. Under norms of rationality, organisations seek to anticipate and adapt to environmental changes that cannot be buffered or levelled (Proposition 4a: if this fails, they resort to rationing).

Proposition 3 concerned the microstrategy of the firm in managing its costs and revenues. This proposition, by contrast, concerns the changes in the macrostrategy in response to wide environmental shifts. The managers of Sinotrans responded to external constraints by moving into regional and international trade on an increasing scale. This strategic move allowed Sinotrans to anticipate the liberalisation of the Chinese economy by securing the experience of operations in economies already liberalised.

Sinotrans has also sought to maintain its close relationship with the government to buffer against uncertainties and to adapt to environmental changes. This includes relationships with both the central government and local and provincial governments. It creates a dilemma for SOE reform, i.e., SOEs seek independence from government in its course of restructuring but have to maintain a close relationship with different layers of government for the sake of business favours and even financial support in case of dramatic change in the external operational environment. This mindset of reliance on government is a reflection of the heritage of Sinotrans-like SOEs, which can only be remedied with further reform in government ownership in SOEs and a radical change of corporate cultures inside firms. Corporate culture (Schein, 1992) is a concept that post-dates Thompson but requires analysis in the context of SOEs reform. The strategy of bargaining is an attempt by the firm to manipulate changes in its environment. This is also a response that was not considered by Thompson, who takes the firm as responding to external stimuli rather than altering them.

Domains of organisational action and the active agent

Proposition 5. Under norms of rationality, organisations seek to minimise the power of task environment elements over them by maintaining alternatives.

The task environment is very similar to the five-forces of Porter (1980) as it includes customers, suppliers, competitors and regulatory groups such as government agencies. Sinotrans experienced a huge downshift in its power over elements of its task environment when it lost its monopoly position as a result of government liberalisation policy. In response to this, Sinotrans tried to reassert its power over customers by exerting influences over local MOFTECS to be the preferred supplier. From the end of the 1970s, Sinotrans used its monopsonistic power to solicit low cost bids from its suppliers. Ironically, this purchasing power increased as liberalisation progressed by increasing competition for contracts to supply

Sinotrans. Before 1984, Sinotrans had no competitors for international freight forwarding. The appearance of competition meant Sinotrans had to work hard to maintain market share. Sinotrans began a programme of branding and advertising in order to secure its non-government customer base. Sinotrans run hundreds of marketing and public relations advertisements on various media nationwide each year, including campaigns to promote Sinotrans as a caring, efficient and responsible corporate citizen, in order to appeal to the widest possible range of customers. At the same time, a major component of Sinotrans' strategy has been to retain and increase government support, to ensure that it has a diversified portfolio of business with both the government and commercial sector.

Proposition 6. Organisations subject to rationality norms and competing for support seek prestige.

The management of Sinotrans has sought prestige by international expansion, by advertising and promotion. They also seek prestige by being nominated as government approved key firms, e.g., Sinotrans was selected as one of the 120 SOEs to pioneer a new wave of organisational reform in 1997. Finally, listing in worldwide stock exchanges is another way of seeking prestige. Part of Sinotrans (Sinotrans Development) has been listed on Shanghai Stock Exchange, and its overseas listing in Hong Kong is underway.

> Sinotrans was the vanguard of China's international trade service sector for decades. We have benefited from this privileged position throughout the different development stages of our country. Under the new circumstances of China's socialist market economy and its accession to the WTO, it is important to maintain our key position amongst internal and external competitors through serving the government goals and promoting ourselves in our society. (One senior manager)

The issue for Sinotrans thus was the *maintenance* of the prestige that came from its previous monopoly position in changing circumstances where competition threatened its status. Sinotrans's actions were therefore designed to maintain 'face' (*mian zi*). This is an example of a Chinese cultural concepts affecting behaviour which is very close to Thompson's notion of 'prestige'.

Proposition 7. When support capacity is concentrated in one or a few elements of the task environment, organisations under norms of rationality seek power relative to those on whom they are dependent.

Managers in Sinotrans are dependent on the state as owner and as regulator, on the Party and on local (provincial) governments. For Sinotrans, the organisational changes it experienced were partially an endeavour to readjust the relationship between itself and the Chinese government. This building of countervailing power (Galbraith, 1956) is in line with this proposition. The separation of government functions from Sinotrans was completed on paper in 1986, officially ending an era in which government functions (as a bureau of MOFTEC) were combined with monopolistic operations (in foreign trade transportation and freight forwarding). As discussed above, the government opened up the market in foreign trade transportation and freight forwarding to local competitors in 1984, at which time its preferential policy towards Sinotrans ceased. However, this does not mean that Sinotrans was an independent business operator. MOFTEC still continued its intervention in Sinotrans' operations as it had done throughout the previous 30 years. Sinotrans still operated as the main subcontractor of MOFTEC. The difference was the creation of a new Bureau of Foreign Trade Transportation, bearing the same name as the previous one, but now excluding Sinotrans' management team. This created hundreds of positions throughout the country to accommodate those in the different administrative layers of the old Sinotrans who were unwilling to be transformed into managers. The administrative relationship between the government and Sinotrans was not broken in the reorganisation in 1986.

In marked contrast, the organisational change of 1997 focused on the transformation of the interventionist relationship into a non-interventionist, equity-based, relationship. The government redefined its role to become the industry regulator, and the sole investor in Sinotrans. The management of business operations was transferred to the managers of the firm. Sinotrans has been corporatised but controlled by the government. Strategic decisions of the management were still be subject to covert government inference.

After 1997, Sinotrans started its new life as one of several government favoured business operators in the foreign trade transportation area. It was left on its own in managing the business and competing in national and international markets. Sinotrans was no longer part of the government, or even the prime business contractor of the government.

In a phrase, Sinotrans had to earn its place in business. The one remaining link with the government was in management appointments. The government sent its representatives to sit in the Board of Directors and, based on its full ownership, appointed managers to fill the top positions of Sinotrans. This indicates that government maintains absolute control over Sinotrans through legitimate business means (Porter, 1996; Martinsons 1999), leaving doors open for Sinotrans to seek invisible favourable support from the government.

Proposition 8. When support capacity is concentrated, but demand is dispersed, the weaker organisation will attempt to handle its dependence through co-option.

This proposition precisely describes Sinotrans, whose support capacity is limited to government agencies within the task environment and whose demand is dispersed. Indeed, Sinotrans has co-opted managers from state government, Local government and has co-opted Party support. It has maintained its love/hate relationship with the government for seeking support and business opportunities. Personnel exchanges with the government have continued. The Chairmanship of the Board of Directors and the position of chief operation officer are normally filled by appointees from the central government. The chairman is normally the secretary of the Party Branch inside Sinotrans. Likewise, the positions of chief operation officers at subsidiary level were appointed by local MOFTEC bureaus in the past, with approval from the local Party Committees. After the organisational change in 1997, the headquarters can appoint its own managers to those positions in subsidiaries. In practice, this has to be taken with prior consultation with local MOFTEC bureaus and local Party Committees. This has resulted in intricate personal connections between Sinotrans and different layers of government and the Party.

Proposition 9. The more sectors in which the organisation, subject to rationality norms, is constrained, the more power the organisation will seek over remaining sectors of its local environment.

This proposition suggests that managers in Sinotrans constrained by government, Party and customers, will seek to control (almost obsessively) its core competencies by internalising its logistical and supply network and the resources that support it. This is shwon in Sinotrans' specialisation in logistics as its core business following environmental changes in the Chinese market. China's economic reform and opening to the outside world began in December 1978. From that point on Sinotrans faced radical changes in its economic environment in which the central government pushed SOEs to transform themselves into efficient business operators.

Therefore, the shift in government policy towards SOEs and the intense competition in the domestic market after the Chinese government introduced competition into the foreign trade businesses in 1984, forced Sinotrans to take the fundamental decision to become a logistics service operator, providing a comprehensive and national distribution service based on a worldwide network. This new aggressive competitive strategy was decided on the fact that the technical as well as managerial capabilities inside Sinotrans would be strong enough to enable it to continue success in the Chinese market. One senior manager commented:

> We recognized that we should switch to logistics as soon as possible several years ago. In pursuit of becoming a logistics service provider, we need to regain the advantage of a national network by reforming the existing corporate organizational system. We rely on network and quality of service in this industry.

Proposition 10. The organisation facing many constraints and unable to achieve power in other sectors of its local environment will seek to enlarge the local environment.

This proposition applies to Sinotrans core logistics business chronologically before Proposition 9, when it was most constrained by government ownership and central planning. The part of Sinotrans' local environment over which it then had complete control was its logistics network. It attempted to enlarge that 'local environment' intra-regionally and internationally in complete comformity with this proposition. It was precisely the 'government's' role as owner and regulator that compelled Sinotrans to expand abroad, as its other outlets were shut off. When diversification restrictions were lifted, Sinotrans over-diversified as Proposition 3 above illustrated.

The sudden lifting of constraints on the active agents caused the managers in Sinotrans to immediately seek to extend their power by diversifying into unrelated businesses. Their excessive enthusiasm is explained by their suppression in previous years.

Organisational design, technology and structure

Proposition 11. Organisations, under norms of rationality, seek to place their boundaries around those activities which, if left to the task environment, would be crucial contingencies.

Sinotrans is compelled to internalise its crucial activities and to protect these from encroachment by other organisations or the market. Through extensive organisational changes the headquarters of Sinotrans was transformed into a governing body, managing its primary and secondary subsidiaries through financial, management and operational controls. One manager confirmed this:

> Actually, control has been achieved in the following areas: human resource management (in particular, appointing managers to subsidiaries), assets (making major decisions at the headquarters), finance and assessing subsidiary performance. In addition, the headquarters are in full control of strategic development. The strategies of subsidiaries must be approved by the headquarters. All these indicate that we are one company now. (A senior manager)

Proposition 12. Organisations employing mediating technologies, and subject to rationality norms, seek to expand their domain by increasing the populations served.

The validity of this proposition in the case of Sinotrans can be demonstrated by Sinotrans' horizontal diversification to serve customers internationally (and international customers). However, its international ambitions have not led to wide and deep internationalisation. From its largely domestic base in the 1970s, Sinotrans added many small outposts worldwide. It remains the largest firm in China to provide a comprehensive and national distribution service. To its 52 domestic subsidiaries, 238 domestic joint ventures, and nine representative offices it has added 67 subsidiaries overseas, employing some 47,000 staff. The total assets of Sinotrans in 1999 were about RMB 22 billion yuan (approximately US$2.6 billion). Following the liberalisation of transportation and related business areas in China since the 1980s, Sinotrans has ceased its governmental functions and experienced several rounds of restructuring with the aim of becoming a competitive global logistics player.

Proposition 13. Organisations with capacity in excess of what the task environment supports will seek to enlarge their domain.

Excess capacity can be interpreted in two different ways. Low utilisation of capital would result in low productivity and pressure to restructure. Alternatively, following Penrose (1959), underutilised resources, particularly management, can be used to extend the operations of the firm, possibly, in new directions.

Under the first interpretation, Sinotrans indeed had excess capacity in comparison with market demand, resulting in low productivity and more pressure to restructure. To survive, Sinotrans undertook a program of restructuring and reform to strengthen its competitiveness for more market share in the Chinese market, and at the same time, set up more foreign subsidiaries than before to secure international market. It improved its service contents as well as quality and strived to provide a comprehensive logistics service to local and international clients. Now, Sinotrans handles logistic support for many world-famous multinational firms in their China operations, such as Motorola, Philips, VW, Ericsson, Panasonic, Hyundai, Samsung and Acer.

Under the second interpretation, we can point to the new strategy of innovating new products in the sense of bonding together services that had previously been separate (e.g. wholesale logistics support).

Proposition 14. Under norms of rationality, organisations group positions to minimise coordination costs.

The application of a networked information system within Sinotrans can be seen as evidence of minimising coordination costs. Operational control was reinforced by the development of a networked information system, linking every subsidiary (including those overseas) with the headquarters. Operational documents (e.g., contracts, progress report, delivery forms, inventory records, customer feedback, etc) were unified and computerised, and software was developed to manage finance, statistics, transportation (land, air and sea) and freight forwarding. Special support was drawn from CA Co. of the USA and IPACS of Singapore to provide logistics-related system solutions. Through operational control, Sinotrans directed its business towards becoming a comprehensive logistics service based on increased control and coordination.

Proposition 15. In the absence of reciprocal and sequential independence, organisations, subject to norms of rationality, seek to group positions homogeneously to facilitate coordination by standardisation.

Thompson, in this proposition, is suggesting an early form of business process re-engineering (Hammer and Champy, 1993) in that similar activities should be grouped under unified rules of operation and connected to other processes by clear linkages. Sinotrans has pursued standardisation to reorganise the company's organisation, management and scope. This is reflected in technical standardisation, quality control, computing network, standardised practice of management (e.g., finance, human resources management, and even culture). Some details are as follows:

(1) The Finance Department in Sinotrans became responsible for group-wide budgeting, designing capital spending rules, making investment decisions, managing project and parent cash flows, and monitoring financial performance of the subsidiaries. These financial rules and procedures have been applied throughout the whole company, which enabled the headquarters to direct the operation of the subsidiaries. It also gave the headquarters the means to encourage the growth of certain business units and differentiated the growth of others by manipulating budgets and attaching differential degrees of financial supervision. As a result, Sinotrans could pool its financial resources to underpin the strategy to become a competitive logistics supplier.

(2) To address the joint-venture-type problems seen inside its local subsidiaries, Sinotrans decided that, from 1997 onwards, all the management appointments of primary subsidiaries should be centralised. This included selection, training, performance evaluation, promotion and new assignments. The centralisation of the power to make management appointments enabled Sinotrans to build up a team of managers in the subsidiaries who were loyal to the headquarters instead of to local governments. This provided an additional route through which to influence the behaviour of their subordinates. Headquarters were also able to develop a set of coherent procedures and practices with respect to human resources management applicable to the whole of the company.

(3) The headquarters withdrew from direct business operation, spinning off business operation units to become specialised primary subsidiaries. Its role now focused on managing subsidiaries. This

was conducted not only through financial and management control, but also by coordinating and directing business activities, setting standards and quality benchmarks, and evaluating individual firm performance. Management reward and incentive schemes were linked to performance to motivate employees at different levels. Operational control was reinforced by the development of a networked information system, linking every subsidiary (including those overseas) with the headquarters. Operational documents (e.g. contracts, progress report, delivery form, inventory record, customer feedback, etc) were unified and computerised, and software was developed to manage finance, statistics, transportation (land, air and sea) and freight forwarding.

Proposition 16. When organisations employ standardisation, which cuts across multiple groupings, they also develop liaison positions linking the several groups and the rule-making agency.

Again, Thompson's analysis accords with the later development of envisaging stages or linked processes across activities within businesses (Buckley and Carter, 1999). A significant complication of Sinotrans' business environment is that many linked processes, which need to be coordinated, are outside the firm. This creates a more open structure, which crosscuts firm and government boundaries as they are conventionally understood in the West. Sinotrans is forced to 'liaise' with local and national state organisations and with the Party. There may be reciprocal 'influence' between the Government as regulator and the Sinotrans management. To cope with this there are extensive personnel exchanges at different levels: at headquarters, the top management team, appointed by the government, is often composed of officials from the government (MOFTEC); at local subsidiaries, it is not uncommon to see MOFTEC and other provincial or municipal officials made managers of Sinotrans. A telling story is that one of the interviewees was an official in MOFTEC before taking his post in Sinotrans. This is not a one-way street, however. Some officials have been promoted to MOFTEC, although this is rarer in comparison with the volume of the contrary direction. One of the reasons why Sinotrans is still subject to extensive government control is the motivations of the top management team to seek promotion into government and Sinotrans has been a vehicle of achieving their ambition. This can be related to the government mindset in Sinotrans' corporate culture.

Boundary spanning activities

Proposition 17. Under norms of rationality, organisations facing heterogenous task environments seek to identify homogeneous segments and establish structural units to deal with each.

There is some evidence inside Sinotrans supporting this proposition. First, Sinotrans has 12 specialised subsidiaries each covering one line of business nationwide (for example, fast delivery). They are independent of Sinotrans' provincial subsidiaries with its own local subsidiaries and representative offices. Second, its provincial subsidiaries can be regarded as structural units in that there are extensive linkages between these subsidiaries based on homogeneous business not heterogeneous business (for example, chartering business cooperation between different units).

Proposition 18. When the range of task environment variables is large or unpredictable, the responsible organisation component must achieve the necessary adaptations by monitoring the environment and planning responses, and this calls for localised units.

Sinotrans has developed an extensive network to monitor changes in its environment arising from changes in government policy. This has arisen from its history, which has taught it that government policy is the key variable producing changes. Sinotrans has a subsidiary in each province and some major cities in China, and an extensive network in the world. In particular, Sinotrans' provincial and local subsidiaries have long connections with local governments, even after restructuring. This is based on the personnel exchanges between them. Maintaining such connections is part of Sinotrans' strategy of winning business deals from local governments and responding to local environmental changes. Therefore, Sinotrans had a considerable degree of localisation, and was in need of strengthening its centralised organisational structure in order to integrate these localised units within the firm. However, Sinotrans has been less successful at forecasting changes in the market where it is less experienced.

> The leadership here and at the subsidiaries is hesitant to make big changes for fear of mistakes. The qualities of the employees differ hugely ... the concept of quality and customer service is far from being in the mindset of everyone. (One senior manager)

Proposition 19. When technical core and boundary spanning activities can be isolated from one another except for scheduling, organisations under norms of rationality will be centralised with an overarching layer composed of functional division.

The organisational reconfiguration of Sinotrans in 1997 was accompanied by a realignment of power between headquarters and subsidiaries. After regaining the 57 subsidiaries formerly under the administration of local MOFTEC bureaus, which is essentially a government-sponsored acquisition, Sinotrans strengthened its control over all of its subsidiaries through increased financial control, management appointments and operational control. This involved increasing the power of functional departments at headquarters.

The headquarters supervise the subsidiaries in business operations, imposing financial control and monitoring the investment made by them. They also appoint managers to the subsidiaries. As a result, the functional departments in the headquarters are more important than in the past. (A senior manager)

The Finance Department in Sinotrans became responsible for budgeting, designing capital spending rules, making investment decisions, managing project and parent cash flows, and monitoring financial performance of the subsidiaries. These financial rules and procedures enabled the headquarters to direct the operation of the subsidiaries. It also gave the headquarters the means to encourage the growth of certain business units and differentiated the growth of others by manipulating budgets and attaching differential degrees of financial supervision. As a result, Sinotrans could pool its financial resources to underpin the strategy to become a competitive logistics supplier.

To address the joint-venture-type problems seen inside its local subsidiaries, Sinotrans decided that, from 1997 onwards, all the management appointments of primary subsidiaries should be centralised. This included selection, training, performance evaluation, promotion and new assignments. The management appointments of secondary subsidiaries became the responsibility of the primary subsidiaries, under the supervision and with the agreement of the Human Resources Department at headquarters.

The centralisation of the power to make management appointments enabled Sinotrans to build up a team of managers in the subsidiaries who were loyal to the headquarters instead of to local governments.

This provided an additional route through which to influence the behaviour of their subordinates. Headquarters were also able to develop a set of coherent procedures and practices with respect to human resources management applicable to the whole of the company.

The headquarters withdrew from direct business operation, spinning off business operation units to become specialised primary subsidiaries. Its role now focused on managing subsidiaries. This was conducted not only through financial and management control, but also by coordinating and directing business activities, setting standards and quality benchmarks, and evaluating individual firm performance. Management reward and incentive schemes were linked to performance to motivate employees at different levels.

Operational control was reinforced by the development of a networked information system, linking every subsidiary (including those overseas) with the headquarters. Operational documents (e.g. contracts, progress report, delivery form, inventory record, customer feedback, etc) were unified and computerised, and software was developed to manage finance, statistics, transportation (land, air and sea) and freight forwarding. Special support was drawn from CA Co. of the USA and IPACS of Singapore to provide logistics-related system solutions. Through operational control, Sinotrans directed its business towards becoming a comprehensive logistics service based on increased control and coordination.

From the above account we can see that the headquarters of Sinotrans were transformed into a governing body, managing its primary and secondary subsidiaries through financial, management and operational controls.

> Actually, control has been achieved in the following areas: human resource management (in particular, appointing managers to subsidiaries), assets (making major decisions at the headquarters), finance and assessing subsidiary performance. In addition, the headquarters are in full control of strategic development. The strategies of subsidiaries must be approved by the headquarters. All these indicate that we are one company now. (A senior manager)

The fact that the headquarters in Sinotrans decide strategies as well as operations of subsidiaries reflects the huge changes experienced by this company in the 1990s. Indeed, Sinotrans has actively pursued the newly identified business strategy of becoming a comprehensive logistics service provider with a global network. Subsidiaries have been driven to attain objectives consistent with this strategy. It indicates that strategic control has been applied to improve the control system of Sinotrans. Strategic control is normally employed in a MNE with a decentralised organisation structure (Hoskisson et al., 1991). Sinotrans, on the contrary, moved from a decentralised structure to a centralised structure as a result of the change in the economic environment. Using strategic control to strengthen grip on subsidiaries in a centralised structure is an integral part of the weaponry possessed by the headquarters following long periods of disintegration and control voids. This shows that strategic control has been viewed as a useful management concept inside Sinotrans.

The specialness of applying strategic control in a centralised structure enriches our understanding of corporate control and restructuring in China and transitional economies.

Changes in Sinotrans' corporate culture over time

Thompson gives a prominent role to culture as a homogenising influence on individual behaviour. Sinotrans' corporate culture before the organisational change in 1997 was a mixture of communist ideas and some slogans concerning higher productivity and output. Being part of the government, employees were educated to serve customers only as a means to serving the country and the Communist Party.

In the 1990s, the notion of corporate culture designed to motivate employee in promoting firm competitiveness was seen as an indication of management modernisation in Sinotrans. This was a result of the dissemination of western management practices to SOEs in the wake of extensive foreign direct investment into China (Ng, 1998). The management team in Sinotrans came to realise that, as an SOE with long history of being a governmental bureau as well as a monopolistic business, resistance to organisational change was found in every business unit. Without a renewed corporate culture cognate with the challenging market and its corporate strategy, the success of its organisational change and the development of its new management model would be unattainable (Schein, 1992). Although a renewed corporate culture can facilitate organisational change, and play an even more significant role in containing resistance to change in such circumstances, Sinotrans mistakenly thought that a new corporate culture could be introduced immediately.

Based on internal discussion and an externally commissioned consultancy report, Sinotrans attempted to change its corporate culture and regarded managing its corporate culture as a crucial part of the overall organisational change strategy. The changed corporate culture was intended to be a set of new norms and values centred on quality, cooperation, efficiency and customer satisfaction. This reflected a complete change of mindset in the top managers regarding the business operation of the firm from dependency on government to serving the customer. This is exemplified in the words of one senior manager:

> Employees need to be aware of the direction of development and the way we do it. Becoming a competitive logistics supplier in today's market is not easy. Each of us should remember the guarantee and promise we have made to the customers, and try our best to excel. This should be part of our corporate culture.

However, the evidence shows that Sinotrans did not fully achieve its objective with respect to using corporate culture to facilitate change. As one interviewee pointed out, equipping every employee with this new corporate culture and applying it in operation remains a distant goal.

> The corporate culture here must connect with the strategy of this firm. However, everybody wants to play safe instead of innovation and change. The leadership here and at the subsidiaries is hesitant to make big changes for fear of mistakes. The qualities of the employees differ hugely ... the concept of quality and customer service is far from being in the mindset of everyone.

The argument of Ghoshal and Westney (1993) and Kilmann, Saxtan and Serpa (1986) that culture is a powerful managerial tool with which to facilitate integration and cooperation, is clearly appreciated in Sinotrans, even though it has not been adequately implemented. We can see that in a SOE in a transitional economy, cultural elements play as important a role in facilitating change as those concrete aspects of an organisation, such as structure, control and strategy (Deshpande and Farley, 2000). After China's admission to the WTO, foreign and local firms will compete directly following the removal of restrictions. The performance gap between foreign and local operators in the service sector will become a critical issue, and cultural change may become an invaluable tool for Chinese SOEs. The wider use of corporate culture could be a way of motivating employees to improve quality and efficiency on top of financial incentives. In the absence of progress on this front, SOEs such as Sinotrans will be placed at a competitive disadvantage as greater competition continues to enter their marketplace.

Discussion

The above longitudinal analysis of Sinotrans' organisational action clearly demonstrates the attempts of the managers in the enterprises to protect their technical core in situations of extreme environmental uncertainty. The conceptual framework offered by Thompson, that any organisation is divisible, has provided a sound starting point for our analysis of Sinotrans. Sinotrans is readily identified as an open system with a business founded on a mediating technology – logistics. Our theoretical review and our case analysis show that these basic general principles can be applied. It has been demonstrated that marketisation trickled into the organisation little by little over a long period of time. The nature of the uncertainty faced by the managers over time changed as the plans, objectives and eventually targets were transmitted to them in a way that eventually reduced the level of uncertainty originating from the government, but this was replaced by market-based uncertainty. This paper has used Thompson's framework to explain the business strategy of an enterprise where radical uncertainty has been the prevailing feature of its environment. In the case of Sinotrans, uncertainty itself is a variable. A further fascinating aspect of Thompson's analysis is that it enables us to understand that firms will attempt to close open systems wherever they impact on the firm including those where personal and political relationships are involved, not just those systems where economic transactions are involved. One of the key strategies of the managers of Sinotrans has been to influence its environment through pressure on Governments and the Party to move it towards a rational, less uncertain, more stable environmental context. Thus, the propositions derived from Thompson stand up very well as explanations of the complex changes within Sinotrans over this turbulent period.

Our longitudinal case study shows that Sinotrans has experienced a punctuated development, precisely because of the dependence of the organisation on decisions taken by the Government and the Party. The government has proven to be the single greatest source of external shock to Sinotrans, and the organisation has necessarily maintained and developed an extensive interface with the administration as a means of survival. The result of this overwhelming pressure from government means that Sinotrans has to divert a great deal of its resources into closing this relationship (Nutt, 2002) and consequently has too few resources available with which to respond effectively to market uncertainties.

The analysis in Thompson (1967) serves well as a basic framework for the analysis of change in a Chinese service state-owned enterprise (SOE). In particular, Thompson's emphasis on the reduction of environmental impact on the technical core of an organisation remains insightful. However, the framework requires modification in the face of the radical uncertainty arising from state ownership. SOEs remain different. The ends and objectives of SOEs are less well known than those of capitalist firms, and so much more interaction with the environment is necessary. The uncertainty engendered by political risk also implies that the means (operational norms) are less knowable, which places a premium on the political, not the commercial, judgment of the key managers in SOEs. The 'norms of rationality' cannot therefore be simply responding to market signals. The inhibition to innovation given by state control and Party interference in management tasks is palpable. The strategies implemented by Sinotrans are designed not only to protect the technical core of the organisation, they are there to protect the stewardship of the managers, too.

Conclusions

This paper has analysed organisational changes and action in Sinotrans utilising a longitudinal case study. As a Chinese state-owned service intermediary, Sinotrans has faced uncertainty arising from political interference from government and party institutions. Over time, it has also faced increasing market pressure, which has caused it to attempt to close off its technical core by income smoothing strategies, such as diversification, which have frequently then been reversed. Thompson's (1967) framework proves to be an excellent means of capturing the dynamics of Sinotrans' actions by focusing on the changing types of uncertainty with which the managers in Sinotrans have attempted to cope.

Thompson provides us with a framework for analysis to make it clear that government interference in the business goals of Sinotrans have the effect of increasing not only the level of environmental uncertainty but also the variability of this level of uncertainty. The outcome of this is that Sinotrans is forever trying to protect itself by identifying and removing certain sources of uncertainty whilst others are continually being imposed upon it.

Acknowledgement

Financial support from the Sino-British Fellowship Trust and the Universities' China Committee in London (UCCL) for conducting interviews in China is gratefully acknowledged.

Note

1. The propositions correspond to Thompson's as follows: 1 = 2.1, 2 = 2.2, 3 = 2.3, 4 = 2.4, 4a = 2.5, 5 = 3.1, 6 = 3.2, 7 = 3.3, 8 = 3.3b, 9 = 3.4, 10 = 3.5, 11 = 4.1, 12 = 4.1b, 13 = 4.3, 14 = 5.1, 15 = 5.1c, 16 = 5.4, 17 = 6.1, 18 = 6.2c, 19 = 6.3.

References

Bryman, Alan (1989) *Research Methods and Organizational Studies*. London: Unwin Hyman Press.

Buckley, Peter J. and Mark Casson (1976) *The Future of the Multinational Enterprise*. London: Macmillan.

Buckley, Peter J. and Martin J. Carter (1999) Managing cross-border complementary knowledge. *International Studies of Management and Organization* 29, no. 1: 80–104.

Casson, Mark C. (1982) *The Entrepreneur*. Oxford: Martin Robertson.

Child, John (1994) *Management in China during the Age of Reform*. Cambridge: Cambridge University Press.

Deshpande, Rohit and John U. Farley (2000) Market-focused organizational transformation in China. *Journal of Global Marketing* 14, no. 1&2: 7–35.

Easterby-Smith, Mark, Richard Thorpe and Andy Lowe (1991) *Management Research: An Introduction*. London: Sage.

Erlandson, David A., Edward L. Harris, Barbara L. Skipper and Steve D Allen (1993) *Doing Naturalistic Inquiry: A Guide to Methods*. London: Sage.

Feldman, Martha S. and Anat Rafaeli (2002) Organizational routines as sources of connections and understandings. *Journal of Management Studies* 39, no. 3: 309–331.

Fligstein, Neil and Kenneth Daube (1989) Structural change in corporate organization. *American Review of Sociology* 15: 73–96.

Galbraith, John Kenneth (1956) *American Capitalism: The Concept of Countervailing Power*. Boston: Houghton Mifflin.

Gates, Robert (2001) Beyond sinotrans: China's distribution infrastructure. *The China Business Review* Jul/Aug: 14–17.

Ghoshal, Sumantra and D. Eleanor Westney (1993) Introduction and overview. In *Organization Theory and the Multinational Corporation*, eds. Sumantra Ghoshal and D. Eleanor Westney. London: St. Martin's Press.

Grant, Robert M. (1991) The resource-based theory of competitive advantage: implications for strategy formulation. *California Management Review* 33, no. 3: 114–135.

Grubel, Herbert G. (1968) Internationally diversified portfolios: welfare gains and capital flows. *American Economic Review* 58: 1299–1314.

Hammer, Michael and James Champy (1993) *Reengineering the Corporation: A Manifesto for Business Revolution*. London: Nicholas Brealey.

Hoskisson, Robert E., Michael A. Hitt and Charles W. L. Hill (1991) Managerial risk-taking in diversified firms: an evolutionary perspective. *Organization Science* 3: 296–314.

Jensen, Michael C. and William H Meckling.1(976) Theory of the firm: managerial behavior, agency cost and ownership structure. *Journal of Financial Economics* 3: 305–360.

Kamps, Jaap and Laszlo Polos (1999) Reducing uncertainty: a formal theory of organizations in action. *American Journal of Sociology* 104, no. 6: 1776–1812.

Kilmann, Ralph H., Mary J. Saxton and Roy Serpa (1986) Issues in understanding and changing culture. *California Management Review* 28, no. 2: 87–94.

Koopmans, Tjalling C. (1957) *Three Essays on the State of Economic Science*. New York: McGraw-Hill.

Kynge, James (2002) Cancer of Corruption Spreads throughout Country. Page 13, *Financial Times*, 1st November.

Leibenstein, Harvey (1976) *Beyond Economic Man*. Cambridge: Harvard University Press.

Martinsons, Maris G. (1999) Management in China after two decades of an open door policy. *Journal of Applied Management Studies* 8, no. 1: 119–126.

Merton, Robert K. (1957) Bureaucratic structure and personality. In *Social Theory and Social Structure*. (enlarged edition 1968), ed. Robert K. Merton. New York: The Free Press.

Meyer, Alan D., Anne S. Tsui and C.R. Hinings (1993) Configurational approaches to organizational analysis. *Academy of Management Journal* 36, no. 6: 1175–1195.

MOFTEC (1996) Notice On Strengthening the Group Based Management of Sinotrans, *Ministry Internal Document* No. 725, MOFTEC, Beijing.

Ng, Rita Mei Ching (1998) Culture as a factor in management: the case of the people's republic of China. *International Journal of Management* 15, no. 1: 86–93.

Nutt, Paul C. (2002) Making strategic choices. *Journal of Management Studies* 39, no. 1: 67–96.

Parsons, Talcott (1960) *Structure and Process in Modern Societies*. New York: The Free Press.

Penrose, Edith T. (1959) *The Theory of the Growth of the Firm*. Oxford: Basil Blackwell.

Porter, Michael E. (1980) *Competitive Strategy: Techniques for Analyzing Industries and Competitors*. New York: Free Press.

Porter, Robin (1996) Politics, culture and decision making in China. In *Management Issues in China: Domestic Enterprises*, eds. D. Brown and R. Porter. London: Routledge.

Schein, Edgar H. (1992) *Organizational Culture and Leadership*. 2nd ed. San Francisco: Jossey-Bass Publishers.

Schilling, Melissa A. and H. Kevin Steensma (2002) Disentangling the theories of firm boundaries: a path model and empirical test. *Organization Science* 13, no. 4: 387–401.

Sinotrans (1990) *Zhong Guo Wai Yun Si Shi Nian* [The Forty Years of Sinotrans]. Beijing: China Workers Press.

Smith, Adam (1776) *An Inquiry into the Nature and Causes of the Wealth of Nations*. London: printed for W. Strahan and T. Cadell.

Steinfeld, Edward S. (1998) *Forging Reform in China: The Fate of State-Owned Industry*. Cambridge: Cambridge University Press.

Strauss, Anselm (1987) *Qualitative Analysis for Social Science*. New York: Cambridge University Press.

Tan, Justin (2002) Impact of ownership type on environment-strategy linkage and performance; evidence from a transitional economy. *Journal of Management Studies* 39, no. 3: 333–354.

Terwiesch, Christian, Christoph H. Loch and Arnoud De Meyer (2002) Exchanging preliminary information in concurrent engineering: alternative coordination strategies. *Organization Science* 13, no. 4: 402–419.

Thompson, James D. (1967) *Organizations in Action*. New York: McGraw-Hill Book Company.

Weber, Max (1947) *The Theory of Social and Economic Organization*. A. M. Henderson and Talcott Parsons (trans), and Talcott Parsons (ed), New York: The Free Press of Glencoe.

Williamson, Oliver E. (1975) *Markets and Hierarchies*. New York: Free Press.

Wu, Sih-Yen (1989) *Production, Entrepreneurship and Profits*. Oxford: Basil Blackwell.

Yin, Robert K. (1994) *Case Study Research: Design and Methods*. 2nd ed. London: Sage.

Section IV

Foreign Direct Investment and Policy

16
Foreign Direct Investment in Ireland: Policy Implications for Emerging Economies

Peter J. Buckley and Frances Ruane

Introduction

The increasingly important role of multinational enterprises (MNEs) in the global economy is linked to questions of how the foreign direct investment (FDI) they control impacts on overall economic activity in the recipient countries. Of specific interest is the policy context in which such FDI flows into the developing country and how a government can influence the impact of those flows. This paper reviews some of the literature in two key contextual areas, namely, when the host country policy regime promotes FDI selectively, and secondly, where it promotes the creation of industrial clusters. It explores the insights of this literature for the development of the strong MNE sector in the Irish economy and draws lessons from the Irish experience for emerging economies.

Ireland is unusual in the extent to which it has consistently promoted export-platform inward investment into the manufacturing sector for over four decades. Starting in the 1970s, it promoted MNEs selectively, and from the mid-1980s, it has sought to develop strong industrial clusters based on MNE investments in key high-tech sectors. MNEs now account for almost 50% of manufacturing employment and are at the centre of the spatial and sectoral restructuring of the Irish manufacturing sector over the past 20 years.

It is appropriate that the analysis of an open economy should be included in a special issue honouring Jagdish Bhagwati's 70th birthday. Bhagwati's consistent championing of openness (Bhagwati, 1988) includes policy prescriptions to free closed economies (Bhagwati, 1993) and this extends to the liberalisation of inward and outward foreign investment (Bhagwati, 2004). Openness to flows of foreign investment is thus a significant part of Bhagwati's extensive and profound *oeuvre*.

Section 2 examines the literature, which underpins the selective promotion of MNEs, i.e., which places MNE behaviour at the centre of theorising about FDI. It then examines how such policy activity has promoted MNEs on a selective basis in Ireland. Section 3 provides an overview of the literature on clustering and examines how Ireland has attempted to establish industrial clusters in manufacturing. Section 4 draws out some specific policy implications for emerging economies from the Irish policy experience.

Selective promotion of MNE investment

There is a long tradition of analysis of international capital flows in trade theory. Since much of the theory until the 1970s was based on the Heckscher-Ohlin (H-O) model, which implied free mobility of capital across sectors, analysis of capital flows into an economy ultimately amounted to analysing the implications of augmenting/reducing the capital stock in an economy. In a seminal article published in 1966, Vernon used the H-O model as a base to develop his product cycle model which set out to explain the foreign activities of MNEs. His starting point was that, in addition to immobile natural endowments and human resources, the propensity of countries to engage in trade also depended on their capability to upgrade these assets or to create new ones, notably technological capacity (Dunning, 1993). The inflow of capital to less-developed or semi-developed countries makes more investment capital available and thus speeds up development, providing as a by-product badly needed foreign exchange. Moreover, by providing a bundle of well tried and tested managerial skills and technology, FDI enables the host country to exploit its comparative advantages more efficiently. The most important effect on FDI recipient countries, according to this perspective, is that FDI is trade enhancing, in that FDI will enhance production and export capacity. Moreover, the product cycle theory predicts that MNEs assist recipient countries in getting access to international markets, as MNEs help these countries to overcome the significant barrier to entry faced by mature products.

The 'Internalisation School' provided a strong link between MNEs and development. In essence, it argued that, since markets for intermediate products such as technology, capital and supporting services do not function well in many developing countries, FDI may assist developing countries through: the provision of capital, the inflow of technology, the inflow of managerial know-how, and their impact on the creation of efficient markets (Buckley, 1988). All these effects derive essentially from the fact that MNEs provide resources that would not otherwise be available in developing host countries (Blomström, 1991; Blomström and Kokko, 1996a). Since MNEs often have privileged access to capital from the international banking sector (Lipsey, 1999), they can give developing countries access to additional capital that would not otherwise have been available. By providing developing countries with an inflow of investment capital and foreign exchange, MNEs may help adjusting some of the macroeconomic imbalances that frequently are major impediments to growth in developing countries.

One of the most frequently cited intangible competencies transferred through FDI is technology (Blomström et al., 1994; Blomström and Kokko, 1996b). Technology transfer can trigger and speed up economic development, for instance, by facilitating the production of goods with higher value-added content, by increasing exports and improving efficiency. MNEs possess the bulk of all patents worldwide, most of the world's R&D takes place within MNEs, and MNEs possess many of the technologies that are pivotal to economic and industrial development. Often these technological competencies cannot be obtained in the market place (e.g., via licensing) and FDI may therefore be the fastest, most efficient and sometimes only way for developing countries to get access to these competencies. MNEs can also play a central role in the transfer of know-how, knowledge and experience to the local workforce through its employment of indigenous professionals and managers (Blomström et al., 1994).

MNEs as organisations are characterised by a high degree of managerial efficiency arising from training, higher standards of recruitment, effective communication with the parent company and other subsidiaries, and a more global outlook. By virtue of these characteristics, they are able to think strategically on a global scale and to organise complex integrated production networks. The integration into this transnational production network can give developing countries advantages (Blomström et al., 2000). MNEs bring with them improvements in storage, logistics and marketing arrangements leading to cheaper delivery, better quality of products and better information about products to consumers. More importantly, developing countries will be able to use the worldwide marketing outlets of MNEs, selling products where huge marketing investments would otherwise have been required. Hence, the presence of MNEs may assist developing countries in penetrating foreign markets.

In the mid-1950s, Ireland began a process of moving from a long-standing autarchic policy, consisting of high rates of tariff protection and prohibition of foreign direct investment (FDI) towards a policy of free trade and direct encouragement of investments by multinational enterprises.[1] MNEs were incentivised to locate in Ireland through the provision of generous financial supports primarily for capital investment, based on the scale of their incremental export activities, and by giving a tax holiday (up to 15–20 years) on the incremental profits generated by export sales.[2] While the tax holiday was automatically earned once the enterprise exported, the financial supports were discretionary up to certain maxima. However, supports operated effectively as automatic capital grants until the end of the 1960s.

Development of policy in Ireland

Ireland benefited from the increased scale of global FDI in the 1960s, by having established a more fiscally- and financially-welcoming environment than other countries in Europe. While intra-EU FDI has been important,[3] Ireland's entry into the European Community in the 1970s enhanced its attractiveness to extra-EU investors, and particularly US investors seeking production bases within the Common External Tariff area. This attractiveness was consolidated in the early 1990s with the creation of the Single Market.[4] In effect, Ireland benefited from Vernon's (1966) product cycle in becoming a low-cost manufacturing base within Europe for maturing US enterprises, which were already exporting new products to the growing European market. In such an environment Ireland has been an attractive base, with its original tax-holiday incentives designed to make it an export platform.

In the early 1970s policy towards FDI became increasingly more selective, encouraging a pattern of investment into the production of modern high-technology (high-tech) goods, leaving Irish entrepreneurs to operate in the traditional sectors.[5] This selectivity was achieved by proactively seeking out investors in high-tech sectors, namely electronics and pharmaceuticals, and by providing higher rates of financial assistance to enterprises in the 'promoted sectors'.[6] Despite having no tradition in these high-tech sectors, policy makers believed that, with its relatively well-educated population, Ireland could be a competitive production base for MNEs as their low per-unit-value transportation costs made them readily suited to exporting from an island economy.[7]

Furthermore, MNEs in these sectors had no domestic competitors and hence there was no opposition to their increasing employment share in these sectors.

As financial aids became increasingly selective, all individual investments were subjected to systematic project appraisal. This reflected a Hymer-type enterprise approach to FDI on the part of policy makers,[8] and resulted in increased flexibility in the scale and type of assistance given. Because of its enterprise approach, Irish policy, uniquely in Europe and perhaps globally, recognised the diversity of MNEs from the outset of its openness strategy. Irish policy makers adopted a sophisticated system of selectivity for influencing the pattern of MNE investment, comprising four stages: (i) finding niche high-value/volume product markets with European growth potential; (ii) identifying enterprises in these markets, which were already exporting large volumes into Europe likely, in terms of the product cycle, to consider a European production base; (iii) persuading these enterprises to consider Ireland as an investment base; and (iv) agreeing an incentives package which would both secure the investment and ensure maximum benefit to Ireland as a host country. This project-based rather than sectoral approach meant that Irish policy makers recognised the heterogeneity of MNEs and their different potentialities. It also laid the ground for the development of a clustering policy in the 1980s (discussed in Section 3).

Irish policy has continued to evolve since the 1980s, in response both to the evolving MNEs and to limitations set by the EU on the use of incentives to attract industry. These limitations led to the replacement of the original tax holiday and grants policy by a low corporate tax rate on all manufacturing profits, and ultimately all profits, and by providing grants which were trade-neutral. More recently, grants in most areas of the country are now limited to training and R&D expenditure. Furthermore, as suggested by Dunning and Narula (1996), the presence of significant MNEs in Ireland had a positive influence on its economic policies in terms of their being rational and pro-competitive.[9] For example, to avoid factor bias, grant maxima were established in terms of both capital and labour, with repayments required if promised targets were not met.[10] Cost-benefit analysis, albeit in a crude form initially, was used systematically to help avoid the worst policy disasters, in terms of both corruption and bad projects.[11] Project appraisal methods have evolved in the last decade to reflect the dramatic change in Ireland from being a high-unemployment to a full-employment economy.

A parallel with China

China is an attractive location for FDI both because of its rapidly growing domestic market and as a low-cost export platform (Buckley and Meng, 2005). Here we briefly review the export platform issues. Like the early experience of Ireland, the coastal clustering of export-orientated FDI in China exacerbates an already existing regional imbalance (Wei, 2004). This is placing severe strains on infrastructure and human capital requirements – even in labour-rich China, there are many skills already in short supply. There is considerable evidence of positive spillovers to the local economy although these are greater from lower-tech FDI from 'overseas Chinese' than from 'Western' MNEs (Buckley *et al.*, 2002). There is also a convincing argument that FDI is a response to capital market imperfections in the host country (Buckley and Casson, 1976). These imperfections inhibit local private companies from accessing capital and thus choking off domestic entrepreneurs from export markets (Huang, 2003). A further effect is to encourage FDI rather than licensing into China and to bias technology transfer into an MNE internalised route within the, rather than by the, market through licensing to local Chinese (exporting) firms (Buckley, 2004). Capital market liberalisation and extension in China is likely (paradoxically) to both raise domestic firms' exports and to reduce FDI (in favour in inward licensing).

Development of clusters

There have been numerous context-specific theories of the siting of particular value-added activities of enterprises and of geographical distribution of FDI. They include the location component of Vernon's product cycle theory (1966), Knickerbocker's 'follow my leader' theory (1973), which was one of the earliest approaches to analysing the clustering or bunching effect of FDI, and Rugman's risk diversification theory, which suggested that MNEs normally prefer a geographic spread of FDI to having all their eggs in the same basket (1975 and 1979). However, researchers extended, rather than replaced, standard theories of location to encompass cross-border value-added activities. In particular, they embraced new location advantages, such as exchange rates, political risks, inter-country cultural differences, and placed a different value on a variety of variables common to both domestic and international location choices, such as wage levels, demand patterns, policy-related variables, supply capacity and infrastructure. These add-on or re-valued variables could be easily accommodated within the existing analytical theories (Dicken, 1998). This marks off older explanations of the location-specific advantage of nations from those of the ownership-specific advantages of enterprises. (For a complete review see Buckley and De Beule, 2005.) The growth of the knowledge-based global economy and asset-augmenting FDI has led to the emergence of a more dynamic approach to both the logistics of the siting of corporate activities, and to the competitive advantages of nations and regions (Dunning, 1998). Enterprises need to take account not only of the presence and cost of traditional factor endowments, of transport costs, of current demand levels and patterns, and of Marshallian types of agglomerative economies; but also of distance-related transaction costs (Storper and Scott, 1987), of dynamic externalities, knowledge accumulation and interactive learning (Enright, 1990, 1998, 2000; Florida, 1995; Malmberg and Solvell, 1996), of spatially related innovation and technological standards (Antonelli, 1998; Sölvell and Zander, 1998; Frost, 1998), of the increasing dispersion of created assets, and of the need to conclude cross-border augmenting and asset-exploiting alliances (Dunning, 1995, 1998). As such, since 1990, location has been taken up in explaining the stickiness of certain locations in an increasingly slippery world (Markusen, 1994). Theories suggest that enterprises may be drawn to the same locations because proximity generates positive externalities or agglomeration effects. Economists have proposed agglomeration effects in the form of both static (pecuniary) and dynamic (technological) externalities to explain industry localisation (Baptista, 1998). Theoretical attempts to formalise agglomeration effects have focused on three mechanisms that would yield such positive feedback loops: inter-enterprise technological spillovers, specialised labour and intermediate inputs (Marshall, 1890).

A distinction should be made between two broad types of agglomeration economies. One relates to general economies of regional and urban concentration that apply to all enterprises and industries in a particular location. Such *external economies* lead to the emergence of manufacturing belts or metropolitan regions (Porter and Sölvell, 1997). These urbanisation economies do not consist of increased efficiency of the enterprises themselves but of reduced transport and search costs for the customers and, therefore, lead to more customers than the individual enterprise would have been able to attract (Pedersen, 1997). A second type of agglomeration refers to *localisation economies*. As advances in transportation and information obliterate distance, cities and regions face a tougher time attracting and anchoring income-generating activities (Markusen, 1996). Economists, geographers and economic development planners have sought for more than a decade for alternative models of development in which activities are sustained or transformed in ways that maintain relatively high wage levels, social contributions and quality of life. They have searched for 'sticky places' in 'slippery space' (Markusen, 1996), examining the structure and operation of these geographic concentrations of interconnected enterprises and institutions.

One extensively researched formulation is that of the flexibly specialised industrial district. In the original formulation of the industrial district Marshall (1890) envisioned a region where the business structure is comprised of small, locally owned enterprises that make investment and production decisions locally. Scale economies are minimal, forestalling the rise of large enterprises. Within the district, substantial trade is transacted between many small enterprises buying and selling from each other for eventual export from the region. What makes the industrial district so special and vibrant, in Marshall's account, is the existence of a pooled market for workers with specialised skills, the provision of specialised inputs from suppliers and service providers, the relatively rapid flow of business-related knowledge between enterprises, which result in what are now called technological spillovers.

All of these factors are covered by the notion of agglomeration, which suggests that the stickiness of a place resides not in the individual location calculus of enterprises or workers, but in the external economies available to each enterprise from its spatial conjunction with other enterprises and suppliers of services. In Marshall's formulation, it was not necessary that any of these actors should be consciously cooperating with each other, in order for the district to exist and operate as such. But in a more recent adaptation (Piore and Sabel, 1984), based on the phenomenon of successful expansion of mature industries in the so-called 'Third Italy' (Goodman and Bamford, 1989), and extended to other venues in Europe and the United States (Scott, 1988; Storper, 1989; Paniccia, 1998), researchers have argued that concerted efforts to cooperate among district members to improve district-wide competitiveness can increase the stickiness of the district. While agglomeration economies signal external economies passively obtained by enterprises located close to each other, collective efficiency (Schmitz, 1989; Pedersen, 1994) indicates advantages, which enterprises may achieve through active collaboration. Localised information flows, technological spillovers, and specialised pools of knowledge and skills will ensure the revitalisation of these seedbeds of innovation in these clusters. Clusters are considered as networks of production of strongly interdependent enterprises, knowledge-producing agents and customers, linked to each other in a value-adding production chain (OECD, 1999).

However, many of the faster-growing regions of the world are not created by small, locally owned, vertically or horizontally specialised enterprises. There exist regions where a number of key enterprises or facilities act as anchors or hubs to the regional economy. These clusters are dominated by one or several large, locally headquartered enterprises, in one or more sectors, surrounded by smaller and less powerful suppliers. These hub-and-spoke districts thrive on market power and strategy rather than on networking (Gray and Golob, 1996; Markusen, 1996). Yet a third variant of rapidly growing industrial districts may be termed satellite platforms (Markusen, 1996), a congregation of branch plant facilities of externally based enterprises. Tenants of satellite platforms may range from routine assembly functions to relatively sophisticated research. They stand alone, and are detachable spatially from either up- or downstream operations within the same enterprise or from agglomerations of competitors and external suppliers or customers (Glasmeier, 1988).

Another way of discerning different clusters is based on the origin of the industry in a specific location: indigenous or transplanted. Some industries grew up as indigenous industries and were afterwards exposed to a globalising economy of increasing levels of international trade and investment. In the beginning, indigenous (hub-and-spoke) clusters are characterised by tightly linked local enterprises and relatively small numbers of foreign-owned subsidiaries. Over time, the number of foreign subsidiaries in indigenous industries increases because of the globalising economy. More specifically, successful industries attract multinationals that set up or acquire local enterprises to have access to the available strategic assets. Other industries originate as a direct result of the increasing levels of international trade and investment between countries and regions. These transplanted (satellite platform) industries are originally characterised by a limited number of local enterprises and by (relatively many) foreign branch plants that are rather weakly embedded in the local economy. Transplated industries are likely to continue to rely on their parent company or network members for key supplies or core technologies for some time, and will only slowly develop strong 'local' ties, set up R&D units and grow to become clusters. Alternatively, the virtuous circle of economic development by embedding foreign plants in the local economy does not materialise and the agglomeration of enterprises remains a satellite district. One would expect to find the relatively high value-adding subsidiaries in industry cluster locations, because they are attractive locations for foreign-owned subsidiaries, both in terms of the opportunities for learning and knowledge transfer and in terms of the specialised inputs and labour they provide. They can be seen as 'tapping into' the sources of knowledge and ideas, and scientific and technical talent which are embedded in cutting-edge regional innovation complexes (Florida, 1995). There will obviously also be foreign subsidiaries in non-cluster locations, but they are more likely to be of the market-seeking type or resource-seeking type (cheap factors of production), rather than the higher value-adding subsidiaries in industry clusters.

These contemporary economic events suggest that the nature and composition of a country or region's comparative advantage, which has always been based on the possession of a unique set of immobile natural resources and capabilities, is now more geared to a distinctive and non-imitable set of location-bound created assets and the presence of strong indigenous enterprises with which foreign MNEs can form alliances to exploit or complement their own core competencies (Dunning, 1996). Research (Porter, 1996; Rosecrance, 1996; UNCTAD, 1997) is suggesting that nation states are not only becoming increasingly dependent on the cross-border activities of their own and foreign-based corporations for their economic prosperity, but that the competitiveness of these corporations is increasingly becoming fashioned by the institutional framework in which they operate. In particular, both nation states and sub-national authorities are recognising the need to provide the appropriate and, where necessary, customised factor inputs, both for their own enterprises to generate the ownership-specific assets consistent with the demands of world markets, and for foreign subsidiaries to engage in the kind of value-adding activities which advances both the technological efficiency and dynamic comparative advantage of the immobile assets within their jurisdiction (Porter, 1994; Peck, 1996; Dunning, 1998).

While there was always a spatial dimension to Irish industrial policy, with financial inducements to MNEs to locate in areas of high unemployment and depopulation, the attempt to build sectoral and spatial clusters only began seriously in the 1980s, and was centred in the two key high-tech sectors, namely, electronics and chemicals/ pharmaceuticals. In terms of the electronics sector, the development of clusters was a natural extension of the policy of sectoral selectivity described above; it built on Ireland's reputation for being pro-MNE and on its existing network of relationships with MNEs. The strategy was to build the MNE electronics sector both vertically and horizontally, so that it would generate agglomeration economies through shared input (especially skilled labour) markets and product linkages, which were increasingly based on tailored inputs.[12] Since the domestic market was not important, Ireland was effectively building an electronics cluster to service the European market (O'Donnellan, 1994).[13]

The approach taken in the electronics sector policy was to attract some key investments into Ireland and then leveraging further MNEs to locate on the basis that these key enterprises had chosen Ireland as a base in Europe. In the 1980s four key segments were identified: microprocessors, software, computer products and printers.[14] Ireland succeeded in attracting the two key global enterprises in microprocessors and software, namely Intel and Microsoft, both of which were dominant in their respective market segments. The computer products segment was much less concentrated internationally and Ireland set out to attract a range of companies in that segment of the market, the most significant of which were Dell, Compaq and Gateway.[15] With the location of Intel and Microsoft, and subsequently Hewlett-Packard in the printing sector, Ireland effectively had an electronics hub and the spokes were quickly populated by dozens of smaller electronics and software enterprises, all of which wanted to interconnect with these key industrial leaders.[16]

As Krugman (1997) pointed out, the Irish economy is a significant beneficiary from the process of clustering, and also of some good luck. But part of this luck was 'made', in the consistency and enterprise-centred approach going back over 25 years previously, and the management of the process of rapid cluster building by policy makers. For example, policy has been highly active in addressing skill needs (including specialised skills) and in managing a good HR environment for incoming investors.[17] Irish education and training policy was also coordinated to ensure that a supply of skilled labour suited to the sector, so that labour costs remained competitive. Several studies have shown the extent of linkages between different enterprises in this sector, which are clustered primarily in two locations: the greater Dublin area and Limerick.[18] The success of winning Microsoft, Intel and Dell was evident in that the average share of US FDI in electronics going to Ireland rose to 27% between 1994 and 2001,[19] compared with a rate of less than 12% for Irish manufacturing as a whole.[20]

There are two other sectors in which industrial clusters have been created. The first is the chemicals and pharmaceuticals sector, which now has plants from most of the world's largest enterprises in this sector. Because of their environmental and resource requirements, enterprises in this sector are much less footloose than those in the electronics sector, and hence the growth of a spatial cluster grew naturally out of the original location of a small number of key plants in the Cork area in the 1970s. In contrast to the electronics sector, there is little evidence of production linkages between the enterprises, and the cluster's development is centred on the natural and built environment, which makes production cost-efficient in that area. The other sector is medical devices, which is spatially centred in the west of Ireland (where significant grants can still be awarded under EU law). This differs from electronics and chemicals/pharmaceuticals in that it is a less concentrated sector and the average enterprise size is much smaller. The skilled labour requirements of the sector match Irish supply, and IDA Ireland (Ireland's FDI promotion agency) has pursued the same leverage approach as it pursued in electronics.

Gleeson *et al.* (2005), analysing the sectoral specialisation and spatial concentration of MNEs in Ireland, argue that since spatial choice is driven entirely by production considerations, MNEs are likely to respond positively to location incentives. Their entropy indices for enterprises and employment for 1985–2001 indicate that both sectoral specialisation and spatial concentration have increased, particularly in the high-tech sectors, which is consistent with MNEs beginning to cluster. They find high correlation coefficients for spatial concentration and low and falling coefficients for sectoral specialisation between MNEs and LEs at county level, suggesting little evidence of MNE-LE clustering to-date. This may reflect the limited incentives for export-driven MNEs to interact with LEs in manufacturing, especially as sub-supply markets increasingly globalise.[21] Thus MNE clusters do not necessarily generate a local LE cluster. These results are broadly consistent with those of Barrios *et al.* (2002), but less so with Barrios *et al.* (2003) who find that MNEs have had an impact on the location choices of LEs.[22]

A parallel with India

India is a diverse country. Its pattern of inward FDI reflects this diversity (Balasubramanyam and Mahambare, 2004). Like Ireland, India had a switch from a protectionist (and dirigiste) regime to a more open one, this process beginning with the Indian reforms of 1991. The most celebrated FDI-centred cluster in India is the software cluster in Bangalore, containing a quarter of the whole Indian software industry (Balasubramanyam and Balasubramanyam, 2000). The Bangalore software cluster conforms to expectations on the rationale for clusters – external (to the firm) economies are present in the creation and circulation of human capital. The cluster has the support of specialist public institutions such as universities and colleges, and social capital exists in the form of publicly available amenities centred on the needs of executives in the industry. This attracts both expatriates and returning Indian migrants to augment the pool of available skilled labour and creates a locationally fixed endowment into which MNEs can participate through FDI or contract-based modes of entry. The role of education policies has been central to the creation of the cluster and it demonstrates the type of endogenous endowment which emerging countries can establish. The very distinctiveness of the Bangalore cluster suggests that its replication is not easy. Barriers to such clusters in other emerging countries (and indeed in the rest of India) include the need for infrastructural support, reductions in red tape, corruption and excessive bureaucracy, lack of an indigenous skill pool, psychic barriers (including local business practices) and open entry and access. The case of Ireland demonstrates the need for continuity and consistency of government policy to support and nurture clusters and emerging clusters.

Implications for FDI policy in emerging economies

There are some very strong similarities between the situation of some of the emerging economies today and Ireland's situation in the late 1960s and early 1970s. Although it was unpopular to say so at the time, Ireland was in fact a semi-developed economy in the early 1970s, exhibiting the characteristics of both developed and less-developed economies. Membership of the EC immediately propelled the economy into a situation where the dominant thrust was the 'developed economy' one, and without a doubt, the inflow of MNE investment (especially from the USA) played a crucial role in Ireland's 'catch-up' with the rest of its EC partners.[23] The Single European Market (SEM) consolidated Ireland's role as a manufacturing base for high-tech, low-weight products within the EU to grow rapidly.

For emerging economies that have no strategic power in trade, Ireland's strategy has some potential relevance. If such economies can accept the lesser control that being 'open' implies, can see the potential benefits of MNEs, and can plausibly create export platform bases, Ireland's portfolio approach, a mixture of sectoral concentration and diversification, has much to commend it. And it also points to recognising that industrial restructuring is continuous and not once-off, as Vernon's product cycle model, means that production bases will change over time. The fact that Ireland is a winner of certain types of investment at one point in time does not guarantee its being a winner for this type of investment in the long term.

Ireland's exceptional success in attracting MNE investment in the past decade is at least in part due to its consistently positive stance towards MNEs over four decades. This was possible because of political consensus regarding the benefits of FDI, and by MNEs not generally competing with LEs on the domestic market. This consensus is now under threat for the first time because (a) Ireland's corporate tax rate strategy is under more pressure in the EU context; (b) with the economy close to full employment, the appropriateness of the current rate of corporate tax (12.5%) is being debated, and (c) two new political parties (Green Party and Sinn Fein) have indicated that they would favour higher tax rates.[24]

Ireland's strategy of developing a long-term business relationship with MNEs means that they see government as assisting rather than constraining them. For example, Enterprise Ireland is now supporting the development of a globally focused sub-supply industry, recognising that 'local outsourcing' by MNEs is much less realistic today than it was for Ireland in the 1960s and 1970s.[25] The Irish experience suggests that it takes time for MNEs to acquire local suppliers, and active policy that can reduce the 'learning phase' about local supply may increase the speed at which linkages occur and assist in building up LEs. Support of supply networks of LEs (which has only recently become a part of Irish policy) would also clearly have potential; however, this is costly in terms of time and effort.[26]

This analysis of Ireland's experience with FDI suggests several implications for policy lessons for emerging economies.

- Host countries can never stop being pro-active.
    MNEs and their FDI policies are constantly evolving and are capable of a rapid response to changing conditions anywhere in the global economy. There can be no room for complacency in host country policy which must evolve both with the changing strategies of MNEs and location-specific advantages, which must be nurtured.

- A package of incentives is superior to a single incentive.
  In general, surveys of MNEs show that they do not rate single incentives highly, even the most generous tax breaks. What is crucial is the whole package of incentives and environment that constitutes the host country 'offer'. Wider aspects such as the ease of doing business are more important than single incentives.
- Host countries should adopt an enterprise-centred approach.
  It is essential that host country policy makers understand the strategies of MNEs, not just local and regional, but also global. There is a great danger that the offer will be based on what the host country has, rather than what the MNE needs. Host countries need to focus on what immobile resources they can offer which combine with the MNE's mobile resources to achieve synergy.
- Sectoral direction requires project selectivity.
  Many emerging countries are insufficiently selective in attempting to attract MNEs. The example of Ireland shows that successful strategies based on clustering and export platform require sectoral selectivity which in turn requires some degree of project selectivity.
- Project selectivity in turn requires:
  - A careful cost-benefit analysis
  - Strategic bargaining
  - Strong governance to avoid corruption.

  There are dangers of corruption in selectivity. A transparent cost-benefit analysis is required to minimise this danger. There will inevitably be bargaining between the host country and the MNE and again strong governance of this process is crucial.
- Policy consistency matters to investors – thus policy should evolve systematically and not add to uncertainty.
  It is the certainty of policy as much as its effect that attracts inward FDI. Rapid switches and changes of direction are harmful. A long-term reputation as a secure base is the fundamental necessity in attracting FDI.
- Performance-based incentives, both fiscal and financial, can combine well.
  In attracting FDI it is essential that both the host country and the MNE perform well. This is best secured by incentives to the MNE designed to ensure that the outcome benefits the host country. Fiscal and financial incentives together need to be designed in line with projected benefits to the host country be they technology, output or export related.

- Projects need to be monitored.
  The corollary of performance-based incentives is that outcomes must be monitored. Clear and transparent goals are required and reporting requirements need to be carefully specified well in advance.
- Limitations of local linkage potential in global production chains.
  A presumption that successful MNE clusters will inevitably lead to linkages with local enterprises cannot be presumed, especially as production supply chains become increasingly global.

Notes

1. It began by announcing its intentions to move progressively towards free trade, starting with the Anglo-Irish Free Trade Agreement in 1965, and culminating in the process of joining the European Community in 1973.
2. The standard tax on income from export sales was around 50% prior to the introduction of the tax holiday, and this rate continued to apply to profits on all domestic sales and pre-incentive export sales levels.
3. German FDI was especially important in the 1960s and 1970s as shortages of labour in Germany in the late 1960s were leading to rising unit wage costs.
4. The reduction in non-tariff barriers was particularly important in sectors like pharmaceuticals as it allowed consolidation of production in the EU, which has hitherto been prevented by country-specific regulations.
5. For example, see Bradley (2004).
6. This amounted to recognition that the food-processing sector, which used the outputs of the large agricultural sector, would not be a key growth sector in the economy.
7. These products are often referred to as 'weightless products'.
8. Hymer (1960) had noted that 'FDI involved the transfer of a package of resources, such as technology, managements, skills, entrepreneurship and not just capital'.
9. An example of this is the telecoms markets in the 1990s. The Irish government sought and got a two-year derogation from deregulating the market, but it deregulated earlier because of pressure from MNEs in the electronics and software sectors.
10. This took some time to happen but has been fully in operation in the past ten years.
11. For example, Ireland turned down the DeLorean car project which the UK government financed with huge losses in Belfast.
12. The development of individually specified personal computers in the late 1990s strengthened these clustering effects.
13. Undoubtedly, Ireland came to benefit from Knickerbocker's (1973) 'follow my leader' theory as US investment piled into Europe in advance of the Single European Market.
14. As networking became increasingly important in the late 1990s, Ireland attracted two of the key players in that sector, namely, Cisco and Lucent.

15 It was recognised that some of these would not survive as this part of the industry consolidated and a large Gateway plant closed in the early part of this decade.
16 Had Ireland not won these projects, it would be an entirely different economy today!
17 The state agency involved in MNE promotion, IDA Ireland, helps new entrants to recruit a good mixture of new and experienced staff, so that no existing enterprise is at risk of losing all its key players to a new arrival.
18 See, for example, Görg and Ruane (2000, 2001).
19 Source: US Department of Commerce, Bureau of Economic Analysis 'U.S. Direct Investment Abroad: Balance of Payments and Direct Investment Position Data'. Data available from http://www.bea.doc.gov/bea/di/di1usdbal.htm
20 A recent paper, Görg (2000) analyses foreign direct investment flows between Ireland and the US, and finds that outward investment from Ireland is primarily in the non-traded sector in contrast with inward investment which is in the traded sectors.
21 The globalisation of sub-supply markets has significant implications for traditional Hirschmantype linkages.
22 This difference may be accounted for by differences in the time period covered.
23 See, for example, Gray (1997) and Braunerhjelm et al. (2000).
24 Their approach is ideologically rather than economically based and, if in a coalition context, either could add to pressure to raise the corporate tax rate.
25 This is becoming easier today than in the past through web technology – and investment in a good system of information provision would seem to have considerable potential as part of any linkage strategy over the coming years.
26 It is often discussed in the Irish case but progress has been slow. This may reflect the historically low manufacturing base. See Cooke (1998) and O'Doherty (1998).

References

Antonelli, C. (1998) 'The Dynamics of Localized Technological Changes. The Interaction between Factor Costs Inducement, Demand Pull and Schumpeterian Rivalry', *Economics of Innovation and New Technology*, 6, 2–3, 97–120.
Balasubramanyam, V.N. and A. Balasubramanyam (2000) 'The Software Cluster in Bangalore', in J.H. Dunning (ed.), *Regions, Globalization and the Knowledge-based Economy* (Oxford: Oxford University Press).
Balasubramanyam, V.N. and V. Mahambare (2004) 'Foreign Direct Investment in India', in Y.A. Wei and V.N. Balasubramanyam (eds), *Foreign Direct Investment – Six Country Case Studies* (Cheltenham: Edward Elgar).
Baptista, R. (1998) 'Clusters, Innovation, and Growth', in P. Swann, M. Prevezer and D. Stout (eds), *The Dynamics of Industrial Clustering: International Comparisons in Computing and Biotechnology* (Oxford: Oxford University Press) 13–51.

Barrios, S., L. Bertinelli and E. Strobl (2003) 'Multinationals and Local Indigenous Development', CORE Discussion Paper 2003/05.
Barrios, S., H. Görg and E. Strobl (2002) 'Multinationals' Location Choice, Agglomeration Economies and Public Incentives', GEP Research Paper 02/33.
Bhagwati, J.N. (1988) *Protectionism* (Cambridge, MA: MIT Press).
Bhagwati, J.N. (1993) *India in Transition: Freeing the Economy* (Oxford: Oxford University Press).
Bhagwati, J.N. (2004) *In Defence of Globalisation* (Oxford: Oxford University Press).
Blomström, M. (1991) 'Host Country Benefits of Foreign Investment', in D.G. McFetridge (ed.), *Foreign Investment, Technology and Economic Growth* (Calgary: University of Calgary Press).
Blomström, M. and A. Kokko (1996a) *The Impact of Foreign Investment on Host Countries: A Review of the Empirical Evidence* (Washington, DC: World Bank).
Blomström, M. and A. Kokko (1996b) *Multinational Corporations and Spillovers* (London: Centre for Economic Policy Research).
Blomström, M., A. Kokko and M. Zejan (1994) 'Host Country Competition, Labor Skills and Technology Transfer by Multinationals', *Weltwirtschaftliches Archiv*, **130**, 3, 521–33.
Blomström, M., A. Kokko and M. Zejan (2000) *Foreign Direct Investment, Firm and Host Country Strategies* (London: Macmillan).
Bradley, J. (2004) 'Changing the Rules: How the Failures of the 1950s Forced a Transition in Economic Policy-making', *Administration*, **52**, 1, 92–107.
Braunerhjelm, P., R. Faini, V. Norman, F. Ruane and P. Seabright (2000) *Integration and the Regions of Europe: How the Right Policies can Prevent Polarisation* (London: Centre of Economic Policy Research).
Buckley, P.J. (1988) 'The Limits of Explanation: Testing the Internalisation Theory of the Multinational Enterprise', *Journal of International Business Studies*, **19**, 2, 181–93.
Buckley, P.J. (1996) 'The Role of Management in International Business Theory: A Meta-analysis and Integration of the Literature on International Business and International Management', *Management International Review*, **36**, 1, 7–54.
Buckley, P.J. (2004) 'The Role of China in the Global Strategy of Multinational Enterprises', *Journal of Chinese Economic and Business Studies*, **2**, 1, 1–25.
Buckley, P.J. and M. Casson (1976) *The Future of the Multinational Enterprise* (London: Macmillan).
Buckley, P.J. and F. De Beule (2005) 'The Research Agenda in International Business: Past, Present and Future', in L. Cuyvers and F. De Beule (eds.), *Transnational Corporations and Economic Development: From Internationalisation to Globalisation* (London: Palgrave).
Buckley, P.J. and C. Meng (2005) 'The Strategy of Foreign Invested Manufacturing Enterprises in China: Export Orientated and Market Orientated FDI Revisited', *Journal of Chinese Economic and Business Studies*, **3**, 2, 111–31.
Buckley, P.J., J. Clegg and C. Wang (2002) 'The Impact of Inward FDI on the Performance of Chinese Manufacturing Firms', *Journal of International Business Studies*, **33**, 4, 637–55.
Cooke, P. (1998) 'Enterprise Support Policies in Dynamic European Regions: Policy Implications for Ireland', in National Economic and Social Council

(ed.), *Sustaining Competitive Advantage: Proceedings of NESC Seminar* (Dublin: NESC) 68–88.
Dicken, P. (1998) *Global Shift: Transforming the World Economy* (London: Paul Chapman).
Dunning, J.H. (1988) *Explaining International Production* (London: Unwin Hyman).
Dunning, J.H. (1993) *Multinational Enterprise and the Global Economy* (Workingham: Addison-Wesley).
Dunning, J.H. (1995) 'The Role of Foreign Direct Investment in a Globalizing Economy', *Banca Nazionale del Lavoro Quarterly Review*, **48**, 193, 125–44.
Dunning, J.H. (1996) 'The Geographical Sources of the Competitiveness of Firms: Some Results of a New Survey', *Transnational Corporations*, **5**, 3, 1–29.
Dunning, J.H. (1998) 'Globalization, Technological Change and the Spatial Organization of Economic Activity', in A.D. Chandler, Jr., P. Hagström and Ö. Sölvell (eds), *The Dynamic Firm: The Role of Technology, Strategy, Organisation and Regions* (Oxford: Oxford University Press).
Dunning, J.H. and R. Narula (1996) *Foreign Direct Investment and Governments: Catalysts for Economic Restructuring* (London and New York: Routledge).
Enright, M. (1990) *Geographic Concentration and Industrial Organization* (Cambridge, MA: Harvard University Press).
Enright, M.J. (1998) 'Regional Clusters and Firm Strategy', in A.D. Chandler, Jr., P. Hagström and Ö. Sölvell (eds), *The Dynamic Firm: The Role of Technology, Strategy, Organization and Regions* (Oxford: Oxford University Press).
Enright, M.J. (2000) 'The Globalization of Competition and the Localization of Competitive Advantage: Policies Towards Regional Clustering', in N. Hood and S. Young (eds), *The Globalization of Multinational Enterprise Activity and Economic Development* (London: Macmillan).
Florida, R. (1995) 'Toward the Learning Region', *Futures*, **27**, 5, 527–36.
Frost, T.S. (1998) 'The Geographic Sources of Innovation in the Multinational Enterprise: US Subsidiaries and Host Country Spillovers: 1980–1990', *Sloan School of Management* (Cambridge, MA: Massachusetts Institute of Technology).
Glasmeier, A. (1988) 'Factors Governing the Development of High Tech Industry Agglomerations: A Tale of Three Cities', *Regional Studies*, **22**, 4, 287–301.
Goodman, E. and J. Bamford (1989) *Small Firms and Industrial Districts in Italy* (London and New York: Routledge).
Görg, H. (2000) 'Outward Direct Investment from Ireland to the US: Evidence and Further Issues', *Journal of the Statistical and Social Inquiry Society of Ireland*, **30**, 33–52.
Görg, H. and F. Ruane (2000) 'An Analysis of Backward Linkages in the Irish Electronics Sector', *Economic and Social Review*, **31**, 3, 215–35.
Görg, H. and F. Ruane (2001) 'Multinational Companies and Linkages: Panel-data Evidence for the Irish Electronics Sector', *International Journal of the Economics of Business*, **18**, 1, 1–18.
Gray, A.W. (ed.) (1997) *International Perspectives on the Irish Economy* (Dublin: Indecon).
Gray, M. and E. Golob (1996) 'Big Firms, Long Arms, Wide Shoulders: The "Hub-and-Spoke" Industrial District in the Seattle Region', *Regional Studies*, **30**, 7, 651–66.

Huang, Y. (2003) *Selling China: Foreign Direct Investment During the Reform Era* (Cambridge: Cambridge University Press).
Hymer, S.H. (1960) *The International Operations of National Firms* (Cambridge, MA: MIT Press).
Knickerbocker, F.T. (1973) *Oligopolistic Reaction and the Multinational Enterprise* (Cambridge, MA: Harvard University Press).
Krugman, P.R. (1997) 'Good News from Ireland: A Geographical Perspective', in A.W. Gray (ed.), *International Perspectives on the Irish Economy* (Dublin: Indecon) 38–53.
Malmberg, A. and Ö. Sölvell (1996) 'Spatial Clustering, Local Accumulation of Knowledge and Firm Competitiveness', *Geografiska Annaler*, **78**, 2, 85–97.
Markusen, A. (1994) 'Studying Regions by Studying Firms', *The Professional Geographer*, **46**, 4, 477–90.
Markusen, A. (1996) 'Sticky Places in Slippery Space: A Typology of Industrial Districts', *Economic Geography*, **72**, 3, 293–313.
Marshall, A. (1890) *Principles of Economics* (London: Macmillan).
O'Doherty, D. (1998) 'Networking in Ireland – Policy Responses', in National Economic and Social Council (ed.), *Sustaining Competitive Advantage: Proceedings of NESC Seminar* (Dublin: NESC) 89–115.
O'Donnellan, N. (1994) 'The Presence of Porter's Sectoral Clustering in Irish Manufacturing', *Economic and Social Review*, **25**, 3, 221–32.
OECD (1999) *Boosting Innovation: The Cluster Approach* (Paris: OECD).
Paniccia, I. (1998) 'One, a Hundred, Thousands of Industrial Districts. Organizational Variety in Local Networks of Small and Medium-sized Enterprises', *Organization Studies*, **19**, 4, 667–700.
Peck, F.W. (1996) 'Regional Development and the Production of Space: The Role of Infrastructure in the Attraction of New Inward Investment', *Environment and Planning A*, **28**, 2, 327–39.
Pedersen, P.O. (1994) 'Clusters of Enterprises within Systems of Production and Distribution: Collective Efficiency, Transaction Costs and the Economies of Agglomeration (Copenhagen: Centre for Development Research).
Pedersen, P.O. (1997) 'Clusters of Enterprises within Systems of Production and Distribution: Collective Efficiency, Transaction Costs and the Economies of Agglomeration', in M.P. Van Dijk and R. Rabellotti (eds), *Enterprise Clusters and Networks in Developing Countries* (London: Cass).
Piore, M.J. and C.F. Sabel (1984) *The Second Industrial Divide* (New York: Basic Books).
Porter, M.E. (1994) 'The Role of Location in Competition', *Journal of the Economics of Business*, **1**, 1, 35–39.
Porter, M.E. (1996) 'Competitive Advantage, Agglomeration Economies, and Regional Policy', *International Regional Science Review*, **19**, 1–2, 85–94.
Porter, M.E. and Ö. Sölvell (1997) 'The Role of Geography in the Process of Innovation and the Sustainable Competitive Advantage of Firms', in A.D. Chandler, Jr., P. Hagström and Ö. Sölvell (eds), *The Dynamic Firm: The Role of Technology, Strategy, Organizations, and Regions* (Oxford: Oxford University Press).
Rosecrance, R. (1996) 'The Rise of the Virtual State', *Foreign Affairs*, **75**, 4, 45–61.
Ruane, F. and J. Sutherland (2005) 'Export Characteristics of Irish Manufacturing Industry' forth-coming in *The World Economy*.

Rugman, A.M. (1975) 'Motives for Foreign Investment: The Market Imperfections and Risk Diversification Hypothesis', *Journal of World Trade Law*, **9** (September–October), 567–73.

Rugman, A.M. (1979) *International Diversification and the Multinational Enterprise* (Lexington, MA: Lexington Books).

Schmitz, H. (1989) *Flexible Specialization. A New Paradigm of Small-scale Industrialization* (Sussex: Institute of Development Studies).

Scott, A.J. (1988) 'Flexible Production Systems and Regional Development: The Rise of New Industrial Space in North America and Western Europe', *International Journal of Urban and Regional Research*, **12**, 2, 171–86.

Sölvell, Ö. and I. Zander (1998), 'International Diffusion of Knowledge: Isolating Mechanisms and the Role of the MNE', in A.D. Chandler, Jr., P. Hagström and Ö. Sölvell (eds), *The Dynamic Firm: The Role of Technology, Strategy, Organization and Regions* (Oxford: Oxford University Press).

Storper, M. (1989) 'The Transition to Flexible Specialisation in the U.S. Film Industry: External Economies, the Division of Labour, and the Crossing of Industrial Divides', *Cambridge Journal of Economics*, **13**, 2, 273–305.

Storper, M. and A. Scott (1987) 'The Wealth of Regions. Market Forces and Policy Imperatives in Local and Global Context', *Futures*, **27**, 5, 505–26.

UNCTAD (1997) *World Investment Report, 1997: Transnational Corporations, Market Structure and Competition Policy* (Geneva: United Nations).

Vernon, R. (1966) 'International Investment and International Trade in the Product Cycle', *Quarterly Journal of Economics*, **80**, 2, 190–207.

Wei, Y.A. (2004) 'Foreign Direct Investment in China', in Y.A. Wei and V.N. Balasubramanyam (eds), *Foreign Direct Investment – Six Country Case Studies* (Cheltenham: Edward Elgar).

17
A Simple and Flexible Dynamic Approach to Foreign Direct Investment Growth: The Canada–United States Relationship in the Context of Free Trade

Peter J. Buckley, Jeremy Clegg, Nicolas Forsans and Kevin T. Reilly

Introduction

In the post-war period the world economy has seen the rise and expansion of regional trading blocs and regional economic integration.[1] The prime example has been the evolution of the European Union since the early 1950s; also significant has been the creation of the Asia-Pacific Economic Cooperation Area in 1989, and development of the North American free trade area, dating also from 1989. This paper will focus on the Canada-United States relationship. While the intentions of the partners to a free trade agreement are clear in the case of trade, the effect on foreign direct investment (FDI) is ambiguous. The question this paper addresses is that of how the North American free trade agreements have affected US foreign investment behaviour in Canada.

The creation of a free trade area creates two classes of foreign investor: those inside and those outside the area. The existing literature suggests that firms outside the area will be motivated by import substitution, while those inside are likely to pursue the rationalisation of production (see Buckley *et al.*, 2003). We have narrowed the scope of this paper to examine only the central relationship between the free trade agreement partners, so leaving the study of outsiders' behaviour to future research. Further, we restrict ourselves to US FDI into Canada, for the years 1955 to 2000, for two reasons. First, in order to identify clearly any impact on FDI from the creation of a free trade area requires that a stable policy environment had previously been maintained for a significant period of time. By way of contrast, the constantly changing rules and membership that has characterised the

European Union would make it difficult to identify the effect of any particular policy shift. Canada and the USA have signed two free trade agreements since 1987: the Canada-US Free Trade Agreement (CUSFTA), implemented on 1 January, 1989, and the North American Free Trade Agreement (NAFTA) implemented on 1 January, 1994. However, it is the first agreement that is the critical one for setting the new policy environment in terms of rules on investment. As Globerman and Shapiro (1999, pp. 517–18) point out, while the NAFTA did introduce changes to investment rules, especially in the area of transparency, the major shift in Canada's policy occurred in 1989 with the first agreement. This stability and 12 years of post-change data opens up the possibility of observing significant effects.

Second, the Canada-US relationship is one of the most important in the world in terms of both trade and investment and level of economic integration. Between 1960 and 2000 the USA exported an average of 18% of its total to Canada. Moreover, the variance of this trade over the period was quite low, with the highest proportion observed being 20.9% in 1976, with the lowest at 15.7% in 1991.[2] This trading relationship is the largest between any two countries in the world (Department of Foreign Affairs, 2003). From 1966 to 2000 United States foreign direct investment (FDI) into Canada fell from 30% of total US FDI abroad to just 10%. However, this was a period of geographical diversification for US multinationals so that, even in 2000, only the United Kingdom received a higher proportion of US FDI than Canada.[3] Further, this decline must be seen in the context of the sectoral distribution of FDI. In 1998 Canada hosted more investment by American multinational firms in the manufacturing and wholesale-trade sectors than any other country, including the United Kingdom (Hanson et al., 2001, p. 47).

This loss of share of US FDI has encouraged both commentators (e.g. Hufbauer and Schoot, 2004, p. 3) and the Canadian Government itself (Department of Foreign Affairs, 2004, p. 29) to believe that, in all likelihood, the signing of the two free trade agreements between the two countries had little or no effect on US FDI into Canada. The possibility that the free trade agreements might have exerted an ambiguous impact on FDI is opened up by the likelihood of the rationalisation of FDI post-FTA. The United Nations Transnational Corporations and Management Division (1993) noted that, in the context of the European Union, the effect of regional economic integration can be positive or negative on FDI, for any or all of the members of a trading bloc. The rationalisation of production arising from the elimination of tariffs within a free trade area can result either in a member state gaining or losing FDI from its partner(s) in the agreement.[4] A free trade agreement represents a significant change in the policy environment in which firms are operating, and should be expected to affect their foreign investment behaviour. This discussion suggests that the key question is not whether the creation of regional trading blocs affect FDI but how, i.e. is the effect positive or negative? The academic literature to date comes down in favour of evidence that the two free trade agreements between Canada and the USA have had a positive effect on FDI in Canada (e.g., Globerman and Shapiro, 1999). The aim of this paper is to contribute to the level of scientific understanding on the role of free trade agreements as a form of regional integration in influencing the foreign investment behaviour of multinational firms.

Research on the determinants of FDI has focused on two different measures of the firm's foreign involvement: the stock (or level) of FDI and the flow (or growth) of FDI. As is now well recognised (Globerman and Shapiro, 1999), there are severe statistical problems in modelling the level of FDI. Generally the series is not stationary, and inferences from an econometric model in this context are misleading at best. In this paper we examine the growth rate of the stock of FDI, thus removing the econometric problems inherent in analysing the stock of FDI. This approximates to studying the flow of US FDI into Canada between 1955 and 2000.

In our empirical implementation we also introduce two innovations in the modelling of foreign investment to the existing literature. Our first is to allow for a simple dynamic structure to the growth in FDI. The previous literature, in both the levels and flows estimations, uses a static framework allowing only current values of the independent variables to determine current values of the dependent variable. This approach fails to recognise the possibility of lags in the investment process, particularly between the decision to invest and its implementation. Any model of FDI should recognise that the growth we observe today may be a function of the value of determinants in an earlier period. The simplest way of allowing for this structure is to utilise a distributed lag set-up in the econometric model, which we implement.

It is customary for a policy innovation to be modelled as an intercept shift in the estimating equation (e.g., Buckley *et al.*, 2003; Clegg and Scott-Green, 1999; Globerman and Shapiro, 1999). This assumes the policy has no effect on the standard behavioural parameters that appear in these equations, such as those for economic growth and the exchange rate. Yet, as Lucas (1976) has pointed out in the forecasting context, we should always view the behavioural parameters of an econometric model as conditional on the existing policy environment.It follows that changes in the environment can result in changes in behavioural parameters. Therefore, our econometric model should allow for the possibility that the introduction of free trade between the USA and Canada might change the parameters of the FDI equation. In this paper we introduce a methodology, structural break analysis, to allow for such changes in explaining the growth in FDI.

The next section reviews the existing literature on the determinants of FDI, with a focus on the flows or growth literature, while introducing our empirical innovations. In particular, it focuses on the results obtained from three of the variables that we use: growth in gross domestic product, changes in the real exchange rate, and changes in the relative interest rate. We examine the time-series pattern of US FDI into Canada between 1955 and 2000. We show that, at the time of the first free trade agreement, the time series pattern of both the level and growth in US FDI changed significantly. We then demonstrate that while the levels series is non-stationary, the growth series is stationary, so we can model the latter series within an econometric framework.

In Section 3 we present the results of our estimation and our overarching conclusion that the introduction of free trade between Canada and the USA resulted in a significant change in the parametrisation of the US-Canadian FDI growth relationship. In particular we document that, prior to 1989, this relationship is best viewed as a static one, in which US investors' decisions are responses only to current growth in the Canadian economy and to current exchange rate movements. A reasonable interpretation of this pre-free trade result is that, for the most part during this period (1955–1988), the motive of US FDI in Canada was to service the existing Canadian market. The parameter estimates on growth in the economy suggests a unitary relationship and our failure to find any role for an interest rate differential variable supports this interpretation. In the post-free trade period (1989–2000) the relationship becomes dynamic in that lagged growth and the interest rate spread become significant determinants along with current growth, changes in the exchange rate and, for the first time, the current interest rate differential. These post-free trade results are evidence that greater product market and financial integration arose between the two economies as a result of the agreement in 1989.

Our concluding section will summarise our results.

Inward foreign direct investment flows and free trade: the US-Canada relationship

In the period 1955–2000 the most important shift in trade and investment policy came with the implementation of the first free trade agreement between the two countries on 1 January, 1989. This was expanded to include Mexico in 1994.[5] The goals of both treaties are relatively limited: the free flow of goods and services and minimisation of the barriers that affect the flow of investment across borders. In particular, as Article 1102, Clause 1, of the North American Free Trade Agreement states: *Each Party shall accord to investors of another Party treatment no less favorable than that it accords, in like circumstances, to its own investors with respect to the establishment, acquisition, expansion, management, conduct, operation and sale or other disposition of investments.* This is the national treatment clause, which requires that US multinational firms be treated just as Canadian firms in terms of Canadian government investment policy. The major exceptions allowed concern the areas of financial services and culture and media. While the North American treaty in 1994 expanded the geographic area covered by the agreement to include Mexico, the fundamental policy environment between the USA and Canada with respect to trade and investment rules has remained stable since the implementation of the 1989 treaty.[6] Stability is critical in order to identify any effect on FDI arising from the adoption of free trade.

Our perspective on the Canada-US relationship leads us to ask four questions. First, should we model the investment process from a stock or flow perspective? Second, what explanatory factors should we use to model the determination of FDI? Third, should we view this process as static, as it is traditionally viewed or as dynamic, as an investment process perspective would suggest? Finally, how should we incorporate the policy change introduced by free trade between the USA and Canada?

Figure 17.1 presents the development of US FDI into Canada between 1955 and 2000. For most of this period there is an upward trend; however, in the early 1990s it appears to increase dramatically. This interpretation is supported by Figure 17.2, which plots the growth rate of US FDI into Canada for the same period. During the 1950s and early 1960s we observe a period of high growth, which after 1967 and until the early 1990s, appears to be on a downward trend. There are eight years of negative growth between 1973 and 1989. In the early 1990s high growth reappears, such that growth rates in US FDI into Canada

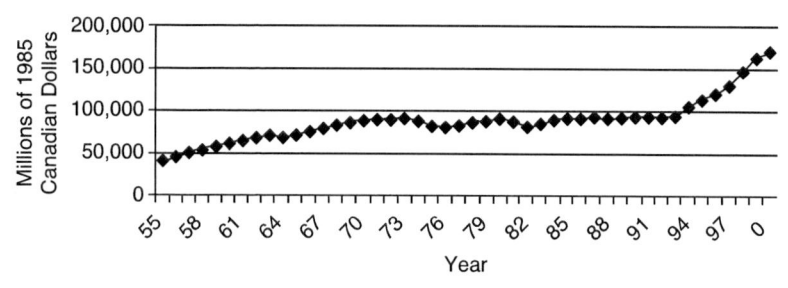

Figure 17.1 Stock of US foreign direct investment in Canada, 1955–2000.

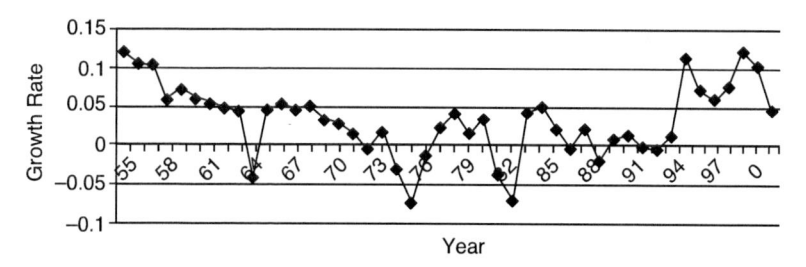

Figure 17.2 Growth rate of US FDI in Canada, 1955–2000.

return to levels only previously observed in the 1950s. Table 17.1 presents this periodic variability. Average for the whole period is 3.3% but this is generated by an average of only 1.3% between 1977 and 1987, and of 4.7% after 1987. Such a pattern in both the level and growth of US FDI into Canada would be expected if Canada had indeed benefited in this sense from the introduction of free trade between the two countries.

However, there is a problem in making the assertion that Figures 17.1 and 17.2 document the impact of the free trade agreement. This pattern could be the result of other factors occurring simultaneously. An obvious candidate is the growth of the Canadian economy which could, in part, account for the changes we observe in the two figures. Between 1980 and 1991 Canadian real GDP grew on average by 2.4%; while, after that, the average growth rate rose to 3.1%. Thus what we observe could be, in part, US multinationals responding to growth in the Canadian markets for their products. This discussion suggests that we need to use a conditional, or regression, framework to disentangle the different effects.

Table 17.1 Growth rate of united states foreign direct investment into Canada.

Period	Mean	Standard Deviation
1955–1964	0.0627	0.0451
1965–1976	0.0142	0.0385
1977–1987	0.0128	0.0369
1988–2000	0.0467	0.0484
1955–2000	0.0336	0.0463

To implement this requires that the measure of FDI we seek to explain is stationary. The reasonably continuous upward trajectory outlined in Figure 17.1 suggests that the stock of US FDI in Canada might be subject to a stochastic trend, and thus not be stationary. Testing for this under the null hypothesis that there is stochastic trend in real US FDI in Canada we find that the Phillips-Perron test statistic for this series is –1.20, with a MacKinnon approximate p-value of 0.934.[7] This does not enable us to reject the null hypothesis that the series is non-stationary, in agreement with Globerman and Shapiro (1999). As with this earlier study, this means we are not able to use a regression technique to examine the determinants of the stock of US FDI in Canada over this period.[8]

Previous researchers have addressed this problem by using FDI flows (Clegg and Scott-Green, 1999; Globerman and Shapiro, 1999) or by normalising the FDI level series using another trended variable, such as GDP (Klein and Rosengren, 1994; Hejazi and Safarian, 1999). We choose to model it in a growth context, and in particular to use:

$$g_t^{K^F} \cong \ln(K^F_t) - \ln(K^F_{t-1}), \tag{1}$$

where:

K^F_j = stock of United States FDI in Canada, $j = t$ or $t - 1$;
$g_t^{K^F}$ = approximate growth rate in the stock in period t.

An advantage of using equation (1) is that the coefficients within a regression context will have a straightforward interpretation. Further, $g_t^{K^F}$ is a stationary series. Table 17.2 reports a Phillips-Perron test statistic for the series of –3.141 with a MacKinnon approximate p-value of 0.024. This allows us to reject the null hypothesis that the series is non-stationary, enabling us to use the growth rate of US FDI into Canada within a regression framework.

Table 17.2 Descriptive statistics.

Variable	Mean	Standard Deviation	Phillips-Perron Unit Root Statistic[a]
Real US FDI into Canada (Millions Canadian $)	87,939.36	25,917.67	−1.200 (0.934)
Growth in Real US FDI into Canada	0.034	0.046	−3.141 (0.024)
Growth in Real Canadian GDP[b]	0.039	0.024	−6.175 (0.000)
Change in Canada-US Exchange Rate	0.008	0.059	−5.603 (0.000)
Change in Difference Real Canadian-US Medium Term Interest Rate	−0.044	1.580	−8.561 (0.000)

Notes:
[a]Newey-West standard errors are used and in parentheses are the MacKinnon approximate *p*-values.
[b]Unit root test includes a time trend in the underlying regressions.

There are two approaches that can be taken when specifying an underlying FDI equation. The first is to follow Stevens and Lipsey (1992) and model a well-specified neoclassical investment process in which the domestic and foreign decisions are jointly determined. While theoretically appealing, and of interest to us in the long run, this structural approach has data requirements that cannot be met at present.[9] The second approach is to use a single-equation specification, which can be loosely referred to as a reduced-form, or hedonic, approach to the foreign investment decision. While lacking theoretical purity in terms of predictions on coefficients, it represents a reasonable starting point and enables the evaluation of our findings in the context of the existing literature.

The empirical model is founded on the perspective of the representative firm facing a choice of methods in foreign market servicing: direct exports, production licensed to a locally-owned firm, or production by an affiliate of the foreign firm (Buckley and Casson, 1976, 1981; Dunning, 1977, 1993). As the size of the local market share attributable to the foreign firm grows in absolute value terms, the cost of local affiliate production (FDI) declines relative to the cost of exporting and licensing (Buckley and Casson, 1981). This local production is better able to avoid or reduce the naturally occurring transport costs, artificially-imposed trade barriers such as tariffs and non-tariff barriers, and transactions costs of operating in the local market. In a simple world, a reduction in such barriers, e.g. via transport innovation, a change in trade policy, or improvement in local intellectual property protection, will tend to reduce the business case for local production via FDI and strengthen that for exports or non-affiliate licensing. Nevertheless, as the firm's sales in the local market grow, a point will arrive beyond which FDI minimises total cost of serving the local market. At this point a standard investment demand function is appropriate, and local market size becomes a key driver of FDI. This suggests we should follow the existing literature and model FDI as conditional on gross domestic product (GDP), which is a reasonable proxy for local market size. Since we are modelling the growth of FDI, we will model the market size effect by the natural log of real GDP (St) and in particular the difference in logs ($\Delta S_t = S_t - St_{-1}$). Translating this into a regression framework within a growth context yields the following simplified representation:

$$g_t^{k^F} = \beta_0 + \beta_1 \Delta S_t + u_t. \tag{2}$$

The Buckley and Casson (1981) argument suggests that we will observe a positive value for β_1. To test this requires that our measure of market size, ΔS_t, is stationary. In Table 17.2 the Phillips-Perron unit root statistic indicates we can reject the null hypothesis that the series is non-stationary.

Findings on the market size hypothesis are mixed (e.g., Aristotelous and Fountas, 1996; Culem, 1988; Lunn, 1983), However, our conclusion is that a positive effect is present when modelling the FDI relationship. When estimating an equation for Canadian FDI inflows, Globerman and Shapiro (1999) find a significant positive effect for change in real GDP. Using industry-level data for Japan; Farrell *et al.* (2003) also find a positive coefficient on a real GDP variable when not controlling for fixed effects. In contrast, the results for FDI into the EU suggest the effect is not present. Clegg and Scott-Green (1999) find predominantly insignificant effects (for US FDI) or significant negative impacts for Japanese FDI. Similar conclusions were drawn by previous EU studies (Pearce *et al.*, 1993; Aristotelous and Fountas, 1996). However, these European studies include potentially non-stationary regressors (e.g., level of GDP) and so cannot be treated as strong evidence against the market growth hypothesis.

The standard expectation is that an appreciation in the host country currency relative to the home currency will lead to a decrease in FDI inflows (Cushman, 1985). However, Stevens (1977) developed three alternative models of FDI behaviour to show that a US dollar devaluation (with the USA as home country) could assume either a positive or negative sign. The theoretical impact of the exchange rate on FDI is also complicated by the fact that there are likely to be several simultaneous influences having opposite effects, even for a single firm. As a consequence, it is difficult to make a solid prediction without an assumption about the dominant character of FDI in question, in particular horizontal local market-seeking versus vertically integrated efficiency-seeking investment. Only market-seeking (import-substituting) FDI would unambiguously associate a host exchange rate appreciation negatively with FDI inflows during initial market entry into the host. The logic is that a host appreciation both renders imports cheaper in terms of host currency and host assets more expensive in terms of foreign currency, thereby reducing the profitability of FDI (Logue and Willet, 1977; and Kohlhagen, 1977). As the exchange rate is often proxied (as in our study) by the number of units of host country currency that can be bought with one US dollar, this would suggest an expected positive sign in the case of market-seeking FDI. To date, the weight of empirical work has concentrated on the USA as the host country (Bailey and Tavlas, 1991; Caves, 1990; Cushman, 1985; Ray, 1989). Overall this evidence suggests an inverse relationship between the exchange value of the host currency and FDI inflows (Stevens, 1993), and therefore that the dominant FDI motive is market seeking. To model the exchange rate effect we include the change in the real Canadian-US exchange rate (ΔE_t) in equation (3):

$$g_t^{kF} = \beta_0 + \beta_1 \Delta S_t + \beta_2 \Delta E_t + u_t. \tag{3}$$

Our discussion suggests that the sign prediction on β_2 is indeterminate, but to test for any exchange rate impact, as with our market size variable, requires that the change in the real exchange rate is a legitimate regressor. The Phillips-Perron unit root statistic for this variable is −5.603 (Table 17.2) and so we can reject the null hypothesis that it is a non-stationary series, permitting us to include it.

As noted above, the relative interest rate is also included as a control variable. When financial markets are to some extent segmented, the international spread in the cost of borrowing should theoretically impact upon the financial component of FDI, so capturing the portfolio-type refinancing of FDI. If the host country cost of borrowing rises relative to the home, then foreign affiliates will tend to reduce their local borrowing and increase their borrowing from the parent firm, thereby increasing the FDI stock and outflow (Boatwright and Renton, 1975). This behaviour falls within the corporate treasury function of

MNEs, and is mimicking within the internal capital market of the multinational firm of the response by portfolio investment to exploit short-lived international differentials in the external capital market (Gilman, 1981). However, most of the impact on FDI of interest rate spread changes occurs within relatively short periods, certainly less than a year, and are temporary, affecting only the *timing* of FDI flows rather than the eventual *amounts* of real investment (Boatwright and Renton, 1975). With only annual data available, much of the important variation in this variable is lost. General insignificance is therefore not surprising, e.g., as found by Culem (1988) and Clegg and Scott-Green (1999) for US FDI in the EU. The relative interest rate is given by the real Canadian minus the real US medium-term interest rates (Δdi_t), valued at year end, where the real rate is the nominal interest rate minus the inflation rate. As Table 17.2 indicates, the change in the difference between real interest rates is a stationary variable. So in spite of the lack of support to date for this hypothesis, it remains theoretically valid as an aggregate control variable for the financial component of FDI flows:

$$g_t^{k^F} = \beta_0 + \beta_1 \Delta S_t + \beta_2 \Delta E_t + \beta_3 \Delta di_t + u_t. \tag{4}$$

Turning to our third question, concerning dynamics, given that the underlying process being modelled is an investment decision, the static assumption that underlies equation (4) is an extremely strong one, even in a context limited to annual data. Theory suggests that firms make investment decisions using the information currently available; however, the actual implementation of these decisions will lie in the future. The investment we observe today will be a function of both current and past information, and therefore a dynamic and not a static process. The simplest method through which to introduce dynamics is to use a distributed lag structure, by including lagged values of the independent variables in the econometric equation:[10]

$$g_t^{k^F} = \beta_0 + \beta_1 \Delta S_t + \beta_2 \Delta E_t + \beta_3 \Delta di_t + \beta_4 \Delta S_{t-1} + \beta_5 \Delta E_{t-1} + \beta_6 \Delta di_{t-1} + u_t. \tag{5}$$

In contrast with equation (4), equation (5) hypothesises that it is not only current but also lagged values of our three explanatory variables that affect growth in US FDI into Canada. The advantage of this simple set-up is that hypothesis testing procedures can be employed to determine whether the lags matter, and whether we require a dynamic structure to explain the data. If a dynamic structure is required, then the cumulative impact of a factor is given by the sum of the relevant individual period effects. So, for example, for the market size variable the total or cumulative impact is:

$$\beta_S^T = \beta_1 + \beta_4. \tag{6}$$

The advantage of a specification in the form of equation (5) is that it allows us to nest the standard static model (equation (4)) commonly used by researchers in the area.

Finally, we turn to modelling the impact of changes in policy. Lucas (1976) argued that the parameters of an econometric model are conditional on the existing policy regime. When a policy regime changes, it is necessary to allow for the possibility that the parameters governing the relationship change. However, customarily within the literature on FDI, authors such as Globerman and Shapiro (1999), Clegg and Scott-Green (1999), Buckley et al. (2001, 2003) have used a dummy variable to capture the effects of policy changes brought about by free trade or regional integration in general. The dummy variable in the context of these studies measures the effect of the policy change only on the intercept. This also applies to equation (5) as it stands, which assumes that the parameters of specified variables are not affected by the free trade agreement. We argue that the free trade agreement, implemented on 1 January, 1989, brought about fundamental policy changes likely to affect the behavioural parameters within our model.

The conventional way of representing the effect of policy changes is encapsulated within the optimal timing of the FDI model (Buckley and Casson, 1981). Here the use of a dummy variable captures the intercept effect. Using a growth approach, we argue that the fixed costs of FDI remain unchanged. What changes are the variable costs of servicing a foreign market through exports, licensing or FDI. This, we argue, is a slope effect as opposed to an intercept effect.

To capture this we treat the implementation of the 1989 Canada-US free trade agreement as a structural break. For example, before the free trade agreement, the effect of current growth in Canada's GDP is β_1, but after this agreement comes into force the coefficient is now β_1^* because of the fundamental change in policy. Therefore, the free trade effect on the parameter can be defined as:

$$\beta_1^{FT} \equiv \beta_1^* - \beta_1. \tag{7}$$

This allows us to estimate β_1 and β^{FT}_1 using a dummy variable:

$$D^{FT}_t = \{1 \text{ if } t \geq 1989; \quad 0 \text{ if } t < 1989. \tag{8}$$

The parameter on any variable interacting with the dummy variable defined in equation (8) yields an estimate of the change in the parameter that results from the introduction of free trade: β^{FT}_1. Its companion variable, not interacted with D^{FT}_t, yields an estimate of the pre-free trade effect (β_1) of the variable on the growth in US FDI into Canada. Using equation (7) we can then derive an estimate of the post-free trade effect (β^*_1). Expanding equation (5) to allow all parameters to be affected by the introduction of the agreement, yields the hypothesised FDI growth equation:

$$g^{KF}_t = \beta_0 + \beta_1 \Delta S_t + \beta^{FT}_1 (D^{FT}_t \times \Delta St) + \beta_2 \Delta E_t + \beta^{FT}_2 (D^{FT}_t \times \Delta Et) + \beta_3 \Delta di_t + \beta^{FT}_3 (D^{FT}_t \times \Delta dit) + \beta_4 \Delta S_{t-1} + \beta^{FT}_4 (D^{FT}_t \times \Delta S_{t-1}) + \beta_5 \Delta E_{t-1} + \beta^{FT}_5 (D^{FT}_t \times \Delta E_{t-1}) + \beta_6 \Delta di_{t-1} + \beta^{FT}_6 (D^{FT}_t \times \Delta di_{t-1}) + u_t. \tag{9}$$

Specifying the relationship using equation (9) allows us to test directly if the provisions of the free trade agreement between the USA and Canada did affect the decision by US multinationals to invest in Canada. This is achieved via a standard significance test on the parameter of the dummy variable-interaction variable. The combination of the distributed lag and structural break innovations affords a flexible methodology. This gives priority to the data to tell us what is and is not important in determining the growth of inward FDI in terms of both dynamic and free trade effects.

Unlike many researchers in the area (e.g., Globerman and Shapiro, 1999; Clegg and Scott-Green, 1999), we refrain from adding further variables. Especially prominent amongst the variables we exclude controls for corporate taxation and wage costs, and this is for two reasons. First, although in each case a theoretical argument can be made for their inclusion there is no evidence, in either the North American or European context, that at the aggregate level they have a significant effect on FDI flows. This implies our results are unlikely to be subject to omitted variable bias. Second, to over-parametrise the equation, as many researchers do, significant effects are being lost due to the increase in the standard errors arising from either partial collinearity between independent variables, or the effect of a dearth of degrees of freedom. So in recognition of the limited degrees of freedom available, there are strong efficiency reasons for following Griliches' (1974) advice to minimise the number of parameters estimated.

Results

Table 17.3 presents the results of five specifications of our model. Column (1) gives the results for the literature's standard static specification, equation (4); the results of a dynamic model (equation (5)) that assumes no free trade effects are presented in column (2); a static model that allows for free trade effects in column (3); a full dynamic specification with free trade effects in column (4), our estimate of equation (9); in column (5) our preferred specification of the relationship. The second part of Table 17.3 presents various tests that allow us to distinguish between the five specifications.

The results in column (1) report that current Canadian GDP growth and the change in the exchange rate have positive and statistically significant parameters. The change in the real interest rate spread parameter has a negative sign, although it is statistically insignificant. The results from this specification are consistent with studies discussed in the previous section and the Ramsey reset test indicates no specification problems. This suggests we could stop at this point; however, this specification test has extremely low power and none of the five specifications in Table 17.3 report a Ramsey reset test statistic indicating a specification problem even though all are significantly different from each other. In this context we will use our simple theoretical arguments developed in the previous section in combination with traditional *t*- and *F*-tests on the parameters to distinguish between the specifications reported in Table 17.3.

The next specification we consider is to allow for dynamic effects in the no-free-trade-effect context, and these results are reported in column (2). The results are inferior to the standard static specification. All lagged terms are individually and jointly [*see Dynamic Test (I)*] statistically insignificant. Further, coefficients on current values of the three variables yield the same conclusion as the pure static model reported in column (1). The effect of introducing the lagged terms is to increase the relative size of the standard errors on all three current variables and thus, via a degrees-of-freedom effect, we have merely reduced the precision of our estimates without changing the conclusions. This suggests that introducing dynamics does not of itself improve the explanation of the growth in US FDI into Canada.

Table 17.3 Growth in United States FDI into Canada and the introduction of free trade, 1955–2000.

Dependent Variable: Growth Rate in United States FDI into Canada

Specification	No Free Trade Effects			Free Trade Effects	
Independent Variables	(1) Static	(2) Dynamic	(3) Static	(4) Dynamic	(5) Dynamic
Current Growth Real Canadian GDP	0.679 (0.297) [0.027]	0.637 (0.285) [0.031]	0.657 (0.291) [0.030]	0.833 (0.294) [0.008]	0.866 (0.231) [0.001]
1st Lagged Growth Real Canadian GDP		0.020 (0.260) [0.938]		0.035 (0.309) [0.910]	
Cumulative Multiplier for Real Growth Canadian GDP		0.657 (0.364) [0.078]		0.868 (0.376) [0.028]	
(Free Trade, 1989) × (Current Growth Real Canadian GDP)			1.271 (0.355) [0.001]	−0.095 (0.393) [0.810]	
(Free Trade, 1989) × (1st Lag Growth Real Canadian GDP)				1.492 (0.498) [0.005]	1.439 (0.371) [0.000]
(Free Trade, 1989) × (Cumulative Multiplier for Real Growth Canadian GDP)				1.396 (0.365) [0.001]	
Current Change in Real Canada $/US $ Exchange Rate	0.295 (0.102) [0.006]	0.231 (0.098) [0.023]	0.312 (0.121) [0.014]	0.291 (0.139) [0.043]	0.316 (0.068) [0.000]

Table 17.3 Growth in United States FDI into Canada and the introduction of free trade, 1955–2000 – continued

Dependent Variable: Growth Rate in United States FDI into Canada

Specification	No Free Trade Effects			Free Trade Effects	
Independent Variables	(1) Static	(2) Dynamic	(3) Static	(4) Dynamic	(5) Dynamic
1st Lag Change in Real Canada $/US $ Exchange Rate		0.187 (0.114) [0.106]		0.099 (0.136) [0.470]	
Cumulative Multiplier for Change in Real Canada $/US $ Exchange Rate		0.419 (0.139) [0.004]		0.390 (0.152) [0.015]	
(Free Trade, 1989) × (Current Change in Real Canada $/US $ Exchange Rate)			−0.229 (0.165) [0.174]	0.063 (0.186) [0.735]	
(Free Trade, 1989) × (1st Lag Change in Real Canada $/US $ Exchange Rate)				0.049 (0.198) [0.806]	
(Free Trade, 1989) × (Cumulative Multiplier for Change in Real Canada $/US $ Exchange Rate)				0.112 (0.200) [0.578]	
Current Change in Difference Canada-US Real Returns	−0.006 (0.005) [0.285]	−0.003 (0.004) [0.431]	−0.003 (0.006) [0.607]	−0.002 (0.007) [0.779]	
1st Lag Change in Difference Canada-US Real Returns		−0.003 (0.004) [0.431]		−0.003 (0.004) [0.473]	

Table 17.3 Growth in United States FDI into Canada and the introduction of free trade, 1955–2000 – continued

Dependent Variable: Growth Rate in United States FDI into Canada

Specification	No Free Trade Effects			Free Trade Effects	
Independent Variables	(1) Static	(2) Dynamic	(3) Static	(4) Dynamic	(5) Dynamic
Cumulative Multiplier for Change in Difference Canada-US Real Returns		0.006 (0.008) [0.740]		−0.005 (0.009) [0.581]	
(Free Trade, 1989) × (Current Change in Difference Canada-US Real Returns)			−0.000 (0.007) [0.965]	−0.007 (0.009) [0.476]	−0.010 (0.003) [0.000]
(Free Trade, 1989) × (1st Lag Change in Difference Canada-US Real Returns)				0.011 (0.007) [0.098]	0.011 (0.003) [0.002]
(Free Trade, 1989) × (Cumulative Multiplier for Change in Diff. Canada-US Real Returns)				0.004 (0.013) [0.352]	0.001 (0.004) [0.805]
Intercept	0.005 (0.014) [0.738]	0.005 (0.014) [0.740]	−0.001 (0.013) [0.951]	−0.013 (0.013) [0.352]	−0.012 (0.013) [0.365]
Specification Tests					
Ramsey Reset Test	1.72 {3.39} [0.178]	1.10 [3.36] [0.360]	0.27 [3.36] [0.848]	1.38 [3.30] [0.276]	1.16 [3.37] [0.339]

Table 17.3 Growth in United States FDI into Canada and the introduction of free trade, 1955–2000 – continued

Dependent Variable: Growth Rate in United States FDI into Canada

Specification	No Free Trade Effects		Free Trade Effects	
Independent Variables	(1) Static	(2) Dynamic	(3) Static	(4) Dynamic	(5) Dynamic
Dynamic Test (I): Static Versus Dynamic		0.97 {3,39} [0.418]		6.80 {6,33} [0.000]	8.20 {2,40} [0.001]
Dynamic Test (II): Static Before Free Trade				0.35 [3,33] [0.791]	
Free Trade Test: Exclusion of Free Trade Interaction Terms			6.85 {3,39} [0.001]	6.69 {6,33} [0,000]	10.20 {3,40} [0.000]
Omnibus Restriction Test: Exclusion of Insignificant Parameters				0.55 {7,33} [0.789]	

Notes:
( ) Standard errors: Static are robust, and Dynamic are Newey-West; [ ] Two-sided probability values;
{ } Degrees of freedom.

Column (3) of Table 17.3 returns to the static specification but now allows all the parameters, except the constant, to change after the introduction of free trade.[11] Our test of the joint significance of the three free trade dummy interaction parameters [see *Free Trade Test*] allows us to reject the null hypothesis that they are jointly insignificant. The estimate of the post-free trade effect of growth in the Canadian economy is large, and indicates that the introduction of free trade between the two countries increased the responsiveness of US multinationals to growth by a factor of two. However, this positive conclusion should be tempered since, on an individual basis, the post-free trade coefficients for the changes in the exchange rate and interest rate differential are statistically insignificant. Further, the results for the three pre-free trade effect coefficients are no different than obtained in our previous results. This suggests we have found a free trade effect on economic growth, but that is all that we have found.

Combining our two empirical innovations, the results with a full set of dynamic and free trade effects are reported in column (4), generating a number of interesting conclusions. First, both our dynamic [*Dynamic Test (I)*] and free trade tests [*Free Trade Test*] indicate we can reject the null hypothesis that all the lags or post-free trade parameters are zero. We now have evidence that the introduction of the distributive lag and structural break specification helps to explain the data better. Second, the post-free trade parameter on lagged growth in real Canadian GDP is large and individually significant. Finally, we now observe a marginally significant effect for the post-free trade parameter on the lagged change in interest rate spread.

However, column (4) reports a number of insignificant parameters, which suggest the specification is over-parametrised. In particular, all the lagged terms estimating the dynamic parameters prior to the introduction of free trade are individually and jointly insignificant [see *Dynamic Test (II)*]. This suggests that part of the over-parametrisation problem is related to imposing a dynamic structure in this earlier period and suggests that a static structure is an adequate representation of the data before the implementation of the agreement. Further, looking at each of the three factors we are modelling, we see other regularities that will simplify the specification. The free trade parameter on current economic growth is insignificant which suggests that free trade had no effect. Further, neither of the post-free trade parameters for the change in the exchange rate is individually significant.[12] Finally, turning to the interest rate spread it is evident that, pre-free trade, both the current and lagged terms are zero from a statistical point of view.[13]

The results from our preferred model are reported in column (5) of Table 17.3 and all the parameters, except the intercept, are statistically significant. Our tests for the presence of dynamic factors [*Dynamic Test (I)*] and parameter shifts as a result of the free trade agreement in 1989 [*Free Trade Test*] both reject the hypothesis that these effects are not present in the data. We should emphasise that the support for the empirical structure proposed in this paper should not be construed as an argument that the relationship under study is either (or both) completely dynamic, or that the free trade agreement altered all parameters. However, our findings suggest that the free trade agreement changed fundamentally the FDI relationship between Canada and the USA.

Our results prior to the free trade agreement are consistent with the US FDI growth relationship being static, whereby only current growth in Canadian GDP and changes in the real exchange rate are influential in the FDI decisions of US multinationals. Prior to 1989 US firms' investment in Canada was driven by growth in the Canadian market as captured by the current market size variable, which exhibits unit elasticity.[14] This may be interpreted as suggesting that increases in FDI were primarily of an expansionary nature, rather than representing the establishment of new projects. There is limited evidence of market-seeking behaviour by US firms from an inspection of the impact of the exchange rate. However, this is very much a second-order effect. Converting the relevant coefficient into elasticity terms results in an effect of only 0.002. Overall the results suggest a reactive mode of decision making by US multinational firms in the pre-free trade period.

From 1989 onwards only changes in the real exchange rate retain the same impact on the FDI growth decision as prior to the free trade agreement. Growth in the Canadian economy now takes on a dynamic structure in which both current and lagged changes now exert significant effects on US FDI. While the impact of current growth in the Canadian economy is unchanged by the introduction of free trade the addition of the lagged effect results in a total effect on the part of Canadian GDP that is significantly larger than the unit elastic response (2.91). Further, US multinationals post-free trade altered their FDI behaviour in, for the first time, reacting to the dynamic (current and lagged) interest rate spread between the two economies. This is a concrete finding for a hypothesis which rarely finds support. It is evident that US multinationals' investment decision making in Canada after 1989 is much more complex, though remaining reasonable, than that exhibited prior to the free trade agreement.

The increase in the coefficient on Canadian GDP growth can be understood as a direct outcome of the provisions under the free trade agreements to remove barriers to trade and investment. It is important here to appreciate that economic integration is only realised through changes in the responsiveness of firms to market conditions in partner countries. Under autarky the impact of market growth on inward FDI would be zero. Under regional integration, the relationship between market growth in the partner countries and inward FDI becomes stronger. In the steady state a position should be reached in which the coefficient on market growth explaining inward FDI from a partner country should approximate that for domestic investment. The result in Table 17.3 therefore testifies to the positive behavioural impact of the removal of trade and investment barriers, via the profitability of FDI.

The impact of the relative interest rate variable is significant in both the current and the lagged period following the implementation of free trade. This significance is almost unprecedented in studies of the financial determinants of FDI using annual data. However, the sign in the current period is negative, which runs counter to expectations, while the sign in the lagged period is positive. The net effect on FDI across the two periods is zero, which is the overall effect generally observed. Our explanation for the negative relationship in the lagged period is that, as we are using annual rather than quarterly (or better) data, our variable is not picking up short-term international movements of funds on intra-company account (the hypothesis for which it was originally designed). Rather, it is the effect of longer-term loans from the parent which are recorded as FDI expenditures only after an investment lag. Loans are increased when the interest rate spread widens. The negative sign in the current period can then be understood as the aggregate behaviour of foreign affiliates in repaying these loans (so reducing the financial component of FDI). The significant change in responsiveness to the interest rate spread can be explained as a behavioural change to economic integration. Following the elimination of barriers in the real sector, the only significant segmentation that remains is that between the capital markets. The greater organisational integration within US multinational enterprises expected with integration would naturally extend to financial strategy.[15]

Conclusions

We began this paper by asking whether US firms' foreign investment decisions with regard to Canada changed with the introduction of a free trade zone between the two countries in 1989. To answer this simple question effectively required us to introduce two empirical innovations. The first is to model the FDI decision in a dynamic rather than the traditional static framework, and is accomplished by using a distributed lag specification of the estimating equation. The second is to generalise the existing methodology for analysing the effect of policy changes on FDI by using a structural break framework, in preference to modelling it simply as an intercept shift, while allowing all parameters in the estimating equation to change. An important advantage of these innovations is that the standard framework is just a special case of the model estimated in this paper. This will be of interest to researchers beyond the specific case of US FDI into Canada pursued here.

With the implementation of these innovations, we answer the question at the centre of the paper by analysing the behaviour of US FDI into Canada in a growth context which, unlike the levels series, is stationary for the period 1955 to 2000. We obtain three key conclusions: first, the introduction of the free trade agreements between Canada and the USA increased the responsiveness of US investors to growth in the Canadian economy by a factor of two. Second, limited dynamics are found in the form of lagged effects in the interest rate spread although, interestingly, this factor only entered into US MNEs' decision making after the first free trade agreement was signed. Finally, the effect of the change in the exchange rate is static and constant over the 1955 to 2000 period, and was unaffected by the introduction of free trade between the United States and Canada.

Our results indicate that the introduction of free trade between the USA and Canada did fundamentally alter the decision-making process of US multinational firms investing in Canada. Prior to the agreement US multinationals' decisions were driven by market size and exchange rate factors in a static way. Following it these firms changed their investment strategy with respect to the Canadian market in a manner consistent with effective product market integration, and their corporate integration as evidenced by the appearance of a significant response to financial market factors. This furnishes scientific evidence that US multinationals' FDI decisions in Canada changed fundamentally with the introduction of free trade, which challenges the view of a number of commentators, including that of the Canadian government.

Appendix A

Variable definitions and data sources

Table A.1 Variable definitions.

Real United States foreign direct investment in Canada:
Growth rate of stock data for the period – as approximated by difference in logs, 1955–2000
(*Source*: United States Bureau of Economic Analysis)

Real Canadian gross domestic product:
Growth rate as approximated by difference in logs, 1955–2000 (Source: IMF)

Real opportunity cost of FDI:
Approximated by the difference between the real Canadian medium-term interest rates (end of year) and US medium-term interest rates, 1955–2000 (*Source*: IMF)

Real exchange rate:
Approximated by [(Canadian$/US$) × (US GDP deflator/Canadian GDP deflator], 1955–2000 (Source: IMF)

Dummy variable:
Equals 1 in 1989 and after, 0 before 1989

Appendix B

Augmented Dickey-Fuller unit root test results

Table B.1 to B.5 present our results for the presence of stochastic trend in the five variables we use in this paper. These tests are the augmented Dickey-Fuller unit root test and are an alternative unit root test to the one presented in the main body of the paper.[16] While the tests differ, the conclusions are the same as those presented in Table 17.2.

Table B.1 Unit root tests for United States (US) foreign direct investment (FDI) into Canada, 1955–2000.

Dependent Variable: Change in US FDI						
Specification	Without Time Trend			With Time Trend		
Independent Variables	(1)	(2)	(3)	(4)	(5)	(6)
1st Lag in US FDI	0.068 (2.59)	0.010 (0.43)	0.012 (0.49)	0.094 (1.71)	−0.060 (1.17)	−0.056 (1.02)
1st Lag Change in US FDI		0.662 (5.15)	0.731 (4.44)		0.747 (5.41)	0.763 (4.65)
2nd Lag Change in US FDI			−0.119 (0.68)			−0.035 (0.19)
Trend				−51.454 (0.53)	128.309 (1.55)	122.652 (1.38)
Constant	−2,958.022 (1.26)	176.758 (0.09)	136.010 (0.07)	−3,942.153 (1.30)	3,035.105 (1.13)	2,869.904 (1.03)
Akaike Information Criteria	16.764	16.327	16.360	16.801	16.315	16.357
Bayes Information Criteria	16.843	16.446	16.519	16.920	16.474	16.556
Observations				46		

Note:
( ) Absolute value of t-statistic.

Table B.2 Unit Root Tests for Growth in United States (US) foreign direct investment (FDI) into Canada, 1955–2000.

Dependent Variable: Change in Growth of US FDI

Specification	Without Time Trend			With Time Trend		
Independent Variables	(1)	(2)	(3)	(4)	(5)	(6)
1st Lag Growth in US FDI	**−0.381** (3.30)	**−0.372** (2.93)	**−0.306** (2.26)	**−0.381** (3.23)	**−0.370** (2.81)	**−0.283** (−1.96)
1st Lag Change in Growth in US FDI		−0.029 (0.20)	−0.105 (0.66)		−0.031 (0.20)	−0.133 (0.78)
2nd Lag Change in Growth in US FDI			−0.194 (1.30)			−0.218 (1.37)
Trend (*1/1,000)				−0.001 (−0.00)	0.198 (0.05)	2.133 (0.47)
Constant	0.012 (1.83)	0.012 (1.69)	0.010 (1.34)	0.012 (0.89)	0.011 (0.76)	0.003 (0.18)
Akaike Information Criteria	−6.583	−6.540	−6.536	−6.539	−6.497	−6.498
Bayes Information Criteria	−6.503	−6.421	−6.377	−6.420	−6.338	−6.299
Observations			46			

Note:
( ) Absolute value of t-statistic.

Table B.3 Unit root tests for growth rate of real Canadian (Can) gross domestic product (GDP), 1955–2000.

Dependent Variable: Change in Real Can GDP Growth

Specification	Without Time Trend			With Time Trend		
Independent Variables	(1)	(2)	(3)	(4)	(5)	(6)
1st Lag in Growth in Real Can GDP Growth	**−0.742** (5.35)	**−0.765** (4.29)	**−0.594** (2.83)	**−0.584** (6.16)	**−0.977** (5.29)	**−0.889** (3.69)
1st Lag in the Change in Real Can GDP Growth		0.030 (0.21)	−0.119 (0.68)		0.142 (1.01)	0.072 (0.39)
2nd Lag in the Change in Real Can GDP Growth			−0.207 (1.49)			−0.083 (0.58)
Trend				−0.001 (2.49)	−0.001 (2.67)	−0.001 (2.22)
Constant	0.029 (4.68)	0.030 (3.98)	0.023 (2.69)	0.051 (4.83)	0.058 (4.61)	0.052 (3.38)
Akaike Information Criteria	−7.504	−7.462	−7.470	−7.595	−7.576	−7.540
Bayes Information Criteria	−7.425	−7.343	−7.311	−7.476	−7.470	−7.341
Observations			46			

Note: ( ) Absolute value of t-statistic.

Table B.4 Unit root tests for change in difference between real Canadian (Can)–US returns, 1955–2000.

Dependent Variable: Change in the Change in Real Canadian (Can) Returns

Specification	Without Time Trend			With Time Trend		
Independent Variables	(1)	(2)	(3)	(4)	(5)	(6)
1st Lag Change in Difference between Can-US Returns	−1.207 (8.31)	−1.290 (5.40)	−1.463 (4.84)	−1.208 (8.23)	−1.293 (5.36)	−1.477 (4.82)
1st Lag Change in the Change in Diff between Can-US Returns		0.055 (0.44)	0.228 (0.99)		0.068 (0.45)	0.239 (1.03)
2nd Lag Change in the Change in Diff between Can-US Returns			0.138 (0.94)			0.145 (0.98)
Trend				−0.087 (0.38)	−0.007 (0.39)	−0.009 (0.49)
Constant	−0.063 (0.27)	−0.060 (0.26)	−0.048 (0.20)	0.087 (0.19)	0.096 (0.21)	0.149 (0.32)
Akaike Information Criteria	0.935	0.974	0.997	0.975	1.014	1.034
Bayes Information Criteria	1.015	1.093	1.156	1.094	1.173	1.233
Observations			46			

Note: ( ) Absolute value of t-statistic.

Table B.5 Unit root tests for change in real United States/Canada (US/Can) exchange rate, 1955–2000.

Dependent Variable: Change in the Change in Real Can/US Exchange Rate

Specification	Without Time Trend			With Time Trend		
Independent Variables	(1)	(2)	(3)	(4)	(5)	(6)
1st Lag Change in Real US/Can Exchange Rate	−0.839 (5.63)	−0.840 (4.19)	−1.050 (4.56)	−0.843 (0.151)	−0.853 (4.16)	−1.077 (4.57)
1st Lag Change in the Change in Real US/Can Exchange Rate		0.001 (0.01)	0.201 (0.167)		0.012 (0.07)	0.223 (1.11)
2nd Lag Change in the Change in Real US/Can Exchange Rate			0.292 (1.74)			0.303 (1.78)
Trend(*1/10)				0.003 (0.43)	0.003 (0.43)	0.004 (0.62)
Constant	0.007 (0.78)	0.007 (0.76)	0.007 (0.85)	−0.001 (0.05)	−0.001 (0.05)	−0.004 (0.18)
$\bar{R}^2$	0.406	0.392	0.419	0.395	0.380	0.411
Akaike Information Criteria	−5.626	−5.582	−5.609	−5.587	−5.543	−5.575
Bayes Information Criteria	−5.546	−5.463	−5.450	−5.467	−5.384	−5.376
Observations			46			

Note: ( ) Absolute value of t-statistic.

APPENDIX C

Free trade intercept results

Table C.1 Growth in United States FDI into Canada and the introduction of free trade, 1955–2000, intercept effect.

Dependent Variable: Growth Rate in United States FDI into Canada

Independent Variables	(1) Static	(2) Dynamic	(3) Dynamic
Current Growth Real Canadian GDP	0.793 (0.345) [0.027]	0.794 (0.362) [0.036]	0.868 (0.280) [0.004]
1st Lagged Growth Real Canadian GDP		0.003 (0.323) [0.933]	
(Free Trade, 1989) × (Current Growth Real Canadian GDP)	0.850 (0.469) [0.078]	−0.076 (0.444) [0.865]	
(Free Trade, 1989) × (1st Lag Growth Real Canadian GDP)		1.717 (0.481) [0.001]	1.429 (0.416) [0.001]
Current Change in Real Canada $/US $ Exchange Rate	0.313 (0.124) [0.016]	0.290 (0.139) [0.046]	0.315 (0.080) [0.000]
1st Lag Change in Real Canada $/US $ Exchange Rate		0.097 (0.140) [0.491]	
(Free Trade, 1989) × (Current Change in Real Canada $/US $ Exchange Rate)	−0.250 (0.183) [0.181]	0.114 (0.169) [0.505]	
(Free Trade, 1989) × (1st Lag Change in Real Canada $/US $ Exchange Rate)		0.046 (0.196) [0.816]	
Current Change in Difference Canada-US Real Returns	−0.003 (0.006) [0.620]	−0.002 (0.007) [0.767]	
1st Lag Change in Difference Canada-US Real Returns		−0.003 (0.004) [0.483]	
(Free Trade, 1989) × (Current Change in Difference Canada-US Real Returns)	−0.001 (0.007) [0.898]	−0.008 (0.009) [0.425]	−0.009 (0.003) [0.001]

Table C.1 Growth in United States FDI into Canada and the introduction of free trade, 1955–2000, intercept effect – *continued*

Dependent Variable: Growth Rate in United States FDI into Canada

Independent Variables	(1) Static	(2) Dynamic	(3) Dynamic
(Free Trade, 1989) × (1st Lag Change in Difference Canada-US Real Returns)		0.013 (0.006) [0.052]	0.011 (0.003) [0.002]
Free Trade, 1989 Dummy Variable	0.019 (0.019) [0.344]	–0.010 (0.023) [0.654]	0.000 (0.019) [0.982]
Intercept	–0.008 (0.019) [0.658]	–0.009 (0.020) [0.655]	–0.012 (0.017) [0.506]

Note: ( ) Standard errors: Static are robust, and Dynamic are Newey-West; [ ] Two-sided probability values.

Table C.2 US foreign direct investment elasticity estimates.

	Elasticity Estimates	
	Before Free Trade Agreement	After Free Trade Agreement
Current Growth Real Canadian GDP	0.852	0.852
1st Lag Growth Real Canadian GDP	0.000	1.439
Total Growth Real Canadian GDP	0.852	2.291
Current Change in Real Canada $/US $ Exchange Rate[a]	0.002	0.002
Current Change in Difference in Real Can-US Returns[b]	0.000	–0.002
1st Lag Change in Difference in Real Can-US Returns[b]	0.000	0.002
Total Change in Difference in Real Canadian-US Returns	0.000	0.000

Notes:
[a] Evaluated using average change in the Real Canada $/US $ Exchange Rate for the whole period, 0.008.
[b] Evaluated using average change in the Difference in Real Medium Canadian-US Returns for the post-free trade agreement period, –0.151.

Notes

1. For a review see Baldwin (1997).
2. These trade figures are for the export of goods and services and income receipts. They were obtained by the authors from the United States Department of Commerce Bureau, of Economic Analysis (BEA), website.
3. These data are for US Direct Investment Abroad and were obtained by the authors from the United States Department of Commerce, BEA, website.
4. See Buckley et al. (2001) for a discussion of this and other points.
5. Students of Canada's foreign investment policy might question this statement on the grounds that on a number of previous occasions the Canadian government had legislated in this area. In defence it can be argued that the Canada-United States Automative Products Agreement of 1965 can be seen as a forerunner of the Canada-US Free Trade Agreement that we are modelling here. The 1965 agreement required that the value of automotive products imported into Canada exactly balance that of Canadian exports to the USA, if penalty tariffs were to be avoided. This is probably best viewed as a 'managed trade' agreement, the existence of which makes less likely an investment effect associated with the implementation of the automotive free trade zone between the two countries. At the same time, the Canadian Foreign Investment Review Act (FIRA) was in operation between 1974 and 1985 and the National Energy Programme between 1980 and 1984. FIRA increased the cost of investment by foreigners through regulation, while the National Energy Programme encouraged Canadian and government ownership of energy industry assets. The possibility that foreign investment was suppressed prior to the implementation of free trade in 1989 makes it more likely that a free trade effect will be observed in the data. However, the evidence to date on the effect of these programmes (Globerman and Shapiro, 1999, pp. 523 and 527) suggests that, at standard significance levels, there had been no impact on foreign investment in Canada.
6. See Globerman and Shapiro (1999, pp. 516–18) for an excellent discussion of this latter issue.
7. An alternative to this is the standard augmented Dickey-Fuller tests and Appendix B documents that this traditional test comes to the same conclusion.
8. In future work we will be turning to a cointegration approach to model the short- and long-run dynamics of the stock of FDI.
9. In particular, as Stevens and Lipsey (1992, p. 45) point out, the researcher requires consistent domestic and foreign investment series, which are not generally available.
10. In this paper we leave the dynamics in terms of the dependent variable as unspecified and correct for the implied autocorrelation.
11. We have considered specifications that include an intercept shift effect for the free trade agreement and in all cases this parameter is insignificant without changing our conclusions. See Appendix C.
12. Further, testing the hypothesis that the pre-free trade lagged term and the two post-free trade changes in exchange rate variables are jointly insignificant can be accepted with a probability value of 0.67.

13 Jointly the restriction that these seven parameters we have identified are zero in this discussion is accepted is documented in the *Omnibus Test* reported in Table 17.3.
14 You cannot reject the null hypothesis that the coefficient on the change in Canadian GDP growth is different from one. Appendix C, Table C2, reports a full set of elasticity results for both periods (pre- and post-free trade).
15 In future work, we will test this directly on the financial components data.
16 Augmented Dickey-Fuller critical values are: Intercept Only: 10% = –2.57; 5% = –2.86; 1% = 3.43 or Intercept and Trend: 10% = –3.12; 5% = –3.41; 1% = 3.96.

References

Aristotelous, K. and S. Fountas (1996) 'An Empirical Analysis of Inward Foreign Direct Investment Flows in the EU with Emphasis on the Market Enlargement Hypothesis', *Journal of Common Market Studies*, **34**, 4, 571–83.

Baldwin, R.E. (1997) 'The Causes of Regionalism', *The World Economy*, **20**, 7, 865–88.

Bailey, M.J. and G.S. Tavlas (1991) 'Exchange Rate Variability and Direct Investment', in M. Ulan (ed.), *The Annals of the American Academy of Political and Social Science: Foreign Investment in the United States* (no. 516, July), 106–17.

Boatwright, B.D. and G.A. Renton (1975) 'An Analysis of United Kingdom Inflows and Outflows of Direct Foreign Investment', *Review of Economics and Statistics*, **57**, 4, 478–86.

Buckley, P.J. and M.C. Casson (1976) *The Future of the Multinational Enterprise* (London: Macmillan).

Buckley, P.J. and M.C. Casson (1981) 'The Optimal Timing of a Foreign Direct Investment', *Economic Journal*, **92**, 361, 75–87.

Buckley, P.J., J. Clegg, N. Forsans and K.T. Reilly (2001) 'Increasing the Size of the "Country": Regional Economic Integration and Foreign Direct Investment in a Globalised World Economy', *Management International Review*, **41**, 3, 251–74.

Buckley, P.J., J. Clegg, N. Forsans and K.T. Reilly (2003) 'Evolution of FDI in the United States in the Context of Trade Liberalisation and Regionalisation', *Journal of Business Research*, **56**, 10, 853–7.

Caves, R.E. (1990) 'Exchange Rate Movements and Foreign Direct Investment in the United States', in D.B. Audretsch and M.P. Claudon (eds), *The Internationalization of US Markets* (New York: New York University Press), 199–229.

Clegg, J. and S. Scott-Green (1999) 'The Determinants of New FDI Capital Flows into the EC: A Statistical Comparison of the USA and Japan', *Journal of Common Market Studies*, **37**, 4, 597–616.

Culem, C.G. (1988) 'The Locational Determinants of Direct Investments Among Industrialised Countries', *European Economic Review*, **32**, 4, 885–904.

Cushman, D.O. (1985) 'Real Exchange Rate Risk, Expectations, and the Level of Direct Investment', *Review of Economics and Statistics*, **67**, 2, 297–308.

Department of Foreign Affairs (2003), *NAFTA @10 A Preliminary Report* (Ottawa, Canada: Minister of Public Works and Government Services Canada).

Department of Foreign Affairs (2004) *Fifth Annual Report on Canada's State of Trade* (Ottawa, Canada: Minister of Public Works and Government Services Canada).

Dunning, J.H. (1977) 'Trade, Location of Economic Activity and the Multinational Enterprise: A Search for an Eclectic Approach', in B. Ohlin, P.-O. Hesselborn and P.M. Wijkman (eds), *The International Allocation of Economic Activity* (London: Macmillan), 395–418.

Dunning, J.H. (1993) *Multinational Enterprises and the Global Economy* (Wokingham: Addison-Wesley).

Dunning, J.H. (1997) 'The European Internal Market Programme and Inbound Foreign Direct Investment – Part II', *Journal of Common Market Studies*, 35, 2, 189–223.

Farrell, R., N. Gaston and J.-E. Strum (2004) 'Determinants of Japan's Foreign Direct Investment: An Industry and Country Panel Study, 1984–1998', *Journal of the Japanese and International Economies*, 18, 2, 161–82.

Gilman, M.G. (1981) *The Financing of Foreign Direct Investment: A Study of the Determinants of Capital Flows in Multinational Enterprises* (London: Frances Pinter).

Globerman, S. and D.M. Shapiro (1999) 'The Impact of Government Policies on Foreign Direct Investment: The Canadian Experience', *Journal of International Business Studies*, 30, 3, 513–32.

Griliches, Z. (1974) 'Comments on Sims', in M.D. Intriligator and D.A. Kendrick (eds), *Frontiers of Quantitative Economics*, Vol. 2 (Amsterdam: North-Holland), 334–6.

Hanson, G.H., R.J. Mataloni and M.J. Slaughter (2001) 'Expansion Strategies of U.S. Multinational Firms', Bureau of Economic Analysis Working Paper (Washington, DC: US Department of Commerce, May, no. 2001-01).

Hejazi, W. and E.A. Safarian (1999) 'Trade, Foreign Direct Investment and R&D Spillovers', *Journal of International Business Studies*, 30, 3, 491–511.

Klein, M.W. and E. Rosengren (1994) 'The Real Exchange Rate and Foreign Direct Investment in the United States: Relative Wealth vs. Relative Wage Effects', *Journal of International Economics*, 36, 3–4, 373–89.

Kohlhagen, S.W. (1977) 'The Effects of Exchange-rate Adjustments on International Investment: Comment', in P.B. Clark, D.E. Logue and R.J. Sweeney (eds), *The Effects of Exchange Rate Adjustments* (Washington, DC: US Government Printing Office), 194–7.

Logue, D.E. and T.D. Willet (1977) 'The Effects of Exchange-rate Adjustments on International Investment', in P.B. Clark, D.E. Logue and R.J. Sweeney (eds), *The Effects of Exchange Rate Adjustments* (Washington, DC: US Government Printing Office), 137–50.

Lucas, R.E. Jr. (1976) 'Econometric Policy Evaluation: A Critique', in K. Brunner and A.H. Meltzer (eds), *The Phillips Curve and Labor Markets*, Vol. 1 of Carnegie-Rochester Conference Series on Public Policy (Amsterdam: North-Holland), 19–46.

Lunn, J. (1983) 'Determinants of US Direct Investment in the EEC: Revisited Again', *European Economic Review*, 21, 3, 391–3.

Pearce, R.D., A. Islam and K.P. Sauvant (1992) *The Determinants of Foreign Direct Investment: A Survey of the Evidence* (United Nations Centre on Transnational Corporations, New York: United Nations).

Ray, E.J. (1989) 'The Determinants of Foreign Direct Investment in the United States: 1979–1985', in R.C. Feenstra (eds), *Trade Policies for International Competitiveness* (Chicago: University of Chicago Press), 53–83.

Stevens, G.V.G. (1977) 'The Effects of Exchange-rate Adjustments on International Investment: Comment', in P.B. Clark, D.E. Logue and R.J. Sweeney (eds), *The Effects of Exchange Rate Adjustments* (Washington, DC: US Government Printing Office), 183–8.

Stevens, G.V.G. (1993) 'Exchange Rates and Foreign Direct Investment: A Note', International Finance Discussion Papers (Washington, DC: Board of Governors of the Federal Reserve System, April, no. 444).

Stevens, G.V.G. and R.E. Lipsey (1992) 'Interactions between Domestic and Foreign Investment', *Journal of International Money and Finance*, **11**, 1, 40–62.

United Nations Transnational Corporations and Management Division (1993), *From the Common Market to EC 92: Regional Economic Integration in the European Community and Transnational Corporations* (Department of Economic and Social Development. New York: United Nations).

Index

Page references in **bold** refer to figures, page references in *italic* refer to tables.

active agent, the   332–3
Africa   93, *135*, 138, 139
agglomeration   371–3
Aiello, P.   169
Aitken, Brian   272, 284, 292, *294*
Alcatel Bell   175–6, 177, 180, 183
Almanac of China's Foreign Economic Relations and Trade   133
American Business Abroad (Kindleberger)   16
Anglo-Irish Free Trade Agreement   380n1
anti-dumping measures   149
Argentina   84, *135*
ASEAN Free Trade Agreement (AFTA)   151, 266
ASEAN-China Expert Group on Economic Cooperation (ACEGEC)   239
Asian Investment Area   151, 266
asset-augmenting FDI   320, 371
asset-seeking FDI   92–3, 103, 110, 156
Association of South East Asian Nations (ASEAN)   239, 240, *241*, *248*, 249, 258, 267n1
asymmetric information   16
AT&T   217
Australia   84, 92, 123, *134*, 138, 139, 148, 158n11, 193–4, 291
automotive industry   *287*
   employees   284
   exports   *287*
   FDI in   285, 285–9
   importance   284
   imports   *287*, 288
   market   285
   production   286, *287*, 288

productivity model   295–7
   sales   284
   sub-sectors   *298*, 300
   volume   *287*
   weaknesses   289
Bank of China   139, 142
banking systems   85
Barrios, S.L.   376
Bartels, F.L.   262
behavioural management practices   166
Behrman, Jack   13n2
Beijing Automotive Works   286, 288
Beijing Jeep   168, 169, *173*, 177, 178–9, 180, 181, 182
Belgium   177, 179
benign effect   255
Bermuda   *136*
Bertschek, I.   284
Bhagwati, Jagdish   365–6
Blomström, M.   220, 230, 284, 290, 291, 291–2, *294*
boundaries   21
brand acquisition   151–4, *152*, *153*
brand awareness   150
brand loyalty   205
Brannen, M.Y.   168
Brazil   111, *135*, 139, 148, 290
Brislin, R.   174
British Virgin Islands   *136*, 268n4
Broadman, H.G.   267n2
Brunei   *241*, 264
Buckley, Peter J.   10, 18–19
Buckley and Casson model   64–71
bureaucratic control   170, 254

419

Cambodia *137*, 139, 151, *241*, 265
Canada 3, 18, 22, 84, 92, *134*, 138, 139, 158n11, 171, 193–4, 291, 292
 American imports 387
 economic growth 391, 399, 404, 406
 Foreign Investment Review Act (FIRA) 415n5
 free trade agreements with USA 387–8, 390, 405, 407, *413–14*, 415n5
 market size 394
 National Energy Programme 415n5
 US FDI 386–408, *400–3*
 US FDI, descriptive statistics *393*
 US FDI, flows 390–9, **391**, *392*, *393*
 US FDI growth 390–2, **391**, *392*, 399, *400–3*, 404–6, *409–14*
 US FDI levels 387
 US FDI, model 388–9
 US FDI stock **391**
Canada-United States Automotive Products Agreement 415n5
Canada-US Free Trade Agreement (CUSFTA) 387
capital 140
 accumulation 299
 flow 366
 intensity 295–6
capital market: access 154
 Hymer on 17–18
 imperfections 85–6
Carter, M.J. 33–4
Casson, Mark 1–2, 17, 18–19, 53–75, 178
Caves, R.E. 193–4, 211n2, 226, 291, *293*
Cayman Islands 268n4
Chang, G.G. 254
change, and costs 54–5
Chen, Z.X. 123
Chile 22, *135*, 138
China International Trust and Investment Corporation (CITIC) 86, 129

China Investment and Trust Corporation for Foreign Economic Cooperation and Trade (FOTIC) 86
China Merchant Holdings 142
China Merchants International 139
China National Nonferrous Metal Industrial Corporation 148
China National Offshore Oil Corporation (CNOOC) 148
China National Petroleum Corporation (CNPC) 92, 148
China Resources 139
Chinese Automotive Industry Yearbook 285
Chinese Diaspora, the 93–4, 158n11
Chrysler 176, 178–9, 182, 183, 288
CITIC 142, 148
Clegg, L. Jeremy 81–112, 165–86, 192–211, 216–36, 239–67, 270–81, 284–302, 305–24, 327–58, 386–408
closed system strategies 331
coal production 158n13
Coase, R.H. 17, 20, 65
Cohen, W.M. 292
collective firms 302n2
communications 21, 170
communism 103
Compaq 375
comparative advantage 374
competition 219, 220, 292, 339–40
competitive advantage 25, 156, 165
Confucian values 170
conglomerate firms 85
Congo *135*
contagion effects 219
control configuration 27–9
 decisions 37, 42–4, 48
 dynamic perspective 47
corporate culture 332, 340
 Sinotrans 340, 351, 355–7
corporate relationships 183–4
COSCO 340–1
cost-benefit analysis 369

Index   421

costs   26
  and change   54–5
  dynamic perspective   45–6
  flow   33–4, 38, 45–6, 47, 48
  growth   58
  labour   246
  marketing   36–7, 45
  operation   34–7, 45–6, 47
  and output   54
  Penrose and   54–5
  production   35–6, 45
  R&D   34–5, 65–6, 74–5
  transaction   121, 258, *259*, *260*,
    265, 338, 371, 393–4
Cross, Adam   81–112, 119–57,
  239–67
cross investment   15
Cuba   *136*
cultural awareness   2, 165–86, **172**,
  173, **175**, **184**
  Chinese cultural characteristics
    166–8
  and corporate and governmental
    relationships   183–4
  data collection, coding and analysis
    172–5, *173*, **174**
  definition   165
  and government support   180–2
  government support   185
  and knowledge transfer   175–7
  literature   166–72
  and long-term vision   182–3
  management model   171–2, **172**,
    184, 184–5
  between partners   168–9
  party and government role
    169–70
  shared mindsets   178–80, 185
  and trust   167–8, 168–9, 177–8,
    185–6
cultural proximity   93–4, 100, 102,
  105, 106, 110
currency depreciation   281n4
Czech Republic   292

data collecting agencies   143–4
Daube, Keith   338
De Beule, Filip   271, 280
Dell   375

demonstration effects   219
demonstration-imitation effect
  290–1
Deng Xiaoping   82, *89*, 94, 102,
  127, *244*
Denmark   *134*
developing country FDI   323–4,
  366–7
  Asian   121–5
  characteristics   125
  distribution of Chinese   138
  flows   123
  governmental role   124–5, 125,
    126
  industrial clusters   370–6
  model   *126*
  policy implications   365–80
  policy lessons of Irish experience
    377–80
  selective promotion of MNEs
    367–8
  theoretical explanations   121–5
development, level of host country
  106, *107–8*, 109
'Direct foreign investment and the
  national interest' (Hymer)   18
direct foreign investment (DFI)
  15–16
disequilibrium   21
distributional effects   219–20,
  311
diversification   65, 68, 342
  geographical   61–4, *64*
Djankov, S.   284, 292, *293*
domestic investment   275–6
Doz, Y.   13n1
Dunning, J.H.   26, 65, 83–4, 86–7,
  121, 218, 271, 309, 369

Eclectic Paradigm, the   26, 83–4,
  86–7, 121, 218, 309
economic development, FDI as tool
  for   323
economic integration, regional   151
economic school of international
  business research   25–49
  literature   26–9
  shortcomings   25–6
The Economist   158n13

'The efficiency (contradictions) of Multinational Corporations' (Hymer)   18–19
efficiency (cost reduction)-seeking FDI   83–4, 154–5, 266, 271, 273
Egger, P.   284, *293*
Egypt   *135*
electronics industry: asset restructuring   228
  capital intensity   228, 230
  categories   222
  exports   230
  FDI   217
  foreign capital share   222, *224–5*, 226
  impact of FDI on productivity   226–32, *227, 229, 231*
  methodology and data   221–6, *223, 224–5, 226*
  productivity   216–36, *223, 224–5, 226, 227, 229, 231*
  special conditions   233–4
  state ownership   233–4
  technology transfer   232, 233, 235
enterprise-centred approaches   379
entrepreneurs   68
environmental uncertainty   331
equity joint ventures   249
Erdener, C.   122, 124
Erlandson, David A.   335
European Union (EU)   8, 140–1, 274, 279, 368, 369, 377, 386, 387
exchange rates   95, 104, 276, 277, 279, 394–5, 404, 405, *412*
expansion: incremental   73–5
  parallel   25
export platform FDI   242, 250, 255–6, 365, 370
exports   95–6, 103–4, 104, 106, 230
  automotive industry   *287*
  country-of-origin effects   271
  and domestic investment   275–6
  econometric analysis   273–6
  impact of FDI   270–81, *274, 277, 277–9, 278*, 280
  and inward FDI   273–6, *274*
  manufacturing   270–81
  performance   *277*, 277–9, *278*
  quotas   149
  spillover effects   279
  structure   *275*, 275
  TNCs and   270
extant theory   87
external market, the   16
externalisation   31

Fabry, N.H.   170
family owned firms   85
Fan, X.   291
FDI flows   388
  developing country   123
  host country   *241*
  inward foreign direct investment   240, *241, 246*, 246, 251, 256
  outward foreign direct investment, Chinese   91
  US to Canada   390–9, **391**, *392, 393*
FDI inflow   119, 240, *241, 246*, 246, 251, 256
FDI stock   132, 133, 240, 262, 388, **391**
Feldman, Martha S.   332
Fiji   *137*, 149
firms *see also* multinational enterprise (MNE): boundaries   21
  collective   302n2
  configuration   25–49
  configuration model   29–47, **30**, *32*
  conglomerate   85
  developing country   121–5
  family owned   85
  flow costs   33–4
  growth   54–61
  integration   17
  international operations   14–16
  marketing costs   36–7
  nationality   14–15
  operation costs   34–7
  Penrose's view of   55
  production costs   35–6
  rates of growth   56–7, 65, 69–70
  regeneration   56
  size   296
First Automotive Works (FAW)   285–6, 288
Fligstein, Neil   338

Index   423

flow costs   33–4, 38, 45–6, 47, 48
flow trends, outward foreign direct investment   131–47, *132*, *134–7*, *142*, *145*
   entry mode   145–7, *146*
   geographic distribution   133, *134–7*
   sectoral distribution   141–5, *142*
follow my leader theory   370, 380n13
foreign affiliates (FA)   305–6, 310, 319, 322
foreign direct investment: definition   112n1
   general theory of   83–4
foreign market penetration   2
foreign market-servicing mode   26
foreign penetration   211, 219–20
foreign presence, measures of   307
foreign-owned enterprises (FOEs)   194–5, 201
Forsans, Nicolas   386–408
forward integration   340–1
Foss, N.J.   53
France   *134*, 289
free trade areas   386–7
free trade, Canada–United States relationship   386–408
Freeman, N.J.   262
Fujian   249
Fung, K.C.   139

Gateway   375, 381n15
geographical distance   96, 104
geographical expansion   61–4, *64*
Georgia   *136*
Germany   *134*, 149, 289
Ghana   21, 22
Ghoshal, Sumantra   356
Gillespie, K.   306
Giorgioni, Gianluigi   284–302
Girrna, S.   284, 292, *293*
global economy, Chinese re-integration with   81
global strategy analysis   7, 8
globalisation   2, 22, 71–2, 239, 371
Globerman, S.   226, 284, 292, *294*, 387, 392, 397

go global (*zou chu qu*) initiative   82, 89, *90*, 120, *128*, 130, 132
Görg, H.   192, 308, 381n20
government support   87, 180–2, 185
governmental relationships   183–4
governmental role   88, 124–5, 125, *126*, 169–70, 176, 280–1, 320, 331, 334, 345–6
Graham, E.M.   246, 249
Graham, G.   21, 23n1
Greenaway, D.   308
growth   239
   costs   58
   limits to   55–6
   and market size   71–3
   Penrose's model   54–61, 64–8
   R&D and   64–8
   rates of   56–7, 65–6, 69–70
   and strategic management   54–61
   value-maximising   59–61
Guangdong   249, 271
Guangzhou Automotive Company   288
Guangzhou Honda   288
guanxi (personal connections)   2, 93–4, 166, 167–8, 169, 171, *172*, 175–7, 179, 182, 183–6

Haddad, M.   284, 291, *294*
Haier   *152*, 152
Hainan Island   *243*
Harrigan, K.R.   168
Harrison, A.E.   284, 291, 292, *294*
Hashai, Niron   1–2, 25–49
Heckscher-Ohlin (H-O) model   366
Henan   263
Hercules Powder Company   53
Hewlett Packard   217
High Technology (HT) products   41–2, 44
Hinings, C.R.   333
Hirsch, S.   27, 34–5
Hitachi   217
Hoekman, B.   284, 292, *293*
home-country embeddedness   140
Honda   288

Hong Kong   84, *89*, 93, 94, 122, 131, *137*, 138–9, 141, 142, 147, 154, 205, 240, *241*, *244*, 246, *248*, 248–9, 251, *257*, 262, 274, 279, 280, 281n3, 306, 308
Hoon-Halbauer, S.K.   168
host country: FDI flows   *241*
   knowledge resources   28
   policy lessons of Irish experience   378
   productivity   216–36, *223*, *224–5*, *226*, *227*, *229*, *231*, 284
host market characteristics   90, 92
host population, ethnic Chinese proportions   94
Huaguang Forest Co. Ltd.   148
hub-and-spoke districts   373
Hui Tan   119–57, 165–86, 239–67, 327–58
human rights   103
Hunan   263
Hymer, Stephen   1, 14–23, 211n3, 380n8
   on the capital market   17–18
   common attributes of phases   20–2
   criticisms of international capitalism   18–20
   on DFI   15–16
   'Direct foreign investment and the national interest'   18
   and internalisation   16, 17
   'Multinational corporations and the division of labour'   21
   phases of work   14, 20–2
   as radical economist   18–20
   Revue Economique   16–18
   'The efficiency (contradictions) of Multinational Corporations'   18–19
   'The internationalisation of capital'   20
   'The multinational corporation and the law of uneven development'   19–20
   thesis   14–16
Hyundai   288

IBM   86, 217
IDA Ireland   381n17
ideology   103
imports   95–6, 104, 256–7, *287*, 288, 395
incentives packages   322, 379
India   84, 111, 123, 125, *137*, 140, 376–7
Indonesia   94, *137*, 139, *241*, 256, *257*, 264, 265, 290
industrial clusters   370–6
   agglomeration economies   371–2
industrial reform   210
inflation rates   95, *102*, 104, 109, 110
information, control of   21
infrastructure   265–6
innovation   68, 68–9, 296, 300–1
innovation-diffusion model   63–4, *64*
input and output transactions   341–2
institutional fabric   87–90, *89–90*
institutional theory   87–8
intangible products   42, 44
Intel   375
intellectual property rights   254
interest rates   15, 395–6, 404–5, 405, 406
internal forward markets   17–18
internalisation   16, 17, 31, 92, 121, 129–30, 145, 348
   Buckley and Casson model   64–71, *66*, 83
   horizontal   61
   and incremental expansion   73–5
   Penrose's model   61–4, *64*
   sequential   63, *64*
   speed of   70–1, 71–3
   theory   2, 7, 10
   vertical   61
Internalisation School   366
international business, domain   7–12, **8**
international business research   7–13
   agenda   1
   economic school of   25–49
   general theories   10–11
   issue driven   8, 12

Index   425

issue–theory interaction   9, 10
levels of analysis   7, **8**
the missing middle   **11**, 12
recursive view   **8**, 8, 10
scholarship   10
theory driven   8, 10, 12
international capitalism, Hymer's criticism of   18–20
international joint ventures (IJV)   124, 125, *126*, 145–6, 320
International Operations of National Firms, The (Hymer)   14–16
internationalisation   25–49, 140, 320
  advantages   26
  alternative firm configurations   *32*
  benefits   25
  control decisions   37, 42–4, 48
  dynamic perspective   44–7
  entry mode   124
  flow costs   33–4
  literature   26–9
  location decisions   37–42, *39–40*, *47*, 48
  marketing costs   36–7
  model   29–47, **30**, 48–9
  operation costs   34–7
  phases   84, 155–6
  production costs   35–6
  and supply and demand   27
'The internationalisation of capital' (Hymer)   20
intra-industry specialisation   266
investment policy, Chinese   242
investment position, outward foreign direct investment   131
investment sources   *248*, 248–9
investment strategy   122–3
investment treaties   140
Inward FDI Performance Index   258, *261*
inward foreign direct investment:
  annual inflows   246, *246*
  Asian domination of   274–5
  benign effect   255
  China as regional driver   262–5
  Chinese advantages   262–3
  Chinese FDI inflow   *241*, 246, *246*
  Chinese patterns   242, 245–7
  Chinese policy   242, *243–5*, 245–6
  Chinese success   239–67, *241*, *243–5*, 246, *247*, *248*, *257*, *259*, *260*, *261*
  and Chinese WTO accession   250–6
  contracted value   *246*, 246
  decline   251
  economic development model   240, 242
  export econometric analysis   273–6
  form   249
  geographic distribution   249–50
  impact on exports   270–81, *274*, *277*, 277–9, *278*, 280
  inflows   240, *241*, 251, 256
  investment promotion measures   265
  and inward FDI   273–6, *274*
  location   *257*, 257–8, 262
  magnetic effect   254
  market access   245, 246, 255
  market growth projections   256–7
  motivation   246–7
  neutral effect   254
  overseas groups   272–3
  Performance Index   258, *261*
  policy responses, Southeast Asia   265–7
  primary sources of capital   242
  sources   *248*, 248–9
  transaction costs   258, *259*, *260*, 265
  western groups   273
Ireland, FDI in   3, 365–80
  chemicals and pharmaceuticals sector   376
  comparison with China   370
  comparison with India   376–7
  education and training policy   375
  electronics sector policy   375
  food-processing sector   380n6
  industrial clusters   370–6
  policy development   368–9
  policy lessons   377–80
  promotion of export platform FDI   365

Ireland, FDI in – *continued*
  sectoral specialisation   375–6
  selective promotion of MNEs   365, 368, 368–9
  spatial dimension   374–6
  taxation   380n2
  telecom markets   380n9
issue–theory interaction, international business research   **9**, 10
Italy   *134*, 289

Jamaica   149
Japan   8, *134*, *248*, 248–9, 274, 284, 289, 308
Japan Bank for International Cooperation (JBIC)   262
JETRO   262
Jiangsu   249
Jinan Automotive Works   286

Kafouros, Mario   270–81
Kamps, Jaap   332, 333
Kay, G.B.   23n3
Kazakhstan   *136*, 148
key industries   302n1
Kholdy, S.   284, 291, *294*
Kilmann, Ralph H.   356
Kim, K.Y.   122
Kindleberger, C.P.   16
Kinoshita, Y.   290, 292
Knickerbocker, F.T.   370, 380n13
knowledge assets   34–5, 42, 48–9, 273, 308
knowledge flow costs   27–8, 33–4, 48
knowledge transfer *see also* technology transfer: and
  corporate and governmental relationships   183–4
  and cultural awareness   165–86, **172**, *173*, **175**, **184**
  data collection, coding and analysis   172–5, *173*, **174**
  government support   180–2, 185
  literature   170–1
  and long-term vision   182–3
  managing cultural awareness   175–7, **184**, 184–5

shared mindsets   178–80, 185
  and trust   167–8, 168–9, 177–8, 185–6
Kogut, B.   168
Kokko, A.   198, 272, 284, 291, 292, *293*
Komaran, R.V.   123
Koopmans, Tjalling C.   333
Kor, Y.Y.   53
Korea, Republic of   *137*
Krugman, P.R.   375
Kumar, K.   122
Kyrgyzstan   *136*

labour   148, 246, 272, 306 *see also* productivity
  costs   84
  international division of   17, 20
  quality   296, 300
labour intensive industries   308–9, 315, 315–18, *316*, *317*
laissez-faire   192, 210
Lam, K.   247
Laos   *241*, 264, 265, 323
Lau, H.   125
Law for the Encouragement of Foreign Investment   243
Lecraw, D.J.   121–2
Lenovo Corporation   86, 152, *152*
Lessard, Donald R.   1, 7–13
Levinthal, D.A.   292
Li, J.   247
liberalisation   88, *89*, 94, 100, 102, 106, 111, *127*, 130, 201, 253, 329, 339, 370
light industries, capital penetration   212n14
Lipsey, R.E.   393
literature: cultural awareness   166–72
  economic school of international business research   26–9
  FDI   119–57
  internationalisation   26–9
  knowledge transfer   170–1
  productivity   289–95, *293–4*
  spillover effects   193, 193–8, 209, 307–11

Lithuania 310
Liu, W. 285
Liu, X. 199, 226
lobbying 183
local government 170, 180–1
localisation 352
locally owned enterprises (LOEs) 192, 194, 197, 198–9, 205, 209, 210–11, 218–19, 305–6
spillover effects 308, 310, 311, *315*, 315–19, *317*
location 26, 27–9, 37–42, *39–40*, *47*, 62, 121, 310
attractiveness *257*, 257–8, 262
decisions 48, 83–4, 110
industrial clustering 370–6
inward foreign direct investment 249–50, 258, 262
long-term vision 182–3
Low Technology (LT) products 41–2, 44
low-cost capital 87
Lucas, R.E. Jr. 389, 397

Macao *137*, 138, 139, 268n3, 274, 279, 280, 306
Machlup, Fritz 53
macrodynamics 18–19
Magee, S.P. 211n3
magnetic effect 254
Mahoney, J.T. 53
Malaysia 88, 94, 123, *137*, *241*, 256, *257*, 263, 264, 265
Mali *135*, 139
management, national differences 7
managerial diseconomies 56
managerial succession 56
manufacturing industry, spillover effects 305–24, *314*, *315*, *316*, *317*, *321*
Marcotte, C. 171
market access 245, 246, 255
market entry, speed of 70–1
market forces 338
market growth projections 256–7
market imperfections 16, 20–1, 370
market information 87
market power 17

market size 70, 71–2, 100, 106, 109, 110
market structure 17
marketing 36–7, 45, 272
markets, internalisation of 10
market-seeking FDI 83–4, 90, 92, 148–51, 242, 251, 257, 263, 264, 271, 273, 395
Markusen, J.R. 308
Marshall, A. 56, 372
Marx, Karl 21
Mauritius *135*, 149
mediating technology 331–2
Mexico *136*, 139, 151, 272, 291, 390
Meyer, Alan D. 333
Meyer, E.K. 306
mianzi ('face') 2, 166, 167–8, 169, 171, **172**, 175–6, 178, 179, 181, 183–6
Microsoft 375
mindsets, shared 178–80, 185
Ministry of Foreign Economic Relations and Trade (MOFERT) *89*, 157n2, *243*
Ministry of Foreign Trade and Economic Cooperation (MOFTEC) *127*, 143–4, 157n2, 327, 329, 345, 351
Ministry of Post and Telecommunications 175–6
Ministry of the Electronics Industry 235
MOFCOM 120, *127*, 130, 131, 133, 143–4, 144
Mongolia *137*
monopoly advantage 121
Morocco *135*, 291
motivation: DFI 15
efficiency-seeking FDI 154–5
export platform FDI 242
inward foreign direct investment 246–7
market-seeking FDI 148–51, 242
natural resource-seeking FDI 147–8
outward foreign direct investment 147–55
strategic asset seeking FDI 151–4

Motorola (China)   *173*, 176, 177, 179, 180, 181, 182–3, 183, 319
'The multinational corporation and the law of uneven development' (Hymer)   19–20
'Multinational corporations and the division of labour' (Hymer)   21
multinational enterprise (MNE)   1–2, 14, 18–19, 121, 145, 365 *see also* firms
  asset-seeking FDI   92–3
  Buckley and Casson model   64–71, *66*, 83
  definition   62
  developing country   121–5
  geographic spread of FDI   370
  growth in number of Chinese   133, 305
  and home origin of FDI   309–10
  impact on LOEs   192
  internalisation and Penrose's model   61–4, *64*
  internalisation theory   2
  managerial efficiency   367
  ownership advantages   121–2
  ownership advantages of Chinese   86–7
  Penrose's 1959 model   53–75
  policy lessons of Irish experience   378
  power   19
  sectoral specialisation   375–6
  selective promotion of investment   365, 366–8, 368–9
  strategic management   53–75
  transaction costs   265
Myanmar   *137*, *241*, 264, 265, 266

Nanjing Automotive Works   286
Narula, R.   369
National Development and Reform Commission (NDRC)   130
nationality   14–15
natural resource endowment   92, 109
natural resource-seeking FDI   147–8
NEC   217
neutral effect   254
New Zealand   *134*, 148

Nigeria   *135*
Niosi, J.   171
non-equilibrium dynamics   21
North American Free Trade Agreement (NAFTA)   151, 155, 387, 390
North American free trade agreements   386
Nutt, Paul C.   332

Olivetti   217
Open Door policies   81, 82, *89*, *127*, 128–9, 145, 217, 240, 305
Open Export Zones (OEZs)   *243*
open system strategies   331
operation costs   34–7, 45–6, 47
organisations, analytical framework   331–4
Organisations in Action (Thompson)   331
Orientation Directory of Industries for FDI   211n7
output, and costs   54
outward foreign direct investment, Chinese   2
  asset-seeking FDI   92–3, 103, 110, 156
  capital market imperfections   85–6
  changes over time   104–6
  cultural proximity   93–4, 100, 102, 105, 106, 110
  data collecting agencies   143–4
  determinants of   81–112, *89–90*, *91*, *98–9*, *101*, *102*, *107–8*
  distance variables   96, 104, 110
  efficiency-seeking FDI   154–5
  entry mode   145–7, *146*
  exchange rates   95, 104
  exports and imports   95–6, 103–4, 104, 106
  flow trends   131–47, **132**, *134–7*, *142*, *145*
  general theory of FDI   83–4
  geographic distribution   *134–7*, 155
  growth rates   119
  host country level of development   106, *107–8*, 109
  host inflation rate   95

host market characteristics   100
inflation rates   95, *102*, 104, 109, 110
institutional factors influencing   87–90, *89–90*
institutional setting   125–31, *127–8*
investment position   131
key periods   88, *89–90*, *126*, *127–8*
lack of data   81
liberalisation   94, 100, 102, 106, 111, *127*, 129–30
market-seeking FDI   90, 92, 148–51
model   97–109
motivation   147–55
natural resource endowment   92, 109
natural resource-seeking FDI   147–8
openness of host country   96–7, 104, 110
outflows, by host region   *91*
ownership advantages of MNEs   86–7
political risk   93, 102–3, 110
sectoral distribution   141–5, *142*, 156
special state fund   112n3
special theory for   84–90
state ownership of investors   82–3
strategic asset seeking FDI   151–4, *152*, *153*
theoretical explanations   121–5
trends   119–57, *126*, *127–8*, *132*, *134–5*
value   *89*, 104, 119, *127*, *128*, 131
variables   90–7, *98–9*
over-capacity   256
ownership advantages   26, 86–7, 121–2, 125, *126*, 194–5, 198, 273, 308, 319

Pang, E.F.   123
Papua New Guinea   *137*
Parsons, Talcott   327, 331
partners: cultural awareness between   168–9
and trust   177–8

Penrose, Edith   2, 53–75
and the Buckley and Casson model   64–71, *66*
definition of firms   55
and foreign subsidiaries   56
and internationalisation   61–4, *64*, 71–3
and multinationality   62
theory of growth   54–61, 64–8
Perez, T.   219–20
Persson, H.   284, 291, *294*
Peru   *135*, 139, 148
PetroKaz   92
Peugeot   288
Pfaffermary, M.   284, *293*
Philippines   *241*, *257*, 264, 266
Philips   217
Pitelis, C.N.   53
Poland   292
policy consistency   379
policy implications, developing country FDI   365–80
political risk   93, 102–3, 110, 358
Polos, Laszlo   332, 333
Porter, Michael E.   13n1, 343
portfolio foreign investment   15
power   19, 20–1
Prahalad, C.K.   13n1
principal-agent theory   332
product cycle theory   7, 28, 44–7, 63, 366, 368, 370
phases   44–5
product diversification   2
product flow costs   33
production costs   35–6, 45
productivity   67, 198–9, 200, 204, 239
direct benefits of FDI   290
and FDI   216–36, *223*, *224–5*, *226*, *227*, *229*, *231*
growth   222, *223*
host country   216–36, *223*, *224–5*, *226*, *227*, *229*, *231*, 284
impact of FDI on   226–32, *227*, *229*, *231*, 284–302, *287*, *293–4*, *298*, *299*
impact of foreign ownership   307
indirect benefits of FDI   290–2
intangible assets   230

productivity – *continued*
  literature 217–20, 289–95, *293–4*
  measuring 295
  methodology and data 221–6, *223*, *224–5*, *226*
  model 295–7
  spillover effects 216–17, 218–20, 226–8, 232, 233, 235, 290–2
profit maximisation 29
project monitoring 380
project selectivity 379
property rights 338

Qian, G. 247

Rafaeli, Anat 332
Ramamurti, R. 306
rationality 331
raw materials, access to 87
Reducing Uncertainty 333
Reilly, Kevin T. 386–408
research and development 28, 296
  costs 34–5, 45, 65–6, 74–5
  growth and 64–8
  and incremental expansion 73–4
  location decisions 38, 41–2, 48–9
resource-seeking FDI 84, 86, 88, 109
restructuring 253–4
Revue Economique (Hymer) 16–18
Riddle, L. 306
risk: diversification 332, 370
  management 140
  political 93, 102–3, 110, 358
Robertson, D.H. 19
Roehrig, M.F. 182
Romania *136*
round-tripping 205, 250, 267n2, 281n3
Ruane, Frances 365–80
Rugman, A.M. 53, 370
Russia 111, *136*, 138, 139

Salk, J.E. 168
Samsung 217
satellite platforms 373
Saxtan, Mary J. 356
Sayre, E. 306
Schilling, Melissa A. 332
Scott, W.R. 122

Second Automotive Works (SAW) 286
Serpa, Roy 356
Shanghai *243*, 249
Shanghai Automotive Industry Corporation 288
Shanghai Baosteel 148
Shanghai Bell *173*, 175–6, 177, 179, 180, 182
Shanghai Volkswagen 168, *173*, 176–7, 177–8, 179, 180, 181, 182, 183, 288
Shannxi Automotive Works 286
Shapiro, D.M. 122, 124, 387, 392, 397
shareholder value 55
Shaver, M.J. 212n8
Sheensma, H. Kevin 332
Shenkar, O. 122–3, 124
Shougang Group 86, 129
Sichuan 263
Sichuan Automotive Works 286
Siemens 217
Siler, Pamela A. 284–302
simultaneity 201, 210
Sinclair, J. 289
Singapore 88, 93, 123, 125, *137*, *241*, 251, 256, *257*, 262, 263, 264, 265, 331–2
Singh, H. 168
Single European Market 141, 368, 377
Sinochem Group 86, 148
Sinopec 148
Sinotrans 3, 327–58
  analytical framework 331–4
  assets 341, 348
  Board of Directors 346
  boundary spanning activities 352–5
  business strategy 354–5
  centralisation 353–5
  competition 339–40
  core business specialisation 346–7, 358
  corporate culture 340, 351, 355–7
  crucial activities 348
  data analysis 337
  data collection 334–6, *336*

Index 431

diversification 342
environmental uncertainty 331
excess capacity 349
expansion 341, 344, 348
Finance Department 350, 353
forward integration 340–1
government control 345–6, 357–8
input and output transactions 341–2
institutional environment 334
local environment 347
localisation 352
management 337–8, 339–40, 346, 351, 353–4
networked information system 349
operational control 354
organisational action 343–7
organisational imperatives 339–43
organisational structure 327–9, 328, 330, 337, 337–8, 348–51, 353–5
origins 327
prestige 344
property rights 338
protection of core technologies 339–40
response to external constraints 342–3
standardisation 350–1
stock market listings 344
subsidiaries 352, 354–5
support capacity 346
task environment 343–5
uncertainty 333, 358
Sit, V.F.S. 285
Sjöholm, F. 220, 230
Smarzynska, B.K. 211n4, 310
Smith, Adam 334
social standing 167
soft budget constraints 85, 140
Song, Shunfeng 281n5
South Africa 135, 139, 148
South Korea 84, 88, 122–3, 124, 125, 284, 289, 324
Southeast Asia 265
advantages 264–5
China as regional driver 262–5
and Chinese accession to WTO 250–6
and Chinese FDI success 239–67, 241, 243–5, 246, 247, 248, 252, 257, 259, 260, 261
policy responses 265–7
rivalry with China 250–4
Soviet Union 285–6, 323
Special Export Zones (SEZs) 242, 243, 244
spillover effects 2, 305–24, 314, 315, 316, 317, 321
appropriability 'problem' 211n3
benefits 193, 197, 211n3
Chow breakpoint test 206
correlation matrix 200, 200–1
curvilinear relationship 201, 204, 209
decline 204–5
demonstration-imitation effect 290–1
descriptive statistics 200, 200–1
distributional effects 311
evaluation 193
and exports 279
and home origin of FDI 309–10
labour intensive industries 308–9, 315, 315–18
labour productivity 198–9, 200
linear relationship 204
literature 193, 193–8, 209, 307–11
locally owned enterprises (LOEs) 308, 310, 311, 315, 315–19, 317
methodology 198–200
negative 195–6, 196, 201, 204, 209, 218–19, 220, 232
positive 194, 195–6, 196, 219–20, 322
productivity 216–17, 218–20, 226–8, 232, 233, 235, 290–2
relationship with FDI 192–211, 196, 200, 202–3, 207
and technological level 206–8, 207, 209
technology intensive industries 309, 315, 316, 317, 318–19, 319–20
theory 307–8

State Administration for Foreign
    Exchange (SAFE)   81, 97, 120,
    127, 131, 141, 143–4, 157n2
State Council   85–6
State Economic and Trade
    Commission   89
State Planning Commission   127
stateowned enterprises (SOEs)   2, 83,
    85, 85–6, 102, 110, 126, 129,
    130–1, 133, 169–70, 233–4, 262,
    306, 311, *316*, 318, 318–21, 334,
    338 *see also* Sinotrans
Steel production   158n13
Steinfeld, Edward S.   338
Stevens, G.V.G.   393
strategic asset seeking FDI   151–4,
    152, *153*
strategic management: and growth
    54–61
    Penrose's 1959 model   53–75
strategic-asset seeking FDI   262
strategy systems   331
Strobl, E.   192
Sturges, D.   306
suborganisations   331
subsidies   87
Sudan   103, *135*, 148
Sun, Haishun   281n5
Sun, X.   267n2
Sung, Y.W.   139
supply and demand   27
support capacity   346

Taiwan   123, 123–4, 125, *244*, *248*,
    248–9, 268n3, 281n3, 306,
    308
Tallman, S.B.   122–3, 124
Tan, Justin   332
Tanzania   *135*, 139
tariffs   149, 393–4
task environment, the   343–5
Taylor, R.   144, 151
TCL-Thomson Electronics   152, *152*
technological capabilities   219
technological investment   158n4
technology gap   292
technology intensive industries   309,
    315, 315, *316*, *317*, 318–19,
    319–20, 322

technology transfer   2, 68–9, 170,
    193, 232, 233, 235, 285, 290–1,
    301, 367 *see also* knowledge
    transfer
Terwiesch, Christian   332
Thailand   94, 123, *137*, 138, *241*,
    256, *257*, 264
Theory of the Growth of the Firm
    (Penrose)   2, 53–75
    and the Buckley and Casson
        model   64–71, *66*
    and internationalisation   61–4,
        64
    theory of growth   54–61
Thompson, James D.   165, 327,
    331–4, 339, 350, 351, 355, 357,
    358
Thomsen, J.   246
Tianjin Automotive Industry
    Corporation   288
Toshiba   217
Toyota   288
transaction costs   121, 258, *259*,
    260, 265, 332, 338, 371,
    393–4
transnational corporations (TNCs)
    228, 234–5, 272
    efficiency   218
    and exports   270
    performance   216
transportation costs   33, 38, 45–6,
    47
Trinidad   22
trust   167–8, 168–9, 177–8,
    185–6
Tsang, E.W.K.   171
Tsui, Anne S.   333
Tung, R.L.   168, 170
Turnover of Working Capital   297

uncertainty   333
UNCTAD   119, 123, 129–30, 140,
    247, 258, 262, 275
United Arab Emirates   *136*
United Kingdom   *134*, 289, 292,
    387
United Nations Transnational
    Corporations and Management
    Division   387

Index 433

United States of America 3, 18, 20, *134*, 139, 141, 148, 149, 150–1, 158n11, *248*, 248–9, 274, 279, 284, 289
  dollar devaluation 394–5
  exports to Canada 387
  FDI in Canada 386–408, *400–3*
  FDI in Canada, descriptive statistics *393*
  FDI in Canada, flows 390–9, **391**, *392*, *393*
  FDI in Canada, growth in 390–2, **391**, *392*, 399, *400–3*, 404–6, *409–14*
  FDI in Canada, levels 387
  FDI in Canada, model 388–9
  FDI stock in Canada **391**
  free trade agreements with Canada 387–8, 390, 405, 407, *413–14*, 415n5
Uppsala theory, the 63, 123–4, 158n12
Uruguay 272
utilised FDI 281n6
Uzbekistan *136*

Vanden Houte, P. 284
Venzuela 292
Verbeke, A. 53
Vernon, R. 13n3, 366, 368, 370
vertical integration 61–2
Veugelers, R. 284
Vietnam *137*, 151, *241*, 264, 265, 266, 323
Voss, Hinrich 81–112, 119–57

Wada, E. 246, 249
Wang, Chengqi 192–211, 216–36, 270–81, *277*, 305–24
Wang, D. 247
Wang, J. 291–2
Wanxiang 150–1
Wells, L.T. Jr. 122
Western Europe *248*, 248–9
Westney, D. Eleanor 356
wholly-owned subsidiaries 124, 146–7
Willmore, L. 290
World Trade Organization (WTO) 81, 130, 149, 186, 239
  Chinese accession 250–6, 280–1, 285, 356
  obligations and commitments 252, 253, 255, 263
Wu, S. *277*

Xin Liu 81–112, 119–57

Yang, D. 123
Yearbook of China's Electronics Industry 222
Yemen *136*
Yumkella, Kandeh 119

Zambia *135*, 139, 148
Zeghni, S.H. 170
Zhan, J.X. 138, 145
Zhang, Honglin K. *277*, 281n5
Zhao, Hongxin 279
Zheng, Ping 81–112, 284–302
Zhou, D. 290, *294*
Zhu, Gangti 279
Zimbabwe *135*
Zukowska-Gagelmann, K. 284, 292, *293*